PSYCHOLOGY IN CONTEXT

PSYCHOLOGY IN CONTEXT

Voices and Perspectives

Second Edition

David N. Sattler
College of Charleston

Virginia Shabatay
Palomar College

HOUGHTON MIFFLIN COMPANY   Boston   New York

Senior Sponsoring Editor: Kerry T. Baruth
Senior Associate Editor: Jane Knetzger
Editorial Assistant: Sarah Gessner
Senior Project Editor: Kathryn Dinovo
Senior Cover Design Coordinator: Deborah Azerrad Savona
Senior Manufacturing Coordinator: Sally Culler
Senior Marketing Manager: Pamela J. Laskey

Cover design: Rebecca Fagan
Cover photographs: Keren Su/Tony Stone Images (calligrapher); Ralph Cowan/FPG International
(ballet class); Michael Goldman/FPG International (maple trees); Lester Lefkowitz/The Stock Market
(brain)

Printed in the U.S.A.

Library of Congress Catalog Card Number: 99-71927

ISBN: 0-395-95962-4

1 2 3 4 5 6 7 8 9-CS-03 02 01 00 99

Brief Contents

Contents

2

SENSATION AND PERCEPTION   28

3

CONSCIOUSNESS   49

4

LEARNING   68

5

MEMORY 87

6

THOUGHT AND LANGUAGE   111

7

HUMAN DEVELOPMENT 135

9

MOTIVATION AND EMOTION   181

Still Me   183
Christopher Reeve

Psychological Concepts: sources of motivation, emotion

Actor Christopher Reeve, who suffered a spinal injury when thrown from his horse, discusses what motivates him to continue working, to be a father and husband, and to raise funds for research in spinal cord injuries.

Dying to Be Bigger   188
D. H.

Psychological Concepts: hormones, testosterone

A high school student, determined to be a football star, decides to take steroids and experiences severe physical and psychological changes.

New Hope for Binge Eaters   192
Harrison G. Pope Jr. and James I. Hudson

Psychological Concepts: eating disorders, anorexia nervosa, bulimia nervosa

A college student develops bulimia nervosa, an illness she finds difficult to cure.

Flow   197
Daniel Goleman

Psychological Concepts: flow, creativity

A noted writer maintains that we are likely to do well at a task when we are fully absorbed in it and have entered a state of "flow."

10

PERSONALITY   201

Asian in America   202
Kesaya E. Noda

Psychological Concepts: self-concept, positive regard

Confused by conflicting cultural and gender issues brought about by her Japanese-American heritage, a young woman struggles to define herself.

Racism Doesn't Grow Up   207

Joyce Lee

Psychological Concepts: reciprocal influences, self-efficacy, self-esteem

A woman who came to the United States from Hong Kong when she was a little girl remembers how she was affected by the necessary adjustments this move required of her.

A Reputation Deserved   212

Arthur Ashe and Arnold Rampersad

Psychological Concepts: Eysenck's personality dimensions, five-factor model, honesty, integrity

A tennis champion discusses the importance of certain personality traits and explains why he values reputation above all.

Handed My Own Life   216

Annie Dillard

Psychological Concepts: phenomenological approach, growth orientation

A noted writer describes how she learned as a young child that her passion and independence would shape her personality.

11

PSYCHOLOGICAL DISORDERS AND TREATMENT   219

The Accident That Didn't Happen   221

Judith L. Rapoport

Psychological Concept: obsessive-compulsive disorder

Suffering from obsessive-compulsive disorder, Dr. S. tells of the anxiety and embarrassment that comes from often doubting his actions and having to constantly recheck them.

I Have Dissociative Identity Disorder   227

Quiet Storm

Psychological Concept: dissociative identity disorder (formerly called multiple personality disorder)

Speaking of herself in first-person plural, a woman who was a victim of child abuse reflects on the anguish of dissociative identity disorder.

12

HEALTH, STRESS, AND COPING   255

Influence   290

Robert B. Cialdini

Psychological Concepts: persuasion, compliance, scarcity principle, psychological reactance

A social psychologist explains why people are so often vulnerable to persuasive techniques and can be easy targets for salespersons and others who wish to influence them.

Black Men and Public Space   297

Brent Staples

Psychological Concepts: stereotypes, prejudice, discrimination, impression formation

An editor for the *New York Times* recalls the prejudice and stereotypes he experienced as he walked the city streets and people ran from him, locked their car doors, and assumed that he was guilty of crimes on the streets.

Why Competition?   301

Alfie Kohn

Psychological Concepts: competition, cooperation, interpersonal relations

Alfie Kohn argues that "competition by its very nature is always unhealthy."

The Revolt on K2   306

Galen Rowell

Psychological Concepts: group dynamics, leadership, fundamental attribution error

From the journals of the team members who set out to climb K2, a noted mountaineer, writer, and photographer records the conflicts that can occur within a group and among its leaders.

Random Acts of Kindness   311

Editors

Psychological Concepts: helping behavior, altruism

Several people share stories of surprise when they experience the kindness of strangers.

Preface

Teaching introductory psychology is an inherently intellectual and emotional enterprise. As professors, we are faced with the challenges of not only presenting theory and research clearly, but also conveying to students our own personal involvement and excitement about the field. We want to show how what we study in the classroom relates to the world outside—in short, bring research and theory to life. Coupled with these challenges are other issues central to excellent teaching: (1) encouraging students to think critically by asking them to reflect on and analyze difficult issues; and (2) exposing students to the complexities of life events, ethical dilemmas, and cross-cultural issues. We suspect that learning is most rewarding when students have clear and vivid examples that relate theory and research findings to personal and interpersonal experiences. We designed this book to help instructors create a dynamic learning environment that shows students the vitality and complexity of the field of psychology.

Our goals for *Psychology in Context: Voices and Perspectives* are the following:

- To promote students' understanding and retention of key psychological concepts and issues.

- To bring theory and research alive through dynamic and insightful first-person accounts and narratives that illustrate psychological concepts and raise important and timely issues.

- To promote active learning by challenging students to consider, think critically about, and discuss the readings as they relate to fundamental psychological principles and concepts.

- To stimulate critical thinking about gender, multicultural, ethical, theoretical, and research issues.

- To expose students to the complexities of the field of psychology and ethical dilemmas.

This book can be used alone or in conjunction with any introductory psychology textbook.

Pedagogical Features

Each chapter contains between four and seven narratives written by popular and scholarly authors. The chapters and narratives each begin with an introduction that orients the reader and presents the main psychological concepts and issues that are illustrated in the reading. In addition, on the first page of each article we present a psychological concept guide, in bold type, that lists the concepts and issues that the article illustrates. The concepts were selected after carefully reviewing more than twenty-five of the best-selling introduction to psychology textbooks and consulting with over twenty instructors who teach the course at a variety of institutions.

After each article, we present a series of questions designed to promote critical thinking and highlight research issues.

- *Response and Analysis* questions ask students to analyze and reflect on the concepts and issues presented in the article. These questions help students learn about the psychological concepts and issues in more detail.

- *Personal Experience and Application* questions ask students to explore their own reactions to and experiences with the issues and to consider how the issues may affect the community (for example, propose an intervention program, outline recommendations for a local school board).

- *Research* questions provide a solid foundation for exploring methodology at an introductory level while also promoting critical thinking. After a brief discussion of a research study, students are asked questions about how they might design the study, develop hypotheses, or interpret the results. They also cover basic methodological concepts, such as identifying and measuring variables, controlling for extraneous variables, and applying ethical research principles. The questions show students that (1) methodology and statistics are important for all areas of psychology; and (2) psychologists studying diverse areas of behavior rely on a common set of scientific methods. Students will find the research questions interesting, in part because they involve issues raised in the readings.

Criteria for Selecting the Readings

We used four primary criteria to select the readings. First, each selection had to illustrate key concepts, issues, and topics that are presented in most introductory psychology textbooks. Second, and equally important, each narrative had to be provocative: It had to arouse us, hold our attention, raise questions, be of interest to students, and promote critical thinking. Third, we favored selections that would broaden students' perspectives on gender, ethnic, and cultural influences. Finally, we chose and edited selections so that they were long enough to be absorbing but short enough that instructors could easily assign them as supplemental readings.

New for the Second Edition

This edition represents a comprehensive revision. We have included fifteen new readings and thoroughly reworked the pedagogical features of the remaining selections. We also reedited several selections.

Two sources of feedback guided this revision. First, several instructors contacted us and offered excellent suggestions. Second, Houghton Mifflin Company surveyed almost twenty instructors who had adopted the first edition of the text. These instructors gave excellent commentary and direction concerning which selections to retain or replace, and offered insight on improving the pedagogy.

Suggestions for the Instructor: How to Use This Book

Psychology in Context: Voices and Perspectives can be used to create an active learning environment in small and large classes. Instructors may assign the readings to correspond to material presented during lecture or in the primary textbook. In addition, instructors using Douglas A. Bernstein's introductory psychology text will find useful suggestions for assigning the readings throughout the Annotated Instructor's Edition that accompanies his text.

This book also can be used to promote class discussions and to develop research projects, writing assignments, and other individual or group projects.

Class Discussion

Students enjoy discussing their reactions to the readings in class.

1. The questions that follow each reading stimulate good class discussion and reinforce students' understanding of psychological concepts. Instructors may ask students to answer the questions prior to or during the class, and to share their responses with the class. This activity also can serve as an excellent way to introduce a topic in class.

   The research questions are a great resource for introducing and discussing research methodology. They teach basic concepts and principles and underscore the importance of methodology and statistics to all areas of psychology.

2. Students often enjoy a class debate. Many of the issues raised by the readings and the questions following each reading serve well for critical thinking and illustrate opposing viewpoints. For example, Richard Rodriguez's essay *A Bilingual Childhood* raises important questions concerning bilingualism. Should schools provide children who are immigrants with classes in their native language? How might the social and personal development of these children be affected by not learning well the language of their new country? What conflicts can occur in families when children adopt the customs of their new land? Elizabeth Loftus and Katherine Ketcham's essay *Witness for the Defense: A Mole and a Stutter—Tyrone Briggs* raises key questions concerning the accuracy of memory and memory contamination. How reliable is eyewitness testimony? What might influence our memories? In *The Revolt on K2*, Galen Rowell, a noted mountaineer and photographer, writes about the conflict that developed among a group that set out to climb one of the world's highest mountains. What problems might develop if a group member decides that he or she does not agree with the decisions of the others? How can the leaders or other group members encourage cooperation? How might competition affect cohesiveness? Students may debate various sides of the same issue in class.

Writing Assignments

Writing assignments allow students to analyze, question, and give personal responses to what they have read, and to develop writing skills. Instructors may require students to answer the questions for a given number of articles and turn in their answers at assigned times during the course or at the end of the semester.

The readings and questions also can serve as a basis for journals or response papers. Instructors might allow students to develop ideas that occur to them after reading the narratives and questions. The writing assignments could be turned in weekly or periodically throughout the course, depending on class size and time available to read and grade them. Instructors could assign grades, satisfactory or unsatisfactory credit, or extra credit as they see appropriate.

Research Projects

Instructors may use the readings to generate creative research projects.

1. Students could work alone or in groups to design a research proposal based on an idea raised in a reading or in the questions that follow each reading. The proposal might include a: (1) statement of the problem or question and why it is interesting or important; (2) summary of previous research exploring the problem or question; (3) statement presenting the hypothesis, independent variable(s), and dependent variable(s); and (4) description of the method (for example, participants, materials, procedures, controls, adherence to ethical standards).

2. Students could work alone or in groups to write a term paper based on one or several of the readings and questions. The term paper might explore the current state of knowledge about the topic. The paper, which might include an introduction, literature review, and discussion, could be turned in during the term or presented in class in a ten- to fifteen-minute presentation.

3. Advanced or honor students could investigate one question or author in detail. For instance, a student could read one or two books or articles by an author whose selection is included herein. They could learn more about the political, social, and economic forces that might have affected the author and/or influenced the issue discussed in the reading. The students could submit a written research report or make an oral presentation to the class.

Group Projects

The readings can be used to generate engaging individual and group projects.

1. Students might work in small groups, and each student in the group could compare his or her responses to the questions. Instructors might provide a rough agenda and time limits. Each group might have a group facilitator, recorder, and reporter. The group could compile and summarize its responses, and the reporter

could give a synopsis to the class. The variability of responses both within and among groups is often instructive.

2. Students working in groups could identify linkages between concepts that are presented in other selections in the same chapter or in different chapters. For example, in the Human Development chapter, Dick Gregory tells how poverty had a negative effect on his ability to learn in school. Students could use this essay to explore development and learning as well as prejudice and stereotypes, concepts that are discussed in the chapter on Social Thought and Social Behavior.

Instructor's Resource Manual

Instructors may wish to quiz students about the readings, psychological concepts, and research issues. The Instructor's Resource Manual contains multiple-choice, short-answer, and essay questions. It is available from your Houghton Mifflin Company representative.

A Final Note: Extending the Borders

In his remarkable book *An Anthropologist on Mars*, Oliver Sacks tells us that he is best able to understand both his patients and their illnesses when he gets out of his office and into their lives, making "house calls at the far borders of human experience." In this way he comes to know them and their conditions from within—as persons, and not merely as patients who have been handed a diagnosis. We believe that students, too, will better understand the issues in psychology if they can extend the borders of the theoretical into the world of human experience. We hope that this book will help them do so.

Acknowledgments

It is a special pleasure to express our appreciation to the many talented and dedicated people who provided creative ideas and suggestions for this book. We have been extremely fortunate in having Douglas A. Bernstein (University of South Florida, University of Surrey) collaborate with us. Doug's enthusiasm for our idea prompted him to put us in contact with Houghton Mifflin Company. His ongoing support, guidance, and contributions have played a significant role in shaping the book. Doug graciously offered his expertise and invaluable suggestions. It is a privilege working with him both professionally and as a friend. We also express our deep gratitude to Geoffrey P. Kramer (Grand Valley State University), good colleague and friend, for his contributions to this edition.

We extend our appreciation to the following individuals for their valuable feedback on revising the text.

Robin A. Anderson, St. Ambrose University
Bette L. Bottoms, University of Illinois at Chicago

Elaine Cassel, Marymount University, Lord Fairfax Community College
Suzanne C. Crawford, McDowell Technical Community College
Reva Dossett, Ivy Tech State College
Robert W. Fisher, Lee University
Lee Fox-Cardamone, Kent State University, Stark
Karen Holbrook, Frostburg State University
Ann McKim, Goucher College
Elizabeth Neumeyer, Kellogg Community College
Richard L. Robbins, Washburn University
Hillary R. Rodman, Emory University
Tracy A. Simonson, Miami University, Middletown
Carole V. Wells, Kutztown University
Elissa Wurf, Green Mountain College

We also thank the following individuals for reading various portions of the manuscript for the first edition and giving insightful suggestions.

Ruth L. Ault, Davidson College
Peter K. Ballantyne, San Diego State University
Wendy J. Beller, Quincy University
Winfield Brown, Florence Darlington Technical College
Thomas Lee Budesheim, Creighton University
Jack Demick, Suffolk University
Kathleen A. Flannery, Saint Anselm College
E. Keith Gerritz, Wilmington College of Ohio
Janet M. Gibson, Grinnell College
Ronald W. Jacques, Ricks College
Sally Holland Kline, Henderson Community College
Geoffrey P. Kramer, Grand Valley State University
Dorothy Ledbetter, Grossmont College
Don Marguilis, Middlesex Community College
Gail Martino, Colgate University
Douglas W. Matheson, University of the Pacific
David G. McDonald, University of Missouri
Joseph L. Miele, East Stroudsburg University
Richard L. Robbins, Washburn University
Connie Schick, Bloomsburg University
Toni Spinelli-Nannen, American International College
Lori Van Wallendael, University of North Carolina at Charlotte

We have enjoyed working with the outstanding staff at Houghton Mifflin Company. Jane Knetzger, Senior Associate Editor, has provided invaluable advice concerning the structure of the book, pedagogy, and its revision. Kerry T. Baruth, Senior Sponsoring Editor, and Kathi Prancan, Editor-in-Chief for Science and Psychology, have been excellent resources. Sarah Gessner, Editorial Assistant, provided outstanding support. We thank them for their professionalism and encouragement. We thank Kathryn Dinovo, Project Editor, for her excellence in overseeing the production of the book, Craig Mertens for helping us secure permissions, and Melissa Lotfy of Books By Design for her assistance with production. We are grateful to Pamela Laskey, Marketing Manager, for her excitement about the book and creative ideas in promoting it. We also thank former Sponsoring Editors Becky Dudley, who originally signed the book, David Lee, who saw the book into its second edition, and Gwen Fairweather and Lou Gum, former Editorial Assistants, who provided good suggestions on the book's development.

We are indebted to Michael Phillips and the staff of the College of Charleston Interlibrary Loan department for helping us obtain books and other materials. We thank Charles Kaiser, Stacy Clark, Conrad Festa, Samuel Hines, and the College of Charleston Psychology Department faculty for their support.

We wish to thank Judy Barkley, good friend and colleague at Grossmont College, for her enthusiasm for this project and for her critical reading of the manuscript. Her responses to the selections and her many helpful comments gave good direction. We also wish to thank Maurice Friedman, scholar, mentor, and long-time friend, for his encouragement and helpful counsel. Our appreciation extends to Yehuda Shabatay for his steadfast support from the inception of this project, for his thorough reading of the manuscript, and for his always-valuable suggestions. We are indebted to Jerome M. Sattler for his wise counsel and unwavering support. Finally, we thank other family members: Heidi, Walter, Nicole, and Justin Philips; Bonnie and Keith Sattler; Debbie Hendrix; Elizabeth, Tom, and Phoenix Voorhies; Deborah and Eli Knaan; and Michael Shabatay.

It has been a delight to work on this book and the *Psychology in Context* series together. The series grew out of our engaging discussions concerning education and society that we have had over the years. To work together as colleagues while being mother and son has been a pleasure twice over.

We always are delighted to hear from students and faculty who use the book. We especially welcome feedback on how to improve the book and suggestions for readings to include in the next edition.

David N. Sattler
College of Charleston
Department of Psychology
Charleston, South Carolina 29424
E-mail: sattlerd@cofc.edu

Virginia Shabatay
Palomar College
Department of English
1140 W. Mission Road
San Marcos, California 92069

About the Authors

David N. Sattler is Associate Professor of Psychology at the College of Charleston. After graduating Phi Beta Kappa with a degree in psychology from San Diego State University, David received his M.A. and Ph.D. in social psychology from Michigan State University. He has held academic positions at the University of California at San Diego, San Diego State University, and Scripps College. His research examines behavior in social dilemmas, and preparation for and responses to natural disasters (for example, coping, social support, and posttraumatic stress disorder). He has published in numerous journals, including *Journal of Personality and Social Psychology*, *International Journal of Stress Management*, *Journal of Applied Social Psychology*, and *Teaching of Psychology*. David is an avid photographer and backpacker.

Virginia Shabatay has a Ph.D. in humanities. She teaches at Palomar College and Grossmont College in San Diego, California, and has held academic positions at San Diego State University, Portland State University, and Lewis and Clark College. She has served as editorial consultant on numerous books, including *Martin Buber's Life and Work* by Maurice Friedman, and has contributed essays to several books. Her most recent publications are "Martin Buber and Sisela Bok: Against the Generation of the Lie," in *Martin Buber and the Human Sciences*, and "The Stranger: Who Calls? Who Answers?" in *Stories Lives Tell: Narrative and Dialogue in Education*. In her leisure time, she likes to read, travel, swim, and take long walks on the beach.

chapter 1

PHYSIOLOGICAL BASES OF BEHAVIOR

What a piece of work is a man! how noble
in reason! how infinite in faculty!
in form and moving how express and
admirable!

WILLIAM SHAKESPEARE, *Hamlet*

The intricacy and detail of human physiology astound us. The human body delights us in its form and in the way it allows us to move and to perceive. Not only are we amazed by how our senses respond to the world, but we marvel at the genius of human creativity: from developing the alphabet to carving the lute to inventing computers. Out of the wonders of physical being come science, art, and literature.

But sometimes part of the body goes awry because of genetics, illness, or accident. In this chapter we present selections written by people who struggle with various conditions that have physiological bases: neurological disorders, such as epilepsy, multiple sclerosis, and Parkinson's disease; stroke; and Alzheimer's disease. These readings underscore, however, the wisdom that a particular condition does not define the person.

Nancy Mairs has multiple sclerosis, yet she is a successful writer, college professor, lecturer, wife, mother, and political activist. A few years ago, wheelchair bound, she was on the front line with others who risked arrest as they protested further nuclear testing in Nevada. Mairs writes candidly about the demands of her daily life and her ability to recognize humorous situations brought on by her illness.

Larry Rose was fifty-four years old when he was diagnosed with Alzheimer's disease. Alzheimer's disease is characterized by a steadily progressive deterioration of intellectual function. Memory disturbance is often the primary feature of the disease, but other symptoms include language and visuospatial disturbances, and personality and mood changes (for example, irritability, apathy, depression, impulsivity). The course of the disease can vary from person to person, with some patients deteriorating rapidly and others slowly. With the aid of a close friend who recorded events, Rose writes about his experiences with Alzheimer's disease. In his extraordinary and lucid account, he describes his struggles to resist the confusion that constantly threatens him.

Parkinson's disease is a slowly progressive condition characterized by tremors, rigidity, and postural instability. Many, but not all, sufferers also experience a decline in cognitive performance. As Sidney Dorros explains in his account of living with the disorder, the physical symptoms alone can have profound social effects; for example, people began to react differently to him because of his facial rigidity. Parkinson's remains one of the most puzzling of cognitive disorders.

When Katherine Lipsitz was a sophomore in college, she was diagnosed with epilepsy. She tried to refuse the diagnosis, but her body wouldn't let her. Lipsitz details the process of her denial, resignation, and eventual recognition that, with medicine, she could live a reasonably normal life.

Rod McLean describes what it was like to have suffered a ruptured aneurysm in the brain (a stroke) that nearly caused his death. What was unusual was that he was barely twenty years old at the time. He recalls the pain, the lack of control, and the rage he experienced. After surgery, McLean was in a coma for three weeks, and his doctors did not think he would be able to communicate again. This selection is testimony to McLean's resilience.

CARNAL ACTS: LIVING WITH MULTIPLE SCLEROSIS

Nancy Mairs

Psychological Concepts
multiple sclerosis, myelin, axon, cell body, dendrite, synapse

Nancy Mairs was a young housewife and mother when she developed multiple sclerosis, or MS. Multiple sclerosis is a serious neurological disease that involves the progressive breakdown of myelin sheaths around nerves. In this process, certain axons that have lost myelin may lose insulation from other axons. As a result, signals in the nervous system may scramble and short-circuit, and the transmission of signals from the brain to the muscles of the arms or legs may be delayed.

MS is a slowly debilitating disease that may result in paralysis. Those afflicted may experience a lack of energy and eventually need to use a cane or wheelchair. Others remain in remission for years and work and live productively.

Mairs, who has talent and grit, speaks of the effects her illness has had on her family, work, and self-image. She credits MS for sparking her sense of humor. How does Mairs describe the progression of her illness? What strategies does she use to cope with her disability?

The beginning of MS wasn't too bad. The first symptom, besides the pernicious fatigue that had begun to devour me, was "foot drop," the inability to raise my left foot at the ankle. As a consequence, I'd started to limp, but I could still wear high heels, and a bit of a limp might seem more intriguing than repulsive. After a few months, when the doctor suggested a cane, a crippled friend gave me quite an elegant wood-and-silver one, which I carried with a fair amount of panache. The real blow to my self-image came when I had to get a brace. As braces go, it's not bad: lightweight plastic molded to my foot and leg, fitting down into an ordinary shoe and secured around my calf by a Velcro strap. It reduces my limp and, more important, the danger of tripping and falling. But it meant the end of high heels. And it's ugly. Not as ugly as I think it is, I gather, but still pretty ugly. It signified for me, and perhaps still does, the permanence and irreversibility of my condition. The brace makes my MS concrete and forces me to wear it on the outside. As soon as I strapped the brace on, I climbed into trousers and stayed there (though not in the same trousers, of course). The idea of going around with my bare brace hanging out seemed almost as indecent as exposing my breasts. Not until 1984, soon after I won the Western States Book Award for poetry, did I put on a skirt short enough to reveal my plasticized leg. The connection between winning a writing award and baring my brace is not merely fortuitous; being affirmed as a writer really did embolden me. Since then, I've grown so accustomed to wearing skirts that I don't think about my brace any more than I think about my cane. I've incorporated them, I suppose: made them, in their necessity, insensate but fundamental parts of my body.

Meanwhile, I had to adjust to the most outward and visible sign of all, a three-wheeled electric scooter called an Amigo. This lessens my fatigue and increases my range terrifically, but it also shouts out to the world, "Here is a woman who can't stand on her own two feet." At the same time, paradoxically, it renders me invisible, reducing me to the height of a seven-year-old, with a child's attendant low status. "Would she like smoking or nonsmoking?" the gate agent assigning me a seat asks the friend traveling with me. In crowds I see nothing but buttocks. I can tell you the name of every type of designer jeans ever sold. The wearers, eyes front, trip over me and fall across my handlebars into my lap. "Hey!" I want to shout to the lofty world. "Down here! There's a person down here!" But I'm not, by their standards, quite a person anymore.

My self-esteem diminishes further as age and illness strip from me the features that made me, for a brief while anyway, a good-looking, even sexy, young woman. No more long, bounding strides: I shuffle along with the timid gait I remember observing, with pity and impatience, in the little old ladies at Boston's Symphony Hall on Friday afternoons. No more lithe, girlish figure: my belly sags from the loss of muscle tone, which also creates all kinds of intestinal disruptions, hopelessly humiliating in a society in which excretory functions remain strictly unspeakable. No more sex, either, if society had its way. The sexuality of the disabled so repulses most people that you can hardly get a doctor, let alone a member of the general population, to consider the issues it raises. Cripples simply aren't supposed to Want It, much less Do It. Fortunately, I've got a husband with a strong libido and a weak sense of social propriety, or else I'd find myself perforce practicing a vow of chastity I never cared to take.

Afflicted by the general shame of having a body at all, and the specific shame of having one weakened and misshapen by disease, I ought not to be able to hold my head up in public. And yet I've gotten into the habit of holding my head up in public, sometimes under excruciating circumstances. Recently, for instance, I had to give a reading at the University of Arizona. Having smashed three of my front teeth in a fall onto the concrete floor of my screened porch, I was in the process of getting them crowned, and the temporary crowns flew out during dinner right before the reading. What to do? I wanted, of course, to rush home and hide till the dental office opened the next morning. But I couldn't very well break my word at this last moment. So, looking like Hansel and Gretel's witch, and lisping worse than the Wife of Bath, I got up on stage and read. Somehow, over the years, I've learned how to set shame aside and do what I have to do. . . .

One may cry harder in the clutches of a troubled existence, but one may laugh harder as well. I had almost no sense of humor at all, particularly with regard to myself; before I started really experiencing difficulties, in the form of depression and MS, I was as sour as a pickle. Now, my life seems full of merriment. Imagine me, for instance, coming home from a shopping trip one winter evening. As I enter the screened porch, Pinto, my little terrier puppy, bounces forward to greet me, throwing my precarious balance off. I spin around and fall over backward, whacking my head on the sliding glass door to the house, but a quick check (I'm getting good at those) suggests no serious damage this time. This is called a pratfall, a burlesque device used in plays and films for a surefire laugh. In keeping with this spirit, I start to giggle at the image of this woman sprawled flat on her back, helpless under the ecstatic kisses of a spotted mongrel with a comic grin who is thrilled to have someone at last get right down to his own level. The night is chilly. George isn't due home for an hour. Pinto's kisses are unpleasantly damp. "Oh Lord," I think, "if I'm too weak to get up this time, it's going to be a long night." Spurred by the cold and the kisses, I get up.

In addition to making me more humorous, I think the difficult life has made me more attentive. In part, this trait is self-defensive: I *have* to watch out for all kinds of potential threats—bumps and cracks, for instance, and small comic dogs lurking in doorways—that others might ignore without courting disaster. But this is only a drill for a more valuable attentiveness to the objects and people around me. I notice more details. I take more delight in them. I feel much more connected to others than I used to, more aware of their troubles, more tolerant of their shortcomings. Hardship can be terrifically humanizing.

The most valuable response I've developed, I think, is gratitude. I don't mean that I'm grateful for having MS. I'm not, not in the least, and I don't see why I should be. What I'm grateful for is that, in spite of having MS, I've fulfilled ambitions I never dreamed I would. When I was first diagnosed, I didn't think I'd see my children grow up, and now I have a foster son in the navy, a daughter in the Peace Corps, and a son in college. I was sure my illness would drive George and me apart, and now we've celebrated our twenty-fifth wedding anniversary. I couldn't imagine that I'd make it through graduate school, but I did—twice. I thought I'd have to give up on being a writer, but here I am, writing for my life. I might have managed all these things—maybe even managed them better—without having MS. Who can tell? But through having MS, I've learned to cherish them as I don't think I could have otherwise. . . .

And so I say, *I'm afraid of having MS: of the almost daily deterioration of my strength; of the loss of control over my own body; of my increasing dependence on others to help me with the simplest personal tasks—tying my shoes, getting out of bed. Where will it all end? I'm afraid. I'm afraid. I'm afraid.* But like other MS people (and on the whole we're not very different from people in general, except perhaps that our fears are more focused and therefore easier to get at if we try), I don't give in to my fears. *If I weren't scared of this catastrophic disease,* I remind myself, *I'd have at least one screw loose somewhere.* So I put my fears to the best use I can, analyzing them to discover how to live carefully and choose my actions wisely. I'm nourished by the encouragement of others, like George, who believe that what's important is not that I'm scared but that I do what I need to do whether I'm scared or not. By speaking my fear aloud, I've reduced it from a giant trampling my interior landscape to an ordinary imp, the kind who dances through everybody's inner house from time to time, curdling the milk and smashing the crockery but leaving the structure basically intact. Surveying the damage, I get out my mop and broom. *This is my life*, I say to myself, *fear and all. I'm responsible for it. And I'd better get on with it, because it matters.*

Response and Analysis

1. The progressive breakdown of myelin sheaths plays a critical role in the development of MS. Define myelin sheaths, dendrite, cell body, axon, and synapse. Why are myelin sheaths important to the transmission of signals along the axon?

2. What is Nancy Mairs's attitude toward having MS? Briefly describe her psychological responses to living with MS, including laughing harder and being grateful. Why does she believe these are valuable responses? How has living with MS affected her view of herself and her self-esteem?

Personal Experience and Application

1. Mairs writes that although her electric scooter significantly increases her mobility, paradoxically it renders her invisible. How is she "invisible" when riding the scooter? What are your first impressions when you see someone riding an electric scooter or a wheelchair? Do you behave differently than you do with an able-bodied person? Why?

2. Briefly describe the daily difficulties that may be associated with living with MS.

Research

Researchers in the field of neuropsychology use a variety of methodological approaches. Suppose you are interested in using a case study to understand how MS affects physical functioning. What are two advantages and two disadvantages of the case study approach? What types of questions or issues cannot be answered with this approach?

Assume that you have scheduled an appointment to interview someone with MS. Make a list of topics that you would discuss with the participant.

SHOW ME THE WAY TO GO HOME

Larry Rose

Psychological Concepts
Alzheimer's disease, hippocampus, limbic system

Larry Rose, an electrical engineer working in Louisiana, began experiencing memory loss and realized that his mental abilities were declining. He thought that a vacation and vitamins would set him right. Gradually, however, his confusion increased—he made mistakes writing checks and remembering friends' faces and names; his thoughts became tangled, he forgot details, and conversations became a challenge. He became sad and anxious about the seriousness of his condition, but his sense of humor and gratitude for a good life helped sustain him. With the support of a special friend, Rose kept notes and recorded his experiences in the early stages of Alzheimer's disease.

Stella became insistent that I see the doctor. She was working in her office one morning and asked me to make her a cup of instant coffee. I went into the kitchen and looked around for a few minutes. Then I went back to her office and asked, "What is instant coffee?" She finally quit laughing when she saw that I was serious. It was then that she came unglued like a two-dollar umbrella.

"I'm going to make an appointment with Dr. Trahan right now. Something is terribly wrong with you, and I have had all of this absent-mindedness I can take."

"*You* have had all *you* can take? You should be looking at it through *my* eyes," I thought to myself. I knew I was in trouble, too, and I had no idea why. . . .

We got a call from Dr. Trahan a few days later, stating that all of the tests looked normal, but there were a few more tests he wanted to do, and he would schedule them later. . . .

The following month, Dr. Trahan called to tell Stella that I should see a neurologist. I had written him a check for six-hundred, seventy dollars to pay a balance of six dollars and seventy cents that the insurance had not paid. He said, "Not only is the check for the wrong amount and the date is wrong, but it looks like it was written by a ten-year-old. At this rate, Larry will be in a nursing home in less than two years!"

Stella made an appointment with the neurologist for a week later. I could hardly wait to see him. I just *knew* that it was nothing serious, and that he would prescribe a pill or something, and I would be all right in a few days.

The examination went well, or so I thought. He checked my reflexes, my vision, and my hearing. He had me read from a *Reader's Digest* and then tell him the gist of the story. I thought I had done well, but I lost the thread of the story several times, and could only get back on track by prompting. . . .

Slowly and painfully, I was becoming aware of the darkness in my mind. I realized that my mental abilities were fading and that I must work to overcome my fear of this loss. Everything that is important to me in life is slowly slipping away. Friends' faces, places, and names are becoming harder and harder to remember. I am preoccupied with time and can never remember what time it is.

I try to face reality. Will I soon forget who I am? Is there a reason for all of this? Why am I living, if there is no purpose to life at all? Will I soon be leading an empty existence? No, I can't be thinking that. A life is never wasted. Even in this helpless state, there has to be a reason. I know that even in the most hopeless situations, there is still a possibility for growth. I must never lose sight of that.

I had tears in my eyes for the first time in years. Stella touched my arm. "Everything will be okay, Larry. We'll go through this thing together." Touch is so very important. It has become an art to Stella—how to touch and guide me. Will there be a day when touch is the only thing left? . . .

The good days were not to last long, however. Stella had asked me to buy her some thin copper wire for a stained-glass project she was working on. Boy, did *that* request stick in my mind. I bought a roll of copper wire every time I went to town. I must have had ten rolls of wire on her workbench when she finally realized what I was doing. Although she told me she had enough wire to last her awhile, that didn't stop me. I still bought a roll every time I thought about it. She finally took all the extra rolls back to the hardware store and got my money back. Then she told the salespeople not to sell me any more copper wire. After that, when I'd try to purchase copper wire, they'd convince me that I didn't need any more. . . .

The weeks passed slowly. I had started carrying a notepad to remind me of important things. I read through it ten times a day and, so far, my notes showed I hadn't done anything stupid.

I found a paper in my pocket one day that read, "Don't forget to give Dr. Trahan back the key to his store." What in hell was I doing with a key to his store? Moreover, where *was* the key? "Maybe," I said to myself, "I just won't mention it, and he won't ask." So far, it's worked.

I am starting to have trouble finding the right words in conversation. Just today, I asked Stella, "Where is the sack of mushrooms?"

"What sack of mushrooms, Larry? We don't have any mushrooms, and anyway, I don't buy them in a sack."

"Sure we do, Stel. I saw them last night, the little, white, fluffy things in the sack."

"Oh, you mean *marshmallows*. They're up in the corner cabinet."

Poor Stella. She really has to stay on her toes when talking to me. Luckily, she is very adroit under pressing conditions. She has learned quickly how to figure out what I mean when I ask something like, "Where is my brown thing (my comb)?" or, "Where is the green stuff (mouthwash)?" Stella always knows.

One night, Stella asked me to sit down. "We need to talk." I hated it when she said that, because it usually meant that I was in trouble. "What do you want for Christmas?" she asked.

"A tombstone," I answered promptly.

"What? What in the world are you talking about? You're not going to be needing one of those for a long time."

"Yes I am. There is only one way to beat this thing in my head, and that is to die. I'm not going to lie in a nursing home with my mouth hanging open, like some Alzheimer's patients I've seen on TV. I just need to find a cool way to check out, like skateboarding down the side of the First National Bank building." . . .

The next morning, I went to Wal-Mart to pick up something or other . . . I forget what. I know it wasn't copper wire! I had taken Stella's Lincoln, because it was parked in front of my pickup. After fifteen or twenty minutes, I came out of the store, but I couldn't find my pickup. I must have looked for over an hour, and walked past the Lincoln ten times. I was beside myself, and dreaded calling Stella to tell her that someone had stolen my pickup. I was walking back to the store to see if I could find a phone, when an old friend and coffee-drinking buddy walked up to me.

"Hi, Larry. How you doing? I see Stella let you drive her car today."

I looked at the keys in my hand. They had Lincoln written all over them. "Oh, yes, I better head for the gas station. She only lets me drive it when it's out of gas." I was thinking fast. I was *thinking*. I was also very relieved. Now I wouldn't have to tell Stella anything. . . .

If that is all Alzheimer's is—a little memory loss, I would be a happy camper. The fact is that Alzheimer's affects the brain, and the brain controls not only memory, but reasoning, walking, sight, and swallowing, as well as many other abilities. . . .

I am becoming more and more withdrawn. It is so much easier to stay in the safety of my home, where Stella treats me with love and respect, than to expose myself to people who don't understand, people who raise their eyebrows when I have trouble making the right change at the cash register, or when I'm unable to think of the right words when asked a question. Maybe it would be easier for them if I didn't look so healthy. . . .

I can feel myself sliding down that slippery slope. I have a sadness and an anxiety that I have never experienced before. It feels like I am the only person in the world with this disease. . . .

I feel that I am walking a precipice alone. No one understands the frustration in my thoughts. I must keep pushing myself to use the abilities I have left, pushing right to the end. How much further do I have to go? How long will it be before I reach that vast canyon of nothingness? . . .

The letter from Social Security came today. I was afraid to open it; Stella looked at it first. I had been approved for the maximum benefits. It was the saddest day of my life. I am sure most people would have been thrilled, and maybe I was too, in a way, but it also meant that this thing in my head is real. Social Security doesn't just give disability benefits for the asking. They really do an investigation; they have good doctors at their disposal, who check every tiny symptom before making their decision. The whole process took just over ninety days. (I must add that I was treated with kindness and respect from everyone at the Social Security offices.) . . .

I feel an anger, a rage inside my head. It is a defused anger, not localized to any substrata—it cannot be narrowed down to any one thing. Mostly, the anger is with myself.

My thoughts are tangled, not in any order. This is hard to bear, since my memory has always been excellent. I can recall when I could read a page in a book, any book, then read it back, from memory, six months later, word for word. I have done it often.

I once told my boss that if he ever wanted me to remember anything, he should tell me that it's important, and tell it to me slowly, and I would remember it, word for word, for as long as I live. So far, I can still remember things that he told me ten years ago, but I can't remember what I did yesterday!

Will there be a day when I won't even know who I am? The things that make me Larry? Will it matter then? The anger goes as quickly as it comes.

I think anger can be justified, at times. It's normal to be angry with Alzheimer's. It's a thief, a murderer, a destroyer of minds. I try to channel my anger in practical ways. The best way for me to do this is to write down my thoughts. Stella's word processor must be jammed by now. I write down my thoughts and experiences almost every day. Some day, my kids, or their kids, might want to know. If the words that I write don't make any sense, I mow the grass. We have the best-groomed grass in the neighborhood. Between writing and mowing, I have neither the time nor the energy for anger.

I try hard not to think of my problems, or why this has happened to me. Carrying a load of resentment inside can only be destructive. . . .

Some time ago, we received an information package from the Alzheimer's Association. In one pamphlet, there was information about a new program called "Safe Return," a nationwide, community-based safety net that helps identify, locate, and return individuals who are memory-impaired. The program provides an identity bracelet or necklace; clothing labels and wallet cards to identify the individual; registration in a national database, and a twenty-four-hour, toll-free 800 number to contact when an individual is lost or found.

Although I have a wallet card and an identity necklace, Stella thought it would be a good idea to register in the new program. They provided an application, which asked for a lot of information, including addresses and phone numbers of friends and family. . . .

One afternoon when I wasn't doing much, I decided to fill in as much as I could. I worked on it for about an hour, then put it aside. A week or so later, I told

Stella that maybe she should finish the application and send it off to the Association. She looked at what I had filled in. I have never heard her laugh so hard in all the years I have known her.

"Larry, what sex are you?"

"What a silly question, Stel," I answered.

"Where the application asks for 'Sex,' you put 'None,'" she said, still laughing.

"They want you to be truthful, don't they?"

"Yes, but you're going to give us a bad image by being *too* truthful!"

"You know, that reminds me of the employment applications I used to get. One lady who was applying for a secretary job wrote down under 'Sex,' 'Only one time, in Baton Rouge.' Another fellow wrote 'Yes' under the question 'Salary desired?' I hired him. He was the only employee I had who knew exactly what he wanted."

We laughed until I could hardly catch my breath.

"Well, I am going to change your answer to 'Male.'"

"Sure. I don't even remember that question," I said, truthfully. . . .

Alzheimer's is not a word you hear every day (unlike AIDS, which you hear about regularly, and which has its own constitution and civil rights). Alzheimer's, it appears, has no agenda in government. It has no "in-your-face" advocates. I'm not even sure it is a disease. It's just a *thing*, a word. It's not caused by a virus or a bacteria. It just is. It's an enigma; and it keeps the afflicted from exerting any control over their own destiny. . . .

I understand that there are nineteen different drug studies going on all over the world right now, aimed at relieving the symptoms of Alzheimer's. I'm participating in one of them—along with a thousand others like me. We are on the cutting edge of research. There are dangers, but it is also dangerous to do nothing. I have been a mover and a shaker all my life. I can't just sit and do nothing. . . .

Although I feel good about myself at times, I strive to remember that, merely because I sometimes feel more at ease, I should not make the mistake of supposing that the danger is over. It comes back soon enough. My thoughts become jumbled, progressing to complete disorientation and confusion, and my speech becomes garbled or slow. The words that once came so fluently must now be thought about for some time. I avoid conversation when I'm in this state of confusion. Past events, as well as recent ones, are often forgotten, and my ability to do everyday tasks is gravely impaired. I work my mind harder now than ever before. . . .

My thoughts drift back to the Alzheimer's patients I have seen in nursing homes, just lying there, gone, for all intents and purposes. Can they still think? What are their thoughts? Are they closer to God than we will ever know? Closer than you and I?

There is so much to do, so little time. My doctors tell me that I am on what is called a "plateau." I am no better, but no worse. I could stay on this plateau for ten years or ten minutes. There is no way of telling. I am going to live every minute like it was my last. If my condition should worsen, no one can say I didn't give life everything I had, that I didn't try everything possible.

There are many people in the world whom I still haven't met. I must get busy. If you are one of the people whom I haven't met, I'm sorry; it's my loss.

If, when you read this . . . you feel a certain sadness, as some have told me they did, let yourself be sad, but not for me. Let yourself feel for all sick people. I have had a good and prosperous life. I have done it all, and I have enjoyed it. If I die tonight, I won't be cheated out of anything. Most of all, I have had the love of some beautiful people . . . and I have loved them, too.

Response and Analysis

1. How does Alzheimer's disease affect Larry Rose's memory? His intellectual functioning? His emotional functioning? Why is Rose sometimes angry with himself? Why does he begin to withdraw from social situations?

2. Research suggests that Alzheimer's disease is associated with degeneration of the hippocampus and other limbic structures. Briefly describe the functions of the hippocampus and the limbic system. What structures are associated with the limbic system? What structures in the limbic system are associated with emotion?

Personal Experience and Application

1. Do you know or have you seen someone who has Alzheimer's disease? Describe his or her cognitive abilities. What short-term and long-term memory difficulties do you notice? How has reading about Larry Rose affected your view of older persons and those with Alzheimer's disease?

2. What problems can a debilitating illness like Alzheimer's pose for the family members who care for an older relative affected by such a disease?

Research

Suppose you are part of a research team that is testing a new drug designed to minimize the mood fluctuations caused by Alzheimer's disease. Assume that your participants are fifty people diagnosed with the disease. You plan to give twenty-five people a new drug for six months and twenty-five people a placebo for six months. After six months, you will assess the frequency of mood fluctuations.

What is the independent variable? What are the two levels of the independent variable? What is the dependent variable? What is your hypothesis? Include the levels of the independent variable in your hypothesis.

PARKINSON'S: A PATIENT'S VIEW

Sidney Dorros

Psychological Concept
Parkinson's disease

Sidney Dorros was in the prime of his life. He was director of the Publications Division of the National Education Association (NEA), was married, and had four children. One day he began to lose dexterity in his fingers. Over a period of several months, his muscles stiffened, his facial expression became somewhat frozen, and he often became restless or impatient. But not until two years after his first symptom would Dorros be diagnosed with Parkinson's, a progressive neurological disease in which cells in the substantia nigra that produce the neurotransmitter dopamine degenerate.

Dorros struggled with issues central to his life: How could he continue to work and provide for his family? What would happen to his relationship with his wife, children, and friends? What treatments could bring him relief? After living with Parkinson's for many years, Dorros learned, with the help of physicians, the love of his family, and his own courage and determination, to accommodate the illness.

Parkinsonism does not suddenly attack its victim. It sneaks up on one—slowly, quietly, but inexorably. Its initial signs are so subtle that Margaret Bourke-White, famous *Life* photographer, in writing about her heroic battle with Parkinsonism, referred to the first evidence of the condition as a "wisp of a symptom."[1] In her case it was a slight dull ache in her left leg which she noticed when she climbed stairs.

In my case it was a slight ache in my left shoulder and then a hint of a tremor in my left arm while raking leaves on a beautiful Indian summer day in October. I attributed the ache to fatigue; my wife thought I wanted to avoid an unappealing task—and we both thought little of it. But the ache in the shoulder did not leave with the leaves of autumn. So I consulted a physician, an internist. He diagnosed the condition as bursitis and suggested a shot of cortisone.

"It only hurts when I do something like rake leaves," I told him. "I'd rather quit raking leaves than risk the possible ill-effects of a drug as strong as cortisone."

"Hmpf!" he snorted, "I can't do anything else for you."

---

[1]Margaret Bourke-White (1963). *Portrait of Myself,* p. 359. New York: Simon & Schuster.

When I told my wife about it, she too said, "Hmpf!" But she did do something to help my shoulder. She raked leaves.

That was the first of many burdens that she took on as the symptoms of Parkinsonism gradually stooped and stiffened me. . . .

When my fingers began to lose their nimble touch-typing pace, I thought it was due to typist's cramp. When my wife pointed out that my shoulders seemed to be more rounded than usual, I thought I was too tired to sit or stand up straight, or perhaps I wasn't getting enough exercise, or maybe I just had bad posture habits. I would often get impatient, nervous, restless, or irritable, which surprised my family and friends. This too was attributed to fatigue.

It was our family physician and friend, Bob Jones, who first recognized that I had symptoms of Parkinsonism. Bob was an ideal general practitioner—broadly knowledgeable, considerate, and available. He lived in the community he served, and he even made house calls. He dealt with the patient and his or her idiosyncrasies, not just the ailment. He had a zest for life that was infectious.

During a routine physical checkup, I told Bob of the slight ache and tremor in my left shoulder and arm. He noticed that I didn't swing my arms freely when I walked, that my movements were a bit slow, and that my facial expression was somewhat frozen; but he didn't announce these observations at the time.

"You may have a neurological problem," he said. "I'd like a neurologist to check you out." . . .

About a week after the initial examination, I got the diagnosis from Bob Jones. He took the time and exercised his skill to minimize the trauma when he broke the news that I had Parkinsonian symptoms. He said that the ailment follows many different courses, and that some cases progress very slowly, or arrest themselves, or are limited in their symptoms. He told me that I didn't require any medication at the time but that there were medicines and exercises that could alleviate the symptoms considerably. . . .

Superficially, I went along with my designation as a Parkinsonian, but deep inside of me a voice said, "It can't be!" And for nearly a year, I really didn't accept the diagnosis. . . .

As I returned home from Bob's office, I wondered why I still doubted the diagnosis of Parkinsonism. I remembered that ever since early childhood, I had harbored a secret desire to accomplish something memorable in service to mankind. Suddenly I understood. I had been afraid that by accepting the diagnosis I would lose all hope of realizing this dream.

I've since come to believe that many other people, for reasons of their own, carry within them equally strong drives and aspirations. These strongly affect a person's reactions to a chronic ailment such as Parkinsonism and need to be recognized, understood, and somehow accounted for by the patient and those who wish to help him. This is not easy when the motivations are well hidden. . . .

I began to get symptoms that were noticeable to others. Slight tremor in my left hand was the first perceptible sign, but this could usually be temporarily alleviated or obscured by moving my hand and arm about or by resting my hand on some surface at the appropriate angle and level. My handwriting also became noticeably smaller and uneven. Sometimes I would have difficulty walking, especially after standing or sitting still for a while. At other times I would be unable to lift either foot. I felt frozen to the spot. But I soon developed a strategy for breaking the ice. I would kneel down and pretend to tie one of my shoelaces. This movement usually loosened my muscles enough to enable me to step out when I stood up. After a while, though, friends began to wonder out loud why I had to tie my shoelaces so often.

Like many Parkinsonians, I was reluctant to tell people that I had the ailment. However, when I thought that they were noticing and wondering about the symptoms I did try to tell them the cause as matter of factly as possible. I learned that people often misinterpret some of the symptoms if they don't know their origin. When I told them about my illness and its effects, it eased some of their concerns. For example, I remember one time while I was interviewing a candidate for a position in the Publications Division of NEA, I got the feeling she was becoming tense. I told her, "I have a chronic ailment of the nervous system called Parkinson's disease which affects my facial expression. So if I appear to be frowning at you or at your papers, please remember that I'm not really frowning. It's just tight muscles." . . .

Despite the tribulations I endured during the . . . years . . . when Parkinsonism first became a serious problem and . . . when it became almost intolerable, I resisted accommodation to limitations imposed by the ailment. Instead, I tried desperately, in the words of Dr. Oliver Sacks, ". . . to transcend the possible, to deny its limits and to seek the impossible . . ."[2] That is, I tried to conduct my life as if I were not ill. My efforts to transcend the impossible resulted in a vicious cycle. The more I ignored my limitations, the greater those limitations became. . . .

I hit new lows: physically, mentally, and in key human relationships that eventually forced me to accommodate to reality—to adjust the style of my life to the conditions of my life.

I was pushed deeper into the valley of despair by pressures at home and at work. At home my wife's buoyant spirit and emotional support weakened as she herself became overwhelmed with problems. About that time her period of menopause began, bringing with it physical discomfort, emotional upset, and depression. I have known women to have been pushed into depression by any one of the problems Debbie faced: adjusting to four independent-minded, adult and teenage children; living with a husband whose frustrating, mysterious illness often made him seem a frightening stranger; and experiencing the trauma of a difficult menopause. Yet most of the time Debbie was able to cope with all three situations at once. Friends and relatives, and even her own children, hardly ever saw her lose her cool. . . .

---

[2]Oliver Sacks (1974). *Awakenings*, p. 226. New York: Doubleday & Company.

But while Debbie appeared to be laughing on the outside, she was sometimes bitterly crying on the inside. . . .

It was during this period that we changed from sleeping together in a double bed to sleeping in separate beds. Perhaps it doesn't seem so serious for husband and wife to sleep in separate beds. Many spouses do it all their lives. But Debbie and I were lonely, isolated, and frightened by the separation. After nearly twenty-five years of togetherness, each of us came to feel rejected by the other. How then did it happen, and why didn't we remedy the situation when we became aware of its implications? Partly because the situation grew slowly and unplanned and partly because it was accompanied by emotional crises that were too strong to overcome.

I previously described the problem of restless nights. At first I used to return to bed, but as the problem continued I found it increasingly difficult to get back to sleep. I was plagued with fears and restlessness, especially in the dark. Debbie was a light sleeper and my tossing and turning disturbed her. We both sought the security of sleeping in each other's arms, but my compulsion to move was too frequent for her to be comfortable. . . .

I had become so emotionally unstable that I would fly into rages upon slight provocation. Despite my wife's tremendous patience and support over a period of years, as my frustrations grew I would blame her for not being sensitive enough. . . .

I found it increasingly difficult to concentrate for long periods of time or to make decisions. It was difficult to tell whether my illness, the side effects of the medication, or emotional reactions to life's problems were responsible.

At work I found dealing with personnel problems and changing organizational and operational conditions increasingly difficult. When asked to draw up a reorganization plan for the publishing function of the organization, I reorganized myself, with the approval of my supervisor, into a consultative position entailing hardly any administrative responsibility. . . .

The most difficult part was getting to and from the office. The twelve-mile drive became too much for me, or too scary for my car-pool associates, and so when my turn came someone else drove. But then a new problem arose. I would often have difficulty walking out to the car or getting from the parking garage to my office. I could sometimes make it only by running. A friend would go ahead of me to clear the way, or follow carrying my briefcase. I was fortunate to have such good and patient friends. Some days they would wait for me because I could not make it to the auto and had to rest or wait for my medication to work. When I had such a bad day that I felt I had to see the doctor on an emergency basis, or just couldn't bear to be at the office any longer, they would take me home early. . . .

"If you get a lemon, make lemonade."

As we learned to adjust to retirement we found some advantages in my relief from the pressures of time and responsibility. Retirement enabled us to enjoy our lives more, to cope more effectively with my ailment, to improve our relationships with our children, and to render increased service to others.

Like many other couples, Debbie and I had feared that too much togetherness might break our already strained marital relationship. However, within a year after retirement our love and respect for each other began to increase. After more than twenty-five years of frustration over differing attitudes and habits on a few crucial matters we began to accommodate to each other. My adjustment to retirement was aided also by the introduction of a new medication that increased my ability to function—not enough to resume remunerative work—but enough to improve my roles as husband and parent. . . .

I tried to arise, eat, move my bowels, exercise, and go to bed at regular times. I also tried to stick to my schedule for taking medication more rigidly than in the past. Instead of taking emergency doses of medication when I felt unable to move, I took emergency rests. . . .

Norman Cousins has publicized the idea that if negative emotions produce negative chemical changes in the body, positive emotions may produce positive chemical changes. . . .

He asks, "Is it possible that love, hope, faith, laughter, confidence, and the will to live have therapeutic values?"[3]

I can attest that they have. I believe it's been love and the other positive emotions listed above that have sustained me as much as medicine since the loss of my wife. First, memories of our love and faithfulness to each other for thirty years helped counteract the grief I continued to feel and still feel over her death. Then, just as new medications have appeared to rescue me each time I have come near the bottom physically, new sources of emotional support came forth when my morale needed boosting.

In addition to the increased attention from my children, and other relatives and friends, members of the Parkinsonian Society provided an important source of emotional support. When the leader of a well-financed but differently organized local Parkinson program in another state came to visit PSGW, he observed: "You don't have as much money to work with as we do, but you have a much more important ingredient. You have love!"

But all the emotional supports mentioned above did not keep me from experiencing many hours of loneliness and depression.

---

[3]Norman Cousins (1979). *Anatomy of an Illness as Perceived by the Patient*, p. 35. New York: W. W. Norton & Company.

Response and Analysis

1. What physical symptoms of Parkinson's disease did Sidney Dorros experience? How might friends or acquaintances of someone with Parkinson's disease misinterpret some of the symptoms? What lifestyle changes does Dorros make to accommodate living with the disease?

2. What is known about the etiology of Parkinson's disease? What is the prognosis?

Personal Experience and Application

1. Imagine that you suffer from hand tremors. What daily activities might be difficult or embarrassing?

2. Describe a few daily difficulties that people with Parkinson's disease may experience.

Research

Neuroscientists have learned a great deal about the relationship between the brain and behavior by studying people who have suffered damage in specific areas of the brain. This research, however, has certain drawbacks; for example, the location and severity of brain damage cannot be controlled, and there are a limited number of human participants available to study.

Because of these limitations, neuroscientists often use animals to study more precisely the relationship between the brain and behavior. Neuroscientists purposely damage portions of animal brains and then study the resulting behavior. Do you think that it is ethical to use animals for this type of research? Why or why not? What other ways might neuroscientists study these questions? How do you think researchers should care for and handle animals that are serving as research subjects?

I REFUSED TO BE SICK . . . AND IT ALMOST KILLED ME

Katherine H. Lipsitz

Psychological Concepts
epilepsy, grand mal seizure, neuron

Katherine Lipsitz was a successful college student "struggling hard for perfection." She had the desires of most young women her age: to enjoy good times with friends, to be attractive, and to succeed in school. But she suffered from muscle spasms and seizures, which she kept secret from others as long as possible. When she was told she had epilepsy, she ignored her doctor's treatment program.

Epilepsy is a serious neurological disorder caused by continual firing of neurons in one area of the brain. The firing rapidly spreads to other areas of the brain; as a result, those with this illness not only have seizures but may speak incoherently and even lose consciousness. Medication is available to control the disease, and most people with epilepsy are able to live reasonably normal lives.

At one point Lipsitz decided "not to be an epileptic." What motivated this decision? What symptoms does she experience? How does she come to accept living with epilepsy?

This is what they say I do: First I lose consciousness. Then my knees buckle and I collapse. Where I am is important when I collapse: I've tumbled down a flight of stairs, fallen on the sidewalk, and slipped under the water in a bath. Many times I go into convulsions. For me, convulsions last three to five minutes and cause a complete loss of muscle control, so that I writhe and shake and sometimes hurt my head. Occasionally, I'm told, I have vomited and lost continence. Afterward, I breathe heavily or snore; it takes a while until I know where I am.

I have never seen another person go through a grand mal epileptic seizure, and I don't remember my own: I black out. But my college roommate and others have described my seizures to me, and I know that they're not pretty.

I must have understood that epilepsy isn't pretty, because the first time a doctor told me I had it, during the summer after my sophomore year at Vassar College, I immediately and passionately denied the diagnosis. I couldn't have epilepsy, I told myself; epileptics are flawed, and I was struggling hard for perfection.

By the time I entered Vassar, I thought I had finally overcome a lifetime of imperfections. I grew up in New York City with a beautiful mother, a successful father—a music producer—and two very intelligent older brothers. For twelve years, I attended an Upper East Side private school. My childhood was privileged; but I was the youngest in my family, the tallest in class—and always overweight. This last flaw was unacceptable. When I was young, classmates called me names. Adults would murmur: "What a shame! She has such a pretty face."

At age fifteen I became thin—by force of will combined with bouts of anorexia and bulimia. I started hanging out with a fast, popular crowd at Studio 54, Area, and Xenon. Yet I continued to feel awkward and out of place—like the fat, ugly kid I thought I'd been.

About this time, I also became dimly aware that something else was bothering me. I began to have muscle spasms, which I later learned were called myoclonus, a pre-epileptic condition. These spasms would happen in the early morning or in moments of stress. I hid them from family and friends. I spent a lot of time alone, dreaming of the day when some man who was smart, kind, and funny would come along and carry me away to happiness.

That first year at Vassar, I began to have full-fledged seizures, though I still didn't know what they were. Amazingly, nobody found out. I was very pleased about that. I also met and began to date a boy who wore a Rolex watch and Bally loafers and was strong-minded, quick-witted, and smart. I was not about to tell him of my seizures or my growing fears. I know I was afraid that he'd leave me, but I think I was even more afraid of admitting to myself that something was very wrong.

I spent the summer after my sophomore year in Spain. I had one seizure before I left home and another after I returned—the latter one I couldn't hide from my parents, who took me to a doctor. The doctor, a neurologist, ruled out a brain tumor and then, describing epilepsy as a mysterious disorder whose causes he couldn't be sure of, cautioned that I'd have to rest every day, abstain from alcohol, and take medicine that would prevent seizures but might also cause weight gain, raise my testosterone level, and promote growth of body hair.

That's when I decided not to be an epileptic. I had worked so hard to be like everybody else; I wasn't about to become the overweight male ape the doctor seemed to be describing. My attitude was: I would drink when I felt like it and sleep only if it didn't interfere with my social life; what the doctor didn't know wouldn't hurt him. I left his office. I never took the pills, and went on with my life as though nothing had changed.

When I returned to school junior year, things were different. The guy I dated had graduated from Vassar and from me. I stopped wearing makeup and caring how I dressed. As I revealed my condition to a few friends, I grew self-conscious about being the only kid I knew who spent quality time with her neurologist. Mostly, I was afraid—not so much of the seizures themselves as of hitting my head during convulsions. I was sure epilepsy would kill me. I believed I should make a will. I didn't think about getting better.

I woke up early one morning junior year facing three men I'd never seen before. "I don't know you," I said. My roommate, stepping forward, explained, "Kate, these men are paramedics. You had a seizure, and you have to go with them." The men took me to the emergency room of the county hospital, where I saw people in real pain, shouting for help. This scared me, but not enough to change. I told myself that all I wanted was to be a normal college kid and I would do it with will-power.

The second semester of my junior year, I met a different kind of guy—no Bally loafers or Rolexes, but I liked him—partly because he liked me. By now I'd gained twenty pounds; whenever I felt sorry for myself I ate, and I'd been feeling very sorry for myself. I was amazed that this boy found me attractive.

Then early one morning, after he and I had gone out drinking and fallen asleep in his dorm room, I woke up feeling strange. I tried to go back to sleep. When I awoke again, my friends the Emergency Medical Technicians were there. The boy had called them. They took me to the Vassar health clinic, where the boy sat with me for hours and held my hand—teaching me a lesson I've never forgotten in how to treat people. Later, he told me how scared he'd been that I would die. I didn't know how to reassure him, because his fears were exactly like my own. So I stopped dating him—stopped dating anyone for the next five years.

Now I know that people experience epilepsy at different times of life and for different reasons, and that it can be controlled. Some people are born with epilepsy; others have their first attack after a blow to the head or similar trauma. I seem to have what's called "idiopathic" epilepsy—literally meaning "cause unknown," but in my case associated with a genetic susceptibility. At the end of my junior year in college, however, I felt as though I were the only person on earth who had this illness, that nothing could be done to stop it, and that no one could accept me with it. The truth is, I couldn't accept myself.

I hit a low point: I wasn't like other college kids. They were experimenting with alcohol while I was experimenting with different combinations of medication. Hard alcohol was poison. And every time I drank, trying to prove I couldn't be something I knew I was, I had a seizure. My friends drove back and forth to New York City; I couldn't even apply for a driver's license until I could prove I'd been seizure free for eighteen months. So I went to classes, watched TV, and ate anything I could get my hands on. I became more isolated. Food took the place of a best friend. Then a new neurologist finally convinced me to give up drinking.

This doctor, whom I still see, saved my life. Highly regarded in his field, and also kind and gentle, he was the first person I met whom I couldn't manipulate or make feel sorry for me. By taking a firm stand, he showed me that the only thing keeping me from getting my epilepsy under control was me.

Under his care, I began to take all my medicine. I graduated from Vassar—sixty pounds heavier than when I'd entered, but also changed in other, more positive ways. I wasn't so arrogant or insistent on perfection; I'd stopped being a spoiled brat. I moved back to New York City and gathered a group of close friends whose idea of a wild night was dinner out. I didn't drink. I rested. And, for the first time since I was fifteen, my seizures stopped.

I got a job as a secretary in a large advertising agency—where I wanted to be. Six months later, two weeks before my twenty-third birthday, I was promoted to junior copywriter. I had lost a few pounds in spite of my medication, and hadn't had a seizure in a year. I felt I had epilepsy beaten.

To prove it, I went to a party on my birthday and drank everything in sight—margaritas, alcohol punch, beer. The next morning I woke early and took my dog for a walk. Out on the street, I suddenly didn't feel well. My knees buckled and I fell to the ground. As in previous days, I woke up in the hospital. I had a blood-stained face, and a doctor was putting stitches in my chin. My mother was there, crying, and my roommate from Vassar, with whom I now shared an apartment, was there asking me if I was okay. That's when it hit me—I wasn't okay, and I knew it. Both these women had always been there for me, putting my welfare above their own concerns, never blaming me or losing patience. And how had I repaid them? By being selfish—never once thinking what effect my careless behavior had on them. For the first time, it was clear to me that I'd have to change—not for a month or a year but for life.

That's how I arrived where I am today—twenty-six years old and free of seizures for the last two years. Some days I still feel shaky, but I take my medicine and know how to manage my illness. I eat fruits and vegetables and brown rice instead of junk food, and I work out five days a week. I've lost forty-five of the sixty pounds I gained in college. I have a driver's license that I don't use much, but that makes me feel free. For a year, I went out with a guy who loved me as I am; now I believe that's in the cards for me.

I have joined the Epilepsy Society of New York City, where I do volunteer work. I've learned a lot there. For one thing, many people find the hardest part of epilepsy is living not with the illness but with the stigma attached to it. This was true of me, and has been true through the ages. In medieval Portugal, epilepsy was considered divine punishment for acts of bestiality committed by a person's ancestors. The Catholic Church once prohibited epileptics from becoming priests, fearing they were possessed by the devil. Until the 1980s, a law barred epileptics from marrying in Missouri. Other myths hold epilepsy a mark of genius. I am neither a possessed person nor a genius, but I am better for having learned to live with epilepsy. It's taught me to be kinder and more empathetic. A few months ago at the Epilepsy Society I met a beautiful, blonde-haired fifteen-year-old girl. We were talking about her boyfriend. "Does he know you have epilepsy?" I asked. "Oh, no. I could never tell him *that*," she said. So I asked her how she would feel if *he* were the one with epilepsy. "I'd keep dating him and love him anyway," she said, a slow smile spreading across her lovely face.

It was the right answer. Though the road is rocky, I hope she learns to love herself as well.

Response and Analysis

1. What were Katherine Lipsitz's physical symptoms during the grand mal epileptic seizure? What changes in consciousness did she experience?

2. According to Lipsitz, why might people develop epilepsy? Why did she deny having epilepsy? What stages of acceptance did she experience? How did she modify her lifestyle to accommodate living with epilepsy?

Personal Experience and Application

1. Lipsitz writes that "many people find the hardest part of epilepsy is living not with the illness but with the stigma attached to it." What stigmas do you believe are associated with epilepsy? How might stereotypes and social pressures make life difficult for someone living with epilepsy?

2. In what ways do you think living with epilepsy taught Lipsitz to be "kinder and more empathetic"?

Research

Most seizure disorders such as epilepsy are caused by one or more regions of scar tissue—seizure foci—that irritate the brain tissue surrounding them. Suppose you are part of a research team that is testing a new drug designed to reduce seizures. Like other research groups, your team is using rats to evaluate the effectiveness of the new drug. Assume that you are using twenty rats and create seizure foci in each rat. You give ten rats the new drug and ten rats the standard drug. You record the number of seizures each rat experiences over a thirty-day period.

Is it important that the rats in both groups live in the same physical environment? Is it important that both groups of rats be fed the same amount of food at the same time? Why or why not? What other factors should you control?

STROKE SURVIVORS

William H. Bergquist, Rod McLean, and Barbara A. Kobylinski

Psychological Concepts
stroke (cerebrovascular accident), lobes (parietal, frontal, occipital, temporal)

Rod McLean was an active, involved college student on his way to a fast-food restaurant with a friend. Suddenly he had difficulty walking. He couldn't see or speak clearly, and he fell. Several of his friends took him to the hospital. McLean had suffered a stroke, which is rare for someone is his twenties.

A stroke, or cerebrovascular accident, occurs when the blood supply to the brain is cut off. When that happens brain cells are damaged because the brain does not receive the oxygen it needs. The location and severity of the stroke largely determine which functions are affected. Some people may have permanent brain damage; others may suffer paralysis in various parts of the body. The resulting physical disabilities may affect stroke victims' psychological well-being and interpersonal relationships.

Particularly impressive is McLean's memory of his stroke. He recalls the intense headache that came on suddenly, his inability to make his friends understand him, and his frustration with losing his balance. What reasons does he give for his survival and recovery?

I'm Rod McLean. I'm a stroke survivor. As a matter of fact, a neurologist described my stroke as a "spontaneous hemorrhage from an angioma or arteriovenous malformation in the left parietal area." In other words, a blood vessel in the left side of my brain had a weak point and burst. And it hurt! I was told later that I was within seconds or minutes of dying. But I guess I was as lucky as I could be, for it just happened that one of the best neurosurgeons in the region was right there when I was carried into the emergency room. He jumped into action to open my cranium and halted the rupture within moments.

The big one! It sure was. I think it was a Wednesday, late afternoon. Patty—a friend of mine—and I decided to walk four or five blocks to the fast-food restaurant. About halfway back, something started happening. It was really strange! I was invaded by an instant and massive headache. Everything started to become different—I didn't know what it was. I looked at my feet, but they didn't seem as though they were mine. I had to concentrate to make sure they would do what they were supposed to, because I noticed that I was having a harder and harder time walking.

At the same time, Patty became aware that something was going on. When she asked me questions, I heard and understood everything, but then I couldn't understand that I was forgetting whatever it was she had said. Not only that, her voice sounded like an echo. I had no reference point and quickly became afraid; I was scared of the unknown. I noticed the sun was too bright and that I was seeing things surrealistically. My walking became wobbly, but Patty helped me get home.

Gary and Rolf, close friends and roommates, were out in the front yard; they saw something was wrong. In a way, I guess I was relieved to see my friends because it gave me a sense of security. They could see that I was afraid and that I appeared disoriented. They asked what was wrong and, to no avail, tried to figure out something to relieve the situation. Meanwhile, I was staggering and falling around. I struggled to answer their questions and pleaded for help and solutions. Looking at Patty, I tried to reach into my right front pocket to get some money to give her so she could go get me some aspirin. But somehow I couldn't find the right words to convey my needs.

I was trying to do all these simple things at the same time, and nothing was working right! My friends didn't know what to do. They carried me upstairs and laid me down on my bed, saying that I would be all right. They left! I was in pain. Everything was so hot; my entire body was drenched with sweat. I tried to sit up to take my shirt off over my head. I had no balance; every time I fought to sit up, I kept falling back down. The last time I hadn't been able to sit up was when I was a baby! Inside I was screaming, but on the outside I had somehow forgotten how to do that. Next, I tried again and again to take my shoes and socks off—that was practically impossible, too. I'd reach for the laces, but my fingers would totally miss them and I'd fall over sideways. Eventually, my friends came back and saw that I was in worse shape than a few minutes ago. They both stared at me in the realization of my anguish, glanced at each other, and agreed that they should take me to the hospital right away.

Lying on my side, I was starting to completely lose it; I was not really in control of anything. About all I could do was force myself to remain conscious—not really alert, but only distortedly aware that something was happening. Gary and Rolf carried me, limp, to the car and poured me in. Gary raced to the emergency room as Rolf held on to me. My body was still sweating and I was so hot that I had to hang my head out the window. It was odd. All the sounds—my friends' voices echoing and the outside sounds, such as the rush of traffic, cars honking, the wind, and everything else—angered me to the point of extreme hatred. I felt like lashing out to destroy and eliminate the grating noises that became an overwhelming irritation. My brain was throbbing, exploding with pain. Everything around me was aggravating the problem. I wanted it all to stop!

When we got to the hospital, they carried me into the Emergency Room and put me on a gurney. I was in tremendous pain. I was lying on the bed—out of control. I wanted out! As I internally screamed to escape, my brain continued to grasp for explanations or solutions. At the same time, I had no control of my body; my limbs and torso were writhing back and forth. My instinctual body was trying to get away from this unbelievable pain, too. But since the brain didn't have control, the body was just fighting it all. A nurse came in and looked at me rolling around, obviously in outrageous pain. She held up two fingers and asked me how many I saw. Remember, I was still in a pure rage. When she made that request, my wrath exploded and destroyed my image of her.

I noticed my vision was warped and distorted, and the colors were skyrocketing and forming different patterns; it was like the grand finale of a fireworks extravaganza, and it was all happening in my mind. When I blinked my eyes again and again, I discovered that what I saw was the same whether my eyes were open or closed. Either way, I was *not* seeing things as they were in reality. "Oh my God, I'm blind!" I thought.

Then, for some reason the writhing and internal chaos seemed to cease. I didn't hurt, feel, or hear anything anymore, though I was still scared. I realized that up to that moment, I had been totally exuding anger and hatred. While I was consumed with this hatred, I felt that if I were physically able, I would have flailed about and crushed anything in front of me.

My thought process shut down. My mind's eye rapidly flashed before me scenes from my entire life—from birth to the present. I was floating away into another dimension as if I were watching myself; maybe my spirit was separating from my body. In retrospect, it all seems so strange. Earlier, my body and mind had been working on instinct as I writhed and contorted, attempting to get rid of the horrendous anguish and all-encompassing pain. I had been fighting against death with ultimate fear. But all of a sudden, my entire being succumbed and then accepted what was happening. At that point, I felt I was floating in the "right" direction; I didn't resist anymore. The battle was over and I comfortably accepted my approaching death. I was exiting. I anticipated a new future in a new dimension. Then, I believe I was brought back to life by the brain surgeon. I was redirected into a deep sleep (or coma) and did not regain consciousness until twenty-one days later, when I awoke into the so-called reality of Tacoma General Hospital's Intensive Care Unit.

Let me explain a bit of what had happened. I had had what's commonly called an *aneurysm*, or ruptured blood vessel in the brain. The brain has many different sections, each with different functions in the overall "system." When the blood vessel exploded in the left hemisphere, a major "glitch" occurred in the communication area—the area that controls our abstract thinking processes as well as our physical movements, fine motor control, sense of balance, and other functions. My aneurysm caused the loss of at least three of the five senses: touch, hearing, and vision. I don't know if I lost smell or taste.

When my stroke happened, it was as if the system shut down. All of the physical components of my body transferred energy to where the emergency was. Unfortunately, this is the sequence that one's body follows, not only when it is reacting to a crisis, but also when it is about to die. I was told later that I had been in critical condition. My parents and friends were informed that I would be dead within ten to fifteen minutes if the brain surgeon didn't operate and snip the area of my brain where the bleeding occurred. The doctors anticipated that I would be confined to a wheelchair and unable to communicate for the rest of my life—a vegetable, a ruta-baga. But I turned out to be an artichoke—"prickly on the outside, with a wonderful heart on the inside" (to quote an extraordinary man and advocate for the disabled, Ed Roberts)!

One thing that was so odd was that the brain attack happened when I was only twenty years old. (The stroke definitely sped up my maturation process!) At that time, I admittedly had no knowledge of what a stroke was; as a matter of fact, I didn't even know what a disability was. At that age, I had no conception of disabilities or fatal traumas—I still had a young adult mind-set and thought I was invincible. I was only beginning to mature.

Response and Analysis

1. What cognitive and physical difficulties did Rod McLean experience before he went to the emergency room and during his time in the emergency room? How did the stroke affect McLean physically and emotionally?

2. McLean says that his stroke occurred in the parietal lobe. What are the functions of the parietal lobe? What changes in behavior or problems might you expect if a stroke occurred in the frontal lobe? In the occipital lobe? In the temporal lobe?

Personal Experience and Application

1. McLean says that at age twenty, he "didn't even know what a disability was." What is your understanding of disability?

2. McLean also says that he thought he was invincible. What does he mean by that? Do you or someone you know feel invincible? Why?

Research

Stroke, heart disease, and cancer are associated with lifestyle behaviors, such as using alcohol, smoking, and diet. Researchers examining the relationship between disease and lifestyle behaviors in humans typically use correlational designs. Why? What are the advantages and disadvantages of using a correlational design?

SENSATION AND
PERCEPTION

A man may see how this world goes
with no eyes. Look with thine ears.

WILLIAM SHAKESPEARE, *King Lear*

Our senses let us enter the world, and we perceive what comes to us in complex ways. This chapter focuses on issues concerning sensation and perception: physical characteristics of sound; auditory transduction; touch and pain sensation; olfaction; aromatic memory; and theories of color vision.

John Hockenberry's senses are all intact except in the area below his lower chest. Hockenberry was injured in an automobile accident when he was nineteen years old. That accident left him a paraplegic. He writes, often in explicit detail and sometimes with anger, about how his paralysis affects his life. Particularly impressive is the strength he has developed in the rest of his body, and the tenacity and stamina he has developed to pursue his career as an international reporter. In this selection, Hockenberry recalls preparing stuffing for a Thanksgiving turkey and placing a hot pan on his lap. Because he had no sensation of pain, he burned one leg badly. He and his doctors did not realize the seriousness of the burn for several months; it nearly cost him his life.

David Wright is deaf. Yet he states that "there is no such thing as absolute deafness." What does he "hear"? Interestingly, Wright says that the world seldom appears silent because "silence is not absence of sound but of movement." Therefore, at a time when not a leaf stirs, he sees the silence; when the wind stirs, he sees and "hears" the motion.

Oliver Sacks worked with a man named Virgil whose vision was partially restored after some forty years. Virgil and his fiancée, Amy, had consulted an ophthalmologist, who agreed that surgery might restore Virgil's sight. The surgery was partially successful, and Virgil was able to see about 20/80 and to discern very large letters. Unfortunately, the restoration of his eyesight proved a mixed blessing. He had difficulty seeing objects in their wholeness and difficulty with depth perception. How difficult might it be to adjust to some renewed vision after having adapted so well without it?

In the final selection of this chapter, Diane Ackerman celebrates the meeting of our senses with the world. Sight, touch, taste, smell, hearing—we use them all for pleasure, warning, and survival. Here Ackerman observes our sense of smell. How does it serve us? Why do certain smells trigger distant memories? Do humans and animals use the sense of smell in different ways?

MOVING VIOLATIONS

John Hockenberry

Psychological Concepts
touch, pain sensation and perception, paraplegia

John Hockenberry, former correspondent for National Public Radio and currently with NBC-TV's newsmagazine program "Dateline," suffered a spinal cord injury at the age of nineteen from an automobile accident. That injury left him a paraplegic without sensation in his legs or abdomen and little in his chest.

Hockenberry is reporter *extraordinaire*. To track a story, he has ridden a mule up a hillside in Iraq and maneuvered his wheelchair through almost intractable stretches of Middle Eastern sand. He applied to be the first journalist in space. Along with frank details about how others sometimes perceive and treat him, Hockenberry writes of the frustrations of limited sensation. In this selection, he tells how he nearly lost his life because of a burn he suffered on his leg when he placed a hot pan on his lap. Unable to feel any pain from the heat, Hockenberry was unaware of the burn that was taking place.

Numbness is a distinct feeling. Just as zero gives meaning to all numbers, numbness is a placeholder of the flesh, the boundary where consciousness and body divide, where life becomes the inanimate vessel we live in. Our lives are played out under an inanimate universe. Sensation is the sideshow, a spotlight inside a tent of darkness. We step in and out of the white circle. It blinds us if we look directly at it. We are just as sightless in the dark.

We worship sensation, longing to make its impressions real. We endow our awareness with the divinity of the creator. We scour our pleasures for a sign that good feelings mean that the universe actually likes us. We make excuses for our pain, insisting that others acknowledge its seriousness. Or we push into our pain, seeking the actual mechanical limits of our bodies. We yearn to equate sense with reality. We discover, every time, that sensation is just the playpen where we have been put. The odd toys handed down to us are all we have to work with. Like a baby, we can throw toys away, but we cannot get any more.

To honor sensation is to honor an illusion. To honor what has none is humanity's original act of faith. My legs have no sensation. Neither does my abdomen or much of my chest. With heart and lungs inside, my chest and abdomen retain their function despite numbness. My legs have lost even that. They are culs-de-sac of blood and bone that carry no weight, must themselves be carried, and justify their existence on the slimmest of pretexts: that regardless of all that, they are still my legs.

Occasionally they will jerk with a spastic, repeating rhythm. The accidental poke of a pen point, the drops of scalding water dribbled from a teapot, an ice cube landing in my lap are sometimes answered by a muscle's spastic movement. Their connection to the spinal cord, if not to the brain above it, is still intact. My legs move by themselves. I feel nothing, but my legs must still feel something akin to pain or pleasure. They remain connected; their nerves do what they have always done. They call home. The phone has been ringing off the hook for nineteen years.

The loss of sensation takes some getting used to. On my left thigh, midway between my knee and my hip, is a scar about six inches long and two to three inches wide. It looks like Madagascar. It also precisely resembles the shape that the bottom of a large Corning Ware baking dish makes when pressed into soft dough, or the soft spongy tissue that used to lie between my lap and my left femur. In 1977 I was cooking stuffing for a Thanksgiving turkey on an electric stove in an apartment in Springfield, Oregon. The Corning Ware dish was taken from the refrigerator first. Its ceramic handles were quite cold, a sensation they conveyed even after several minutes on the hot burner of an electric range.

If this had been a metal pot, a few minutes on the burner would have conducted heat all over its surface and into the air around it. A metal pot would have broadcast its temperature, conveying immediately that it was an object to keep well away from the skin. On any other body but mine, if the pot had made accidental contact, pain would have made sure the pot was swiftly moved. But ceramic is not a conductor of heat. Just a few minutes out of the refrigerator, the dish was cold to the touch everywhere but underneath, where the burner of the stove was beginning to cook the bread cubes, spices, and melting butter. On the bottom of the dish, next to the burner, it was probably three hundred degrees. It was certainly close to that temperature when I picked up the dish, and holding its still-cold handles set it down absently and squarely on my lap.

With a wooden spoon, I mixed the crumbs and spices and butter while I held the dish steady. The aroma of cooking rose from inside the dish. I felt nothing. With no saucepan resting on its element, the electric burner I had taken the dish from moments before began to glow red. Its heat hit my face. I continued to stir. I added a little milk and heard a sizzling sound as the liquid contacted the hot bottom of the plate. I still felt nothing and continued stirring and adding spices, and talking to whomever else was in the room.

When I removed the dish, my left leg trembled. The spasticity was odd. Normally my legs had coarse, slow movements when they were spastic. This time their motions were tiny and very fast. There was no sensation, but a slight queasiness passed over me. Something was wrong, but the idea that I had actually set a hot pan on my lap and had been calmly stirring its contents for several minutes was so absurd that even then I did not think I had burned my leg severely. It seemed impossible that such a thing could have happened.

It was only after I could see a slight outline of fluid on my pants leg that I suspected something terrible might have happened. I looked at the leg. Its motions now were more pronounced, erratic, and unknown to me. I had not seen this kind of motion before. From my detached position, looking down, it was as though I was watching a horror movie. My legs appeared to be in agony. It was clear even without sensation that the legs were now trying to account for an act of the creator above that seemed senseless and cruel. I felt embarrassed and foolish. Then, as the stain on my thigh became more apparent, I felt scared.

Removing my trousers revealed the place where the hot dish had sat for perhaps two full minutes. It was something to see, and even more shocking to watch, without feeling the slightest pain. The skin was gathered into a leathery, shrunken depression on the top of my thigh. The hairs had all been cooked into a blistered white wound. The root of each hair was a raised dot where the glands beneath the skin had simply exploded from the heat. There was no blood, for reasons that would become apparent later. The wound looked unearthly. It was just as unusual to the doctors at the local hospital who examined it and concluded that it was only a second-degree burn.

If I had any sensation about this whole affair, it was embarrassment. To go to the hospital over something that didn't hurt at all seemed like complaining. I laughed about it with the doctors. I was ashamed to have done such a stupid thing. I was trying to be a good paraplegic and not make silly mistakes. I felt sorry for wasting the doctors' time. That I felt nothing, and was so apologetic about what appeared to be a pretty serious burn, made the doctors suspicious. They began to ask about my life at home. Perhaps there was some more sinister explanation for the burn. "Did anyone get mad at you this morning?" a nurse asked. They asked about drugs or some angry relative who might have wanted to punish me. I told them I lived alone. They called my house to make sure it was so. One of the doctors asked if this burn might have been self-inflicted. "Yes," I said, "I told you it was." He looked at me again. "Is there anything you want to tell me?"

The burn no longer scared me. This emergency room intern who thought I might have tried to kill myself with a Corning Ware dish filled with bread cubes and butter pats was suddenly making me very nervous. He was so convinced that this was a plausible explanation for my leg burn that for a moment I thought I might be in shock, and that someone had actually tried to cook me that morning but that I was just blocking it out. "Look, I just made a stupid mistake with the dish. It felt cold on the top. I couldn't feel that it was hot on the bottom. I set it on my lap for a minute. I won't do it again. Can I go now?"

In their haste to establish some explanation for the burn other than that I had accidentally cooked my thigh while preparing a turkey, they missed just how serious a burn it was. The numbness in my legs threw them off. A third-degree burn is rarely the result of a moderate amount of heat applied over a period of minutes. More commonly, it is an extremely high temperature contacting the skin for a short period of time. A slowly cooked leg is not a textbook injury. It suggests torture, an unusual malady in Springfield, Oregon, in 1977. The doctors did what they normally would for a second-degree burn—they gave me a large bandage, some iodine, and sent me home.

The wound did not heal for months. For a while it shed large chunks of dead tissue and a brown fluid totally unlike anything I had ever seen emerge from my body. I tried to get it to scab over, or heal under a bandage. It simply got worse. Each morning and night I would look at a wound that, if I could feel it, would have been infinitely more painful than anything that had happened in my accident. I stared down at it from above as though I were on some leisurely balloon ride. I had no sensation, yet I worried about the leg. I felt sorry for its pain. It could not tell me how it felt, it could not do anything for me. I became sentimental about all of the times my legs had helped me. I wanted to help them. But I was also fascinated by the invulnerability of numbness. There was no urgency about this wound because I felt no pain. I slept normally. I ate normally. I had to bandage the leg before going out to prevent it from staining my pants, but otherwise I could go about my life without much concern that my thigh was dangerously infected.

This was still the case three months later, so I went to the only doctor I knew by name in Oregon. Dr. Ellison was a urologist who handled all of the local crips' catheter problems and said he would be glad to look at this burn trouble I was having. He told me to remove my pants. He eyed the size of the bandage as I started to untape it from the skin around the wound. When he saw the wound, he stopped cold. He told his nurses to shut all of the doors to the examination rooms and to scrub him for surgery. He declared the room I was in in quarantine and began spraying the air with antiseptic. When the nurse asked if he needed anesthetic, he nodded and then caught himself. "No, I guess I won't be needing it this time."

Without anesthesia, and for nearly an hour while I calmly watched, Dr. Ellison poked and scrubbed and pulled away dead skin. For the first time since Thanksgiving, my leg began to bleed profusely. When he was finished, he wrapped my leg in gauze and removed a surgical mask he had put on. "You would have lost your leg if you had waited much longer." He shook his head as he took my temperature. "If you had started to run a fever, you could have died."

All of this had happened with me as a spectator feeling no pain. I did feel guilty that I might have put my legs through a nearly fatal ordeal. With the wound cleaned and its dead tissue removed, my leg began to heal. The circulation came back. My thigh returned to its normal pink color. In a matter of weeks, the wound was fully closed. All that remained of the trauma was a spectacular scar. On my last visit to the doctor he noted that while the wound had healed well, the nerves in the thigh were probably damaged beyond repair. "There will be no feeling here ever again," he said gravely as he probed the scar with his finger.

It was odd to think that my legs and I shared numbness now. Two degrees of sensation: my own loss of feeling in the parts of me below the break in my spinal cord, and the loss of nerves in the skin on my thigh. With my fingers I could feel the cold, leathery numbness of the scar surrounded by warm, healthy skin. Numbness has a feeling and a texture. Doctor Ellison suddenly realized his mistake. "I'm sorry, I forgot for a moment that you can't feel anyway. I guess it doesn't really matter," he said.

Response and Analysis

1. John Hockenberry raises an important issue regarding sensation when he says: "We yearn to equate sense with reality." What does he mean by this? How do sensation and numbness affect Hockenberry's perceptions of reality? His sense of self-identity? Give examples from his narrative to support your ideas.

2. Briefly describe Hockenberry's limits to feeling pain below his chest. Briefly discuss one theory that explains how the spinal cord influences the amount of pain that reaches the brain.

Personal Experience and Application

1. Describe the daily difficulties that may be associated with not being able to walk or have sensation below the waist. Do you think people behave differently when they interact with someone in a wheelchair than with an able-bodied person? Why or why not?

2. Are all areas on your campus accessible to persons in wheelchairs? In your community?

Research

The procedures of an experiment must be ethical and protect the rights and dignity of the participants. One of the challenges to conducting research on pain is designing a procedure that does not hurt or harm the participants. How might you ethically examine how we perceive pain?

DEAFNESS:
AN AUTOBIOGRAPHY

David Wright

Psychological Concepts
hearing, physical characteristics of sound

What might it be like to suddenly be cut off from the world of sound? Do the other senses compensate for the loss? In what way?

Poet David Wright, born in 1920 in Johannesburg, South Africa, became deaf from scarlet fever when he was seven years old. At the age of fourteen he went to England, where he attended a school for the deaf, and in 1942 he graduated from Oxford University. If deafness was to be his "destiny," Wright observes, he was fortunate to have already developed language skills. He could speak and had a vocabulary that could easily be developed further by reading. These advantages helped him personally and professionally.

In this selection, Wright points out what might at first seem a contradiction: he can't hear, yet he doesn't live in complete silence. His explanation helps us understand what kinds of sounds break up his silent world.

About deafness I know everything and nothing. Everything, if forty years' first-hand experience is to count. Nothing, when I realize the little I have to do with the converse aspects of deafness—the other half of the dialogue. Of that side my wife knows more than I. So do teachers of the deaf and those who work among them; not least, people involuntarily but intensely involved—ordinary men and women who find themselves, from one cause or another, parents of a deaf child. For it is the non-deaf who absorb a large part of the impact of the disability. The limitations imposed by deafness are often less noticed by its victims than by those with whom they have to do.

Deafness is a disability without pathos. Dr. Johnson called it "the most desperate of human calamities." Yet its effects are slapstick:

"Where's the baby?"

"I put it in the dustbin."[1]

There is a buffoonery about deafness which is liable to rub off on anybody who comes into contact with it. Having to shout at the hard of hearing is not ele-

---

[1] To a lip reader the words *baby* and *paper* are almost indistinguishable.

gant, nor is finger-spelling or the mouthing of words to magnify lip movements for those whose eyes are their ears. . . .

Very few are absolutely deaf. Their experience must necessarily be different from that of the severely deaf, the partially deaf, and the merely hard of hearing. The partially deaf, it seems to me, have the worst of both worlds. They hear enough to be distracted by noise yet not enough for it to be meaningful. For the merely hard of hearing there is the strain of extracting significance from sounds that may be as loud as life yet out of focus; what comes through is an auditory fuzz. Of course there are hearing-aids, but not everybody can profit from these.

Yet what is crucial is the age at which hearing is lost. Those who have been born deaf, whether completely or partially, must always be at a disadvantage compared with those who lose hearing later in life. The deaf-born cannot pick up speech and language naturally like ordinary children. They have to be taught, a difficult and slow process, the slower and more difficult the later the teaching begins. For the most intense activity of the brain takes place in the first few years of one's life, and thereafter—from the age of about three—gradually decreases. That is why small children quickly and easily pick up foreign languages while older children and adults find it an effort. But the born deaf and those who become deaf in early childhood have the compensation that they do not feel the loss of a faculty they never had or cannot remember. They are at least spared the painful effort of adjustment. The later in life one loses hearing, the sharper the test of character and fortitude: because adaptability lessens with age. On the other hand, the years of hearing are so much money in the bank. Those to whom deafness comes late do not have to acquire with pain and struggle the elements of language, vocabulary, speech. These assets—pure gold—are theirs already. . . .

I do not live in a world of complete silence. There is no such thing as absolute deafness. Coming from one whose aural nerve is extinct, this statement may be taken as authoritative.

Let me attempt to define the auditory limits of the world I inhabit. They are perhaps less restricted than may be imagined. Without entering into technicalities about sones, decibels, and so on, it may be said that all sound is vibration and that the ear, roughly speaking, is a highly specialized organ for the reception of air-vibrations or sound-waves. But other things besides air conduct vibration and therefore sound—wood for instance. If I stand on a wooden floor I can "hear" footsteps behind me, but not when standing on a floor made of some less resonant substance—for example stone or concrete. I can even partially "hear" my own voice. This is not surprising, for people hear themselves talk mainly by bone-conduction inside their heads (but other persons by air-conduction; that is why people find their own voices sounding surprisingly different when thrown back at them by a tape recorder). Yet like nearly all deaf people I cannot judge the loudness or quality of my own voice. To some extent I can do so by putting a finger against my Adam's apple or voicebox. This is well known as one of the ways in which the deaf can be made to "hear" something of a speech-instructor's voice. Likewise I "hear" a piano if I place a finger on it while it is being played; a radio and gramophone too, when touching the sound box or amplifier. (The gramophone needle gives best results, but this isn't good for the record.) Such "hearing" is selective; I receive only the low notes of the scale, the high ones elude me. No matter how loud the volume is turned on what comes through is a bent or incomplete version of actual sound. In "touch-hearing" most music, and all speech, comes across as a blurry bumble of noise.

Nevertheless there is some music that I enjoy after a fashion. But it has to be produced by stringed instruments (harp, guitar, piano, double-bass, and so on) as I cannot hear wind-instruments (flute, bagpipes, oboe). Percussive instruments like drums are naturally well inside my range. I have a passion for military bands, though hearing little except the drumtaps, a sad boom-thud from the big drum and a clattering exhilaration from the kettledrums. . . .

To get on with the list of things audible, or at least interfering with the silence that might be expected to compensate a totally occluded ear, let me tabulate the following: gunfire, detonation of high-explosives, low-flying aeroplanes, cars backfiring, motor-bicycles, heavy lorries, carts clattering over cobblestones, wurlitzers, pneumatic drills. There can't be much that I miss of the normal orchestration of urban existence. I should add that I also once heard the human voice. One day in 1963 I was at Lord's cricket ground; Ted Dexter had just come in to bat against the West Indies. He put a couple of runs on the board with the air of a man who means to get another ninety-eight before lunch. Suddenly he was bowled. While the bails were still flying, coats, hats, cushions, umbrellas, sandwiches, for all I know babies even, were hurled into the air by some nine or ten thousand West Indians in the free seats where I was watching. Up went a simultaneous roar of delight. Hearing that sound, for me not very loud but like a croaking bark, was a queer and spooky experience. I have never forgotten it.

It will be seen that the world a deaf man inhabits is not one of complete silence, which is perhaps the chief complaint he has to make about it. There is another point. Though noise, as such, does not obtrude to the extent that the above catalogue would seem to imply, the world in which I live seldom *appears* silent. Let me try to explain what I mean. In my case, silence is not absence of sound but of movement.

Suppose it is a calm day, absolutely still, not a twig or leaf stirring. To me it will seem quiet as a tomb though hedgerows are full of noisy but invisible birds. Then comes a breath of air, enough to unsettle a leaf; I will see and hear that movement like an exclamation. The illusory soundlessness has been interrupted. I see, as if I heard, a visionary noise of wind in a disturbance of foliage. Wordsworth in a late poem exactly caught the phenomenon in a remarkable line:

A soft eye-music of slow-waving boughs

which may have subconsciously derived from an equally cogent line in Coleridge's *The Eolian Harp:*

A light in sound, a sound-like power of light.

The "sound" seen by me is not necessarily equivalent to the real one. It must often be close enough, in my case helped by a subliminal memory of things once heard. I cannot watch a gale without "hearing" an uproar of violent movement: trees thrashing, grassblades battling and flattened; or, at sea, waves locked and staggering like all-in wrestlers—this kind of thing comes through as hubbub enough. On the other hand, I also live in a world of sounds which are, as I know quite well, imaginary because non-existent. Yet for me they are part of reality. I have sometimes to make a deliberate effort to remember I am not "hearing" anything, because there is nothing to hear. Such non-sounds include the flight and movement of birds, even fish swimming in clear water or the tank of an aquarium. I take it that the flight of most birds, at least at a distance, must be silent—bar the creaking noise made by the wings of swans and some kinds of wild geese. Yet it *appears* audible, each species creating a different "eye-music," from the nonchalant melancholy of seagulls to the staccato flitting of tits.

This is not to subscribe to the irritating theory that the loss of one sense is compensated for by the quickening of another. There are no compensations; life is not like that. At best we are offered alternatives. We have no choice but to take them.

This is by no means a complete picture of the world I live in, or of any other deaf person's, come to that. Almost nothing has been said about the major hurdle of deafness, the problem of communication. It is simply an attempt to convey what deafness is like physically, or at least what it's like so far as one deaf man is concerned, before I go on to tell the story of how I lost my hearing, how I reacted, how I was educated, and the various stratagems necessity forced me to adopt to get on and get by in a non-deaf world.

For I am now, after forty years of what we will term silence, so accommodated to it (like a hermit-crab to its shell) that were the faculty of hearing restored to me tomorrow it would appear an affliction rather than a benefit. I do not mean that I find deafness desirable, but that in the course of time the disability has been assimilated to the extent that it is now an integral condition of existence, like the use of a hand. By the same token the restoration of my hearing, or the loss of my deafness, whichever is the right way of putting it, would be like having that hand cut off.

Response and Analysis

1. Briefly discuss the types of sounds that David Wright can hear. How is Wright able to "hear" footsteps and his own voice?

2. Describe the physical characteristics of sound (for example, amplitude, wavelength, and frequency).

3. Why does Wright believe that the age at which hearing is lost is crucial to language acquisition and speech?

Personal Experience and Application

1. Do you or does someone you know have a hearing impairment? At what age did the hearing difficulties begin? What speech and communication difficulties do you observe?

2. Excessive exposure to sounds that are 85 decibels and louder can cause hearing loss. Here is a brief list of common sounds and their approximate intensities: normal conversation: 60 decibels; vacuum cleaner: 70 decibels; city traffic: 80 decibels; power lawn mower: 90 decibels; subway train from a distance of 20 feet: 100 decibels; jackhammer: 110 decibels; amplified rock music: 120 decibels. The average intensity of music that college students play over headphones is about 88 decibels (Brody, 1982). List the sounds you hear every day that may be 85 decibels or louder.

Research

Suppose you conduct a year-long longitudinal study to investigate the impact of repeated exposure to loud music on hearing ability. The participants are thirty eighteen-year-old rock musicians who practice with their band at least twice a week and perform at a music club at least twice a month. You measure their hearing ability on the first day of each month. Unfortunately, during the year half of the musicians move out of the area and discontinue their participation in your study. At the end of the year, you have complete data for only fifteen musicians. Might the loss of the fifteen musicians affect your conclusions? Why or why not?

TO SEE AND NOT SEE

Oliver Sacks

Psychological Concepts
top-down processing, trichromatic theory of color
vision, opponent process theory of color vision

What if, after some forty years of blindness, you were to have your sight restored? How would you feel? Would you expect to have any difficulties, and, if so, what might they be?

Oliver Sacks tells the story of a man who regained partial eyesight in midlife. Virgil was fifty years old and had been blind since early childhood. He was soon to be married, and his fiancée, Amy, had taken him to her ophthalmologist for an examination. The couple learned that through a relatively simple operation Virgil might be able to see again. Virgil consented to the surgery and, when the bandages were removed, some of his sight was restored.

However, Virgil faced many difficulties: shadows confused him, and stairways became a hazard because of problems with depth perception. When Tibbles, his cat, came to him, Virgil struggled to see the ears and head, body and tail, as all of a piece so that he could see Cat. About one month after surgery, "he often felt more disabled than he had felt when he was blind" (p. 121).[1] Virgil's story illustrates the difficulties that may occur when one's sight is restored after so long a time.

When we arrived at the house, Virgil, caneless, walked by himself up the path to the front door, pulled out his key, grasped the doorknob, unlocked the door, and opened it. This was impressive—he could never have done it at first, he said, and it was something he had been practicing since the day after surgery. It was his show-piece. But he said that in general he found walking "scary" and "confusing" without touch, without his cane, with his uncertain, unstable judgment of space and distance. Sometimes surfaces or objects would seem to loom, to be on top of him, when they were still quite a distance away; sometimes he would get confused by his own shadow (the whole concept of shadows, of objects blocking light, was puzzling to him) and would come to a stop, or trip, or try to step over it. Steps, in particular, posed a special hazard, because all he could see was a confusion, a flat surface, of parallel and crisscrossing lines; he could not see them (although he knew them) as

---

[1]In this and all subsequent introductions, quotations that are not in the excerpt itself can be found in the unabridged version of the selection.

solid objects going up or coming down in three-dimensional space. Now, five weeks after surgery, he often felt more disabled than he had felt when he was blind, and he had lost the confidence, the ease of moving, that he had possessed then. But he hoped all this would sort itself out with time.

I was not so sure; every patient described in the literature had faced great difficulties after surgery in the apprehension of space and distance—for months, even years. This was the case even in Valvo's highly intelligent patient H.S., who had been normally sighted until, at fifteen, his eyes were scarred by a chemical explosion. He had become totally blind until a corneal transplant was done twenty-two years later. But following this, he encountered grave difficulties of every kind, which he recorded, minutely, on tape:

> During these first weeks [after surgery] I had no appreciation of depth or distance; street lights were luminous stains stuck to the window panes, and the corridors of the hospital were black holes. When I crossed the road the traffic terrified me, even when I was accompanied. I am very insecure while walking; indeed I am more afraid now than before the operation.

We gathered in the kitchen at the back of the house, which had a large white deal table. Bob [an ophthalmologist] and I laid out all our test objects—color charts, letter charts, pictures, illusions—on it and set up a video camera to record the testing. As we settled down, Virgil's cat and dog bounded in to greet and check us—and Virgil, we noted, had some difficulty telling which was which. This comic and embarrassing problem had persisted since he returned home from surgery: both animals, as it happened, were black and white, and he kept confusing them—to their annoyance—until he could touch them, too. Sometimes, Amy said, she would see him examining the cat carefully, looking at its head, its ears, its paws, its tail, and touching each part gently as he did so. I observed this myself the next day—Virgil feeling and looking at Tibbles with extraordinary intentness, correlating the cat. He would keep doing this, Amy remarked ("You'd think once was enough"), but the new ideas, the visual recognitions, kept slipping from his mind.

Cheselden described a strikingly similar scene with his young patient in the 1720s:

> One particular only, though it might appear trifling, I will relate: Having often forgot which was the cat, and which the dog, he was ashamed to ask; but catching the cat, which he knew by feeling, he was observed to look at her steadfastly, and then, setting her down, said, So, puss, I shall know you another time. . . . Upon being told what things were . . . he would carefully observe that he might know them again; and (as he said) at first learned to know, and again forgot, a thousand things in a day.

Virgil's first formal recognitions when the bandages were taken off had been of letters on the ophthalmologist's eye chart, and we decided to test him, first, on letter recognition. He could not see ordinary newsprint clearly—his acuity was still only about 20/80—but he readily perceived letters that were more than a third of an inch high. Here he did rather well, for the most part, and recognized all the commoner letters (at least, capital letters) easily—as he had been able to do from the moment the bandages were removed. How was it that he had so much difficulty recognizing faces, or the cat, and so much difficulty with shapes generally, and with size and distance, and yet so little difficulty, relatively, recognizing letters? When I asked Virgil about this, he told me that he had learned the alphabet by touch at school, where they had used letter blocks, or cutout letters, for teaching the blind. I was struck by this and reminded of Gregory's patient S.B.: "much to our surprise, he could even tell the time by means of a large clock on the wall. We were so surprised at this that we did not at first believe that he could have been in any sense blind before the operation." But in his blind days S.B. had used a large hunter watch with no glass, telling the time by touching the hands, and he had apparently made an instant "crossmodal" transfer, to use Gregory's term, from touch to vision. Virgil too, it seemed, must have been making just such a transfer.

But while Virgil could recognize individual letters easily, he could not string them together—could not read or even see words. I found this puzzling, for he said that they used not only Braille but English in raised or inscribed letters at school— and that he had learned to read fairly fluently. Indeed, he could still easily read the inscriptions on war memorials and tombstones by touch. But his eyes seemed to fix on particular letters and to be incapable of the easy movement, the scanning, that is needed to read. This was also the case with the literate H.S.:

> My first attempts at reading were painful. I could make out single letters, but it was impossible for me to make out whole words; I managed to do so only after weeks of exhausting attempts. In fact, it was impossible for me to remember all the letters together after having read them one by one. Nor was it possible for me, during the first weeks, to count my own five fingers: I had the feeling that they were all there, but . . . it was not possible for me to pass from one to the other while counting.

Further problems became apparent as we spent the day with Virgil. He would pick up details incessantly—an angle, an edge, a color, a movement—but would not be able to synthesize them, to form a complex perception at a glance. This was one reason the cat, visually, was so puzzling: he would see a paw, the nose, the tail, an ear, but could not see all of them together, see the cat as a whole.

Amy had commented in her journal on how even the most "obvious" connections—visually and logically obvious—had to be learned. Thus, she told us, a few days after the operation, "he said that trees didn't look like anything on earth," but in her entry for October 21, a month after the operation, she noted, "Virgil finally put a tree together—he now knows that the trunk and leaves go together to form a complete unit." And on another occasion: "Skyscrapers strange, cannot understand how they stay up without collapsing." . . .

Although Virgil could recognize letters and numbers, and could write them, too, he mixed up some rather similar ones ("A" and "H," for example) and on occasion, wrote some backward. (Hull describes how, after only five years of blindness in his forties, his own visual memories had become so uncertain that he was not sure which way around a "3" went and had to trace it in the air with his fingers. Thus the numeral was retained as a tactile-motor concept, but no longer as a visual concept.) Still, Virgil's performance was an impressive one for a man who had not seen for forty-five years. But the world does not consist of letters and numbers. How would he do with objects and pictures? How would he do with the real world?

His first impressions when the bandages were removed were especially of color, and it seemed to be color, which has no analogue in the world of touch, that excited and delighted him—this was very clear from the way he spoke and from Amy's journal. (The recognition of colors and movement seems to be innate.) It was colors to which Virgil continually alluded, the chromatic unexpectedness of new sights. He had had Greek salad and spaghetti the night before, he told us, and the spaghetti startled him: "White round strings, like fishing line," he said. "I thought it'd be brown."

Seeing light and shape and movements, seeing colors above all, had been completely unexpected and had had a physical and emotional impact almost shocking, explosive. ("I felt the violence of these sensations," wrote Valvo's patient H.S., "like a blow on the head. The violence of the emotion . . . was akin to the very strong emotion I felt on seeing my wife for the first time, and when out in a car, I saw the huge monuments of Rome.")

We found that Virgil easily distinguished a great array of colors and matched them without difficulty. But, confusingly, or confusedly, he sometimes gave colors the wrong names: yellow, for example, he called pink, but he knew that it was the same color as a banana. We wondered at first whether he could have a color agnosia or color anomia—defects of color association and color naming that are due to damage in specific areas of the brain. But his difficulties, it seemed to us, came simply from lack of learning (or from forgetting)—from the fact that early and long blindness had sometimes prevented his associating colors with their names or had caused him to forget some of the associations he had made. Such associations and the neural connections that underlay them, feeble in the first place, had become disestablished in his brain, not through any damage or disease, but simply from disuse.

Response and Analysis

1. Briefly describe Virgil's ability to identify objects on the day his bandages were removed. Which objects were easy and which were difficult for him to identify? How might Virgil's expectations influence his perception of objects, including the physical appearance of a cat or a dog?

2. What were Virgil's impressions of color? Describe his difficulty in naming colors. Why might he have had this difficulty?

3. What are the main features of the trichromatic theory of color vision and the opponent process theory of color vision? Why are both theories useful?

Personal Experience and Application

1. Imagine that glasses and contact lenses are not available. What visual, cognitive, and emotional difficulties might someone who needs corrective lenses experience? How might life change for this person?

2. Suppose you are blindfolded and walk through your house or neighborhood. How would you orient yourself? What senses might you rely on, and for what purpose?

Research

Suppose you want to examine how experience modifies the visual system that detects movement. You train twenty participants to detect extremely small movements by having them look at very small dots on a computer screen. Four screens present dots that make extremely small movements in the same direction: up, down, left, or right. The fifth screen presents stationary dots. The participants watch only one screen for thirty minutes each day for four days. On the fifth day, you measure their ability to detect movements by presenting dots that move in all four directions. You find that the participants are better at detecting movement for the direction in which they were trained; the training did not affect their ability to detect movement in the other three directions.

Why was it necessary to have the participants look at only one screen rather than at all five screens? What might happen if the participants watched more than one screen? On the basis of your findings, what might you conclude about how experience influences perception?

A NATURAL HISTORY OF THE SENSES

Diane Ackerman

Psychological Concepts
olfaction, aromatic memory, pheromones

Do certain fragrances activate your memory? Does suntan lotion? The salt air of the sea? A pine forest? What memories do these scents evoke? Our olfactory sense bears a mysterious quality. We can't touch, see, or hear it, yet it is as vital as any of our other senses. A delectable aroma coming from the kitchen makes us hungry, while burning food inhibits our appetite. Smoke can be a warning and perfume a pleasure. A strange scent may make us curious or cautious.

"Smell," writes Ackerman, "is the mute sense, the one without words" (p. 6). Although we can describe smells as floral, musky, resinous, ethereal, foul, or acrid, this cataloging does not convey what the smell of a gardenia is like. Nevertheless, being an astute observer, Ackerman manages to write about this powerful sense and makes us more aware of its importance.

We each have our own aromatic memories. One of my most vivid involves an odor that was as much vapor as scent. One Christmas, I traveled along the coast of California with the Los Angeles Museum's Monarch Project, locating and tagging great numbers of overwintering monarch butterflies. They prefer to winter in eucalyptus groves, which are deeply fragrant. The first time I stepped into one, and every time thereafter, they filled me with sudden tender memories of mentholated rub and childhood colds. First we reached high into the trees, where the butterflies hung in fluttering gold garlands, and caught a group of them with telescoping nets. Then we sat on the ground, which was densely covered with the South African ice plant, a type of succulent, and one of the very few plants that can tolerate the heavy oils that drop from the trees. The oils kept crawling insects away, too, and, except for the occasional Pacific tree frog croaking like someone working the tumblers of a safe, or a foolish blue jay trying to feed on the butterflies (whose wings contain a digitalis-like poison), the sunlit forests were serene, otherworldly, and immense with quiet. Because of the eucalyptus vapor, I not only smelled the scent, I felt it in my nose and throat. The loudest noise was the occasional sound of a door creaking open, the sound of eucalyptus bark peeling off the trees and falling to the ground, where it would soon roll up like papyrus. Everywhere I looked, there seemed to be proclamations left by some ancient scribe. Yet, to my nose, it was Illinois in the 1950s. It was a school day; I was tucked in bed, safe and cosseted, feeling my mother massage my chest with Vicks VapoRub. That scent and memory brought an added serenity to the hours of sitting quietly in the forest and handling the exquisite butterflies, gentle creatures full of life and beauty who stalk nothing and live on nectar, like the gods of old. What made this recall doubly sweet was the way it became layered in my senses. Though at first tagging butterflies triggered memories of childhood, afterward the butterfly-tagging *itself* became a scent-triggerable memory, and, what's more, it replaced the original one: In Manhattan one day, I stopped at a flower-seller's on the street, as I always do when I travel, to choose a few flowers for the hotel room. Two tubs held branches of round, silver-dollar-shaped eucalyptus, the leaves of which were still fresh—bluish-green with a chalky surface; a few of them had broken, and released their thick, pungent vapor into the air. Despite the noise of Third Avenue traffic, the drilling of the City Works Department, the dust blowing up off the streets and the clotted gray of the sky, I was instantly transported to a particularly beautiful eucalyptus grove near Santa Barbara. A cloud of butterflies flew along a dried-up riverbed. I sat serenely on the ground, lifting yet another gold-and-black monarch butterfly from my net, carefully tagging it and tossing it back into the air, then watching for a moment to make sure it flew safely away with its new tag pasted like a tiny epaulet on one wing. The peace of that moment crested over me like a breaking wave and saturated my senses. A young Vietnamese man arranging his stock looked hard at me, and I realized that my eyes had suddenly teared. The whole episode could not have taken more than a few seconds, but the combined scent memories endowed eucalyptus with an almost savage power to move me. That afternoon, I went to one of my favorite shops, a boutique in the Village, where they will compound a bath oil for you, using a base of sweet almond oil, or make up shampoos or body lotions from other fragrant ingredients. Hanging from my bathtub's shower attachment is a blue net bag of the sort French-women use when they do their daily grocery shopping; I keep in it a wide variety of bath potions, and eucalyptus is one of the most calming. How is it possible that Dickens's chance encounter with a few molecules of glue, or mine with eucalyptus, can transport us back to an otherwise inaccessible world? . . .

Smells spur memories, but they also rouse our dozy senses, pamper and in-dulge us, help define our self-image, stir the cauldron of our seductiveness, warn us of danger, lead us into temptation, fan our religious fervor, accompany us to heaven, wed us to fashion, steep us in luxury. Yet, over time, smell has become the least necessary of our senses, "the fallen angel," as Helen Keller dramatically calls it. Some researchers believe that we do indeed perceive, through smell, much of the same information lower animals do. In a room full of businesspeople, one would get information about which individuals were important, which were confident, which were sexually receptive, which in conflict, all through smell. The difference is that we don't have a trigger response. We're aware of smell, but we don't auto-matically react in certain ways because of it, as most animals would.

One morning I took a train to Philadelphia to visit the Monell Chemical Senses Center near the campus of Drexel University. Laid out like a vertical neigh-borhood, Monell's building houses hundreds of researchers who study the chemis-try, psychology, healing properties, and odd characteristics of smell. Many of the news-making pheromone studies have taken place at Monell, or at similar institu-tions. In one experiment, rooms full of housewives were paid to sniff anonymous underarms; in another study, funded by a feminine hygiene spray manufacturer, the scene was even more bizarre. Among Monell's concerns: how we recognize smells; what happens when someone loses their sense of smell; how smell varies as one grows older; ingenious ways to control wildlife pests through smell; the way body odors can be used to help diagnose diseases (the sweat of schizophrenics smells dif-ferent from that of normal people, for example); how body scents influence our so-cial and sexual behavior. Monell researchers have discovered, in one of the most fascinating smell experiments of our time, that mice can discriminate genetic differ-ences among potential mates by smell alone; they read the details of other animals' immune systems. If you want to create the strongest offspring, it's best to mate with someone whose strengths are different from yours, so that you can create the maxi-mum defenses against any intruder, bacteria, viruses, and so on. And the best way to do that is to produce an omnicompetent immune system. Nature thrives in mon-grels. *Mix well* is life's motto. Monell scientists have been able to raise special mice that differ from one another in only a single gene, and observe their mating prefer-ences. They all chose mates whose immune systems would combine with theirs to produce the hardiest litters. Furthermore, they did not base their choices on their perception of their own smell, but on the remembered smell of their parents. None of this was reasoned, of course; the mice just mated according to their drive, unaware of the subliminal fiats.

Can it be possible that human beings do this, too, without realizing it? We don't require smell to mark territories, establish hierarchies, recognize individuals or, especially, know when a female is in heat. And yet one look at the obsessive use of perfume and its psychological effect on us makes it clear that smell is an old warhorse of evolution we groom and feed and just can't let go of. We don't need it to survive, but we crave it beyond all reason, maybe, in part, out of a nostalgia for a time when we were creatureal, a deeply connected part of Nature. As evolution has phased out our sense of smell, chemists have labored to restore it. Nor is it something we do casually; we drench ourselves in smells, we wallow in them. Not only do we perfume our bodies and homes, we perfume almost every object that enters our lives, from our cars to our toilet paper. Used-car dealers have a "new-car" spray, guaranteed to make a buyer feel good about the oldest tin warthog. Real estate dealers sometimes spray "cake-baking" aromas around the kitchen of a house before showing it to a client. Shopping malls add "pizza smell" to their air-conditioning system to put shoppers in the mood to visit their restaurants. Clothing, tires, magic markers, and toys all reek with scent. One can even buy perfume discs that play like records, except that they exude scent. As has been proven in many experiments, if you hand people two cans of identical furniture polish, one of which has a pleasant odor, they will swear that the pleasantly scented one works better. Odor greatly affects our evaluation of things, and our evaluation of people. Even so-called unscented products are, in fact, scented to mask the chemical odors of their ingredients, usually with a light musk. In fact, only 20 percent of the perfume industry's income comes from making perfumes to wear; the other 80 percent comes from perfuming the objects in our lives. Nationality influences fragrances, as many companies have discovered. Germans like pine, French prefer flowery scents, Japanese like more delicate odors, North Americans insist on bold smells, and South Americans want even stronger ones. In Venezuela, floor-cleaning products contain ten times as much pine fragrance as those in the United States. What almost all nationalities share is the need to coat our floors and walls with pleasant odors, especially with the smell of a pine forest or lemon orchard, to nest in smells.

Response and Analysis

1. What does Diane Ackerman mean when she writes that "we each have our own aromatic memories"? Briefly describe one of Ackerman's aromatic memories. What anatomical features might account for the relationship between olfaction and memory?

2. Briefly describe the experiments being conducted at the Monell Chemical Senses Center that investigate the relationship between smell and mood. Why might smell influence mood and the way we evaluate objects? Why might smell influence social behavior and mate selection in animals?

Personal Experience and Application

1. Think about an experience in which a smell triggered a distant memory. Briefly describe the scent and the memory that you associated with it. How did you feel when you recollected the memory? Why?

2. Many industries, such as wineries, perfumeries, and food manufacturers, need expert smellers. Suppose the Human Resources Department at a perfumery asks you to make a few recommendations for teaching newly hired employees to detect and identify various smells. What recommendations might you offer?

Research

Suppose you want to conduct an experiment to explore whether people in certain cultures can detect and identify odors better than people in other cultures. You decide to use a scratch-and-sniff test with various odors, and you ask the participants (1) if they can smell the scent and (2) to identify the scent. You plan to administer the scratch-and-sniff test in four countries: England, Singapore, Japan, and Kenya. The participants will be second-year male and female college students who were born in their countries. How might their experiences with the odors in your study influence their ability to detect and identify those odors?

chapter 3

CONSCIOUSNESS

*Octavio Paz cites the example of
Saint-PolRoux, who used to hang the
inscription "The poet is working" from his
door while he slept.*

ANNIE DILLARD, *The Writing Life*

What is consciousness? Can our minds be at work while we sleep, as Saint-PolRoux suggests? In this chapter, we present narratives about consciousness: sleep deprivation, the influence of drugs and alcohol, and hypnosis.

Does sleep deprivation affect our ability to think clearly and perform tasks? Lydia Dotto tells of the difficulties she had concentrating on various tasks when she went for long periods without sleep. The findings of the study in which she took part have important implications for those who work long hours.

Luis Rodriguez was a gang member in Los Angeles. As a teenager, he wanted to escape the misery of poverty by changing his state of consciousness with drugs and chemicals. Not until drugs almost killed him was he able to quit using them and leave the gang.

When Los Angeles Dodgers pitcher Bob Welch used alcohol, his perceptions of the world changed. He believed that alcohol liberated his inhibitions and subdued his anxieties. Though Welch was rich and successful, he still felt he needed alcohol. Under pressure from his team, he sought help and eventually was able to admit that he had become an alcoholic.

The case of Julie demonstrates how hypnosis can be used to relieve pain. Julie lost a leg in an accident and suffered from phantom limb syndrome. With the help of hypnotherapists who used visualization, direct suggestion, and posthypnotic suggestion, she was able to lessen and eventually eliminate her pain.

ASLEEP IN THE FAST LANE

Lydia Dotto

Psychological Concepts
sleep deprivation, functions of sleep, REM sleep

Could you go a day without sleep? Two days? What abilities would fail first if you had to stay awake for twenty-four hours? Would your reaction time be slower? Could you still balance your checkbook? When would your vision become blurred and your hearing strained?

Researchers at the Defence and Civil Institute of Environmental Medicine in Toronto, Canada, conducted studies examining the effects of sleep deprivation on task performance. The project findings may have important implications for air traffic controllers, doctors, firefighters, and others who must be alert for long periods of time. Lydia Dotto, a participant in one of the studies, tells of the difficulties she and the other participants had while concentrating and performing various tasks after going without sleep for extended periods of time. What enables Dotto to improve her performance under these conditions? What states of consciousness does she experience when she goes without sleep?

It has taken just two days and two nights to reduce me to this sorry state—a fact that annoys me no end, because I'd started the experiment determined not to let it get the better of me. How difficult can it be to last two days without sleep, I'd asked myself as I checked in at the Defence and Civil Institute of Environmental Medicine (DCIEM) in Toronto shortly before noon on a Tuesday in early April. At that point, it was not hard to feel self-confident. I'd been awake only four hours, having awakened at 8:00 A.M. after sleeping a full eight hours the night before. I felt alert and mentally geared up for the challenge ahead.

The researchers are rather bemused by my enthusiasm for this project. Most of their subjects are paid volunteers recruited from the ranks of the Canadian Forces. "We don't usually get subjects who are looking forward to the experience," Bob Angus, Head of Applied Psychology at DCIEM, comments wryly.

He takes me down to the sleep lab, located in the basement off a drab, narrow hallway barricaded at both ends with Do Not Disturb signs. The lab consists of a suite of four small rooms in which the subjects work and a control room filled with computer equipment as well as a bank of small closed-circuit TV monitors lining one wall. Here the researchers, working in shifts, maintain an around-the-clock watch on the subjects. Drooping eyelids and nodding heads are picked up by wall-mounted TV cameras in each room, and within moments, one of the researchers is headed down the hall to nudge the subject awake. As the hours wear on, these trips become more frequent. "I just kind of scratch on the door before I go in, to give them a chance to fool me," says Bob. . . .

It's about 8:00 P.M. on Tuesday night, and I have now been awake for twelve hours.

During the first ninety-minute session, I feel very alert—quite hyped up, in fact, and ready to face whatever challenges the computer throws my way. At the first break, between 9:30 and 10:00 P.M., I'm still feeling pretty good, and I note into the tape recorder that my motivation remains strong: "I really want to keep things under control and to keep myself awake and alert." But by the time the second break rolls around, just before midnight, I'm beginning to feel fatigued and my concentration is slipping: I become annoyed and frustrated if I can't understand something right away. The repetitive tasks are becoming both boring and irritating, eliciting a reaction of "Oh, Lord, not this one again." Being confronted with a test that I don't like to do provokes a few episodes of fist-waving at the terminal. Ross later observes that the frequency of these displays of temper, which have been duly witnessed on the closed-circuit TV, seems to be increasing.

Periodically during sessions, the computer instructs me to sit with my eyes closed for four minutes. Now, as I enter the wee hours of the first night of sleep loss, I find myself drifting toward sleep during these closed-eyes sessions and I comment that although "I still feel I'm on top of the tasks, I'm glad when the breaks come." The computer also inquires solicitously from time to time about my mood and the degree of sleepiness and fatigue I feel. The sleepiness scale contains seven statements, starting with *alert, wide awake* through *foggy, slowed down, beginning to lose interest in remaining awake* to *fighting sleep, losing the struggle to remain awake.* The fatigue checklist asks me to record whether I am *better than, the same as,* or *worse than* a series of statements ranging from *very lively* and *extremely peppy* to *slightly pooped* and *ready to drop.* And the mood scale asks me to describe my feelings in terms such as *carefree, cheerful,* and *full of pep* or *dull, drowsy,* and *defiant.*

By 7:00 A.M. on Wednesday, *dull, drowsy,* and *defiant* don't even come close to describing how I feel. Now approaching twenty-four hours without sleep, I am not in a happy frame of mind. My subjective feelings of sleepiness and fatigue have increased sharply, and my mood, along with my performance, has begun to deteriorate badly. The words *cheerful* and *peppy* are no longer in my vocabulary. Although I can still remain reasonably alert during the war game exercises, I'm beginning to struggle against falling asleep during the more boring tasks. "Sleep is starting to ambush me," I report into the tape recorder. "I find myself staring into space. I just kind of blank out; it's like I vanish, disappear."

I know that sometime during this experiment, I'll be allowed to have a nap. Periodically, the computer taunts me with questions like "If you could sleep now, would you do so?" For the first time, I start hinting that I wouldn't turn down a nap if it were to be offered. It isn't. The computer, it seems, is only interested in knowing if I'd *like* a nap, not in actually satisfying my wish.

During the next break, which I have calculated occurs during early morning, Ross appears looking suspiciously well scrubbed and wearing a cheerful grin. He does not look like a sleep-deprived person and this makes me feel distinctly grumpy. I find that I'm also depressed. I "hit the wall" during the last work session, and as a result, I've broken my rule not to think too far ahead. The certain knowledge that there's at least another full day and night of this to get through induces a state of mild despair, and for the first time I wonder if I'm going to make it. Julia is also beginning to despair about her ability to carry on, reflecting, "It's this rough now and I have to make it through another night." Ours is a typical response to "the first-night effect." Subjects hit a low point between about 4:00 and 6:00 A.M. after the first night of lost sleep, says Ross. "They feel very depressed because they think, 'If I'm feeling this tired and it's only the first night, I'll never make it. I'm going to die.'"

Certainly, I'm beginning to wonder how I'm going to marshal the resources needed to go back into that room. As it happens, however, I don't have to. At the end of the break period, about 10:00 A.M. on Wednesday, Ross announces that it's nap time. When I was six years old, these were dreaded words; now they couldn't have been more welcome.

Julia and I bed down on cots in two of the unused rooms. We're allowed to remove the belts of tape recorders, which are laid beside the beds trailing their wires. The electrodes have to stay on, of course, but it hardly matters; I've reached the stage where nothing's going to keep me awake, not even the sensation of having my head in a vise.

The nap occurs between 10:00 A.M. and noon on Wednesday. For me, it comes at just the right time, rescuing me as I'm about to hit rock bottom. As I settle gratefully into the bed and close my eyes, I experience a momentary anxiety that I won't be able to sleep on demand, even though—or perhaps because—I desperately want to. But, given my advanced state of exhaustion, and perhaps the fact that I am used to napping in my "regular" life, I manage to fall asleep very quickly, even under these unusual circumstances.

Julia, though also highly fatigued, is less happy than I about the timing of the nap. She's a morning person and by midmorning is usually at the height of alertness. Even though she's in a sleep-deprived state, her biological rhythms had begun to climb by 10:00 A.M. and she had trouble falling asleep. "I'd have preferred the nap earlier on, say at 4:00 A.M., because that was my really low point," she commented later. But she began to pick up after the early-morning break during which we had breakfast: "I was awake by the time the nap came along because that's my high point of the day. It wasn't when I craved sleep. I hadn't geared up to having a nap; I was not thinking, 'I've just got to last till the nap.' I think that's why I had such difficulty getting to sleep." She too put psychological pressure on herself, knowing the nap would be her only opportunity to sleep until the end of the experiment. "I knew the nap was two hours long and I was saying, 'C'mon, got to get to sleep, got to make the most of this two hours of sleep.'" In the end, she managed about 1½ hours of sleep.

The nap helped both of us tremendously. I woke up feeling completely re-freshed and in a greatly improved frame of mind—feeling, in fact, pretty much as I had when the experiment began. Even though she did not sleep for the full two hours, Julia felt the nap helped her too. "If I hadn't had it, I'd be dead by now," she said during the last break before the end of the experiment. Ross asked her if she felt the nap had allowed her to do better on the computer tasks. "I felt better, yes, but whether I did better or not, I don't know."

In fact, the nap had a significant impact on our performance of the tasks. Our scores on the logical reasoning and serial reaction time tasks improved by more than 40 percent after the nap, and in one case, Julia's score almost doubled. Equally important, for a period of more than twelve hours after the nap, our performance was maintained well above the levels to which they'd dropped before the nap. At times, our performance after the nap was nearly equal to—and occasionally even better than—our performance when we first started the experiment. In some cases, our scores did not fall below their prenap lows until about 5:30 A.M. on the second night of lost sleep, some 17½ hours after the nap.

Studying the effect of napping on performance was the whole point of this experiment, one of a series of such studies conducted by Angus and his group in recent years. They're focusing on factors that affect the performance of military personnel under battle conditions (referred to as "sustained operations"), when they might have to function for days on end with only brief snatches of sleep. However, these studies on napping—currently one of the hottest new fields of sleep re-search—have much wider implications. The knowledge gained about human sleep/wake patterns may someday help others—doctors, pilots, athletes, air traffic controllers, firefighters, nuclear plant operators and astronauts, to name just a few—whose jobs demand high levels of alertness over long periods of time and/or sus-tained high-quality performance under extremely demanding conditions. These studies may also help people with more normal but still stressful jobs, such as execu-tives who work long hours or travel a lot, and millions of people trying to cope, often unsuccessfully, with shift work.

Reviewing the data from my experiment, Angus noted with satisfaction that "the nap seemed to give you almost a whole day. It really helped." But it couldn't sustain me indefinitely. Both Julia and I began to disintegrate during the early-morning hours after the second night of sleep loss, and toward the end, we both exhibited a sharp roller-coaster pattern on the tests, performing moderately well—though with ever-diminishing accuracy—immediately after a break but falling apart rapidly in the middle of the ninety-minute work sessions. These extreme swings are a striking feature of work sessions during the second day or so without sleep. Ross commented that when subjects are well rested, breaks don't make much difference in their performance because they're already very alert. But as time wears on and fatigue starts to build, the breaks do have a brief noticeable effect, causing the roller-coaster performance pattern. Ultimately, however, they lose their effective-ness and "after you've been awake two or three days, they don't make much difference."

There were many similarities in the way Julia and I reacted to extreme sleep deprivation, but there were also some intriguing differences. While I experienced sensations of blanking out and "disappearing," Julia felt that her thoughts were wandering aimlessly. "My mind would shoot off and I had no control over it," she said. "My thought patterns were going off in different directions." Often, she could not comprehend words printed on the screen because they seemed to be spelled wrong. "They looked totally weird and I thought, 'What is this word?' When you look at a word for a long time, it just appears to be odd. That kept capturing my attention, rather than what I was supposed to be doing." She also had some mild hallucinatory experiences; sometimes she was uncertain whether she was actually doing a task or merely dreaming that she was doing it, and at times she felt as though there was someone in the room. "I got quite worried about the shadows around me. I kept on thinking that somebody's in the room with me because I see shadows on the walls. My vision's a bit iffy."

Like me, she was easily annoyed by the computer's "damn fool questions," but, she added, "I was less grouchy than I thought I was going to be."

Response and Analysis

1. Briefly describe Lydia Dotto's cognitive abilities, task performance, and mood at the beginning of the study and after being awake for twenty-four hours. How did a nap affect these same factors? How might sleep during a nap differ from a normal night's sleep?

2. What are the main functions of sleep? What is REM sleep? What are the functions of REM sleep?

Personal Experience and Application

1. What is the longest amount of time you have gone without sleeping? What changes in mood and cognitive ability did you notice?

2. Automobile accidents and injuries on the job are often related to lack of sleep. What practical benefits might result from the study of sleep deprivation?

Research

Sleep studies have implications for people whose "jobs demand high levels of alertness over long periods of time and/or sustained high-quality performance under extremely demanding conditions." Would the study in which Dotto participated be considered applied or basic research? Why? What are the main goals of applied research and basic research?

ALWAYS RUNNING: GANG DAYS IN L.A.

Luis J. Rodriguez

Psychological Concepts
psychoactive drugs, drug dependence, hallucinations

Luis Rodriguez gives a piercing account of "the crazy life" of gangs with which some American youth are involved. What could make a child join a group that organizes criminal activity? Rodriguez gives two possible reasons. First, he believes that poverty and racism lead to violence and despair—all of which may lead to the formation of gangs and illegal activities. Second, some children engage in criminal activities without thinking—*de volada*—on impulse. What could open the way for a child to use illegal drugs and sniff chemicals? *De volada*.

Rodriguez, also known as Chin, grew up in a harsh world. He remembers wanting to run from being "this thing of bone and skin." When Chin sniffed spray to escape, "the world became like jello, like clay, something which could be molded and shaped. Sounds became louder, clearer. . . ." What physical and psychological effects and changes in consciousness did the drugs have on him?

Some readers may find portions of Rodriguez's account disturbing because of the language that these young people use and the behavior in which they engage.

Not going to school meant a lot of free time. Sniffing became my favorite way to waste it. I stole cans of anything that could give a buzz: carbono, clear plastic, paint, or gasoline. Sometimes I'd mix it up in a concoction and pour it on a rag or in a paper bag we sniffed from.

Behind the school, on the fields, inside the tunnel, at Marrano Beach, and alongside the concrete banks of the San Gabriel River: I sniffed. Once I even climbed on top of a back hoe at a construction site, removed the lid off the gas tank and inhaled until somebody checked out the noise and chased me away.

Spray was dangerous; it literally ate your brain. But it was also a great escape. The world became like jello, like clay, something which could be molded and shaped. Sounds became louder, clearer—pulsating. Bodies removed themselves from bodies, floating with the sun. I sought it so desperately. I didn't want to be this thing of bone and skin. With spray I became water.

Once I sniffed with Chicharrón and Yuk Yuk behind the "Boys" Market in San Gabriel. I don't remember the trip, but they told me I suddenly stood up and proceeded to repeatedly bang my head against a wall. Pieces of hair and skin scraped on the brick. Chicharrón walked me home; refused to give me any more spray.

While on spray I yelled. I laughed. I clawed at the evening sky. I felt like a cracked egg. But I wouldn't stop.

Then another time Baba, Wilo, and I gathered in the makeshift hideout we had alongside the Alhambra Wash, next to the drive-in. We sat ourselves down on the dirt, some blankets and rags nearby to lie on. We covered the entrance with banana leaves and wood planks. There were several cans of clear plastic—what we called *la ce pe*—around us. We each had paper bags and sprayed into them—and I had already dropped some pills and downed a fifth of Wild Turkey. I then placed the bag over my mouth and nose, sealed it tightly with both hands, and breathed deeply.

A radio nearby played some Led Zeppelin or Cream or some other guitar-ripping licks. Soon the sounds rose in pitch. The thumping of bass felt like a heart-beat in the sky, followed by an echo of metal-grating tones. I became flesh with a dream. The infested walls of the wash turned to mud; the trickle of water a vast river. The homeboys and I looked like something out of Huckleberry Finn or Tom Sawyer. With stick fishing poles. The sparkle of water below us. Fish fidgeting below the sheen.

Dew fell off low branches as if it were breast milk. Birds shot out of the tropical trees which appeared across from us. Perhaps this trip had been the pages of a book, something I read as a child. Or saw on TV. Regardless, I was transported away from what was really there—yet it felt soothing. Not like the oil stains we sat in. Not like the factory air that surrounded us. Not this plastic death in a can.

I didn't want it to end. As the effect wore thin, I grabbed the spray and bag, and resumed the ritual. Baba and Wilo weren't far behind me.

Then everything faded away—the dew, the water, the birds. I became a cartoon, twirling through a tunnel, womb-like and satiated with sounds and lines and darkness. I found myself drifting toward a glare of lights. My family called me over: Seni, Mama, Papa, Tía Chucha, Tío Kiko, Pancho—everybody. I wanted to be there, to know this perpetual dreaming, this din of exquisite screams—to have this mother comfort surging through me.

The world fell into dust piles around me. Images of the past pitched by: my brother tossing me off rooftops, my mother's hearty laughter, my father's thin and tired face, the homeboys with scarred smiles, and the women with exotic eyes and cunts which were the churches I worshipped in. Everything crashed. Everything throbbed. I only knew: I had to get to the light, that wondrous beacon stuffed with sweet promise: Of peace. Untroubled. The end of fear. *Don't close the door, Mama. I'm scared. It's okay, m'ijo.*[1] *There's no monsters. We'll be here. Don't be scared.*

No more monsters. Come to the light. I felt I would be safe there—finally. To the light. The light.

Suddenly everything around me exploded. An intense blackness enveloped me. A deep stillness. Nothing. Absolute. No thinking. No feeling. A hole.

---

[1]*m'ijo*: my son.

Then an electrified hum sank its teeth into my brain. Hands surrounded me, pulled at me, back to the dust of our makeshift hideaway.

A face appeared above me. It leaned down and breathed into me. Images of leaves, crates, stained blankets came into view. Wilo pulled back and looked into my eyes. A haze covered everything. I felt dizzy. And pissed off.

"Give me the bag, man."

"No way," Baba said. "You died, Chin—you stopped breathing and died."

I tried to get up, but fell back to the ground. A kind of grief overwhelmed me. I was no longer this dream. I was me again. I wished I did die.

"You don't understand," I yelled to the homeboys. "I have to go back."

I crept toward a paper bag, but Baba kicked it out of my reach. Later I found myself stepping down a street. Baba and Wilo had pointed me in the direction of home and I kept going. I hated being there. I didn't know what to do. God, I wanted that light, this whore of a sun to blind me, to entice me to burn—to be sculptured marble in craftier hands.

Wilo's sister Payasa liked me and told him. She was okay, I guess, a real *loca*[2] when it came to the 'hood. She had the high teased hair, the short tight skirts, the "raccoon" style makeup, and boisterous presence. I ended up going with her. Mostly for Wilo's sake at first.

After I got expelled from school, Payasa and I spent time together during the day since she refused to go to classes herself. We'd walk to Garvey Park. She would hand me some *colies* which I'd drop and soon start to sway, talk incoherently, and act stupid.

"Oh, you'll get over it," Payasa said. "Eventually."

She always said that.

After a time, whenever a car crashed, a couple argued, or somebody tripped and fell, we'd look at each other and say at the same time: "Oh, you'll get over it . . . eventually."

When Wilo and I sniffed aerosol spray, sometimes Payasa joined us.

"Why do you let your sister do this?" I asked.

"That's her," Wilo shrugged. "I can't stop her."

Payasa was always high. The higher she got, the more bold she became. One time we were sniffing in the tunnel beneath the freeway. I started tripping: Snakes crawled from the sides, as well as melted faces and bolts of lights and a shower of shapes. She brushed up to me and pulled off her blouse. Erect nipples confronted me on firm breasts. I kissed them. She laughed and pulled me away.

"Oh, you'll get over it," she said. "Eventually."

I was too fucked up to care.

One time in the park she said she wanted to take her pants and underwear off.

"Right here? Right now? . . . in front of everybody?"

"Yeah, why not?" she responded. "You dare me."

"Sure—I dare you."

She did.

---

[2]*loca*: crazy girl.

Sniffing took the best out of her. Sometimes I'd walk through the tunnel and she would be there, alone, with a bag of spray, all scuffed up, her eyes glassy.

Payasa became a *loca* because of her older brothers. They were Lomas *veteranos*, older gangsters. Because Wilo and Payasa were younger, they picked on them a lot; beating them to make them stronger.

Payasa fought all the time at school. Whenever she lost, her older brothers would slice her tongue with a razor. She wasn't ever supposed to lose. This made her meaner, crazier—unpredictable.

As a girlfriend Payasa was fun, but she couldn't be intimate unless she was on reds, spray, or snort.

I had to break with her. I loved the spray and shit but Payasa became too much like the walking dead. So I told her I didn't want to see her anymore. She didn't say anything, just turned around and left. I faintly said to myself, "Oh, you'll get over it . . . eventually."

She was later found in a daze, her arms with numerous deep cuts all the way to her elbows. Nobody would let me see her after she was taken to a rehabilitation hospital for teenage addicts. Wilo suggested I let it go.

"That's Payasa, man," Wilo said, and shrugged his shoulders.

Response and Analysis

1. Briefly describe one of Chin's hallucinations after he sniffed clear plastic, paint, or gasoline. What changes in consciousness did Chin experience?

2. What are hallucinogens (also known as psychedelic drugs)? How do hallucinogens alter brain chemistry?

3. Do you think that Chin was psychologically and/or physically dependent on drugs? Why or why not? What is the difference between psychological and physical dependence? Why did Chin conclude that "spray was dangerous"?

Personal Experience and Application

1. Do you know someone who decided to drink a large quantity of alcohol or take illegal drugs? How might psychological and social factors have influenced that decision?

2. Suppose you are a member of a committee whose mission is to reduce drug abuse among students on your college or university campus. The committee chairperson asks you to help design a program to decrease drug abuse on campus. Discuss a few of your recommendations. Why do you believe your recommendations will be effective?

Research

Suppose a committee whose mission is to reduce drug abuse among students asks you to conduct a study to determine the percentage of students on campus who are abusing drugs. Because you do not have the time to interview every student, you ask a small group of students to participate. How would you select the students? How can you be fairly sure that the information you gather will generalize to the entire student body? How many students would you interview? Why?

THE COURAGE TO CHANGE

Dennis Wholey

Psychological Concepts
alcohol abuse, expectations of drug effects

Baseball star Bob Welch began drinking in his early teens and always chose friends who were heavy drinkers. What Welch wanted from the alcohol was instant transformation as he "guzzled the thing, looking for the effect." He didn't worry about becoming an alcoholic, for he thought alcoholics were failures or were people passed out on the street. They were not celebrated ball players or his friends.

In this interview with Dennis Wholey, Welch tells how he used emotion, thinking, and social influence to justify his drinking. How did he use these same forces to help him quit?

I thought an individual who had a problem with alcohol could not be successful, especially as a major league pitcher who could purchase anything he wanted at a very young age, as I could. I thought an alcoholic had to be lying on a street corner on skid row. That was my definition of an alcoholic. I didn't believe I was one. When someone would raise the question and say, "Well, I think you're an alcoholic," he'd grab my attention, but he'd pissed me off more than anything. "Maybe I have a little problem with drinking," I said to myself many times, but there was no way I could be an alcoholic. I didn't believe it until I got over to the treatment center and saw what it was like for someone at my young age to have the characteristics of an alcoholic. By the time I got there, I was well on my way to drinking a fifth or a quart a day. That was three or four years ago.

My girlfriend, Mary Ellen, had no idea. She wasn't knowledgeable. She didn't know about the disease, what an alcoholic was. And I never paid attention to the fact that I might be causing my mother and father and my girlfriend some pain.

When I was fifteen years old some friends and I went out to a park, and I drank a bottle of Mogen David blackberry wine. I liked it. I liked what it did for me because I was able to speak with girls a lot more easily. That was important to me at that time. After the first time, I didn't need anyone to pull on me and say, "Hey, let's go have a beer." It just snowballed.

I was shy. I was scared to death of girls. But when I got drunk I could tell a girl I liked her. I couldn't wait for the weekend because I thought maybe I'd get a chance to talk to a girl and even kiss her. I also thought that if you didn't like a girl and she didn't like you, you could drink to cover it up. Very early on, I started running from my feelings, hiding instead of talking. I covered up my feelings by drinking.

As I look back now, I see that the friends with whom I first started drinking at fifteen were heavy drinkers. I started choosing such friends even before I started going to college. They had to be people who drank and acted and talked the same way I did. But whether it was in class or on a baseball team, if my friends didn't want to go get drunk with me, I'd go to a bar alone. I did that from the time I started drinking. I didn't go out to drink socially. I went out to drink for the effect, for what it gave me. I knew what I was going to be able to do after I drank—go to the football games, be able to talk a lot more, maybe even go to a party and dance with a girl.

I built up a reputation as both a great baseball player and a very good drinker at a young age.

In college I wanted to prove to people that I was the best baseball player, and when I was done playing, I wanted to show them that I was the best drinker. My mother told me at the treatment center that when I left to go to college the one thing she was worried about was that I was going to turn into an alcoholic. She had this insight when I was seventeen.

When I got to college, I was away from my mother and father and didn't have to worry about coming home, sneaking in the back room, or driving their car. It was a perfect setup for someone who enjoyed drinking. I had some friends there with whom I played baseball in the summertime, and I knew exactly which ones would drink like I did. Then I started finding people over at my dormitory. When I wanted to get away from baseball players, I'd go to these individuals. At seventeen I knew exactly what I was doing. I knew the people who lived in certain bars. There is a bar up in Ypsilanti where the gentlemen are full-fledged practicing alcoholics. I knew that I could go over there and fit right in with those guys. They liked me. I used to go in there and talk about playing baseball. They're probably still sitting there. I didn't associate with people who didn't drink and I didn't want anybody to look at me and question me about how much I drank.

I didn't drink and sip it. I didn't want to see what happened. It was boom! I guzzled the thing, looking for the effect. You like it or dislike it. I happened to like it.

If I pitched a game and lost, I went out and got drunk. I drowned my sorrows or my aggravation or my anger in drinking. If we won, I could celebrate. On both ends, I always had it covered.

I got to the majors by the time I was twenty-one. I'd go out and get drunk whenever I wanted to. In baseball, you don't even have to go anywhere. They have the beer in the clubhouse. It was a perfect setup. I started pitching once every five days. You start mapping out your strategy. You know exactly when you can get drunk, and you know how much time it takes you to recover. The thing that was difficult about baseball for me was that it gave me an opportunity to drink just about every day. I could stay out until three o'clock and sleep until three o'clock. I had plenty of time to rest. There were many times I said, "I'm not going out drinking tonight," but I was right back out there.

Everybody wants to be associated with a professional baseball player. They all want to party with you and buy you drinks, and they all want to push other types of drugs on you. In Los Angeles, where I was living, I knew who was going to get drunk, just like in college.

I'd get drunk four out of five days, get sober the night before pitching, and go back out drinking that night. I didn't wake up in the morning and have a drink or drink at a definite time daily, and I didn't drink every day, but 85 to 95 percent of the times that I started to drink, I couldn't stop. I'd drink until I was drunk or passed out or there was nothing left.

I had pitched in 1978 and done very well. I played in the World Series. In 1979 I participated for about two months and hurt my arm. I knew I wasn't going to play, and I was traveling to all these towns, so I'd get drunk during the games. I'm not going to play, I thought, so let's pop a few cans of beer. Not just one or two, but three or four or five or six. I justified sitting on the bench by saying, "Hell, I'm going to have a few beers and root and at least enjoy myself." I was terribly hurt that I wasn't playing, and feeling bad because one part of the team wasn't doing so well. I wanted to put myself in there and I just couldn't. I covered that up by drinking all the time.

On the way to the park, I'd know I wasn't going to pitch, so I'd say to myself, Why not have a nice little drink on my way there? I'm going to sit in traffic and I'm going to be itchy and edgy. I've got to have a drink. I'm going to have one on the way. Toward the end of the season, I really was not taking care of myself and not being concerned too much with my occupation because I was drinking so heavily. My girlfriend was beginning to hear some whispers. Friends and family members and wives of other baseball players were saying, "Hey, do you hear what your boyfriend does?" I could barely speak to her. My family was beginning to be concerned, too. I could tell not so much by what they were saying, but when I got around them they would look at me when I was drinking. They were concerned about how much I was drinking and where I was going. My health really wasn't affected too much. Basically, I took care of myself, but my ability to prepare myself to play baseball was starting to go downhill.

There was one time in San Francisco, after I was injured, that I had a chance to pitch. They wanted me to start a couple of games at the end of the season. I went out there and my elbow was feeling terrible. It was cold and windy in San Francisco. I gave up a home run. My pitching was a disaster. I went out that night and had a few drinks, went home, and went to bed. I really didn't get drunk. I woke up the next morning and I, another player, and a gentleman we knew in San Francisco went out to this place and had lunch. I started drinking, and I must have drunk three bottles of wine at lunch. The guy on our team went home. I stayed out there and drank ten more Seven and Seven's and a few more beers. I went back to the hotel about a quarter to five. Our bus was leaving about five o'clock. I went upstairs, drank a bottle of wine, guzzled it in about five minutes, then went down and got on the bus. There were a lot of reporters. I just started raising hell. I was screaming and hollering at the manager, making an ass out of myself, embarrassing everybody.

I got to the ball park and fell asleep by the stall. One of my teammates woke me up and started helping me get dressed and tried to hide it from my manager. Everybody knew I was drunk. I thought it was funny. A couple of my teammates helped me out. I went out on the field and started a few fights with the guys on the Giants. I got out there in center field and then started a couple of fights with my own teammates. My manager called me in and said, "Hey, you've got to take off your uniform and stay inside." I was never so embarrassed in my life.

Before I went home to Michigan that winter, the Dodgers called me into their office and said, "We fine you for being drunk at the park. We want you to know that we want you to be a part of this club next year, and we're not going to finish last or next to last. We want you to be ready. We want you to take a look at your drinking." I told them all to go shit in their hats and leave me alone. I told them it was their fault, anyway, that if I didn't pitch in the bullpen, I wouldn't be getting drunk, I would have been healthy. "It's your fault," I said, "so why don't you get out of my life and leave me alone? If I don't pitch here, I'll pitch somewhere else."

I came home that winter and tried to quit drinking, but couldn't do it. I stopped for about two to three weeks, until Thanksgiving. That was a deadly time, because I liked to drink and there were a lot of parties in our family. I had my first drink and then I think I was drunk until after Christmas.

A telephone call came from the Dodgers on about January tenth. "We want you to come out here and speak to some people and meet with us." I knew exactly what it was all about. They didn't have to say anything about drinking. I knew what the hell was going on. I knew what was going to happen the next day. I flew out to L.A., and when I arrived I smoked a couple of joints, then stopped at a place and grabbed a six-pack. I went to the Biltmore, went to sleep, woke up the next morning, and met with a gentleman who was a recovering alcoholic.

It was really the first time that someone knew exactly how to handle me, knew exactly what to say. It wasn't "Hey, you have a problem." It was "I have a problem." He sat down and shared his story with me, the story of what it was like when he was young, how his drinking had caused great pain to his family, how he had made an ass out of himself and embarrassed himself many, many times. Boy, I could see myself in that same category. I knew this was my time. I really wanted to do something about my drinking, and this gentleman helped me out by sharing his own story, not by saying, "You have a problem. What are you going to do about it?" It was more or less, "I care. There are things you can do." . . .

I was in treatment for thirty-six days. When I first came out, I had the idea that just because I didn't drink, it was OK to smoke a joint or pop a few pills. I almost killed myself running into the back end of someone's car. I was on Valium. Until I eliminated everything, I really didn't get a good foundation. What helped was being in the AA program, and wanting to stay sober. I'm really just now getting to the point where I can finally give in. I don't care if I never take a drink again. I don't care if I don't get high again. It's OK to be right here, to be sober, not get high; that's fine. I've struggled for quite a while now. It doesn't seem hard not to drink.

Response and Analysis

1. Give examples of how Bob Welch used emotion, thinking, and social influences to justify drinking and then used them later to break his addiction. What physical and psychological effects of alcohol abuse did Welch suffer?

2. How do alcohol and other depressant drugs affect the nervous system and the brain? How can expectations about the effects of alcohol influence behavior?

Personal Experience and Application

1. Have you ever been in a situation in which you drank alcohol but did not want to? Why then did you drink? If you had a friend who did not want to drink but was going to a party where alcohol would be available, what advice would you offer so that he or she might feel less pressure to drink?

2. Do you think alcohol use on your campus is a problem? Why or why not? When do students usually drink alcohol? List the reasons why you believe they drink alcohol.

Research

Suppose you want to replicate a study examining how expectations about alcohol influence aggressive behavior. All participants will be given the same amount of a beverage. Half will drink tonic water and half will drink alcohol that does not taste when it is mixed with tonic water. Participants drinking alcohol will receive enough alcohol to become legally intoxicated. Before you hand out the beverage, you tell half of the participants who receive both tonic water and half who receive tonic water and alcohol that they are drinking tonic water; you tell the other half that they are drinking alcohol. That is, one quarter of the participants will:

*   expect alcohol and drink alcohol,
*   expect alcohol but drink tonic water only,
*   expect tonic water but drink alcohol, or
*   expect tonic water and drink tonic water.

After the participants drink the beverage, your research assistant will pretend to be a participant and irritate and annoy the real participants. Then you will give the participants an opportunity to deliver electric shocks to your research assistant. The degree of electric shock delivered is your measure of aggression. In fact, no shocks will be delivered to the assistant; the participants do not know that the shock-generating machine is not operational.

Do you think that knowledge of having consumed (or not consumed) alcohol would affect participants' aggressiveness? Why or why not? Is it ethical to have people drink alcohol without their foreknowledge? If not, how can a researcher inform potential participants without creating expectations about how they should behave? Is it ethical to tell participants that they have delivered electric shocks to someone when no shocks were delivered? How might a researcher debrief his or her participants regarding these issues? Do you think that the human participants Institutional Review Board at your college or university would approve this study? Why or why not?

PRACTICAL
CLINICAL HYPNOSIS

Robert G. Meyer

Psychological Concepts
hypnosis, hypnotherapy, pain control

Can hypnotherapy help reduce pain? Julie, a twenty-seven-year-old nurse, lost her leg in an automobile accident and suffered from phantom limb syndrome, a response that occurs because the brain attempts "to seek the stimulation of the (now-departed) nerves that had been sending information from the limb." As a result, Julie was depressed, anxious, and no longer saw herself as attractive or desirable.

The hypnotherapists whom Julie consulted treated her for pain she felt in her leg, even though it had been amputated. They used several techniques, including self-hypnosis. What other techniques did they teach to control, alleviate, and eliminate the pain? What guided imagery did they suggest?

We had occasion recently to treat a woman who had lost her left leg in an automobile accident. Julie, a twenty-seven-year-old nurse, came seeking hypnotherapy to deal with a condition referred to as phantom limb. This often occurs when a limb is amputated and is due to the brain's attempting to seek the stimulation of the (now-departed) nerves that had been sending information from the limb. This condition can last for some time, even years, and it can be uncomfortable or even painful. Julie had been without her leg for almost nine months at the time she [came] for her first session.

We first got a history of her symptom and the factors surrounding it. She was experiencing a lot of anticipatory anxiety because she did not know when the pain would begin, but she usually felt it each day for a few hours. If it happened at work, it could be incapacitating. In the middle of the night, it was simply painful and frightening. There was also the issue of Julie's self-esteem and self-image, which were severely damaged by her accident. She had lost confidence in her ability to do the things she had loved to do, although her doctors assured her that with the new prosthetics available, she could jog, ride a bicycle, and even play tennis. Depression was thus part of the picture.

We decided together that we would work on the anxiety and pain first and then deal with the depression, trying to get Julie back into the swing of her life.

Julie was an excellent hypnotic subject, as is often the case with pain clients. She achieved a deep trance during our first session, using the eye fixation method[1] and testing the depth via glove anesthesia.[2]

We had agreed that she should have an imaginal refuge she could retreat to when she was feeling anxious or if the pain was beginning. Julie would use this "safe place" only when she was not at work, not driving, and not in other situations where she needed to be alert. The safe place served two functions. First, she had an autohypnotic technique[3] she could use to relax and avoid pain, and second, it gave her confidence in her ability to cope with her condition.

Julie had grown up in the state of Washington and fondly recalled walks on the beach as a youngster. Therefore, we set her safe place on a beach she loved, on a warm, summer day, with a cool breeze blowing the salt smell of the ocean on her face. Direct suggestions were used to set the imagery.

Guided Imagery

Julie, you are feeling warm and comfortable. It is a summer day, and you can feel the sun on your face. You are sitting on a picnic table near the sandy beach, and you decide you want to go for a walk down that favorite path. You stand up, and as you do, you feel the breeze blowing across your face; you smell the salt spray from the sea, the scent of the kelp, and the mustiness of the warm sand. What do you smell? [At this point, it is a good idea to check for the sensory hallucinations. If the client is not smelling and experiencing the hallucination, deepening through more progressive relaxation or another technique will help.]

Good. Now you are proceeding down the beach to your safe place, the cove on the west side of the inlet. You see the cove. You feel relaxed and comfortable. Proceed to your favorite spot, and indicate to me when you are there by raising your finger. [Once we established that she was there, we could proceed with one of the pain reduction techniques we used.]

Julie, I want you to look around you on the beach. You will see a bottle half buried in the sand. Pick it up. There is a piece of paper in your pocket, as well as a pencil. Take them out. Write "my pain" on the paper. Now roll the paper up and put it in the bottle. Now stand up and throw the bottle as far out to sea as you can. You will count to ten as you see the bottle get farther and farther away. With each count, your pain becomes less and less, until at the count of ten you feel no pain from your leg. You will realize that the bottle is likely to come back in. The tide and waves will bring it back. All you have to do is pick up the bottle and throw it back out to sea, and count from one to ten.

---

[1]eye fixation method: a method of inducing hypnosis by having the client focus on an object, such as a spot on the wall or a pendulum.
[2]glove anesthesia: a process in which the therapist makes a suggestion to the client that his or her hand is becoming numb and insensitive, and transfers this new perception of numbness to a part of the body that is experiencing discomfort.
[3]autohypnotic technique: also known as self-hypnosis, when an individual induces hypnosis in himself or herself.

It is important to note that the dialogue did not follow this straight-through pace. Throughout the process, we were making sure she was experiencing the imagery and feeling the sensation by asking simple questions and looking for a finger movement in response.

This technique was very successful for Julie; however, we needed to deal with her pain in a less complex manner for those times when she could not go into autohypnosis and retreat to her safe place, where she could throw the pain away. We did this by transferring a glove anesthesia to her missing leg—not to the missing leg, obviously, but to a spot on her thigh that, when numb, would not allow any pain messages from the phantom limb. This was the suggestion we gave:

Direct Suggestion

Julie, I want you to notice that your hand is getting numb. As I touch it, you notice that you are feeling less and less sensation from it, as though it is covered in a protective covering. I could be touching the chair, and you would not know the difference. I want you to be aware of the fact that you are controlling the feeling in this hand. You are making it numb. Now I want you to use that power to make another spot numb. I am going to touch you on the left thigh, and on that spot you will notice you will lose sensation. I am touching your thigh with one finger, and I want you to take that numbness and extend it around your thigh in a band, just as if you have a tourniquet around your thigh that is cutting off the feeling instead of the blood supply. Now that loss of feeling means that no sensation below it will get by; no loss of sensation will occur above the ring of numbness.

Two approaches were used in posthypnotic suggestions. To alleviate the pain directly and indirectly, Julie was given posthypnotic suggestions that she would be able to control the pain and that if she experienced pain it would be tolerable.

Therapist

Julie, you have indicated to me that you experience pain at certain times during the day, such as in the morning, late in the afternoon, and in the evening just before you retire. In the morning after you rise, you will feel refreshed and invigorated. You will be aware of the fact that you often have felt the pain of your leg at these times, but you will feel no apprehension about it. If you begin to feel pain, you will use the anesthetic technique you have learned to eliminate the pain. You will feel the pain and make it go away by using the band of numbness you have control over. The pain will never be so severe that you will not be able to tolerate it.

The direct techniques that we used with Julie were successful in helping her to deal with her loss. In addition to hypnosis, we used interpersonal process techniques[4] to help Julie regain her lost self-esteem and deal with her depression. But

---

[4]interpersonal process techniques: a general term for psychotherapy.

direct suggestions were used throughout the therapy to reinforce and enhance the psychotherapy.

Direct suggestions have an important place in hypnotherapy, especially since cognitive-behavioral and behavioral therapies have been shown to be so effective in treatment of specific disorders. The extent to which direct suggestions and post-hypnotic techniques may be used in hypnotherapy is bounded only by the imagination of the therapist. Entering into a therapeutic alliance in which the input and motivation of the client is encouraged and supported is fertile ground for a direct approach. Direct suggestions and posthypnotic techniques benefit motivated clients by giving them the tools they need to change and by showing them that change occurs through efforts they ultimately have control over. In medical and dental applications, direct suggestions and posthypnotic techniques work not only to alleviate the pain of the procedures but also to reduce the associated anxiety, and thus they may make it more likely that the patient will comply with the treatment.

Response and Analysis

1. How did the therapists help Julie create a "safe place" to cope with pain? Where was the safe place? What is a posthypnotic suggestion? Briefly describe the posthypnotic suggestion that the therapists gave to Julie to help her relieve her pain.

2. Briefly discuss one theory that suggests and one theory that does not suggest that hypnosis represents an altered state of consciousness. Do you believe that people who are hypnotized experience an altered state of consciousness? Why or why not?

Personal Experience and Application

1. Have you seen someone being hypnotized? Briefly describe the hypnotist's instructions. What behaviors did the hypnotist have the person perform? How did the person describe the experience? Did the person believe he or she was in an altered state of consciousness? Why or why not?

Research

Suppose you want to use the case study approach to examine the effectiveness of a new technique using hypnosis to relieve pain. You work with one client continuously for six months and find that the client's perceptions of pain have diminished significantly. How could you determine whether your findings would be equally effective for other people with similar problems?

chapter 4

LEARNING

*There is only one thing more powerful than
learning from experience and that is not
learning from experience.*

ARCHIBALD MacLEISH, in Marian Wright Edelman,
The Measure of Our Success

What makes us want to learn, and how do we learn most effectively? Psychologists have made valuable contributions to our understanding of learning principles. This chapter illuminates learning principles and concepts at work: classical conditioning, operant conditioning, positive and negative reinforcement, observational (social) learning, role models, and cooperative learning.

Various disadvantages, whether physical, emotional, or environmental, make constructive learning onerous. Our first selection presents an individual who surmounted her disabilities with the personal involvement of an extraordinarily devoted teacher. Helen Keller, who was blind and deaf from the time she was eighteen months old, says she would never have been able to know the world she lived in so fully without the superb instruction of her beloved teacher, Anne Sullivan.

Positive reinforcement is an effective learning tool. The second selection presents a fascinating interview with an expert who describes how animal trainers work and play with killer whales. Chuck Tompkins of Sea World explains how important it is for trainers to develop positive relationships with whales when teaching them to perform.

Susan Goodwillie gathered interviews conducted by teenagers with other teenagers who come from families and neighborhoods of poverty and violence. Their powerful stories tell of inadequate role models, of learning not to learn, and of gaining the wrong sort of knowledge. In this selection a young man from Brooklyn tells how he was able to turn away from drugs and gangs. He would like to get a high school diploma, but he believes he has little chance because of his unstable life.

Jaime Escalante well deserves the awards he has received as an outstanding teacher. What Escalante accomplished teaching advanced mathematics to students in East Los Angeles is exemplary of the finest educator; his approach is richly portrayed in the film *Stand and Deliver*. Here he discusses how he uses passion, devotion, and cooperative learning to inspire students to become excited about learning.

EVERYTHING HAD A NAME

Helen Keller

Psychological Concepts
association, repetition

How does a person who is deprived of sound and sight learn language? This was the challenge for Helen Keller. Blind and deaf from an illness she contracted at the age of eighteen months, Keller was cut off from the knowledge that language brings until Anne Sullivan, a great teacher, came into her life.

Until she was almost seven years old, Keller lived "in the still, dark world" where "there was no strong sentiment or tenderness." Neither had she yet conceived of thought. By being patient and gentle, intuitive and understanding, Sullivan was able to show Keller how to give shape to thought, how to name and identify. Here Keller tells how Sullivan taught her sign language that enabled her to understand concepts and labels. Gradually, she was able to join in conversations with people beyond her immediate family.

The most important day I remember in all my life is the one on which my teacher, Anne Mansfield Sullivan, came to me. I am filled with wonder when I consider the immeasurable contrasts between the two lives which it connects. It was the third of March, 1887, three months before I was seven years old.

On the afternoon of that eventful day, I stood on the porch, dumb, expectant. I guessed vaguely from my mother's signs and from the hurrying to and fro in the house that something unusual was about to happen, so I went to the door and waited on the steps. The afternoon sun penetrated the mass of honeysuckle that covered the porch, and fell on my upturned face. My fingers lingered almost unconsciously on the familiar leaves and blossoms which had just come forth to greet the sweet southern spring. I did not know what the future held of marvel or surprise for me. Anger and bitterness had preyed upon me continually for weeks and a deep languor had succeeded this passionate struggle.

Have you ever been at sea in a dense fog, when it seemed as if a tangible white darkness shut you in, and the great ship, tense and anxious, groped her way toward the shore with plummet and sounding-line, and you waited with beating heart for something to happen? I was like that ship before my education began, only I was without compass or sounding-line, and had no way of knowing how near the harbour was. "Light! give me light!" was the wordless cry of my soul, and the light of love shone on me in that very hour.

I felt approaching footsteps. I stretched out my hand as I supposed to my mother. Some one took it, and I was caught up and held close in the arms of her who had come to reveal all things to me, and, more than all things else, to love me.

The morning after my teacher came she led me into her room and gave me a doll. The little blind children at the Perkins Institution had sent it and Laura Bridgman had dressed it; but I did not know this until afterward. When I had played with it a little while, Miss Sullivan slowly spelled into my hand the word "d-o-l-l." I was at once interested in this finger play and tried to imitate it. When I finally succeeded in making the letters correctly I was flushed with childish pleasure and pride. Running downstairs to my mother I held up my hand and made the letters for doll. I did not know that I was spelling a word or even that words existed; I was simply making my fingers go in monkey-like imitation. In the days that followed I learned to spell in this uncomprehending way a great many words, among them *pin, hat, cup* and a few verbs like *sit, stand,* and *walk.* But my teacher had been with me several weeks before I understood that everything has a name.

One day, while I was playing with my new doll, Miss Sullivan put my big rag doll into my lap also, spelled "d-o-l-l" and tried to make me understand that "d-o-l-l" applied to both. Earlier in the day we had had a tussle over the words "m-u-g" and "w-a-t-e-r." Miss Sullivan had tried to impress it upon me that "m-u-g" is *mug* and that "w-a-t-e-r" is *water,* but I persisted in confounding the two. In despair she had dropped the subject for the time, only to renew it at the first opportunity. I became impatient at her repeated attempts and, seizing the new doll, I dashed it upon the floor. I was keenly delighted when I felt the fragments of the broken doll at my feet. Neither sorrow nor regret followed my passionate outburst. I had not loved the doll. In the still, dark world in which I lived there was no strong sentiment or tenderness. I felt my teacher sweep the fragments to one side of the hearth, and I had a sense of satisfaction that the cause of my discomfort was removed. She brought me my hat, and I knew I was going out into the warm sunshine. This thought, if a wordless sensation may be called a thought, made me hop and skip with pleasure.

We walked down the path to the well-house, attracted by the fragrance of the honeysuckle with which it was covered. Some one was drawing water and my teacher placed my hand under the spout. As the cool stream gushed over one hand she spelled into the other the word *water,* first slowly, then rapidly. I stood still, my whole attention fixed upon the motions of her fingers. Suddenly I felt a misty consciousness as of something forgotten—a thrill of returning thought; and somehow the mystery of language was revealed to me. I knew then that "w-a-t-e-r" meant the wonderful cool something that was flowing over my hand. That living word awakened my soul, gave it light, hope, joy, set it free! There were barriers still, it is true, but barriers that could in time be swept away.

I left the well-house eager to learn. Everything had a name and each name gave birth to a new thought. As we returned to the house every object which I touched seemed to quiver with life. That was because I saw everything with the strange, new sight that had come to me. On entering the door I remembered the doll I had broken. I felt my way to the hearth and picked up the pieces. I tried vainly to put them together. Then my eyes filled with tears; for I realized what I had done, and for the first time I felt repentance and sorrow.

I learned a great many new words that day. I do not remember what they all were; but I do know that *mother, father, sister, teacher* were among them—words that were to make the world blossom for me, "like Aaron's rod, with flowers." It would have been difficult to find a happier child than I was as I lay in my crib at the close of that eventful day and lived over the joys it had brought me, and for the first time longed for a new day to come. I had now the key to all language, and I was eager to learn to use it. Children who hear acquire language without any particular effort; the words that fall from others' lips they catch on the wing, as it were, delightedly, while the little deaf child must trap them by a slow and often painful process. But whatever the process, the result is wonderful. Gradually, from naming an object we advance step by step until we have traversed the vast distance between our first stammered syllable and the sweep of thought in a line of Shakespeare.

At first, when my teacher told me about a new thing I asked very few questions. My ideas were vague, and my vocabulary was inadequate; but as my knowledge of things grew, and I learned more and more words, my field of inquiry broadened, and I would return again and again to the same subject, eager for further information. Sometimes a new word revived an image that some earlier experience had engraved on my brain.

I remember the morning that I first asked the meaning of the word "love." This was before I knew many words. I had found a few early violets in the garden and brought them to my teacher. She tried to kiss me; but at that time I did not like to have any one kiss me except my mother. Miss Sullivan put her arm gently round me and spelled into my hand, "I love Helen."

"What is love?" I asked.

She drew me closer to her and said, "It is here," pointing to my heart, whose beats I was conscious of for the first time. Her words puzzled me very much because I did not then understand anything unless I touched it.

I smelt the violets in her hand and asked, half in words, half in signs, a question which meant, "Is love the sweetness of flowers?"

"No," said my teacher.

Again I thought. The warm sun was shining on us.

"Is this not love?" I asked, pointing in the direction from which the heat came, "Is this not love?"

It seemed to me that there could be nothing more beautiful than the sun, whose warmth makes all things grow. But Miss Sullivan shook her head, and I was greatly puzzled and disappointed. I thought it strange that my teacher could not show me love.

A day or two afterward I was stringing beads of different sizes in symmetrical groups—two large beads, three small ones, and so on. I had made many mistakes, and Miss Sullivan had pointed them out again and again with gentle patience. Finally I noticed a very obvious error in the sequence and for an instant I concentrated my attention on the lesson and tried to think how I should have arranged the beads. Miss Sullivan touched my forehead and spelled with decided emphasis, "Think."

In a flash I knew that the word was the name of the process that was going on in my head. This was my first conscious perception of an abstract idea.

For a long time I was still—I was not thinking of the beads in my lap, but trying to find a meaning for "love" in the light of this new idea. The sun had been under a cloud all day, and there had been brief showers; but suddenly the sun broke forth in all its southern splendour.

Again I asked my teacher, "Is this not love?"

"Love is something like the clouds that were in the sky before the sun came out," she replied. Then in simpler words than these, which at that time I could not have understood, she explained: "You cannot touch the clouds, you know; but you feel the rain and know how glad the flowers and the thirsty earth are to have it after a hot day. You cannot touch love either; but you feel the sweetness that it pours into everything. Without love you would not be happy or want to play."

The beautiful truth burst upon my mind—I felt that there were invisible lines stretched between my spirit and the spirits of others.

From the beginning of my education Miss Sullivan made it a practice to speak to me as she would speak to any hearing child; the only difference was that she spelled the sentences into my hand instead of speaking them. If I did not know the words and idioms necessary to express my thoughts she supplied them, even suggesting conversation when I was unable to keep up my end of the dialogue.

This process was continued for several years; for the deaf child does not learn in a month, or even in two or three years, the numberless idioms and expressions used in the simplest daily intercourse. The little hearing child learns these from constant repetition and imitation. The conversation he hears in his home stimulates his mind and suggests topics and calls forth the spontaneous expression of his own thoughts. This natural exchange of ideas is denied to the deaf child. My teacher, realizing this, determined to supply the kinds of stimulus I lacked. This she did by repeating to me as far as possible, verbatim, what she heard, and by showing me how I could take part in the conversation. But it was a long time before I ventured to take the initiative, and still longer before I could find something appropriate to say at the right time.

The deaf and the blind find it very difficult to acquire the amenities of conversation. How much more this difficulty must be augmented in the case of those who are both deaf and blind! They cannot distinguish the tone of the voice or, without assistance, go up and down the gamut of tones that give significance to words; nor can they watch the expression of the speaker's face, and a look is often the very soul of what one says.

Response and Analysis

1. How did Anne Sullivan use association and repetition to teach Helen Keller sign language? What other lessons did Sullivan teach Keller?

2. Do you think that classical conditioning was at work when Helen Keller learned to finger-spell the word *water*? Why or why not? What processes may have been involved in her learning to finger-spell *water*?

Personal Experience and Application

1. Think of a time when you learned something through classical conditioning, such as a fear or food aversion. Briefly describe the situation and what you learned.

2. What problems in learning language are likely for someone born deaf or who lost her or his hearing in early childhood? What difficulties may be involved in teaching language to someone who was born deaf and blind?

Research

Suppose you want to investigate how advertisers use classical conditioning to form positive associations with their products. How might you determine (1) what types of positive images are associated with various products; and (2) the degree to which advertisers use classical conditioning on television?

POSITIVE REINFORCEMENT IN ANIMAL TRAINING

David N. Sattler and Chuck Tompkins

Psychological Concepts
operant conditioning, reinforcement, shaping, reinforcers, successive approximation

Chuck Tompkins, vice-president of animal training at Sea World of Florida, began working with animals as a child. Whenever somebody had an injured animal, Tompkins says that he was the kid on the block to whom everyone turned because he always found the right person or the right way to get the animal back on its feet. Training animals didn't become a serious love for Tompkins until he began working at Disney World. Soon thereafter, he joined Sea World as an apprentice trainer and has been there ever since.

In this selection, Tompkins answers a number of intriguing questions, including how trainers are able to get close enough to a six-thousand-pound killer whale to scratch its belly and live to tell about it. He explains that this is possible by using learning principles and developing a strong, trusting relationship with the whale. For Tompkins, the way to achieve this relationship is through positive reinforcement.

Working with killer whales is one of the most rewarding experiences I've ever had. I came to Sea World eighteen years ago, and my work is as exciting as it was when I first began. When I'm in the water interacting with the whales and we are working together as a team, it is absolutely exhilarating.

Before we begin training a new whale, we make sure that the animal is in good physical condition and is adapting well to its new environment. Then we start working on our relationship. We start by asking the animal to come over to us, and we give the animal things we know it will like. We make certain that we pair ourselves with the positive things that the animal wants in its environment, such as food, attention, body rubs, and toys. Every killer whale likes a particular part of its body scratched. We use these body rubs as reinforcement. For killer whales a toy could be a fifty-five-gallon barrel; a one-hundred-foot-long, six-inch rope, with which we play tug-of-war; the mirrors we bring to the side of the pool so they can look at themselves; or a water jet. The whales love to be sprayed on the body, and they associate these reinforcers with the trainer who is giving them. In a very short time, interacting with a trainer becomes a positive event. . . .

We only use positive reinforcement to train our killer whales. We know that the behavior we want to increase needs to be immediately reinforced, so during the training process we teach the whales a signal we call a "bridging stimulus" because it bridges the time gap between when the animals have performed correctly and when we are able to deliver a reinforcement. Many times we can reach out and give immediate reinforcement when an animal performs the correct behavior. But when we're working in a pool as large as our Shamu performing pool, we use the sound of a dog whistle to let the whale know immediately that it has performed the correct behavior. Then, when the animal returns to the trainer, the reinforcer is given. The sound of the whistle is always paired with positive reinforcement and therefore becomes a secondary reinforcer.

After we establish the bridging stimulus, we bring out the tools of training. One of the main tools is a long white pole with a ball at the end. We call this the target. We teach the whales to touch their rostrum (an area of the whale's nose) to the end of the pole. By teaching the animals to follow the white ball, we can use the movement of the target to manipulate the whales' body movements. Positive reinforcement and successive approximation training—reinforcing small steps—help the whales to understand that they should turn when the ball turns or that they should jump out of the water if the ball rises up out of the water. We manipulate the whale's body posture, its position in the pool, and its swimming speed by moving the target and reinforcing the whale for following it very closely. We then pair a hand signal with the behavior we're trying to train. Eventually, we fade out the target, and the hand signal becomes the stimulus to perform the behavior. Depending on the complexity of the behavior and the experience of the trainer, this process can take months.

We don't rely just on food and other primary reinforcers to reinforce behavior. Experienced trainers also use secondary reinforcers effectively. They might be able to elicit an entire interaction without giving food—using only the relationship as the reinforcer. A trainer who has developed a strong relationship with an animal doesn't need to use many primary reinforcers because the animal enjoys interacting with the trainer. If that experienced animal were to interact with a less experienced trainer, I would expect the trainer to have to use more primary reinforcers because he or she would not yet have developed a strong relationship with the whale. A strong relationship with a killer whale takes anywhere from two to five years to develop. Without trust and respect, a trainer entering the water with a killer whale could be in an extremely dangerous situation.

At Sea World, we feel strongly about not using negatives in our animals' environments. Unfortunately, some facilities and trainers around the world still use punishment and food deprivation to modify behavior. When I first started training eighteen years ago, we used these negatives to some degree to modify behavior, but we learned quickly that negatives create frustrated animals and have the potential of getting people hurt. We then decided to use only positive reinforcement. As most people have probably experienced, behavior can be quickly modified by using punishment, but most people also don't realize the long-term effects that punishment can have on behavior. By using negatives, people can lose the trust and respect they have developed with their animals.

The way we handle whales' incorrect behavior at Sea World is very simple. When an animal does something incorrectly, we just do not offer a reinforcing stimulus. So when the animal returns to the trainer after performing incorrectly, the trainer uses extinction—by ignoring the whale for three seconds. After the three seconds we have the option of signaling the whale to repeat the behavior or of signaling the next behavior in a sequence. We have found that by using extinction to deal with incorrect behavior and by providing reinforcement for correct behavior, we most easily teach the animals to perform correctly.

People ask us when training begins with our baby killer whales. The training process begins within the first few days after their birth. We begin reinforcing the baby by touching it and swimming with it. Obviously, the baby is still nursing, but when we play with it on stage or in the water, our attention becomes a reinforcer. The mother allows us to interact with her and the newborn in the water because of the strong trust we have developed with her. As the baby matures it will begin to mimic the mother. The trainers will reinforce this mimicry and eventually the young animal will acquire its own behavioral repertoire.

One of the greatest rewards of working with animals is developing a relationship with them. There are times when we put on the scuba gear and enter the pool with our killer whales and simply play with them. I can't explain in words what it feels like to play with a killer whale under water. We rub their bellies and scratch them. They pull us around the pool while we hold on to their dorsal fin and pectoral flippers. It's a fantastic experience.

Response and Analysis

1. According to Chuck Tompkins, why do the animal trainers pair themselves with positive items? Why is it important for trainers to use secondary reinforcers? How do they use successive approximation to shape behavior? How do they use extinction?

2. Take the whale's point of view. In what ways have the whales "shaped" the trainers to treat them as they want to be treated? What punishing consequences do the whales have at their disposal? What reinforcements can they supply to the humans?

Personal Experience and Application

1. Suppose you want to train a puppy to sit. How might you use shaping, secondary reinforcement, and a schedule of reinforcement?

2. Do you believe trainers should use punishment when working with animals? Why or why not? What are the advantages and disadvantages of punishment compared to positive reinforcement? Do you think parents should use punishment with their children? Why or why not?

Research

Suppose you want to determine whether pigeons learn to walk in a circle faster when they are on a variable ratio schedule or a variable interval schedule of reinforcement. You train five birds under each schedule of reinforcement. What is the independent variable? What are the levels or conditions of the independent variable? What is the dependent variable?

VOICES FROM THE FUTURE: OUR CHILDREN TELL US ABOUT VIOLENCE IN AMERICA

Susan Goodwillie (Editor)

Psychological Concepts
observational (social) learning, role models, violence

Manny learned to be violent from the time he was five years old, when his mother remained indifferent to him and his stepfather began beating him. Although he often did well in school, Manny, now twenty years old, says that he received no praise, and he began to doubt whether an education could help him. Because he was always getting into fights, Manny was expelled from school when he was in the ninth grade. He turned to the streets of Brooklyn, became involved in gangs, and served time in jail. Now Manny is trying to survive and would like to have a better life. After Manny's story, we include a brief discussion among other teenagers on role models and what hopes they see for teenagers in America.

I guess I've known violence all my life, since I was about five or six when my stepfather started brutalizing me. I guess I did violence because that's all I knew. And drugs somehow seemed to make it better.

I grew up in Brooklyn. It's tough in Brooklyn. You have to be dressed hip and be down with everybody else, and if they get into a fight with a bunch of white kids, you have to get involved in it. You have to do stupid things like steal, rob, you know, all that crap, take drugs and things like that. I do admit it, when I was younger, I took drugs and hung out in a gang.

But then, as I grew older, I started learning that drugs and hanging out and being in gangs, it's not going to help me in life. It's not even gonna save my ass, 'cause in the streets, it's like . . . it's hectic. You know, the only way you could survive is to be yourself. Avoid problems. Avoid certain kinds of people you know that's gonna cause problems. Like if you see a certain group of kids hanging out, go around them. Don't go through them, 'cause if you go through them, you're going to get into serious trouble.

Right now, I'm trying to sell my Rollerblades for fifty bucks 'cause, well, it's hard to find a job. It's not easy finding jobs, especially if you ain't got a high-school diploma. I got kicked out of school in ninth grade—you know, too much fighting, carrying knives and guns and things like that to school. And I would pick fights to get kicked out of certain schools. I didn't want to be in that school. I even fought teachers. I fought a principal. I punched the principal in the mouth when I was young.

If I didn't fight, I wasn't satisfied. It was like a daily habit for me. And then I hit seventeen and I got locked up for a year because of fighting and assault charges and things like that. Came out, started learning, you know, jail is not the place, streets is not the place. The only place that it can be is through yourself, in your heart.

Now I'm drug-free. I just did it with willpower because I was realizing it was killing me and I was wasting too much money on drugs. I would spend two to three hundred dollars a day taking cocaine and smoking pot. That shit almost killed me. The only drug I take now is smoking cigarettes and drinking coffee. That's caffeine and nicotine. It's still bad, but it's a slow death.

I basically raised myself in the streets 'cause my mother wasn't there for me. She was home, but she wasn't there. She could be in the living room, I could walk into the house, and she wasn't there. She would not treat me like I was there, you know? She literally threw me out when I was younger so her boyfriend could live there.

And my stepfather, he used to beat me. He used to make me bend over the bed, naked, and beat me with a leather belt until I bled. Now, that's kinda crazy, you know what I mean? He used to do that to me and my brother, and then he would tell us if we did good in school he would buy us something, like clothes. We'd do good in school, and he wouldn't buy us shit. He'd leave us without buying anything. We were kids with no clothes, nothing.

So me and my brother started doing stuff to make money and live. We started stealing, 'cause that was the only way of survival. And then my mom and my stepfather would say that we were no good and all this and that and I said, If you would have helped us when we was younger, we wouldn't have been in this area where we are now.

They said, Oh, we did everything for you, we did this and we did that, and then they would send me to a psychiatrist. I tell the psychiatrist what they did to me and he would ask my parents if it was true and they would deny it and then when I got home I'd get beat again. Then I would go to school with beat marks and my parents would say I fell down the stairs—you know, that old line—so in other words, I was child-abused.

I turned rebellious against them at the age of fourteen and that's when I started hanging out in the streets and doing all this other shit because nobody will help me. I would do good in school, hoping I'd get something. But I would never get anything, so I said, Fuck it. I'm not going to go to school if I'm not gonna get nothin' for it, you know what I mean? I didn't realize how much I needed school.

I was living in the streets for a while, but then I said, That's not gonna help me. I said, Let me go home. 'Cause I was hungry, I'd go into the house when my mother wasn't there and steal food and take my bath, wash myself, change, and then go back in the streets. Every day I would do that and then I started stealing money from them. I stole two hundred dollars from my grandmother 'cause nobody would buy me toys, and I played with the money, but then I gave it all away to my friends because I couldn't take it home.

You know, a lot of these kids have broken lives. They don't have nobody to take care of them. They don't have nobody helping them. They have to do it all their life, practically helping themselves. Some of them came from good families and they're still fucked up. Me, I came from a bad family and I'm fucked up, anyway.

Now, basically, I'm a collector. I collect comics, I buy things and then sell them. Just to survive, I sell my comics. I keep them or make trade-offs. Like I give someone a bunch of comics that's worth three dollars and they'll give me a comic that's worth twenty dollars and I'll sell it for fifteen or ten dollars, and that way I can get a profit. That's a way of living, you know, you gotta survive that way.

You come out here every day, you're going to see how crazy it is. And how hard these people work just to survive. In a way it's good, 'cause we learn, we learn experience 'cause we're in the street and you learn from the streets, you learn to survive. Like some homebound kids, they're in the house, they don't know much about the streets. If you left them out in the streets for about a week without a place to live, they'd probably go crazy. They wouldn't know how to survive.

You know, you tell somebody something, they don't learn their lesson until they see it happen to themselves. Like when my big brother used to tell me, Don't take drugs anymore, man. Chill out with it, don't do this shit anymore. I didn't want to listen to him, I was like, You did it for so many years, man, you're gonna tell me now not to do it? But then I started getting locked up, getting beat up, getting robbed, and I started realizing, Now I know how those people that I beat up feel, because I got beat up. I started realizing a lot of shit because what I did to people, they did to me. They say what goes around comes around and, I might say, it came around to me.

So, right at this moment, I just try to survive. Later on in the future, I don't know what's going to happen to me. For what I know, I could be dead tomorrow. But I'm really going to try to straighten out my life, try to make it somewhere. I'd like to get a high-school diploma, but I can't right now because I really don't have a stable environment. I have a permanent address but not a permanent residence.

I try to live day by day now. Buy my comics, read my comics, then sell them. If I die, at least I died reading my comics, you know, I did something I enjoy. . . .

Note: The reporters for *Children's Express* are teenagers and were asked to discuss the following issue:

Do you think there's any hope for kids and teenagers in America in the future?

Amy: When I talked to those kids, they didn't know that they could do things with their lives. No one ever told them, You can make good grades, you can go to college, or you can *be* anything. Their parents could care less that they quit school or that they come home and smoke pot, or not go to school at all. It is so sad, all those parents who just don't care.

Sarah: Without parents to support kids, they have no one to go to. So they look up at the people who are in gangs, and then they get in the gang and then they have to sell drugs because that's their job in the gang, and they have to steal cars and they have to do all this stuff. It takes like ten years and then they wonder, Why am I doing this? I did it because I needed someone to help me. I needed friends. And then they realize, by the time they're twenty-five, I want to go back. I want to get my GED. I want to get a job. But there are no jobs for people who haven't been in high school because that's just the way our country is. It's all really bad.

There really aren't very many role models anymore. I think the most important role model for someone is their parents, and I know there are tons of kids who live in foster homes, or nowhere, who don't have any parents to look up to. If you don't have someone to guide you and tell you what's right and wrong, then how are you going to find out? You're going to find out on the streets, or from your friends in school who are in the same situation as you are.

If your parents aren't serious, if you're doing bad in school and the teacher calls your parents and they don't do anything, they don't care, why should you care? You're a kid. You don't know what to do.

We need to reevaluate what we feel is important in society. Right now violence is a very important thing in our society. For some reason, everyone loves it. People go to the movies to see people get shot and killed. They like to see blood. That's what sells. Violence and sex and all that stuff. It sells. If that's the way our society is going to continue to go, we're just not going to make it.

Amy: Every time I'd interview someone, I'd ask, Who's your role model, who do you look up to? And usually they'd say, My big brother, he's in a gang, he beats up people every day. And I was like, Don't you look up to your parents? And they'd say stuff like, My mom sleeps all day or my dad sells drugs. I just can't imagine not having *any*one to look up to who's a positive influence in your life.

TJ: I think that's why gangs are formed, because there's nobody to look up to. Gangs are a substitute when families aren't there. If there could be somebody in the community they could go to and look up to, instead of gangs, maybe it could start to change things.

Hector: You have to live a positive life, don't always think that everything is going to turn on negative. If you live a negative life, you're never going to get anywhere. How do you expect to become something in life if you're saying, Oh, I'm not going to make it, I'm not going to do this and I'm not going to do that? . . .

Sarah: I think violence relates to poverty because if you don't have any money, you have to steal things so that you can have them. Or you can sell drugs. So we need to help people who are poor, more than we're doing now. I'm really glad we have a new president, because the other two weren't doing anything except making it a lot worse.

Kids shouldn't have to grow up with violence in their homes or on their streets or in their schools or anywhere. It's ridiculous that you need a metal detector to get into school. A school is a place where kids are supposed to learn and then go to the next school. It's not a place for drugs and guns and knives and things like that. It just really angers me that our world has come to this.

Hector: I think television is also a big problem. When you see this family, like on "Beverly Hills, 90210," living this good life and all their problems get solved and they have a car and people say, Why should I not have a life like that? I'll do anything to get that way, and that's like another way to promote violence. I'm never going to be like those people, so I'll just push my way through. And if you have this mentality, that you're harder than everyone else, you're definitely not going to do it by education. You're going to do it by force. You're going to fight your way up there, use your hands, kill people, deal drugs.

Sarah: I have hope for a lot of kids in America but not for all. I'm really upset about all the crack babies that are born. When they're born they already have something against them. They're already addicted to a drug. And no one wants them. Their mothers, their fathers, no one wants them. No one wants to adopt babies with AIDS, either.

I don't know what we can do, but every person that wants to help makes it better. I think we have to work together and figure out something to do. Bill Clinton cannot make our country not violent. He's one person. Even his administration is just going to be a bureaucratic organization. What are they going to do? Write laws. But laws obviously haven't gotten us anywhere. It's the law that you can't steal. You can't kill. You can't rape. You can't do all these things. But it doesn't matter. It's against the law to sell drugs, but that doesn't help.

I don't think putting people in jail is the answer to all our problems, either. A lot of the violence is happening inside jails. I think we all need to find out our values again. I'm not saying I want it to be like the fifties with the mom and the dad and the mom stays home all day and bakes cookies and they have a little dog and a picket fence. That's not what I want. I just want everyone to be a little kinder instead of trying to be against everybody else who you don't even know.

Response and Analysis

1. Manny says that he has known violence since the age of five or six. What were his experiences with violence at home? Who were Manny's role models? What did he learn from them?

2. According to the reporters of *Children's Express,* who were the role models for the young people they interviewed? What effects do the reporters believe the role models had on the children? How can observational, or social, learning influence socialization and violent behavior?

Personal Experience and Application

1. Who are your role models? Do you think they have a positive or negative influence on

your life? Why or why not? List a few public figures who may be role models for children. Do you believe these public figures have a positive or negative influence? Why?

2. Suppose the principal at a local elementary school invites you to help develop a program to provide positive role models for the children. Whom might you choose? Why? Briefly discuss two activities in which the students and the role models might participate.

Research

Suppose you want to interview students at your college or university about their experiences with violence. What demographic information would you request? Write ten questions you would ask the students. Now suppose you want to interview students at a local high school about their experiences with violence. What demographic information would you request? Write ten questions you would ask the students.

GANAS: USING TEAMWORK AND GOAL-SETTING IN THE CLASSROOM

Jaime Escalante and Jack Dirmann

Psychological Concepts
goals, cooperative learning

What excites us and makes us willing to work hard to learn? What student or teacher does not ask this question? As a graduate student in La Paz, Bolivia, Jaime Escalante discovered that "children learn faster when learning is fun, when it is a game and a challenge." A successful high school teacher in California, Escalante often recruited students for his math program who were known for causing problems on campus. All he asked of those who joined his class was an eagerness to succeed. He provided them with the concern and support that enabled them to discover the pleasures of learning. Today, Escalante, now in his sixties, is teaching other teachers and raising money for scholarships.

In 1952, while still an undergraduate in La Paz, Bolivia, I began teaching mathematics and physics—first at one high school, then a second, and finally a third. I found early in my career that children learn faster when learning is fun, when it is a game and a challenge. From the beginning, I cast the teacher in the role of the "coach" and the students in the role of the "team." I made sure they knew that we were all working together. . . .

Few students today have not been lectured on the necessity and importance of a good education; but the dictum "get a good education" may be too nebulous a message for easily distracted young minds. Their focus easily shifts to other more pressing problems, particularly when they are living in poverty. The AP test provides the formidable outside "opponent" that galvanizes the students and teacher in a united charge toward a tangible and inexorable deadline—the second week of May. Over the years I have found it easy to focus student attention on this challenge and its very real rewards of possible college credit and advanced placement in college mathematics courses.

Not all students who take the test score a "three" or better, which enables them to receive college credit at over 2,000 colleges and universities, but those who sit for the exam have already won the real game being played. They are winners because they have met a larger challenge than any single examination could present. They have attained a solid academic background in basic skills, especially math and science, and are prepared to move on and compete well against the challenges of both higher education and life. Many of my former students who have gone on to college mathematics or calculus courses often call me. "Kimo," they say ("Kimo" is the shortened, student-preferred spelling of "Kemo Sabe," the nickname I was given by one of my gang kids in the 1970s), "this was easy after your course."

As the number of students enrolled in my program has grown to between 140 and 200 studying calculus alone, Advanced Placement at Garfield High School has also exploded in other technical subjects such as physics, chemistry, biology, and computers. Many of my students now take two, three, and sometimes even four AP tests in various subjects. In 1989 the school set a record with over 450 AP tests administered in 16 different subjects. By comparison, in 1978, the year before I started my AP program, only 10 tests were administered for the entire school and not one student sat for the calculus examination.

A growing number of junior high school students who wish to be part of the program enroll early and participate in their first math class during the summer program at East Los Angeles College (ELAC) between their ninth grade year (last year of junior high school) and their tenth grade year. Thus, by the time these students enter the tenth grade they are prepared to take geometry. Currently, six Escalante program students are studying math analysis at a local junior high school. By the time they reach the twelfth grade, they will be ready for third-year college math.

I have been able to reach down into the three feeder junior high schools and establish an unofficial recruiting network within their math departments. We are constantly trying to pick out promising kids with *ganas* (*ganas* translates loosely from Spanish as "desire," or the "wish to succeed") while they are yet junior high school students, so that they can enter the program before or just as they arrive at Garfield.

I do not recruit these students by reviewing test scores or grades, nor are they necessarily among the "gifted" or on some kind of "high IQ track," because I believe that tracking is unworkable and unproven as a guarantee that students will be channeled into the program of classes best suited to them. My sole criterion for acceptance in this program is that the student wants to be a part of it and sincerely wants to learn math. I tell my students, "The only thing you need to have for my program—and you must bring it every day—is *ganas*." If motivated properly, any student can learn mathematics. Kids are not born as bad students; however, the school and the student's home and community environment can combine to produce a bad student. The teacher is the crucial point in this equation. It is up to the teacher to bring out the *ganas* in each student.

Today, the junior high school teachers in our locale have a much better idea of what we need for our program. I often tell the following story to show the difference between the attitude of junior high school math teachers when I first started teaching at Garfield ten years ago and their attitude today. In 1979, when junior high school teachers would tell me, "Take Johnny, he's gifted in math," I would almost always ignore them. Such a recommendation was almost a guarantee that I would pass that child over. If the child was in fact gifted, I figured he or she would need less help from the teacher. Secondly, few of the "gifted" were appreciably different from the "average"—except in their ability to score high on tracking tests. Instead, I often chose the rascals and kids who were "discipline problems," as well as those who simply liked math. I found that the "class cut-ups" were often the most intelligent, but were extremely bored by poor teaching and disillusioned by the perceived dead-end that school represented for them. Sometimes they showed themselves to have the most *ganas* when their "learning light" finally switched on. . . .

I exhibit deep love and caring for my students. I have no exclusive claim to these attributes; they are as natural as breathing to most parents and teachers. The power of love and concern in changing young lives should not be overlooked.

A few months ago I surveyed a large number of students in each of my six classes. I asked them, "What do you want from your parents?" There was a variety of answers, but those that appeared most often really surprised me and made me think twice. They were:

1.   unconditional love; that is, with no strings attached;
2.   peace at home;
3.   to be understood;
4.   trust, and the freedom of choice that such trust implies.

I believe that unconditional love must be extended to each student. This happens when a teacher loves to motivate and teach the difficult students as well as the good ones. I make sure that my students know that I believe in them. I know that the strong intention I communicate to them to succeed must be great enough to overcome the combined negativity of their previous failures, the prejudices of others who predict their likely future failures, and the lack of preparation in mathematics with which they are burdened after nine years in our education system.

Response and Analysis

1. Why does Jaime Escalante believe that students of any race or economic status will work to their potential when they have teachers who challenge them and believe in them? Why does he believe that exhibiting love for students is important to learning? How might cooperative learning (that is, a team approach) facilitate learning?

2. What is *ganas*? Why does Escalante believe *ganas* is important? How does he use *ganas* to motivate his students?

Personal Experience and Application

1. Think about one teacher who motivated or inspired you to learn. What did she or he do to inspire or motivate you? How did your new inspiration or motivation influence your performance in other courses?

2. Suppose a teacher at a local high school invites you to give a lecture to his or her class. The teacher asks you to present the information on operant conditioning that is in your psychology textbook. There will be twenty-five sophomore students in the class. How might you create interest in the topic and generate *ganas* among the students?

Research

Suppose you want to identify teaching techniques that motivate junior high school students to excel in their studies. You decide to interview high school teachers in your community about successful techniques they use. Is it important to randomly select teachers from your community to participate in your study? Why or why not? Would you interview a similar number of male and female instructors? Why or why not? Would you interview many instructors at the same school, or fewer instructors at the same school but many from several schools? Why?

chapter 5

MEMORY

My forgetter works very well.

NELLYE LEWIS, age 92,
personal communication

To what extent can we rely on our own memory or on the memories of others? In this chapter we examine the following concepts: memory acquisition, retention, and retrieval; short- and long-term memory; memory contamination; eyewitness testimony; amnesia; and exceptional memory.

In the first two selections, psychologist Elizabeth Loftus and Katherine Ketcham describe fascinating accounts of trials for which Loftus served as an expert in eyewitness testimony. One is the case of Tyrone Briggs, a man accused of assault and rape in Seattle. Loftus demonstrates how memory can be subject to suggestibility, how it can vacillate under stress, and how, in the case of Briggs, numerous errors in recall can work to bring a conviction against an innocent man.

Loftus and Ketcham also present the case involving serial murderer Ted Bundy, who was eventually executed in Florida. A woman who was abducted by Bundy still remembered his face and certain other details after eleven months, yet there were inconsistencies and gaps in her testimony. Loftus discusses the problems that can be associated with short- and long-term memory and eyewitness identification. However, in this case the witness was correct: It was Bundy who had abducted her.

Very different from having inaccurate memory is having little or no memory at all. Dr. Tony Dajer tells of a woman who lost her memory for only twenty-four hours. Dajer describes his patient's sudden confusion and the various conditions that might have caused her attack. What caused her memory loss and how did she recover?

In the former Soviet Union in the first half of the twentieth century, A. R. Luria worked for several years with a young man of unusual memory whom he called "S." S. was able to remember long series of words and numbers and seemed to have no limit to how much or how long he was able to retain what he had learned. He was equally gifted in his ability to recall extensive details about minutiae, events, conversations, and scenes. Could such a memory pose problems as well as offer benefits?

WITNESS FOR THE DEFENSE:
A MOLE AND A STUTTER—
TYRONE BRIGGS

Elizabeth Loftus and Katherine Ketcham

Psychological Concepts
eyewitness memory, memory contamination

In November 1986, a series of assaults, robberies, and attempted rapes began near the Yesler Terrace Housing Project in Seattle, Washington. Outraged, the public demanded that the perpetrator be found and convicted. One victim worked with a police artist until a sketch of the suspect took form. This drawing was published in local papers and shown on television. Two months later, a woman who lived in the housing project said that the sketch looked like a boy who lived nearby. Thus was Tyrone Briggs, a nineteen-year-old high school basketball star, targeted. Before long evidence against him accumulated.

By March 1987, defense attorney Richard Hansen had phoned Elizabeth Loftus, a psychologist and an expert in the fallibility of eyewitness testimony, to appear as an expert witness. The case ended in mistrial, only to be opened again. In December 1987, the second jury declared Briggs guilty, and he was sentenced to sixteen years and three months in prison. But in July 1989, Briggs's conviction was reversed on the basis of a juror misconduct issue. When the case went to trial again, the jury ended in deadlock. The charges were dropped and the case was not retried.

In looking at the details that Hansen and Loftus gathered for the first trial, what impresses you most about the findings, the effects of suggestibility on witnesses' memory, and the reliability of memory?

"The police have made a grievous error," Richard said. "They were under intense pressure to find someone—a black man was out there attacking white and Asian professional women—and Tyrone happened to look something like the man in the artist's sketch. From that point on, it's been a tragedy of errors."

Tragedy of errors. I liked that.

"Tyrone is nineteen years old, a high school basketball star, living in an apartment in the Yesler Terrace Housing Project with his family. He's the sweetest kid you could imagine. And he's got a terrible stutter. It's the worst stutter I've ever heard."

Richard wouldn't be relating that little fact without a reason. I waited, enjoying the suspense.

"Not one of the victims mentioned a stutter," he continued. "Not one. In fact, from the victims' initial descriptions, it would appear that the attacker couldn't stop talking. He was calm, he didn't whisper or shout but spoke in a 'normal conversational tone.' If you could hear Tyrone speak, you would know that this could not be the same man—he's had a severe stutter ever since his parents can remember. I'm talking severe—it takes him nearly a minute to say his name and address."

Stutter, I wrote on a piece of note paper.

"But that's not the only problem with the prosecution's case. The victims' initial descriptions of the attacker are so far off the mark it's like the proverbial shotgun that can't hit the side of a barn. One victim described a man with a receding hairline, a short Afro, about 190 pounds; another described a full-grown man in his mid-twenties, between five eight and five nine. The most detailed description was given by the last victim, who described her attacker as twenty-two to twenty-five years old, five nine to five ten, with yellow crooked teeth, a space between the two front teeth, a bushy Afro tinted red, and a ski-jump nose. At the time of the attacks, Tyrone Briggs was barely nineteen years old, wore his hair in jeri curls—the Michael Jackson look—weighed about 155 pounds, had straight, white teeth, a very large nose, very large lips, and a prominent mole above his right lip. Not one of the eyewitnesses mentioned a mole. In fact, the only detail that consistently fits is the fact that Tyrone is black. I'll send this stuff to you by messenger, and we can discuss it after you've had a chance to review it. I've got to be in court in"—a slight pause while Richard cupped the receiver against his shoulder and looked at his wristwatch—"ye gods, in five minutes. Gotta run. Call me."

I spent that evening in my office going through the Briggs file, making my little checkmarks in the margins, scribbling my notes, sifting, sorting, and separating the facts into the relevant categories. Right away three things bothered me about the case. First and most obvious, five women victims and a male eyewitness had identified Tyrone Briggs as the Harborview attacker. Eyewitness testimony is problematic, but when you have six positive witnesses pointing their fingers at the same man, even a skeptic like me begins to believe there might be something to it.

The second problem had to do with the available lighting conditions when the attacks took place. In daylight or artificial lighting conditions, we process more information into memory and thus have more information to pull out of memory later, when we are asked to recall an event. Even though it was gray and rainy in Seattle and close to the shortest day of the year when these attacks took place, there was, theoretically at least, enough light available for the victims to see their attacker.

The third problem concerned the duration of the attacks. The longer a person has to look at something, the better his or her memory will be, and only one of the attacks could be considered "fleeting"; several of the women were with the attacker for at least a minute or two.

I sipped my coffee and stared at the sheets of paper covering my desk. This just wasn't one of those cases that came hurtling at me, screaming of injustice. It didn't hit me, for example, like the recent case I'd worked on in Florida, where a teenager was accused of attempted rape and attempted murder after stabbing a twenty-four-year-old woman in the stomach with an eight-inch butcher knife. On the night she was attacked, the victim told a detective that her assailant was a teenager who wore braces; later she identified eighteen-year-old Todd Neely, who had never worn braces and who had an ironclad alibi confirmed by credit card receipts that showed that he was eating dinner at a restaurant with his family when the crime occurred. Police claimed Neely left the restaurant early, although they had no proof; moreover, the victim changed her testimony about her assailant's braces. In court she said she might have seen a reflection of the indoor light off his teeth and mistaken that for braces. Neely was convicted in a nonjury trial and sentenced to fifteen years.[1]

When the Florida lawyer sent me the police reports and preliminary hearing transcripts, I became convinced that Todd Neely was a victim of mistaken identification. But with Tyrone Briggs I wasn't so sure. I kept thinking—six eyewitnesses. *Six.* I knew of cases where five, six, seven, even as many as fourteen eyewitnesses were wrong, but these were the unusual, highly publicized cases that occurred once in a blue moon. Most of the cases I work on involve just one or two eyewitnesses.

But, I reminded myself, if one person can make a mistaken identification, so can five. The odds may go up, but it can happen. It had happened before.

I began a more careful reading of the police reports, incident reports, and lineup statements, looking specifically for contamination. Our memories are not, as so many people believe, perfectly preserved in our brains, frozen in time. Like other organic substances, memories can go "bad" when exposed to polluting influences.

I put on my glasses and went to work.

On January 20 Tyrone Briggs was tentatively identified from the police artist's sketch by a Yesler Terrace resident. "That looks something like him," she told Detective Clark. Briggs was arrested on an outstanding traffic ticket, his picture was taken and included in a stack of twenty-one photographs that was then shown to Karl Vance, the man who held the gun on the attacker in the December 18 attack. Vance positively identified Briggs, signing this statement:

> Today Detective Clark showed me a photo montage of twenty-one pictures. I positively picked picture numbered four as the person I saw dragging a lady into an apartment and I stopped him as he was trying to rape her. As soon as I saw the picture, I picked it up and knew it was the same person. I am absolutely positive that that is the person.

A lineup was scheduled for the morning of January 23; but newspaper and TV reporters discovered that the police had arrested a suspect in the Harborview attacks and arrived en masse at the Public Safety Building, cameras loaded and ready

---

[1]On August 24, 1990, charges against Todd Neely were dropped and he was cleared after an appeals court ruled that prosecutors withheld crucial evidence in the case. "We can't get it through our heads that it's over," Neely's stepfather told the *Palm Beach Post*. "It's sort of like being on a battlefield when the shelling stops. The silence is deafening." The four-and-a-half-year ordeal cost the Neely family approximately $300,000.

to shoot, a hastily assembled, celluloid firing squad. Four of the five victims were brought into the lineup room, a small auditorium on the fifth floor of the building. At that time, Richard wrote in his notes, a police sergeant prepared the women for the shock of seeing their attacker in person. "It is not uncommon for a person to have an emotional reaction upon seeing a suspect again for the first time," he said. "Those feelings manifest themselves in a lot of different ways. Some people get a chill down the spine, a rumbling in the stomach, palpitations, some people sweat, some people get frightened all over again."

This was already a kind of memory contamination. The police sergeant had, in effect, told the victims that they were about to see the man who attacked them. He had set them up, communicating to them that the police had a definite suspect.

The sergeant left the room, then, and returned some time later to apologize for the delay. He explained to the victims that they couldn't get enough people together to make sure that the person they had in custody—another not-so-subtle clue that the police had a definite suspect waiting in the wings—would get a fair lineup. They would have to do a photo montage instead.

The witnesses were kept waiting while a photo montage was hastily assembled. Robin Clark, the detective in charge of the investigation, took a ball-point pen and marked a mole on every photograph, being careful to make it match in size and shape the mole above Tyrone Briggs's right lip.

Now this was tricky. It's a well-established psychological finding that unusual features or objects draw our attention. When people try to recall the details of Mikhail Gorbachev's face, for example, they might first mention the prominent birth mark on his forehead. In a photo lineup, it's standard police practice to either cover up an unusual facial feature or to make sure that everyone has it. If a suspect has a strange hairdo, the police will cover the "distractors'" heads with a hat; if the suspect wears braces, the police would ask the suspect and others in the lineup to keep their mouths closed; if the suspect has a deep scar on his face, the scar should be concealed or the distractors should have a similar scar.

When Detective Clark drew a mole on the other five faces in the montage she was actually following standard police procedure designed to protect the suspect from bias or prejudice. Nevertheless, there were two significant, potentially serious problems stemming from this act. First, not one victim ever mentioned a mole on the attacker, but since every face in the photo montage had a mole, it would not take great powers of deduction to conclude that the police had a suspect who had a mole. The eyewitnesses' original memories, exposed to this potent source of postevent information, might then undergo change and contamination. Their minds would simply use their own mental pen to draw a mole on the face in their memory. Just like that, with little or no conscious thought, the memory would change to incorporate the new information.

The second problem would come later, in the actual in-person lineup. If Tyrone Briggs was the only person in that lineup with a mole, then the whole identification procedure would be tainted. After the photo identification, the eyewitnesses would be left with the impression that the suspect had a mole. When they viewed the in-person lineup, they would notice the man with the mole. They might, then, pick him out as the attacker not necessarily because he *was* the attacker, but because he was the man with the mole.

I wanted to jump ahead and look through the in-person lineup statements and photographs, but I forced myself to proceed slowly, going step by step, inch by inch through the evidence, sifting through the facts.

I found the Xerox copies of the victims' "montage identification statements." All five victims identified Tyrone Briggs as their attacker, but in every case the victims expressed reservations and uncertainty; in their written statements, they indicated that they arrived at their choice through the process of elimination.

The Seattle University student who had been assaulted on November 28 wrote: "I picked picture number 4 as the person who looks like and could be the person that assaulted me. His lips in the front view look thick but I don't really remember the lips. Everything else about his face looks right. It is definitely not any of the other five photographs."

The victim of the December 3 robbery wrote: "I am not positive it is number 4, he could be the person. It is definitely not numbers 1, 2, 3, 5, or 6."

According to the December 4 victim: "It seems more like number 4 because number 1 is not heavy enough, and number four is lighter complected and has smoother features. However, I am not positive that it is number 4."

The December 15 assault victim wrote: "I feel that it is number 4. I don't remember a mole being there, but I don't remember it not being there."

According to the December 18 assault victim: "It is definitely not numbers 1, 2, 3, 5, and 6. I am sure that it is number 4, but I don't remember the mole on his face, but I do remember a spot on his face."

Every one of these statements reflected a response that was closer to a guess than a positive statement. Guessing can be extremely dangerous, because when a witness is uncertain, guessing may actually fill the gaps in the initial skeletal representation of the event, causing an actual change in the underlying memory. Later, when searching her memory, the witness may incorrectly recall something that had earlier been merely a guess as an entrenched part of memory. Furthermore, while an initial guess may be offered with low confidence, later, when the witness mistakes the guess for a real memory, the confidence level can rise. The witness is no longer able to distinguish the original facts from the subsequent guesses, and in her mind she "sees" the entire construction as the truth. The facts have been cemented together through guesswork.

Imagine a memory as a pile of assorted bricks (details, facts, observations, and perceptions) piled up in a big mound. Guessing is the cement slapped on the bricks, allowing them to become a solid, cohesive structure. In the beginning, the guesswork may be liquid and malleable, but it can harden over time, becoming firm and resistant to change. Each time the memory is recalled, it becomes more vivid, more colorful, more *real*, and the witness becomes more confident that this is, indeed, the way things were.

In an actual criminal identification procedure, police and prosecutors often exert a subtle but profound pressure on their witnesses to be complete and accurate; under such pressure, a guess can quickly solidify into a certainty. Witnesses will also put pressure on themselves, for it is a general characteristic of human nature that we will try to avoid looking uncertain or confused. Once we have offered a response, we tend to stick by it, becoming increasingly more confident as time goes by. Any attempt to get us to rethink or question a statement that we have offered as fact may be perceived as an assault on our honor and integrity.

One other factor may have affected the witnesses' identifications of Tyrone Briggs. Three of the victims were Caucasians, two were Asians, and the assailant was black. It's a well-established fact that people are better at recognizing faces of people of their own race than they are at recognizing people from different races. This phenomenon, known as cross-racial identification, has been observed in numerous psychological experiments, yet many people remain unaware of its effects.

Response and Analysis

1. Briefly describe the three features of the Tyrone Briggs case that bothered Elizabeth Loftus. Why did they concern her? What does Loftus mean when she writes that our "memories can go 'bad' when exposed to polluting influences"?

2. How might the instructions during the lineup and the unusual face mole have influenced the memory of the eyewitnesses? How can guessing about a memory or feeling pressure to give complete and accurate details influence memory?

Personal Experience and Application

1. Have you ever thought about a past event over and over, trying to remember details? What was the event? Do you believe that in doing so your memory of the event became more accurate or less accurate? Why?

2. Suppose the police department in your community asks you to offer two recommendations to minimize the contamination of eyewitness memories during an interview. Briefly discuss each recommendation and why it would be effective.

Research

Suppose you want to examine how cultural experiences influence memory. You expect that people will more accurately remember information that is consistent with their own cultural experiences. You discover that Americans and Nigerians have markedly different experiences with funerals. You speculate that Americans and Nigerians will more accurately recall details of funerals in their respective countries than those of funerals in the other country.

You recruit participants from a university in Nigeria and from your own institution. A professor at the Nigerian university will help you recruit participants from his or her university. The participants will read a description of either a traditional American funeral or a traditional Nigerian funeral. After reading the description, they will write an essay describing what they remember.

Suppose you suspect that the participants know a great deal about how funerals in the other country are conducted. How might this knowledge influence their memory of the essay? What could you do to be sure that the participants did not know very much about how funerals in the other country are conducted? What other problems in conducting the study do you foresee?

WITNESS FOR THE DEFENSE:
THE ALL-AMERICAN BOY—
TED BUNDY

Elizabeth Loftus and Katherine Ketcham

Psychological Concepts
stages of memory (acquisition, retention, retrieval),
eyewitness memory, experiences and memory

Is eyewitness testimony reliable? Can leading questions alter our memory? Psychologist Elizabeth Loftus points out that our memories are vulnerable to suggestibility and suffer from the effects of time. In addition, what we originally perceive may be influenced by the amount of stress we are under, by conditions of weather and light, and by our own selectivity.

In 1975, Dr. Loftus received a call from John O'Connell, a defense attorney in Salt Lake City, who wanted her to work as an expert in eyewitness testimony in the case of Ted Bundy. In the early 1970s, the "Ted cases" had become well known in the Northwest, which had been beset with the murders of several young women.

Loftus and O'Connell examined the way memory, bias, and perception influence a witness's allegations. Although there were conflicting statements about the accused in the testimony of the woman who survived Bundy's attack, the judge did not believe Bundy and sent him to prison. He was later transferred to a jail in Colorado, from which he escaped, and eventually he was arrested in Florida for the murders of two women at Florida State University. Bundy was indeed the serial killer who had murdered several women in the Northwest and elsewhere.

Loftus had many qualms about having worked for Bundy's defense. But her devotion to being a social scientist who carefully analyzes testimony in order to aid justice and to keep innocent people from being convicted prompted her to become involved with the case.

Now that I think back on it, I don't remember John O'Connell ever telling me that his client, twenty-three-year-old law student Ted Bundy, was innocent. I have a letter from O'Connell in which he refers to the kidnapping charge against Bundy as "one of the more interesting cases involving eyewitness identification." I remember a phone conversation in which he talked about the "extremely weak case" against his client. He often stressed the confusion and uncertainty of the kidnapping victim—the only eyewitness, it would turn out, who lived to tell about her few moments of terror with Ted Bundy.

But when I dredge up the strange and painful memories of my involvement with Ted Bundy, I have no recollection of John O'Connell insisting with his characteristic passion and intensity that his client was innocent. Maybe that particular silence should have given me a clue.

The name Ted Bundy meant nothing to me back in December 1975 when John O'Connell first contacted me about the kidnapping charge against his client. The name might as well have been anyone's. But one comment in O'Connell's letter did set off an alarm system in my memory. It was the second line of his five-page, single-spaced letter.

> Dear Dr. Loftus,
> I am representing Ted Bundy on a charge of aggravated kidnapping here in Salt Lake. Mr. Bundy is a law student from the Seattle area and has achieved a great deal of notoriety there because this case has made him a prime suspect in the "Ted cases." . . .

I knew all about the "Ted cases": I'd be willing to bet that every woman living in the state of Washington knew about the "Ted cases." Beginning in January 1974, young women in their late teens and early twenties, all pretty, all with long brown hair parted down the middle, began to disappear. Every month another woman would vanish. The media, in a hideous display of insensitivity, began referring to the missing women as "Miss February," "Miss March," "Miss April," and "Miss May."

In June 1974 the pace speeded up as two more women disappeared, and in July two women vanished on the same day from the same park at Lake Sammamish, twelve miles east of Seattle. But now, finally, there were witnesses who told police that an attractive, polite young man calling himself "Ted" and wearing his left arm in a sling approached several women and asked for their help in lifting a sailboat onto his car. He couldn't do it himself, he explained with a shy grin, because of his sprained arm.

The disappearances seemed to stop then, but the grisly discoveries began. In September the remains of three women were discovered by a grouse hunter near an abandoned logging road twenty miles east of Seattle. The next spring another "dumping site"—a favorite media expression—was discovered by two forestry students hiking on the lower slopes of Taylor Mountain near the town of North Bend. Four skulls and assorted bones would eventually be unearthed there, each cranium fractured by a heavy blunt instrument wielded with tremendous force and fury.

I turned to page 2 of O'Connell's letter, where he described the kidnapping incident, and continued on to page 3 where he discussed Bundy's arrest on a traffic charge almost ten months after the kidnapping.

> There is no other evidence whatsoever connecting the defendant to this crime except that he has type O blood and some type O blood was found sometime later on the victim's clothing. All this, despite the fact that Ted Bundy has been subjected to the most

thorough police investigation that I have ever seen. Due to the great time lapse, we are unable to establish an alibi for the time concerned.

O'Connell included with his letter a twenty-page police report and typed transcript of a taped statement the victim made the night of the incident. Throughout both the police report and the transcript, O'Connell used a thick black pen to underline certain words and phrases and scrawl notes in the margins. I began reading.

OFFENSE: Abduction
DATE OF OCCURRENCE: 11-8-74
SUSPECT: Male, white, American, 25–30 years, brown hair, medium length, approximately six feet tall, thin to medium build, moustache neatly trimmed. Wearing green pants and sports jacket, color unknown. Patent leather, shiny black shoes.

An arrow led from the underlined word to the left-hand margin where O'Connell had scrawled, "See taped statement—reddish brown shoes."

I leafed through the remaining pages of the police report, noting the other underlined parts.

Victim believed that she scratched suspect, probably on either the hands or arms, that she did note some blood on her hands that must have come from the suspect, that she was not injured herself. However, does not remember actually hurting the suspect.

 In talking to victim, she states she believes she could identify suspect if she saw him again, that she spent approximately 20–30 minutes with him in the mall and walking through the parking lot and in the vehicle. Victim taped a report which will be included as a supplement of this report.

The supplementary report contained the transcript of a conversation between the victim, Carol DaRonch, and Detective Riet. . . .

"Let's review the major eyewitness issues in this case," I said.

O'Connell searched through some papers on his desk and handed me a lined, legal-size piece of paper with "Loftus—Main Points" handwritten at the top of the page. "I took notes from our telephone conversations," he explained, grinning at me.

I read the first point.

Perception and memory do not function like TV camera and videotape. Only that which was perceived can be remembered—i.e., memory cannot be "replayed" to get details which were not noted in original perception. Analogy to watching football play. If observer did not notice great block because concentrating on runner, cannot replay and recall from memory the block as one could do with the videotape of the same play.

"Nice analogy," I said.

"I'm a great football fan," O'Connell said, puffing on his pipe. "Why don't you explain this videotape concept to me again."

I'd given this particular lecture dozens of times to college students; I was on automatic pilot. "Most theoretical analyses of memory divide the process into three separate stages," I began. "First, the acquisition stage, in which the perception of the original event is put into the memory system; second, the retention stage, the period of time that passes between the event and the recollection of a particular piece of information; and third, the retrieval stage, in which a person recalls stored information.

"Contrary to popular belief," I continued, "facts don't come into our memory and passively reside there untouched and unscathed by future events. Instead, we pick up fragments and features from our environment and these go into memory where they interact with our prior knowledge and expectations—information that is already stored in our memory. Thus experimental psychologists think of memory as being an integrative process—a constructive and creative process—rather than a passive recording process such as a videotape."

I switched from the general to the specific. "All the 'I don't knows' and 'I don't remembers' in Carol DaRonch's testimony could mean that the information was never stored in the first place—there was a failure, in other words, in the acquisition stage. Or it could mean that the information was stored but then forgotten—a failure in either the retention stage or the retrieval stage. There's really no way of telling exactly what happened."

I looked at O'Connell's list and read number 2: Memory deteriorates at an exponential rate.

"The accumulation of research shows that memory decays or deteriorates as time goes by," I explained. "After a week, memory is less accurate than after a day. After a month, memory is less accurate than after a week. And after a year, memory will be less accurate than after a month."

"Eleven months is presumably one hell of a long time for Carol DaRonch to hold a memory of Ted Bundy's face in her mind," O'Connell observed.

"That's right," I agreed, "although many people are under the mistaken impression that memory for faces lasts a lifetime. The distinction—and it's an important one—must be made between memory for faces of people we've known for years and memory for the face of a stranger whom we see once, for a short period of time. Many people do remember the faces of friends whom they haven't seen for years or even decades. We graduate from high school, go off on our own, and twenty years later come back to a reunion where we immediately recognize the faces of our former friends.

"But this is not the same thing as remembering the face of a stranger. When it comes to strangers—people seen only briefly and only once—the overwhelming trend is that memory deteriorates as time passes. Most of the studies have used periods of time much shorter than eleven months and have shown great deterioration of memory for faces."

O'Connell nodded his head and looked at the paper, reading over my shoulder. "Some stimulation improves perception and memory, but great stress interferes. Fear to the point of hysteria has a negative effect on memory."

"This third point refers to the relationship between stress and memory," I said, "which is explained by the Yerkes-Dodson law, named after the two men who first noted the relationship back in 1908. At very low levels of arousal—for example, when a person is just waking up in the morning—the nervous system may not be fully functioning and sensory messages may not get through. Memory is not functioning very well. At moderate levels—say if you were slightly nervous about an upcoming trial or anxious about a confrontation with your teenage son—memory performance will be optimal. But with high levels of arousal, the ability to remember begins to decline and deteriorate."

"Tell me, Elizabeth," O'Connell said. "If you were in a car with a man who had identified himself as a police officer but who was driving the wrong way to the police station in a rundown Volkswagen, who then ran the car up onto the curb, snapped handcuffs on your wrist, brandished a gun, and raised a crowbar in an effort to hit you over the head—would you rate that as a high level of stress?"

"Yes, I would," I said. "But I should warn you about a potential problem."

O'Connell raised his eyebrows at me.

"Carol DaRonch wasn't under great emotional stress for the first five or ten minutes that she was with 'Officer Roseland,' " I said. "Part of that time she walked around with him in a well-lighted mall. It could be argued that she was under a moderate level of emotional arousal, which tends to produce alertness and fairly good recall."

"The prosecutor will be sure to pick up on that," O'Connell said. "Still, if you put all the facts together, we've got a good case for reduced accuracy of memory." He pointed to number 4 on the list. "Difficult to maintain separate visual images without transference and merging."

"This point refers to a process known as unconscious transference," I said, "a phenomenon in which a person seen in one situation is confused with or recalled as a person seen in a second situation. Again, with reference to this particular case, when the police showed Carol DaRonch two different photos of Ted Bundy—a mug shot and then, within a few days, a driver's license photo—they could have created a memory for her. 'Planted it in her brain,' as you once said."

O'Connell nodded his head. He understood that point well enough.

"Point 5," I said, reading the last paragraph on the list. "Effect of interviewer bias—particularly unintentional cueing and reinforcing. Support proposition that increasing excitement and activity of peace officers from September 1 (original photo selection) to October 2 (lineup) had effect of changing weak identification to positive identification."

"Do you always refer to the police as peace officers?" I asked.

"Yup," he said. "That's what I call them, because that's what they're supposed to be." But in this case O'Connell believed that the "peace officers" had gone too far and biased their witness, transmitting through words, gestures, or other "cues" their belief that Ted Bundy was, in fact, the kidnapper. After DaRonch tentatively identified Bundy's photo on September 1, 1975, and then more firmly identified him a few days later from a different photograph, the police may have communicated to her, intentionally or unintentionally, the feeling that they had "a live one." In her desire to help the police and finally put an end to her ordeal, DaRonch might have picked up on the signals and decided in her own mind that Bundy was, in fact, her abductor. Questions suggested answers that encouraged more sharply detailed questions until the whole thing picked up speed, steamrolling neatly ahead, with Bundy—guilty or innocent?—trapped beneath the wheels. . . .

In the beginning had I been fooled, as so many others were fooled, by the all-American boy with the polite manner and the deep smile lines? Unaccustomed to evil, could I not recognize it when it stared me in the face?

Response and Analysis

1. Elizabeth Loftus provides examples from Carol DaRonch's testimony to illustrate how perceptions of one's surroundings interact with prior knowledge. How can expectations influence memory? According to Loftus, what are the main features of the acquisition, retention, and retrieval stages of memory?

2. According to Loftus, how might an interviewer's questions affect memory? What theoretical model might best explain how this happens? How can stress affect memory?

Personal Experience and Application

1. Describe in as much detail as possible the face of a television news anchorman or anchorwoman. Then watch the news program. Which of the features that you listed were accurate? Which features did you omit? What does this suggest about memory?

2. Suppose you are a member of a jury. The case involves a convenience store robbery that occurred in the middle of the night. The clerk presents eyewitness testimony. What factors might influence the quality of the clerk's recollections? Why do you think these factors might influence the clerk's memory?

Research

Suppose you want to replicate an experiment examining how memory can be altered (Loftus & Palmer, 1974). You show a videotape of a car accident to students in an introduction to psychology class. You then ask the participants what they saw in the videotape. You ask half of the students, "About how fast were the cars going when they *hit* each other?" You ask the other half, "About how fast were the cars going when they *smashed* into each other?" Then you dismiss the participants. Seven days later, you ask the participants whether they remember seeing broken glass in the accident. In fact, there was no broken glass. Which group do you think would "recall" seeing more broken glass—the participants hearing the word *hit* or those hearing the word *smashed*? Why might one group recall seeing more broken glass than another group? Do you think this study adequately illustrates how memories can be distorted? Why or why not?

THE LOST TWENTY-FOUR HOURS

Tony Dajer

Psychological Concepts
amnesia (retrograde, anterograde), hippocampus

Imagine that one day you suddenly lose your memory. You don't remember what day it is, whether it is time for lunch, or why groceries are sitting on the table. That is what happened to Mrs. Duke, a woman in her mid-sixties, whose story is told by Dr. Dajer, her physician. In the thirty minutes it took her husband to go shopping one morning, Mrs. Duke became confused and unable to recall important details. The next twenty-four hours became "lost." While she was in the hospital and the doctors looked for the source of her amnesia, Mrs. Duke's spirits remained positive. Note the characteristics of her conversations, and Dr. Dajer's reactions to her. How would you describe the interaction between them during that twenty-four-hour period? Does Mrs. Duke show signs of reconnecting to the life she had before her memory loss?

For an emergency room, the scene seemed almost too tranquil: a couple in their mid-sixties were chatting quietly in a small exam cubicle. The man had his right elbow perched atop a cabinet; the woman sat on the stretcher, still wearing her street clothes.

"Hello, I'm Dr. Dajer," I said, walking in. "How can I help you?"

Mr. Duke spoke first. "My wife is confused."

While his wife paid close attention—as if hearing a recap of the first half of a movie she'd missed—he very precisely recounted the events of the previous two hours: He had left the house for thirty minutes to buy groceries; his wife had taken a bath. When he'd returned, she had seemed fine, but then she had started asking odd questions.

"What day is it?" for instance. Or, "Is it time for lunch yet?" (She'd already had lunch.) Then, "What are the groceries for?"

She should have known: it was her favorite niece's birthday, and they'd been planning the party for weeks. When he answered her, she didn't seem to know what to do next. A few minutes later she began asking the same questions all over again.

"So I called my daughter—she's a nurse—and she told me to bring my wife to the emergency room right away," Mr. Duke concluded.

"Sounds like your daughter was right," I replied, trying to look more intrigued than concerned.

I turned to Mrs. Duke. She was a silver-haired sixty-six-year-old but seemed ten years younger. We chatted a bit about her daughter, whom I happened to know. While she spoke—coherently and easily—I scrutinized her face for the telltale drooping eyelid or asymmetrical smile of a transient ischemic attack, or TIA, some-times called a ministroke, that might have accounted for her mental lapse. She ap-peared perfectly normal, though.

"Okay with you if we do a once-over-lightly?" I asked her. I quickly listened to the heart and lungs, palpated the abdomen, then zeroed in on the neurological exam. I tested the cranial nerves, the ones controlling the facial muscles we use to move our eyes and smile, which are typically affected in TIAs. Then I checked the muscle strength in her arms and legs, examined her reflexes and ability to feel a sen-sation like a pinprick, and tested her coordination. But I couldn't find the slightest abnormality.

Last came the mental-status exam, which measures cognitive functions like rea-soning and memory.

"Mrs. Duke," I began, "do you know where you are right now?"

She took a look around and replied, "Why, in the hospital, I think."

"Do you know what day it is?"

"Of course." She opened her mouth to answer, but then she stopped. "Well, isn't that strange? I don't know."

I kept an encouraging note in my voice: "Sometimes I don't even know myself. How about the month?"

"July?" she answered, tentatively.

"September, actually."

"Oh dear." She pressed three fingers to her forehead, as if urging herself to concentrate a bit more.

"Do you know who the president is?" (She didn't.) "Is there some trouble with a country in the Middle East right now?" (The Iraqi invasion of Kuwait had been in the headlines for a month.)

She didn't know. Each time she would start to answer the question as if she were opening a familiar cupboard, only to find it unexpectedly bare. With every miss her husband's lips pressed tighter together.

"Let's try this," I ventured. "I'm going to name three objects. In five minutes I'll ask you to repeat them back to me, all right?"

She smiled bravely. "I'll do my best."

I glanced around the room: "Bed, chair, sink. Got it?"

"Bed, chair, sink. Yes."

"Okay, I'll be back in a few minutes and ask you to repeat those objects."

"Bed, chair, sink," she intoned as I left the room.

"Bed, chair, sink," I whispered to myself as I went to examine another patient. Then I walked back in.

"Well, Mrs. Duke," I boomed heartily, "what were the three objects?"

She peered at me for a second, then in a bewildered tone asked, "Who are you?"

I stopped in my tracks. "I'm the emergency room doctor. I was here just five minutes ago. Don't you remember?"

"Oh dear. I'm sorry. Should I?"

Her husband took her hand. "That's how she's been since I came home from shopping," he told me. "It's as if nothing sticks."

Amnesia. Absence of memory. Few medical phenomena have so intrigued the imagination or shaped so many plots as the idea that we can forget our past, even forget who we are. Most fictional cases, of course, don't fit medical fact (for example, the spy in Robert Ludlum's thriller *The Bourne Identity* couldn't possibly forget his entire life history and still fully assimilate new information). But there are enough holes in our knowledge of how the brain processes and stores memories—and how it loses them—to leave room for poetic license.

Imagine if the brain remembered absolutely everything, if every thought, impression, and sensation, no matter how trivial, was indelibly recorded. Then imagine that a past event could be recalled only by sorting through each and every event that came after it. Retrieving a childhood memory would take hours. Clearly, the brain must edit and file memories to make them retrievable and useful.

Crucial to this complicated process is the hippocampus, a curled, sea-horse-shaped structure that is tucked inside the brain's temporal lobes. First it appears to gather new information and store it as a short-term memory. Then it edits, or consolidates, the short-term memory and after a while files the boiled-down product permanently in other parts of the brain. Finally, it helps retrieve those files when needed later. Thus the hippocampus acts both as a way station for recent memories—a monkey whose hippocampus has been destroyed can't remember tasks learned two weeks earlier—and as a retrieval system for old memories.

Although Mrs. Duke could speak and reason normally, her memory acted like a faulty computer in which each new entry erased the one ahead of it—before it could be stored. In short, her hippocampus could construct no new memories. Nor could it recall the events in the recent past, such as the invasion of Kuwait. Finally, her inability to recollect long-established facts such as the president's name suggested her file-retrieval system was jumbled.

The question we needed to answer was whether the amnesia was permanent—the result of a tumor in the hippocampus or of a large blood clot causing a major stroke. The other, much more hopeful possibility was transient global amnesia, a rare condition that is probably caused by a small clot passing through the arteries that feed the hippocampus. Like any other TIA, this disturbance usually resolves itself within twenty-four hours. Only time and the CT scan could reveal what was the matter with Mrs. Duke. And neither verdict would be in till morning.

I arranged for Mrs. Duke's admission into the intensive care unit. With child-like trust, she agreed to be hospitalized when her husband suggested it, though she herself felt nothing was wrong: she literally couldn't remember that she kept forgetting. Every time I reentered the room, to her it was the first time. All she knew was that she could rely on her husband to decide what was best, even if she couldn't remember why or how or even what he had decided.

That night, Mrs. Duke kept asking the nurses the same questions: "Why am I here?" And, most disconcerting of all, "Who are you?" It was as if she kept waking up in an unfamiliar room.

When I got off my emergency room shift at 7 A.M., I went up to see her. She seemed more alert than twelve hours before. Tentatively, I asked the questions she should have been sick of hearing by now.

"Do you know where you are?"

She smiled. "Why, in the hospital."

"Do you remember coming into the hospital yesterday?"

A small frown. "No."

"What's the last thing you do remember?"

"Breakfast, I think. We were getting ready for my niece's birthday." (She had clearly made progress—though the twenty-four hours after that would remain a permanent blank to her.)

"Do you think you could remember three objects if I listed them for you?"

"I'll try."

We repeated yesterday's exercise. I went into the hall for five minutes, then returned. "Well?" I prompted.

"Bed, chair, sink," she replied.

Her hippocampus, apparently, had clicked back on. That meant she'd almost certainly had transient global amnesia, not a massive clot or a tumor. Her prognosis was excellent: unlike other TIAs, this temporary condition is not a harbinger of strokes to come, and better yet, it rarely repeats itself.

"We still need to do that CT scan, just to be sure," I told her. "But I think you're going to do just fine."

"Well, that's nice of you to say so," she replied, as if I had paid her a compliment.

As I took my leave, though, it struck me that maybe her recovery was too good to be true, that by repeating the same list, I'd "primed" her too well. I stopped and retraced my steps. Would she remember me if I took her by surprise?

I poked my head back into the room.

"Hello, Mrs. Duke."

"Oh, hello, Dr. Dajer." She smiled solicitously. "Is there something you've forgotten?"

Response and Analysis

1. What problem did Dr. Dajer suspect caused Mrs. Duke's amnesia? Did Mrs. Duke's experience resemble retrograde amnesia or anterograde amnesia? Why?

2. Briefly describe Mrs. Duke's difficulty recalling short-term and long-term memories. What is the role of the hippocampus in short-term and long-term memory? Briefly describe two other brain structures involved in memory.

Personal Experience and Application

1. Do you know someone who has experienced temporary or long-term memory loss, such as from an automobile accident or stroke? Briefly describe his or her ability to recall events that occurred within a few minutes and from many years in the past. What difficulties did this person experience because of his or her memory impairment? What was done to help the person remember?

2. Imagine that you are a victim of amnesia. How might anterograde amnesia affect your life? Retrograde amnesia?

Research

Suppose you design a study to examine how anxiety (low, medium, high) and noise (soft, loud) affect the ability to retrieve and remember information. In this study, what are the independent variables? What are the levels or conditions of each independent variable? What is the dependent variable?

THE MIND OF A MNEMONIST

A. R. Luria

Psychological Concepts
exceptional memory, mental imagery, mnemonist

What advantages or disadvantages might there be in not forgetting anything you have learned? Might people who remember nearly everything one day find their "memory disk" overloaded? Indeed, are there people haunted by thorough and accurate memories?

The distinguished Soviet psychologist A. R. Luria presents the famous case of S., a man who had unusual mnemonic and perceptual abilities. When S. was a journalist and was given instructions by his editor, he was able to remember everything he had been told without taking notes. He assumed that everyone had that ability. S. was also able to repeat a list of numbers or words of any length that Dr. Luria presented to him—even when the sessions were days, weeks, and even years apart. More fascinating were S.'s responses to sounds, decibels, words, and scenes. Upon hearing one particular individual speak, S. said, "What a crumbly, yellow voice you have."

After you read Dr. Luria's portrayal of S., imagine that you are S. and then listen to numbers or voices. Do any colors or images come to you?

When I began my study of S. it was with much the same degree of curiosity psychologists generally have at the outset of research, hardly with the hope that the experiments would offer anything of particular note. However, the results of the first tests were enough to change my attitude and to leave me, the experimenter, rather than my subject, both embarrassed and perplexed.

I gave S. a series of words, then numbers, then letters, reading them to him slowly or presenting them in written form. He read or listened attentively and then repeated the material exactly as it had been presented. I increased the number of elements in each series, giving him as many as thirty, fifty, or even seventy words or numbers, but this, too, presented no problem for him. He did not need to commit any of the material to memory; if I gave him a series of words or numbers, which I read slowly and distinctly, he would listen attentively, sometimes ask me to stop and enunciate a word more clearly, or, if in doubt whether he had heard a word correctly, would ask me to repeat it. Usually during an experiment he would close his eyes or stare into space, fixing his gaze on one point; when the experiment was over, he would ask that we pause while he went over the material in his mind to see if he had retained it. Thereupon, without another moment's pause, he would reproduce the series that had been read to him.

The experiment indicated that he could reproduce a series in reverse order—from the end to the beginning—just as simply as from start to finish; that he could readily tell me which word followed another in a series, or reproduce the word which happened to precede the one I'd name. He would pause for a minute, as though searching for the word, but immediately after would be able to answer my questions and generally made no mistakes.

It was of no consequence to him whether the series I gave him contained meaningful words or nonsense syllables, numbers or sounds; whether they were presented orally or in writing. All he required was that there be a three-to-four-second pause between each element in the series, and he had no difficulty reproducing whatever I gave him.

As the experimenter, I soon found myself in a state verging on utter confusion. An increase in the length of a series led to no noticeable increase in difficulty for S., and I simply had to admit that the capacity of his memory *had no distinct limits;* that I had been unable to perform what one would think was the simplest task a psychologist can do: measure the capacity of an individual's memory. I arranged a second and then a third session with S.; these were followed by a series of sessions, some of them days and weeks apart, others separated by a period of several years.

But these later sessions only further complicated my position as experimenter, for it appeared that there was no limit either to the *capacity* of S.'s memory or to the *durability of the traces he retained.* Experiments indicated that he had no difficulty reproducing any lengthy series of words whatever, even though these had originally been presented to him a week, a month, a year, or even many years earlier. In fact, some of these experiments designed to test his retention were performed (without his being given any warning) fifteen or sixteen years after the session in which he had originally recalled the words. Yet invariably they were successful. During these test sessions S. would sit with his eyes closed, pause, then comment: "Yes, yes. . . . This was a series you gave me once when we were in your apartment. . . . You were sitting at the table and I in the rocking chair. . . . You were wearing a gray suit and you looked at me like this. . . . Now, then, I can see you saying . . ." And with that he would reel off the series precisely as I had given it to him at the earlier session. If one takes into account that S. had by then become a well-known mnemonist, who had to remember hundreds and thousands of series, the feat seems even more remarkable. . . .

Our curiosity had been aroused by a small and seemingly unimportant observation. S. had remarked on a number of occasions that if the examiner said something during the experiment—if, for example, he said "yes" to confirm that S. had reproduced the material correctly or "no" to indicate he had made a mistake—a blur would appear on the table and would spread and block off the numbers, so that S. in his mind would be forced to "shift" the table over, away from the blurred section that was covering it. The same thing happened if he heard noise in the auditorium; this was immediately converted into "puffs of steam" or "splashes" which made it more difficult for him to read the table.

This led us to believe that the process by which he retained material did not consist merely of his having preserved spontaneous traces of visual impressions; there were certain additional elements at work. I suggested that S. possessed a marked degree of *synesthesia*.[1] If we can trust S.'s recollections of his early childhood . . . these synesthetic reactions could be traced back to a very early age. As he described it:

> When I was about two or three years old I was taught the words of a Hebrew prayer. I didn't understand them, and what happened was that the words settled in my mind as

---

[1] synesthesia: the stimulation of one sense evokes another sense, as in visualizing a color when hearing a particular sound.

puffs of steam or splashes. . . . Even now I *see* these puffs or splashes when I hear certain sounds.

Synesthetic reactions of this type occurred whenever S. was asked to listen to *tones*. The same reactions, though somewhat more complicated, occurred with his perception of *voices* and with speech sounds.

The following is the record of experiments that were carried out with S. in the Laboratory on the Physiology of Hearing at the Neurological Institute, Academy of Medical Sciences.

Presented with a tone pitched at 30 cycles per second and having an amplitude of 100 decibels, S. stated that at first he saw a strip 12–15 cm. in width the color of old, tarnished silver. Gradually this strip narrowed and seemed to recede; then it was converted into an object that glistened like steel. Then the tone gradually took on a color one associates with twilight, the sound continuing to dazzle because of the silvery gleam it shed.

Presented with a tone pitched at 50 cycles per second and an amplitude of 100 decibels, S. saw a brown strip against a dark background that had red, tongue-like edges. The sense of taste he experienced was like that of sweet and sour borscht, a sensation that gripped his entire tongue.

Presented with a tone pitched at 100 cycles per second and having an amplitude of 86 decibels, he saw a wide strip that appeared to have a reddish-orange hue in the center; from the center outwards the brightness faded with light gradations so that the edges of the strip appeared pink.

Presented with a tone pitched at 250 cycles per second and having an amplitude of 64 decibels, S. saw a velvet cord with fibers jutting out on all sides. The cord was tinged with a delicate, pleasant pink-orange hue.

Presented with a tone pitched at 500 cycles per second and having an amplitude of 100 decibels, he saw a streak of lightning splitting the heavens in two. When the intensity of the sound was lowered to 74 decibels, he saw a dense orange color which made him feel as though a needle had been thrust into his spine. Gradually this sensation diminished.

Presented with a tone pitched at 2,000 cycles per second and having an amplitude of 113 decibels, S. said: "It looks something like fireworks tinged with a pink-red hue. The strip of color feels rough and unpleasant, and it has an ugly taste—rather like that of a briny pickle. . . . You could hurt your hand on this."

Presented with a tone pitched at 3,000 cycles per second and having an amplitude of 128 decibels, he saw a whisk broom that was of a fiery color, while the rod attached to the whisks seemed to be scattering off into fiery points.

The experiments were repeated during several days and invariably the same stimuli produced identical experiences.

What this meant was that S. was one of a remarkable group of people, among them the composer Scriabin, who have retained in an especially vivid form a "complex" synesthetic type of sensitivity. In S.'s case every sound he heard immediately produced an experience of light and color and . . . a sense of taste and touch as well.

S. also experienced synesthetic reactions when he listened to someone's *voice*. "What a crumbly, yellow voice you have," he once told L. S. Vygotsky while conversing with him. At a later date he elaborated on the subject of voices as follows:

> You know there are people who seem to have many voices, whose voices seem to be an entire composition, a bouquet. The late S. M. Eisenstein had just such a voice: Listening to him, it was as though a flame with fibers protruding from it was advancing right toward me. I got so interested in his voice, I couldn't follow what he was saying. . . .
>
> But there are people whose voices change constantly. I frequently have trouble recognizing someone's voice over the phone, and it isn't merely because of a bad connection. It's because the person happens to be someone whose voice changes twenty to thirty times in the course of a day. Other people don't notice this, but I do. (Record of November 1951.)
>
> To this day I can't escape from seeing colors when I hear sounds. What first strikes me is the color of someone's voice. Then it fades off . . . for it does interfere. If, say, a person says something, I see the word; but should another person's voice break in, blurs appear. These creep into the syllables of the words and I can't make out what is being said. (Record of June 1953.)

"Lines," "blurs," and "splashes" would emerge not only when he heard tones, noises, or voices. Every speech sound immediately summoned up for S. a striking visual image, for it had its own distinct form, color, and taste. Vowels appeared to him as simple figures, consonants as splashes, some of them solid configurations, others more scattered—but all of them retained some distinct form.

When S. read through a long series of words, each word would elicit a graphic image. And since the series was fairly long, he had to find some way of distributing these images of his in a mental row or sequence. Most often (and this habit persisted throughout his life), he would "distribute" them along some roadway or street he visualized in his mind. Sometimes this was a street in his home town, which would also include the yard attached to the house he had lived in as a child and which he recalled vividly. On the other hand, he might also select a street in Moscow. Frequently he would take a mental walk along that street—Gorky Street in Moscow—beginning at Mayakovsky Square, and slowly make his way down, "distributing" his images at houses, gates, and store windows. At times, without realizing how it had happened, he would suddenly find himself back in his home town (Torzhok), where he would wind up his trip in the house he had lived in as a child. The setting he chose for his "mental walks" approximates that of dreams, the difference being that the setting in his walks would immediately vanish once his attention was distracted but would reappear just as suddenly when he was obliged to recall a series he had "recorded" this way.

This technique of converting a series of words into a series of graphic images explains why S. could so readily reproduce a series from start to finish or in reverse order; how he could rapidly name the word that preceded or followed one I'd select from the series. To do this, he would simply begin his walk, either from the beginning or from the end of the street, find the image of the object I had named, and "take a look at" whatever happened to be situated on either side of it. S.'s visual patterns of memory differed from the more commonplace type of figurative memory by virtue of the fact that his images were exceptionally vivid and stable; he was also able to "turn away" from them, as it were, and "return" to them whenever it was necessary.

When S. read a passage from a text, each word produced an image. As he put it: "Other people *think* as they read, but I *see* it all." As soon as he began a phrase, images would appear; as he read further, still more images were evoked, and so on.

As we mentioned earlier, if a passage were read to him quickly, one image would collide with another in his mind; images would begin to crowd in upon one another and would become contorted. How then was he to understand anything in this chaos of images? If a text were read slowly, this, too, presented problems for him. Note the difficulties he experienced:

> . . . I was read this phrase: "N. was leaning up against a tree. . . ." I saw a slim young man dressed in a dark blue suit (N., you know, is so elegant). He was standing near a big linden tree with grass and woods all around. . . . But then the sentence went on: "and was peering into a shop window." Now how do you like that! It means the scene isn't set in the woods, or in a garden, but he's standing on the street. And I have to start the whole sentence over from the beginning. . . . (Record of March 1937.)

Thus, trying to understand a passage, to grasp the information it contains (which other people accomplish by singling out what is most important), became a tortuous procedure for S., a struggle against images that kept rising to the surface in his mind. Images, then, proved an obstacle as well as an aid to learning in that they prevented S. from concentrating on what was essential. Moreover, since these images tended to jam together, producing still more images, he was carried so far adrift that he was forced to go back and rethink the entire passage. Consequently a simple passage—a phrase, for that matter—would turn out to be a Sisyphean task. These vivid, palpable images were not always helpful to S. in understanding a passage; they could just as easily lead him astray.

Response and Analysis

1. Why did A. R. Luria believe that there was no limit to S.'s memory? What were S.'s short-term and long-term memory capabilities? Briefly describe one of S.'s responses (for example, seeing colors) when listening to someone's voice.

2. Briefly describe how S. would "elicit a graphic image" when he "read through a long series of words." What images did he create? How does his use of mental imagery explain, in part, his exceptional memory?

Personal Experience and Application

1. Do you know someone with an exceptional memory? What types of special techniques does he or she use to remember? What kinds of information is he or she able to remember?

2.   Suppose the psychology club at your college or university asks you to give a five-minute presentation on improving memory and study skills. Write a brief talk that addresses the following questions: Should a student study in the same location for an exam? Should the study area be quiet rather than noisy? Should a student study for an exam over a period of several days or "cram" for an exam?

Research

Luria's case study revealed that S. was an unusual person, both for his ability to remember and for his synesthesia. Can psychologists generalize what they learn about extraordinary people to normal people? Why or why not? What are the advantages and disadvantages of doing research on extraordinary people?

chapter 6

THOUGHT AND LANGUAGE

But if thought corrupts language, language also corrupts thought.

GEORGE ORWELL,
Politics and the English Language

How does language draw us together? How do the words we use and the manner in which we speak contribute to misunderstandings we may have with one another? This chapter explores several key issues that pertain to language and thought: conflict between the sexes, cultural misunderstandings, some effects of bilingualism, and the power of thought.

Are men or women more often perceived as being too bossy? Too emotional? Poor listeners? Linguist Deborah Tannen explores how men and women use language and how misunderstandings may result from different conversational styles. Women may use conversation to establish rapport whereas men may use it to preserve independence and status. By becoming aware of their different conversational styles, men and women gain insight into the intentions of each other and can thus work hard toward better communication.

Nancy Masterson Sakamoto experiences another form of miscommunication because she married a man from Japan and moved to Tokyo. Sakamoto, an American who knows Japanese, was puzzled why her in-laws often became silent whenever she spoke with them. She discovered that they were not personally affronted but were confused by the different conversational style of Americans. Such differences can affect social interaction for those who don't know the "rules."

Although being bilingual can have great advantages, Richard Rodriguez describes how it can also be problematic. For Rodriguez, Spanish was the "family language," a language of intimacy, whereas English was a public language, the primary language of the country. As Rodriguez became more proficient in English, he entered a world less accessible to his parents. He thus discovered that language can both join and separate people.

Psychologist Daniel Wegner examines the power that thoughts can have over us. When thoughts trap us, how do we escape? Through distraction? Suppression? Where do our thoughts go when we send them packing? Wegner observes how people deal with unwanted thoughts and speculates about effective and ineffective ways of controlling them.

Two years before she became an Olympic silver medalist, Michele Mitchell was terrified each time she had to dive off a three-story-high diving board. She realized that either she would have to give up a sport she loved or she would have to overcome her fears. Determined not to succumb to fear, Mitchell did some self-analysis and decided on several ways to deal with her reactions to fear. In this selection she details the stages she went through in making this decision, including the techniques she uses when she is practicing and competing, and she reflects on how her decisions have enabled her to succeed.

"PUT DOWN THAT PAPER AND TALK TO ME!": RAPPORT-TALK AND REPORT-TALK

Deborah Tannen

Psychological Concepts
communication, gender socialization

Do the different conversational styles of men and women contribute to misunder-standings between the sexes? Deborah Tannen bases much of her work on that premise. What are those styles? We know some of the complaints men and women level against one another: women talk too much, men are too bossy, women's talk is emotional, men clam up and are poor listeners. Tannen suggests that, for most women, conversation is primarily a way of establishing rapport, whereas for men it is primarily a way of preserving independence and status. She traces these differences to the ways boys and girls are raised and says that often misunderstand-ings are based on these different styles. Knowing this, each group has an opportunity to understand the other and to change in a constructive way.

I was sitting in a suburban living room, speaking to a women's group that had in-vited men to join them for the occasion of my talk about communication between women and men. During the discussion, one man was particularly talkative, full of lengthy comments and explanations. When I made the observation that women often complain that their husbands don't talk to them enough, this man volun-teered that he heartily agreed. He gestured toward his wife, who had sat silently be-side him on the couch throughout the evening, and said, "She's the talker in our family."

Everyone in the room burst into laughter. The man looked puzzled and hurt. "It's true," he explained. "When I come home from work, I usually have nothing to say, but she never runs out. If it weren't for her, we'd spend the whole evening in si-lence." Another woman expressed a similar paradox about her husband: "When we go out, he's the life of the party. If I happen to be in another room, I can always hear his voice above the others. But when we're home, he doesn't have that much to say. I do most of the talking."

Who talks more, women or men? According to the stereotype, women talk too much. Linguist Jennifer Coates notes some proverbs:

A woman's tongue wags like a lamb's tail.

Foxes are all tail and women are all tongue.

The North Sea will sooner be found wanting in water than a woman be at a loss for a word.

Throughout history, women have been punished for talking too much or in the wrong way. Linguist Connie Eble lists a variety of physical punishments used in Colonial America: Women were strapped to ducking stools and held underwater until they nearly drowned, put into the stocks with signs pinned to them, gagged, and silenced by a cleft stick applied to their tongues.

Though such institutionalized corporal punishments have given way to informal, often psychological ones, modern stereotypes are not much different from those expressed in the old proverbs. Women are believed to talk too much. Yet study after study finds that it is men who talk more—at meetings, in mixed-group discussions, and in classrooms where girls or young women sit next to boys or young men. For example, communications researchers Barbara and Gene Eakins tape-recorded and studied seven university faculty meetings. They found that, with one exception, men spoke more often and, without exception, spoke for a longer time. The men's turns ranged from 10.66 to 17.07 seconds, while the women's turns ranged from 3 to 10 seconds. In other words, the women's longest turns were still shorter than the men's shortest turns.

When a public lecture is followed by questions from the floor, or a talk show host opens the phones, the first voice to be heard asking a question is almost always a man's. And when they ask questions or offer comments from the audience, men tend to talk longer. Linguist Marjorie Swacker recorded question-and-answer sessions at academic conferences. Women were highly visible as speakers at the conferences studied; they presented 40.7 percent of the papers at the conferences studied and made up 42 percent of the audiences. But when it came to volunteering and being called on to ask questions, women contributed only 27.4 percent. Furthermore, the women's questions, on the average, took less than half as much time as the men's. (The mean was 23.1 seconds for women, 52.7 for men.) This happened, Swacker shows, because men (but not women) tended to preface their questions with statements, ask more than one question, and follow up the speaker's answer with another question or comment.

I have observed this pattern at my own lectures, which concern issues of direct relevance to women. Regardless of the proportion of women and men in the audience, men almost invariably ask the first question, more questions, and longer questions. In these situations, women often feel that men are talking too much. I recall one discussion period following a lecture I gave to a group assembled in a bookstore. The group was composed mostly of women, but most of the discussion was being conducted by men in the audience. At one point, a man sitting in the middle was talking at such great length that several women in the front rows began shifting in their seats and rolling their eyes at me. Ironically, what he was going on about was how frustrated he feels when he has to listen to women going on and on about topics he finds boring and unimportant.

Who talks more, then, women or men? The seemingly contradictory evidence is reconciled by the difference between what I call *public* and *private speaking*. More men feel comfortable doing "public speaking," while more women feel comfortable doing "private" speaking. Another way of capturing these differences is by using the terms *report-talk* and *rapport-talk*.

For most women, the language of conversation is primarily a language of rapport: a way of establishing connections and negotiating relationships. Emphasis is placed on displaying similarities and matching experiences. From childhood, girls criticize peers who try to stand out or appear better than others. People feel their closest connections at home, or in settings where they *feel* at home—with one or a few people they feel close to and comfortable with—in other words, during private speaking. But even the most public situations can be approached like private speaking.

For most men, talk is primarily a means to preserve independence and negotiate and maintain status in a hierarchical social order. This is done by exhibiting knowledge and skill, and by holding center stage through verbal performance such as storytelling, joking, or imparting information. From childhood, men learn to use talking as a way to get and keep attention. So they are more comfortable speaking in larger groups made up of people they know less well—in the broadest sense, "public speaking." But even the most private situations can be approached like public speaking, more like giving a report than establishing rapport. . . .

The difference between public and private speaking, or report-talk and rapport-talk, can be understood in terms of status and connection. It is not surprising that women are most comfortable talking when they feel safe and close, among friends and equals, whereas men feel comfortable talking when there is a need to establish and maintain their status in a group. But the situation is complex, because status and connection are bought with the same currency. What seems like a bid for status could be intended as a display of closeness, and what seems like distancing may have been intended to avoid the appearance of pulling rank. Hurtful and unjustified misinterpretations can be avoided by understanding the conversational styles of the other gender.

When men do all the talking at meetings, many women—including researchers—see them as "dominating" the meeting, intentionally preventing women from participating, publicly flexing their higher-status muscles. But the *result* that men do most of the talking does not necessarily mean that men *intend* to prevent women from speaking. Those who readily speak up assume that others are as free as they are to take the floor. In this sense, men's speaking out freely can be seen as evidence that they assume women are at the same level of status: "We are all equals," the metamessage of their behavior could be, "competing for the floor." If this is indeed the intention (and I believe it often, though not always, is), a woman can recognize women's lack of participation at meetings and take measures to redress the imbalance, without blaming men for intentionally locking them out.

The culprit, then, is not an individual man or even men's styles alone, but the difference between women's and men's styles. If that is the case, then both can make adjustments. A woman can push herself to speak up without being invited, or begin to speak without waiting for what seems a polite pause. But the adjustment should not be one-sided. A man can learn that a woman who is not accustomed to speaking up in groups is *not* as free as he is to do so. Someone who is waiting for a nice long pause before asking her question does not find the stage set for her appearance, as do those who are not awaiting a pause, the moment after (or before) another speaker stops talking. Someone who expects to be invited to speak ("You haven't said much, Millie. What do you think?") is not accustomed to leaping in and claiming the floor for herself. As in so many areas, being admitted as an equal is not in itself assurance of equal opportunity, if one is not accustomed to playing the game in the way it is being played. Being admitted to a dance does not ensure the participation of someone who has learned to dance to a different rhythm.

Response and Analysis

1. According to Deborah Tannen, what are the main similarities and differences between the communication styles of men and women?

2. Briefly discuss two communication problems that occur between women and men. What remedies might Tannen suggest?

Personal Experience and Application

1. Think about two of your close friends—a male and a female. Make a short list of the main topics that you talk about with them. Are they similar? Why or why not?

2. Suppose you are invited to give a five-minute presentation on improving communication in intimate relationships to an introduction to psychology class. List three recommendations you would offer. Why do you think these recommendations could improve communication?

Research

Suppose you want to examine the communication styles of boys and girls. You are interested in whether three- to five-year-old boys and girls include others in the decision-making process when they play doctor. You hypothesize that boys will issue orders such as "Give me your arm" and "Sit down," whereas girls will propose activities such as "Let's do this. . . ." After the Institutional Review Board at your college or university approves your study and the parents agree to let their children participate, you have one boy and one girl of the same age come to your lab, which is a small room with a two-way mirror. In the room is a doctor's toy medical kit, a variety of toy medical instruments, and a doctor's smock. You tell the children that you would like them to play doctor. You randomly select one child to be the doctor and the other to be the patient. You tell the "doctor" that she or he can wear the doctor's smock and can use the toy medical instruments. Finally, you tell the children that they may begin playing and that you will return in a few minutes.

You observe the children through the two-way mirror.

After observing thirty boys and thirty girls, you tabulate the data. The results suggest that boys issued more orders than girls, and girls pro-posed activities more than boys. Would you conclude that the findings support your hypothesis? Why or why not? If you were to repeat the study, what would you do differently? Why?

CONVERSATIONAL BALLGAMES

Nancy Masterson Sakamoto

Psychological Concepts
cross-cultural communication, miscommunication

As infants, we receive cues about how others respond to our sounds and how long they will tolerate our cries. As we get older, we learn how to carry on a conversation and to pick up the rhythms of give and take. How do we know whose turn it is to talk and how much time we have to speak? Do conversational styles vary from group to group even within a country?

What seldom occurs to us is that there are acceptable and unacceptable styles of engaging in conversation in different parts of the world. Israelis, for example, may expect everyone to speak up; they may look for an active exchange, as do most Americans. Nancy Masterson Sakamoto, however, often shocked her Japanese in-laws into silence when she visited with them. Here Sakamoto explains why she needed to learn more than the Japanese language to be comfortable speaking in her second homeland.

After I was married and had lived in Japan for a while, my Japanese gradually improved to the point where I could take part in simple conversations with my husband and his friends and family. And I began to notice that often, when I joined in, the others would look startled, and the conversational topic would come to a halt. After this happened several times, it became clear to me that I was doing something wrong. But for a long time, I didn't know what it was.

Finally, after listening carefully to many Japanese conversations, I discovered what my problem was. Even though I was speaking Japanese, I was handling the conversation in a western way.

Japanese-style conversations develop quite differently from western-style conversations. And the difference isn't only in the languages. I realized that just as I kept trying to hold western-style conversations even when I was speaking Japanese, so my English students kept trying to hold Japanese-style conversations even when they were speaking English. We were unconsciously playing entirely different conversational ballgames.

A western-style conversation between two people is like a game of tennis. If I introduce a topic, a conversational ball, I expect you to hit it back. If you agree with me, I don't expect you simply to agree and do nothing more. I expect you to add something—a reason for agreeing, another example, or an elaboration to carry the idea further. But I don't expect you always to agree. I am just as happy if you question me or challenge me, or completely disagree with me. Whether you agree or disagree, your response will return the ball to me.

And then it is my turn again. I don't serve a new ball from my original starting line. I hit your ball back again from where it has bounced. I carry your idea further, or answer your questions or objections, or challenge or question you. And so the ball goes back and forth, with each of us doing our best to give it a new twist, an original spin, or a powerful smash.

And the more vigorous the action, the more interesting and exciting the game. Of course, if one of us gets angry, it spoils the conversation, just as it spoils a tennis game. But getting excited is not at all the same as getting angry. After all, we are not trying to hit each other. We are trying to hit the ball. So long as we attack only each other's opinions, and do not attack each other personally, we don't expect anyone to get hurt. A good conversation is supposed to be interesting and exciting.

If there are more than two people in the conversation, then it is like doubles in tennis, or like volleyball. There's no waiting in line. Whoever is nearest and quickest hits the ball, and if you step back, someone else will hit it. No one stops the game to give you a turn. You're responsible for taking your own turn.

But whether it's two players or a group, everyone does his best to keep the ball going, and no one person has the ball for very long.

A Japanese-style conversation, however, is not at all like tennis or volleyball. It's like bowling. You wait for your turn. And you always know your place in line. It depends on such things as whether you are older or younger, a close friend or a relative stranger to the previous speaker, in a senior or junior position, and so on.

When your turn comes, you step up to the starting line with your bowling ball, and carefully bowl it. Everyone else stands back and watches politely, murmuring encouragement. Everyone waits until the ball has reached the end of the alley, and watches to see if it knocks down all the pins, or only some of them, or none of them. There is a pause, while everyone registers your score.

Then, after everyone is sure that you have completely finished your turn, the next person in line steps up to the same starting line, with a different ball. He doesn't return your ball, and he does not begin from where your ball stopped. There is no back and forth at all. All the balls run parallel. And there is always a suitable pause between turns. There is no rush, no excitement, no scramble for the ball.

No wonder everyone looked startled when I took part in Japanese conversations. I paid no attention to whose turn it was, and kept snatching the ball halfway down the alley and throwing it back at the bowler. Of course the conversation died. I was playing the wrong game.

This explains why it is almost impossible to get a western-style conversation or discussion going with English students in Japan. I used to think that the problem was their lack of English language ability. But I finally came to realize that the biggest problem is that they, too, are playing the wrong game.

Whenever I serve a volleyball, everyone just stands back and watches it fall, with occasional murmurs of encouragement. No one hits it back. Everyone waits until I call on someone to take a turn. And when that person speaks, he doesn't hit my ball back. He serves a new ball. Again, everyone just watches it fall.

So I call on someone else. This person does not refer to what the previous speaker has said. He also serves a new ball. Nobody seems to have paid any attention to what anyone else has said. Everyone begins again from the same starting line, and all the balls run parallel. There is never any back and forth. Everyone is trying to bowl with a volleyball.

And if I try a simpler conversation, with only two of us, then the other person tries to bowl with my tennis ball. No wonder foreign English teachers in Japan get discouraged.

Now that you know about the difference in the conversational ballgames, you may think that all your troubles are over. But if you have been trained all your life to play one game, it is no simple matter to switch to another, even if you know the rules. Knowing the rules is not at all the same thing as playing the game.

Even now, during a conversation in Japanese I will notice a startled reaction, and belatedly realize that once again I have rudely interrupted by instinctively trying to hit back the other person's bowling ball. It is no easier for me to "just listen" during a conversation than it is for my Japanese students to "just relax" when speaking with foreigners. Now I can truly sympathize with how hard they must find it to try to carry on a western-style conversation.

If I have not yet learned to do conversational bowling in Japanese, at least I have figured out one thing that puzzled me for a long time. After his first trip to America, my husband complained that Americans asked him so many questions and made him talk so much at the dinner table that he never had a chance to eat. When I asked him why he couldn't talk and eat at the same time, he said that Japanese do not customarily think that dinner, especially on fairly formal occasions, is a suitable time for extended conversation.

Since westerners think that conversation is an indispensable part of dining, and indeed would consider it impolite not to converse with one's dinner partner, I found this Japanese custom rather strange. Still, I could accept it as a cultural difference even though I didn't really understand it. But when my husband added, in explanation, that Japanese consider it extremely rude to talk with one's mouth full, I got confused. Talking with one's mouth full is certainly not an American custom. We think it very rude, too. Yet we still manage to talk a lot and eat at the same time. How do we do it?

For a long time, I couldn't explain it, and it bothered me. But after I discovered the conversational ballgames, I finally found the answer. Of course! In a western-style conversation, you hit the ball, and while someone else is hitting it back, you take a bite, chew, and swallow. Then you hit the ball again, and then eat some more. The more people there are in the conversation, the more chances you have to eat. But even with only two of you talking, you still have plenty of chances to eat.

Maybe that's why polite conversation at the dinner table has never been a traditional part of Japanese etiquette. Your turn to talk would last so long without interruption that you'd never get a chance to eat.

Response and Analysis

1. According to Nancy Masterson Sakamoto, what are the main differences between American-style and Japanese-style conversations? Why does Sakamoto believe that it is "almost impossible to get a western-style conversation or discussion going" with Japanese students who are taking an English class?

2. What types of misunderstandings might occur when people of different cultures converse?

Personal Experience and Application

1. Have you tried to communicate with someone who did not speak your language? What difficulties did you experience? Did you or the other person understand the context in which the words were spoken—the idiomatic expressions and the way a word was used in a sentence? What nonverbal behaviors helped you communicate?

2. Suppose the outings club on your campus asks you to be one of five guides on a ten-day tour of the Grand Canyon. The tour group will consist of German and Chinese college exchange students who have had three English classes. What communication difficulties might you expect? What might you do to facilitate communication? What nonverbal cues could you use to convey important information?

Research

Sakamoto suggests that cultural customs influence how people talk with and understand others. Suppose you want to replicate a study examining how experiences influence the way people understand and interpret new events. You wonder whether college students with different interests and experiences might perceive the same situation differently. You recruit fifty music majors and fifty business majors at your college or university to participate. The participants read a paragraph containing ambiguous words. Here is a brief excerpt from the paragraph:

> Every Saturday night, four good friends got together. When Jerry, Mike, and Pat arrived, Karen was sitting in her living room writing some notes. She quickly gathered the cards and stood up to greet her friends at the door. They followed her into the living room but as usual they couldn't

agree on exactly what to play. Jerry eventually took a stand and set things up. Finally, they began to play. Karen's recorder filled the room with soft and pleasant music. (Anderson et al., 1977)

Next, you ask the participants to tell you how they interpreted the material. Write three ques-tions that you might ask to determine if the students' majors affected how they interpreted the information.

Which words do you believe are ambiguous? Why? Why might a student's major influence how she or he interprets the information?

A BILINGUAL CHILDHOOD

Richard Rodriguez

Psychological Concept
bilingualism: cognitive and social effects

What are the challenges for a child who goes to school not speaking the language of the land? Richard Rodriguez grew up in a Spanish-speaking section of Sacramento, California, and was caught between two cultures: that of his family and that of the culture outside of his home. The nuns of his school strongly urged that Richard develop his skill with English, and that the family speak English in their home. This was not easy for the parents, but, wanting their children to succeed, they consented. Thus did the boy take on the language of *los gringos* (the Americans or the "foreigners"). Once he began using English and moved into the public domain, his life with his parents and his intimate, protected world of home and barrio changed. What does the boy gain and what does he lose by adopting a new language?

I remember, to start with, that day in Sacramento, in a California now nearly thirty years past, when I first entered a classroom—able to understand about fifty stray English words. The third of four children, I had been preceded by my older brother and sister to a neighborhood Roman Catholic school. But neither of them had revealed very much about their classroom experiences. . . .

Because I wrongly imagined that English was intrinsically a public language and Spanish was intrinsically private, I easily noted the difference between classroom language and the language at home. At school, words were directed to a general audience of listeners. ("Boys and girls . . .") Words were meaningfully ordered. And the point was not self-expression alone, but to make oneself understood by many others. The teacher quizzed: "Boys and girls, why do we use that word in this sentence? Could we think of a better word to use there? Would the sentence change its meaning if the words were differently arranged? Isn't there a better way of saying much the same thing?" (I couldn't say. I wouldn't try to say.)

Three months passed. Five. A half year. Unsmiling, ever watchful, my teachers noted my silence. They began to connect my behavior with the slow progress my brother and sisters were making. Until, one Saturday morning, three nuns arrived at the house to talk to our parents. Stiffly they sat on the blue living room sofa. From the doorway of another room, spying on the visitors, I noted the incongruity, the clash of two worlds, the faces and voices of school intruding upon the familiar setting of home. I overheard one voice gently wondering, "Do your children speak only Spanish at home, Mrs. Rodriguez?" While another voice added, "That Richard especially seems so timid and shy."

That Rich-heard!

With great tact, the visitors continued, "Is it possible for you and your husband to encourage your children to practice their English when they are home?" Of course my parents complied. What would they not do for their children's well-being? And how could they question the Church's authority which those women represented? In an instant they agreed to give up the language (the sounds) which had revealed and accentuated our family's closeness. The moment after the visitors left, the change was observed. "*Ahora*, speak to us only *en inglés*," my father and mother told us.

At first, it seemed a kind of game. After dinner each night, the family gathered together to practice "our" English. It was still then *inglés*, a language foreign to us, so we felt drawn to it as strangers. Laughing, we would try to define words we could not pronounce. We played with strange English sounds, often overanglicizing our pronunciations. And we filled the smiling gaps of our sentences with familiar Spanish sounds. But that was cheating, somebody shouted, and everyone laughed.

In school, meanwhile, like my brother and sisters, I was required to attend a daily tutoring session. I needed a full year of this special work. I also needed my teachers to keep my attention from straying in class by calling out, *"Rich-heard"*—their English voices slowly loosening the ties to my other name, with its three notes, *Ri-car-do*. Most of all, I needed to hear my mother and father speak to me in a moment of seriousness in "broken"—suddenly heartbreaking—English. This scene was inevitable. One Saturday morning I entered the kitchen where my parents were talking, but I did not realize that they were talking in Spanish until, the moment they saw me, their voices changed and they began speaking English. The gringo sounds they uttered startled me. Pushed me away. In that moment of trivial misunderstanding and profound insight, I felt my throat twisted by unsounded grief. I simply turned and left the room. But I had no place to escape to where I could grieve in Spanish. My brother and sisters were speaking English in another part of the house.

Again and again in the days following, as I grew increasingly angry, I was obliged to hear my mother and father encouraging me: "Speak to us *en inglés.*" Only then did I determine to learn classroom English. Thus, sometime afterward it happened: One day in school, I raised my hand to volunteer an answer to a question. I spoke out in a loud voice and I did not think it remarkable when the entire class understood. That day I moved very far from being the disadvantaged child I had been only days earlier. Taken hold at last was the belief, the calming assurance, that I *belonged* in public.

Shortly after, I stopped hearing the high, troubling sounds of *los gringos.* A more and more confident speaker of English, I didn't listen to how strangers sounded when they talked to me. With so many English-speaking people around me, I no longer heard American accents. Conversations quickened. Listening to persons whose voices sounded eccentrically pitched, I might note their sounds for a few seconds, but then I'd concentrate on what they were saying. Now when I heard someone's tone of voice—angry or questioning or sarcastic or happy or sad—I didn't distinguish it from the words it expressed. Sound and word were thus tightly wedded. At the end of each day I was often bemused, and always relieved, to realize how "soundless," though crowded with words, my day in public had been. An eight-year-old boy, I finally came to accept what had been technically true since my birth: I was an American citizen.

But diminished by then was the special feeling of closeness at home. Gone was the desperate, urgent, intense feeling of being at home among those with whom I felt intimate. Our family remained a loving family, but one greatly changed. We were no longer so close, no longer bound tightly together by the knowledge of our separateness from *los gringos.* Neither my older brother nor my sisters rushed home after school any more. Nor did I. When I arrived home, often there would be neighborhood kids in the house. Or the house would be empty of sounds.

Following the dramatic Americanization of their children, even my parents grew more publicly confident—especially my mother. First she learned the names of all the people on the block. Then she decided we needed to have a telephone in our house. My father, for his part, continued to use the word gringo, but it was no longer charged with bitterness or distrust. Stripped of any emotional content, the word simply became a name for those Americans not of Hispanic descent. Hearing him, sometimes, I wasn't sure if he was pronouncing the Spanish word *gringo,* or saying gringo in English.

There was a new silence at home. As we children learned more and more English, we shared fewer and fewer words with our parents. Sentences needed to be spoken slowly when one of us addressed our mother or father. Often the parent wouldn't understand. The child would need to repeat himself. Still the parent misunderstood. The young voice, frustrated, would end up saying, "Never mind"—the subject was closed. Dinners would be noisy with the clinking of knives and forks against dishes. My mother would smile softly between her remarks; my father, at the other end of the table, would chew and chew his food while he stared over the heads of his children.

My mother! My father! After English became my primary language, I no longer knew what words to use in addressing my parents. The old Spanish words (those tender accents of sound) I had earlier used—*mamá* and *papá*—I couldn't use any more. They would have been all-too-painful reminders of how much had changed in my life. On the other hand, the words I heard neighborhood kids call their parents seemed equally unsatisfactory. "Mother" and "father," "ma," "papa," "pa," "dad," "pop" (how I hated the all-American sound of that last word)—all these I felt were unsuitable terms of address for *my* parents. As a result, I never used them at home. Whenever I'd speak to my parents, I would try to get their attention by looking at them. In public conversations, I'd refer to them as my "parents" or my "mother" and "father."

My mother and father, for their part, responded differently, as their children spoke to them less. My mother grew restless, seemed troubled and anxious at the scarceness of words exchanged in the house. She would question me about my day when I came home from school. She smiled at my small talk. She pried at the edges of my sentences to get me to say something more. ("What . . . ?") She'd join conversations she overheard, but her intrusions often stopped her children's talking. By contrast, my father seemed to grow reconciled to the new quiet. Though his English somewhat improved, he tended more and more to retire into silence. At dinner he spoke very little. One night his children and even his wife helplessly giggled at his garbled English pronunciation of the Catholic "Grace Before Meals." Thereafter he made his wife recite the prayer at the start of each meal, even on formal occasions when there were guests in the house.

Hers became the public voice of the family. On official business it was she, not my father, who would usually talk to strangers on the phone or in stores. We children grew so accustomed to his silence that years later we would routinely refer to his "shyness." (My mother often tried to explain: Both of his parents died when he was eight. He was raised by an uncle who treated him as little more than a menial servant. He was never encouraged to speak. He grew up alone—a man of few words.) But I realized my father was not shy whenever I'd watch him speaking Spanish with relatives. Using Spanish, he was quickly effusive. Especially when talking with other men, his voice would spark, flicker, flare alive with varied sounds. In Spanish he expressed ideas and feelings he rarely revealed when speaking English. With firm Spanish sounds he conveyed a confidence and authority that English would never allow him.

The silence at home, however, was not simply the result of fewer words passing between parents and children. More profound for me was the silence created by my inattention to sounds. At about the time I no longer bothered to listen with care to the sounds of English in public, I grew careless about listening to the sounds made by the family when they spoke. Most of the time I would hear some-one speaking at home and didn't distinguish his sounds from the words people uttered in public. I didn't even pay much attention to my parents' accented and ungrammatical speech—at least not at home. Only when I was with them in public would I become alert to their accents. But even then their sounds caused me less and less concern. For I was growing increasingly confident of my own public identity.

I would have been happier about my public success had I not recalled, sometimes, what it had been like earlier, when my family conveyed its intimacy through a set of conveniently private sounds. Sometimes in public, hearing a stranger, I'd hark back to my lost past. A Mexican farm worker approached me one day downtown. He wanted directions to some place. "*Hijito,* . . ." he said. And his voice stirred old longings. Another time I was standing beside my mother in the visiting room of a Carmelite convent, before the dense screen which rendered the nuns shadowy figures. I heard several of them speaking Spanish in their busy, singsong, overlapping voices, assuring my mother that, yes, yes, we were remembered, all our family was remembered, in their prayers. Those voices echoed faraway family sounds. Another day a dark-faced old woman touched my shoulder lightly to steady herself as she boarded a bus. She murmured something to me I couldn't quite comprehend. Her Spanish voice came near, like the face of a never-before-seen relative in the instant before I was kissed. That voice, like so many of the Spanish voices I'd hear in public, recalled the golden age of my childhood.

Response and Analysis

1. How did not knowing English affect Richard Rodriguez's school work, his social life, and his life with his family? How did his learning English change his life as he was growing up?

2. Psychologist Walter Lambert distinguishes between additive and subtractive bilingualism. With additive bilingualism, an individual respects both the native language and the secondary language and is proficient in both languages. With subtractive bilingualism, an individual becomes proficient in the second language, loses proficiency in the first language, and eventually, the second language replaces the first language. As Rodriguez became more proficient in English, do you think he became more or less proficient in Spanish? Why?

Personal Experience and Application

1. More than six million children in the United States come from homes in which English is not the primary language. It is estimated that the number of bilingual children will triple in the twenty-first century. Suppose your local school board is developing a new policy on how to instruct elementary school children who are not proficient in English. The board members tell you that some schools in the district have as many as twenty different languages spoken by the student body. They ask you to offer a few recommendations on how to instruct non-English-speaking students. List five recommendations. Why do you believe each recommendation would be effective?

2. Some children learn to speak two languages at the same time. How do you think learning two languages simultaneously might influence the cognitive development of young children? Why?

Research

Suppose you plan to conduct a study to examine the effects of bilingualism on children. You want to know if bilingual children have similar intelligence test scores as monolingual children. When choosing children to participate in your study, you make sure that you have a similar number of bilingual and monolingual boys and girls of the same age, that they have a similar number of brothers and sisters, and that they have lived in the United States for a similar number of years.

Unfortunately, you have difficulty matching the participants on socioeconomic status: the bilingual children live in upper-class neighborhoods and the monolingual children live in lower-class neighborhoods. After securing the approval of the Institutional Review Board at your college or university and permission from the children's parents, you administer an intelligence test to each student. You find that bilingual children have higher intelligence test scores than monolingual children. Can you conclude that bilingualism is beneficial? Why or why not? What other factors may have influenced the relationship between bilingualism and the intelligence test score? If you were to repeat this study, what changes would you make to minimize these problems?

WHITE BEARS AND
OTHER UNWANTED THOUGHTS

Daniel M. Wegner

Psychological Concepts
mental image, elements of thought, distraction

Are we able to control our thoughts? Do we want to? Psychologist Daniel Wegner demonstrates how difficult it can be to keep some thoughts at bay. He tells of the time he and his wife were going on vacation to Florida to "soak up some sun." The day they were leaving, Wegner says, "a good friend came back from a dermatology appointment sporting several scars where minor skin cancers had been removed. He casually pointed to a spot on my arm and said, 'Hey, that's just like one of them.'

This totally ruined my vacation." Wegner's mind had been "high-jacked" for ten days!

If someone says to us, "Don't think of a white bear," what do we think of? How can we get rid of that bear? Wegner suggests that we do have some options. In varying ways, suppression, self-distraction, and absorption may turn our attention away from disturbing or unwanted thoughts.

When I first learned there was such a thing as an indelible pencil (I think it was in third grade) I was overwhelmed. Its purplish marks could *never be erased.* This finality was too much for my young sensibilities. Erasing was my life, the center of a daily eternity of smudges, errors, and regret played out under the eye of my teacher, a universal master of human penmanship. As it happened, of course, I learned that many things are as good as indelible, from bounced checks to auto wrecks, and I have come to accept this as a necessary part of life on earth.

There is still one slight problem. Although reality can't be erased, it seems only fair that our *thoughts* about things might be erasable. We can change our mind, get new ideas, see things in different ways, and easily move our attention from one thing to another. In other words, it usually seems that we can control what we think. When we try not to think about something, though, our thoughts can be as indelible as the marks made by that purple pencil. Unwanted thoughts—about food when we're on a diet, about that little lump that could be cancer, about a lost love whose absence we grieve, even about the mutton-headed thing we said to the boss yesterday—often seem etched permanently in our mind. The silliest little thought can be this way. Try right now, for instance, not to think of a white bear. Really. Put down the book and look away and stop thinking of a white bear. I'm serious. Try it.

The White Bear   Welcome back. How successful were you? Did you avoid a white bear for a few seconds or a minute? Did it return to your mind even once after you had wished it away? Most people report one or more returns, and some of them also stop at this point and remark that it is a cute trick, maybe good for a full minute of entertainment at children's birthday parties. There may be something to learn, however, on taking seriously the observation that people do not do a good job of avoiding an unwanted thought, even a warm fuzzy one like a white bear. . . .

Why *shouldn't* we be able to suppress a thought? Suppression seems like a simple, obvious, and important ability, as basic as thinking itself, and we don't seem to have it. Imagine—we are drawn to the very item we are attempting to avoid, clambering desperately away from the thought only to stumble back upon it again and again. Like a moth drawn to a flame, or a chicken entranced by a line drawn in the dirt, the person attempting to avoid an unwanted thought doesn't seem very smart. We can do so much—our minds so flexible and imaginative and complex—but all the IQ points in the world don't keep us from puzzling repeatedly over one thought. . . .

Distracting oneself seems easy enough. In fact, this is what I've been doing all day prior to writing this chapter. First I dawdled over coffee, read the newspaper, and became involved in an unusually thorough tooth-flossing project. I used my own teeth, so this didn't cause nearly the uproar or delay that it could have. Then, I went to the office, read my mail, made a phone call, and . . . hard to believe but it's three in the afternoon and I have to quit soon to get the baby from the sitter's. Procrastination is a kind of self-distraction, an engagement in trivial activities when we wish to avoid a more important task that looks too much like work.

Now that I've gotten myself started, I can point out that the kind of self-distraction I did this morning was the easy kind. I slipped into it without any planning or effort. When we wish to avoid a disturbing unwanted thought, however, self-distraction is not something we can do so naturally or effectively, and it can escalate into a major chore. Try distracting yourself, for instance, when you are looking down from a great height, or when the itch of an insect bite is begging for a nice rough scratching. Self-distraction is one of the key strategies we use to keep our mind away from our fears, worries, secrets, forbidden ideas, and even itches, and for this reason it is important that we understand how to do it well.

Children are not very skilled at self-distraction, so they become quick victims to whatever grabs their attention. They can cry interminably as the result of a broken dolly, or become overwrought with a "boo boo" on their finger. They seem to be able to whine for hours about one thing, and always tend to become interested in what will soon spill or explode. Parents must learn, then, to supply distracters on a regular basis, helping the child to redirect attention away from things that can cause grief and toward more benign points of interest. After flying cross-country in a crowded plane with my toddler on my lap, I was convinced that the ability to distract is one of the great skills of parenting. All the passengers nearby agreed. The most effective parents I know are able to guide their children from the brink of hell to a state of bemused puttering in a matter of moments. Eventually, of course, the child must learn to do this for himself or herself, and self-distraction becomes one of the key abilities we have that gets us through adulthood—and through flights crowded with other people's children. . . .

A Change of Plans   We have learned that "naked" suppression is not possible. Our mental apparatus is not built to clear itself, to think "I will not think of X" and then in fact immediately stop thinking of X forever. Indeed, it seems that the more energy we invest in the attempt to suppress, the more likely is the attempt to fail, landing us directly in that untidy spot in the road we were trying to step over. If all we ever did on encountering an unwanted thought, then, was to try direct suppression, we would make no progress at all. Trying not to think of X makes us think of X, as vividly, frequently, and efficiently as if we had decided to think of X from the start.

Suppression thus requires a mental transformation of the task. We move from "I will not think of X" to "I will think of Y." This is the basic form of self-distraction. It is a metacognitive strategy, a move from one way of metathinking about a thought to another. Admittedly, this mental transformation is a precarious one, in that trying to think of Y can remind us of why we undertook this task, and so bring us back to "avoid X." However, the movement to "think of Y" has a number of benefits that can make it a useful first step in shaking loose the unwanted thought of X. In particular, the self-distractive thought does not automatically bring us back to X. Back when we were thinking "avoid X," the more effort we expended on our thought, the more it all backfired. But now in the "think Y" mode, the more cognitive effort we expend, the more we will focus on Y—and thus actually stay away from X.

This is a critical feature of self-distraction. As long as we attempt suppression only, then the harder we try, the deeper we get ourselves into the soup. When we attempt self-distraction, in contrast, our efforts can get us somewhere. Although we may still be reminded of the unwanted thought from time to time, there is at least some room in self-distraction for a brief respite, a time during which we can focus on something other than the unwanted idea. At least now, when we try harder to think, we do not find our thoughts defeating their own purposes. And it is in this time that our automatic perception and memory processes may edge the conscious window away from the whole mess, toward a more pleasing view that can hold our attention.

This way of understanding self-distraction helps us get a grip on the effects of stress and activity on unwanted thoughts. It helps us to understand why being busy (because of stress or just plain activity) can sometimes increase the occurrence of unwanted thoughts and at other times will seem to push them away. I've wondered about this a lot because of the odd things that vacations can do to my mental state. Sometimes going away and relaxing clears my mind wonderfully, whereas other times leaving the activities and stresses of my usual routine produces a unique sensitivity to worry and makes me wish I were home. The difference between these effects seems to hinge on whether one is trying to suppress or trying to self-distract.

Consider what happens when you go on vacation right after you have a major argument with your boss. With this nasty incident fresh in your mind, you set off to the beach. An argument like this has not happened before, so you probably have not had the occasion to try to distract yourself from such problems. In all likelihood, then, you will simply try to suppress the thought when you're on the vacation. And if so, you will find that you are refreshingly distracted by the water, the beach, and the surroundings. These things keep you from even trying to suppress the thought, and as a result the thought is swept away and you are left in peace. You wonder at this time how a vacation could ever *promote* an unwanted thought, and you scoff at the idea.

The next year, though, you go to the mountains. This time, the boss has been after you for some time to straighten up your act, and things at work are very unpleasant. To deal with this, you have taken to watching TV a lot at home and following the programs very carefully. Sure, it is not very exciting—but it keeps your mind off the mess at work and also keeps you up to date on all the fine bargains that your local retailers have to offer. In the cabin in the mountains, there is also a TV. But you don't watch it very much and instead you hike, take pictures, and enjoy the breathtaking views. Amidst all this, you find that the turmoil at work keeps coming to mind. You see a DON'T FEED THE BEARS sign and imagine your boss mauling a tourist. The vacation, rather than taking your mind off your worries, has taken your mind off your distractions—and so leaves you oddly worried even though you have come to "relax."

An important mental transition occurs when we change strategies—from the strategy of suppressing a thought to the strategy of distracting ourselves from that thought. This changes the rules by which external distractions influence the occurrence of unwanted thoughts. Such a rule change must be common, however, because when people are asked what they do to avoid unwanted thoughts, they mention self-distraction nearly every time. And when people who identify themselves as chronic worriers are asked what they're doing wrong, they blame their inability to distract themselves from the targets of their worry. The change from suppression to self-distraction is natural, the path we follow away from the thoughts we desire to avoid, but it also changes the way our mental efforts influence our thoughts. When we are suppressing, attention to what we are doing is injurious to our plan; when we are self-distracting, attention to what we are doing is exactly what we need.

Can Distraction Work?   Most of what we currently know about the effectiveness of distraction comes from experiments on pain. Dentists and physicians would love it if their patients would just stop whining, not to mention that the patients might be pleased as well, so pain control is an issue that has received a fair amount of scientific attention. In these studies, people are exposed to something painful—a real dental or surgical procedure, or a somewhat analogous discomfort such as keeping a hand in ice water for several minutes. They are asked to report when they begin to feel pain, how strong it is, whether they can continue, or the like, and these judgments are taken as measures of the degree of pain they are feeling. This is really all we have to go on, as there is no special "pain behavior" in the body that we can monitor to see how much discomfort the person is feeling. Wiggling and hopping and saying "Yipes!" are signs, but even they are unreliable at times.

If there is a general rule that emerges from pain studies, it is that distracters work best when they are absorbing. For instance, music piped in during a dental procedure doesn't seem to make that much difference, whereas allowing the patient to play a video game reduces pain reports quite a bit. You might argue that the kind of Muzak most dentists play can cause minor pain before you even sit in the chair. And it is true that a rendition of one's favorite music on a good stereo system might turn out to be more engaging than even a video game. These seemingly minor variations in the quality of the distracter could have a critical influence on the degree to which the distraction can hold one's attention away from the unwanted thought.

Response and Analysis

1. When Daniel Wegner asks you not to think of a white bear, what do you think about? Do you have a mental image of a white bear? If so, briefly describe that image. Mental images are one of several elements that make up thought. Discuss two other elements.

2. According to Wegner, what is distraction? Briefly describe a few techniques that Wegner offers for controlling unwanted thoughts. Why might distraction "suppress" unwanted thoughts?

Personal Experience and Application

1. Are you sometimes bothered by thoughts that will not go away? What do you do to get rid of them? When you are trying to get to sleep, how do you get rid of distracting thoughts that keep you awake?

2. Often people use the same solution to solve different problems, even if there is an easier solution. This is referred to as a "mental set." Briefly describe a situation in which you or someone you know used a familiar but less effective solution to solve a problem. Were you or the person aware of the simpler solution? If so, why didn't you or the person you know use it?

Research

Suppose you want to investigate how often people use mental imagery as a form of distraction. You have one hundred students at your institution record their mental images every day for one month. The participants will list their mental images for each of the five senses—hearing, taste, vision, smell, and touch—and indicate whether they used the image as a way to distract themselves. Which of the five senses do you believe will be reported most frequently? Why? Does this study have an independent variable or a dependent variable? Why or why not?

FEAR

Michele Mitchell

Psychological Concepts
decision making, thinking strategies

Michele Mitchell, who won the 1984 Olympic silver medal for the ten-meter platform dive, was terrified of diving from great heights. Driven to succeed at a skill she was good at, yet terrified of jumping off the diving board, Mitchell had to make a choice. She did not want to give up diving. Neither did she want fear to affect her physically, make her unable to concentrate, or deprive her of enjoying the camaraderie of her fellow athletes. Mitchell analyzed her anxieties and developed several methods to overcome them. The strategies she uses to overcome her fear show courage and determination.

Diving off a platform the height of a three-story building and falling at speeds of up to thirty-three miles per hour requires me to work through my fears every day. I'm afraid every time I go up there, but getting through the fear makes me feel stronger; it makes me feel that I can achieve any goal I put my mind to.

But that realization didn't come naturally. Two years before the Olympic Games I was almost paralyzed every time I climbed up to the ten-meter platform. There were days, after years of practice from that height, when I couldn't even look over the edge. And there were times that I couldn't go off the tower. It was as if all of my potential had been sealed in a jar by my own subconscious fears of the "what if."

Finally one day after I had climbed down the tower in disgust, I decided that if I was going to continue diving, I would have to study my complex reactions to fear and find ways to conquer it.

I realized that stress evoked three changes in me: physical, mental, and attentional. Physically, my heart would pound, my respiratory rate would increase, my stomach would hurt, I would feel shaky and weak, and my adrenalin levels would rise. Worst of all, my muscles would become so tight that I could hardly move, let alone attain the flowing style required in diving.

Mentally, too, I would become very rigid. I felt shaky, unable to control my thoughts. I'd see visions of landing incorrectly in the water or hitting my hand on the edge of the board. The more I tried to shut out those thoughts, the more severe they became.

Later I realized that this thinking was a result of my skewed attentional focus. Instead of relaxing and enjoying the circumstantial rewards of training, such as the social life or the humor, I'd be focusing on my pounding heart and my shaking hands. I became a victim of my own tunnel vision. At other times, instead of concentrating on one or two important parts of a dive, I would be paying attention to occurrences that I had no control over. I'd watch cars passing on the street or people walking under the tower even as I stood, ready to launch myself into the air.

After a few weeks of self-analysis I began some deep contemplation of how I could deal with my responses to fear. The techniques I started then are the ones I am still using in every practice session and every competition I'm in, even today.

I always begin by writing my short, intermediate, and long-term goals on a piece of paper. On one side of each goal I list the fears I will have to overcome to achieve that goal. On the other side I write down the rewards I'll receive at the completion of each goal. Obviously the harder the goal, the higher the reward I place next to it. The rewards can be anything from a dinner out on the town to a gold medal. This makes a systematic method of achieving those things I set out to do.

Next I force myself toward the positive. The first step is to remember that I am not unique in this situation. When I begin getting mentally and physically tense, I start a conversation about it with my teammates who experience the same fears.

Putting my ego to work also helps. If I want to impress someone who is watching me, I acknowledge that to myself and use it to fuel the fires to burn up my fears. A bet with a teammate can do the trick as well. Last fall two of us had to learn a new dive on the same day and both of us were nervous. So, at the beginning of practice we each put a $100 bill on the deck. If each of us did our new dive we would take back our money; however, if only one of us did the dive, she would be $100 richer. Guess what? The bet worked. Neither of us lost the bet, and both of us got through the fear to gain a new dive.

Defining positively reinforcing words also works for me. For instance, Webster defines courage as "the attitude of facing and dealing with anything recognized as dangerous." Being able to repeat that definition when I am trying to summon up my courage is reassuring. I also have other standard comments such as, "Yes, I'm nervous, but it's okay; I've felt this way before and I'm still alive," or "I may be scared but I *am* going to do it!"

Time for general relaxation is crucial. On competition days or tough training days I always try to walk slowly rather than hurrying, talk calmly rather than chattering, and focus my eyes rather than allowing them to dart from object to object.

As I am actually walking or driving to the pool I always make sure to have a relaxing radio station or tape playing. After awhile it gets to the point that even humming a tune actually calms me down. Finally, I always try to shake the last little bit of tension out of my arms and legs. Some slow stretching and deep breathing never hurt, either. These activities coupled with positive statements and a quick review of previous successful experiences always prepare me mentally, physically, and attentionally. From that feeling on, I'm set. All I have to do is launch myself into the air and go for it, because at that point, I *know* I can do it.

Response and Analysis

1. Describe the process Michele Mitchell uses to understand her fear of diving. What positive and negative aspects of diving influence her decision to dive? How does "tunnel vision" affect her thoughts about diving?

2. What techniques and thinking strategies does Mitchell use to control her fear? Why might these techniques reduce her fear?

Personal Experience and Application

1. Do you know someone who has a fear that is difficult to overcome? How does the fear inhibit the person? Does the fear serve a useful purpose? If so, what is it? What thinking strategies might the person use to control or overcome the fear? Do you believe that thinking alone can help someone overcome a fear? Why or why not? In what ways can "thinking" be helpful?

2. Suppose the director of the Learning Skills Center at your college or university asks you to give a five-minute talk on reducing test anxiety. The director tells you that some students become anxious when taking an exam and may experience a racing heart and perspire. They may attribute these physiological reactions to their anxiety about taking the exam. Offer two recommendations that students might use to reduce test anxiety. Why do you think these recommendations will be effective?

Research

Suppose the swimming coach at your college or university asks you to design a program to help a few team members overcome their fear of diving into a swimming pool from a three-story-tall platform. Before making any recommendations, you decide to interview team members to understand how they attempt to control their fears. Make a list of questions that you would ask the swimmers.

chapter 7

HUMAN
DEVELOPMENT

*A few nights in your life, you know this
like the taste of lightning in your teeth:
Tomorrow I will be changed. Somehow
in the next passage of light, I will shed
reptilian skin and feel the wind's friction
again. Sparks will fly. It's a hope for the
right kind of fear, the kind that does not
turn away.*

KIM R. STAFFORD, *Having Everything Right*

What physical, emotional, and cognitive changes can we expect as we grow from one stage to another? This chapter highlights the experiences of people who are at different stages in life: infancy, childhood, adolescence, midlife, and late adulthood.

Brian Hall is enchanted with his newborn daughter, Madeleine. During her first two years, Madeleine learns to connect sounds with language, to communicate in more complex ways, and then to combine play, imagination, and language. She enjoys playing with her stuffed animals and doll baby and having her parents read to her. When Madeleine puts the baby on the floor and says to her parents, "Shh," Hall wonders whether she is merely imitating what she has learned, or whether she understands that language has meaning and that she can express her own feelings and thoughts. Before long, he is convinced that Madeleine can "turn the loose cannon of her mind" towards all sorts of fanciful play as she grows into a delightful child.

Dick Gregory writes of how a physically, socially, and economically impoverished environment can affect development. Because he came from a poor family, he often went to school without breakfast. His inability to concentrate contributed to his poor work, and he was typecast by his teacher as a boy who was always fooling around and getting into trouble.

Author Nora Ephron describes her entry into puberty. She becomes convinced that her worries over being feminine will end once her breasts grow. But, compared to her peers, Ephron is slow to develop. She goes though much of her adolescence waiting, comparing herself unfavorably to her peers. There is much variability in the timing of puberty during adolescents, and many adolescents, like Ephron, are self-conscious about being outside of the averages. Sometimes the effects of early or late maturation on one's identity can last well into adulthood. With the benefits of years, Ephron is able to look back and take a more objective view of her adolescence.

Adults in midlife are sometimes called the "sandwich generation." H. Michael Zal shows how parents in this middle-aged group are often caught between their children, who may be young adults and may still need some kind of parental support, and their elderly parents, who also may need care.

Malcolm Cowley shares his view on living in his eightieth year. "The year from seventy-nine to eighty," he writes, "is like a week" of time when he was a boy. His body, too, sends messages. It often can't or won't do what Cowley would like. Yet there are rewards. Simple needs "become a pleasure to satisfy."

MADELEINE BEGINS TO TALK

Brian Hall

Psychological Concepts
sensorimotor period, language development, imagination

Writer Brian Hall presents a rich account of his daughter Madeleine's first few years of life. Hall is fascinated by Madeleine's developing language skills. He observes how she listens to the songs he and his wife sing to her, how she mimics words, and how she delights in using her voice. When will she begin to connect sounds with language? When will "da da da" mean "daddy" to her? Madeleine's vocabulary continues to expand during her second year. When she pushes a toy car around and makes the sound of "Brrm!", is she imitating her father or using this vocalization to represent the sound of a real car? When, Hall asks, does learning become "indistinguishable from insight?"

Madeleine's Imagination Begins to Develop

I had been watching out for the beginnings of make-believe ever since her first birthday. . . .

Madeleine as a baby had been awash in wild imaginings, delusions, projected fears. It was only as she began to grasp, within her tight lit spot of expertise, what was real and what was not that she could turn the loose cannon of her mind toward intentional delusion, projecting hopes instead of fears (but fears, too, digging channels for them to drain the swamps), filling the mute world of her dependable things with voices, with the verbs that were missing from *Baby's World*.[1] . . .

At fourteen months she pushed a wooden car around the floor and said "Brrm!"Aha! I thought. But once again, the evidence was tainted. When I had first given her the car, I had pushed it around myself and said "Brrm." (All self-respecting researchers, throw up your hands.) It occurred to me to wonder if I was viewing the learning process backward, anyway. I had assumed that she would eventually accomplish the conceptual leap from toy car to real car, and that she would then express that understanding by making the toy car act like a real car. But perhaps it went the other way around: I gave her the wooden car; she had no idea it represented the large object in our driveway; I moved it around, saying "Brrm"; she imi-

---

[1]*Baby's World:* One of Madeleine's books.

tated me; after several days or weeks of making the little wooden thing act like a car, she gradually came to associate it with the real car. Body taught mind, rather than vice versa. Rote learning was absorbed until it became indistinguishable from insight.

She hugged her stuffed animals, but that didn't mean she was pretending they were alive, since she also hugged pillows and fluffy balls. . . . One of her cows mooed when it was turned over, and her reaction of anxious surprise suggested she knew perfectly well the thing wasn't alive and she didn't appreciate it pretending otherwise. . . .

At sixteen months, Madeleine was with us in a toy store when she spotted a two-year-old boy holding a doll. This doll was only six inches long, with an almost spherical head, full cheeks, and wide-open blue eyes. . . . It could not have looked more like Madeleine if it had been modeled on her. . . .

Madeleine carried Bald Baby everywhere. Her small cloth body was easy to hold in one hand, and Madeleine enjoyed an occasional contemplative suck on the smooth round head of soft plastic (which made her look a bit unnervingly like Kronos eating his own children). With a good deal of tugging and tweezering finger work, Bald Baby's sleeper was removable, and the only thing Madeleine liked better than putting it on was taking it off again. I assumed off always eventually won out over on, because it felt more intimate to Madeleine, more secure. She had probably already come to associate underwear or nakedness with home, and in the coming months would strip all her favorite dolls as far as she could. Bald Baby, lying around in her unremovable underwear, was not only clearly a good friend of ours, she also was evidently not about to go anywhere.

During Madeleine's baths, in the big tub with me or Pamela, Bald Baby sat on the rim and watched, and was later dropped into the plastic tub, pulled out, dropped again. Before Madeleine ate, she stuffed Bald Baby into the mouth of an upright cardboard cylinder (part of a building set) so that only the doll's head, arms, and feet stuck out. "Hai-ch'," Madeleine explained. Highchair. Apparently, Bald Baby functioned somewhat like a voodoo doll in reverse. Instead of causing things to happen to Madeleine, she confirmed what had already happened. Not only could Madeleine look from her own highchair to Bald Baby on hers and think, "I am here, I am eating," but she could do to Bald Baby what we did to Madeleine. Of her several incorporations, this internalization of authority was perhaps the most important to her self-constructing sense of self. Certainly it was the one she would practice most assiduously, or rather, compulsively, in the months to come. (When she learns the word, perhaps she will call it her conscience.)

Naturally I couldn't know whether Madeleine had really just made a conceptual breakthrough or had merely progressed physically to the point where I could infer her thoughts from her actions. Whichever was the case, soon after I noticed her breathing life into her dolls, I saw her do it to other things. Perhaps it had taken a mirror image to unlock her empathy, but once unlocked, empathy obeyed its own logic and flowed everywhere. She pushed raisins around on her highchair tray, saying "Brrm," and I wondered whether she was imagining they were cars, like the one in our driveway, or wheeled wooden blocks, like the one she had in her toy chest, or both. She jumped the raisins over little puddles of milk, and here I recognized a moment from a book we had just read, in which two rabbits were jumping over daisies.

Madeleine Improves Her Language Skills and Shows Signs of Autonomy

Madeleine's words at nineteen months sketched out a portrait of Madeleine's world, a guide to what was important to her.

"Ba-bö" was diaper. When I opened hers up, if there was poop I bugged out my eyes and dropped my jaw the way I did when I saw her tummy, and I announced "Poop!" and she joyfully shouted "Poop!" and rocked back, flinging up her legs to hold her feet. "Wawa" was the water in the cup, and "bukreh" was one of the wiping cloths that I indecorously called butt rags. With her new diaper on, Madeleine flushed the toilet herself, waving her poop goodbye. . . .

Madeleine would hold Bald Baby up to me and say "Poop!" . . . "Ba-bö—*aw!*" Diaper—*off!* Madeleine's make-believe had now become sophisticated enough that she didn't always need a prop (although she preferred one), and she accepted from my hand motions that I was removing an invisible diaper, bugging my eyes out at the voluminous, indeed well-nigh incredible contents, sloughing them into an invisible toilet, flushing and waving goodbye. If I tried to put on a new diaper immediately, Madeleine objected, "Bukreh!", and I had to back up, wipe Bald Baby's butt, dry her off, apply some oil. "Ba-bö—*aw!*" Diaper—*on!* I would mime it and hand Baby Bald over with a silent prayer. But usually in vain. "Poop!" Madeleine would announce, handing her back. (The fact that she used "aw" to mean both "on" and "off" facilitated another self-perpetuating game: she was interested in the putting on and taking off of her shoes, and could simply shout "Aw!" at me continually as I went though a number of cycles.) . . .

"Ch'" meant chair. Chairs loomed large in Madeleine's mind as the loci of important activities. "Hai-ch'" was where she ate. "Aunh-ch'" (armchair) was where she looked at books with us during the day. "Raw-ch'" (rocking chair) was where we read in the evenings and sang to her. She has measured her physical progress in terms of chairs. Back in her crawling days, her instinctual urge to climb had sent her repeatedly up into her own miniature chair, where she would get stuck, straddling the summit. Later she drafted the full-size chairs into service as makeshift walkers, and pushed them shuddering around the house. Now that she could climb into the rocking chair, we often found her there, blissed out on the motion. We bought a rocking horse, which she also loved, and also called "raw-ch'." . . .

She now had the core family words well in hand. At eighteen months, she had switched from "Dada" to "Daddy," as the months of evidence from her ears finally penetrated that inner sanctum of preverbal utterances. Pamela remained "Mama," since that was the word we used. "Baby" had multiple uses. Bald Baby was "baby," and so was Big Baby. Real babies were baby. A small version of some familiar object, such as an undersized vegetable, was baby. . . .

The most important meaning of "baby" was this particular baby, Madeleine. She knew that folding her arm back toward herself meant "This is me," so for extra emphasis, just to make sure, she folded it as tight as she could and stuck her index finger in her armpit, her elbow bobbing like a chicken wing: "Baby!" Now that she had a clear word for herself, and a percussive one at that, she wielded it like a baseball bat, asserting her will. If I handed her a cracker, she flapped her arms in desperate disapproval and rained *b*'s down on me, boxing my ears, "Baby! Baby!"—meaning that baby must get the cracker out of the bag herself. This demand was not merely to show me, and herself, that she was physically capable of reaching into the bag, but to exercise choice. Confronted constantly with her own powerlessness—carried wherever Pamela or I needed to go, eating what we gave her, unable to do this and forced to do that for unfathomable reasons—naturally she needed to exercise power in the tiny areas allowed her. At this age, alas, those were often areas in which her choice not only didn't matter, but *obviously* didn't matter, yet she had learned how to pretend, and make-believe is the toddler's therapy, so by God she would pretend, and believe, that the choice was crucial, that the world hung on it. Baby certainly did not want *that* cracker. What on earth did I take her for? Ahh, yes, *this* one. . . .

For Madeleine, immersion in language began in rituals of rhythm and song. . . . Madeleine's first sound of my voice was as a bad Placido Domingo, crooning "Un Dì Felice" through the uterine wall. Later, Pamela rocked her to sleep with lullabies: "I Gave My Love a Cherry," "Shenandoah." I preferred pacing to rocking, and ballads to lullabies: "Barbara Allen," "Henry Martin," and an obscene sixteenth-century number entitled "The Bonny Black Hare" (don't ask), which I had to remind myself, a couple of years later, not to sing anymore. . . .

But songs were only a fraction of it. Virtually every time I spoke to Madeleine I used a voice that seems to come unbidden to parents, a rhythmic, rhyming chant, as though I were summoning her spirit or coaxing a new one out of myself. The altered cadence must be useful to the infant, a signal that these words, hopping and bopping out of the background chatter, are meant for her. I found myself speculating about this one day after I had spent five minutes bouncing Madeleine in my arms and asking her, in a dotted rhythm arranged in bars of 2/4: "Who's this little | ba-by with the | stuffed-up | nose?" . . .

Pamela relied less on rhythm in speaking to Madeleine and more on pure ardor. She called her Sweetest Girl, Love Child, Love Bug, Buglet. She was counterbalancing my simple-minded doggerel with simple-hearted Homeric epithets. We didn't know it at the time, but we were filling stereotypical complementary roles, since mothers tend to soothe their babies and fathers tend to stimulate them. The mother strokes, the father pokes. The mother hymns, the father rhymes.

I thought more about this when Madeleine began to speak in clear syllables. All over the world, babies begin with the same basic repertory of utterances. This initial vocabulary, reasonably enough, consists of the easiest sounds to produce: the vowel sound *ah*; the labial consonants *p*, *b*, and *m*; and the tongue taps *t* and *d*. It is no coincidence that the core family words "mama," "baba," "papa," "dada," and "tata," which occur throughout the world, are constructed out of these sounds. But individual babies vary as to which of these sounds they use most, and Madeleine's preference was unequivocal: "Da!"

She would say it upon spotting an object, a terse, tense sound, as though exclaiming "There!"—a word that is, in fact, a relative of the Germanic *da*. Once we had handed the object to her, she would emit a "Da-da-da-da," a ripple of satisfaction descending like a sigh. As she lay in her crib, just awake from a nap, she would say "Da da?" with a contemplative upward drift, and it would sound so uncannily as though she were addressing me that I would only half jokingly answer, "Yes, honey?" and hover for a moment on the edge of a surreal expectation, until she tripped back down the scale: "Da da da da." . . .

Madeleine's next step was to discover that vocalization—this stick with which she tapped objects, or beat out a rhythm to beat back not-Madeleine—could also be used to communicate, as her hands, in waving, were learning to do. Perhaps it made sense, then, that her first understanding of the call-and-response possibilities of sound seemed to come in conjunction with the hand. When Pamela, one day, hummed to her while dribbling an index finger over her lips. Madeleine picked it up almost immediately. Now, from across a room, she could make me stop whatever I was doing to wave to her with one hand and dribble my lips with the other. . . .

To the parents this is all a game, but the fact that the baby also laughs does not prove it's a game to her. Surely for the baby it is real language and a whole language, expressive of all the concepts she knows: I am here, I am here (and I'm hungry), I am here (and you're not paying attention to me), we are here, you are here. Her laughter is also language, a response to the parent's call: we are happy to be here, we are relieved to be here. And the intent stare that accompanies the baby's call, the disconcerted look that comes with the failure of response, suggest that this is not merely language but the word that calls into being the thing it names, the primal chant in which nomen and numen are one. We are here because we say we are.

At six months, Madeleine loved this: I would touch my head to hers and sing a tone. She, wide-eyed, concentrating, would match it. The tone would vibrate through both our heads. I would nudge my pitch up or down and a pulse would begin, as the two nearly identical sound waves throbbed in and out of phase. Madeleine, imitating me, would adjust her note as well. If we eased the pitches further apart the pulse quickened into a blur, if we brought them back toward each other it slowed, to a run, a walk, a wary standstill. Everything was combined here: pitch, rhythm, communication, touch. The slow pulse in our heads was like the heartbeat in the womb, that first music of that first sphere, but this was music of two spheres, social instead of solipsistic, the rhythm in each impossible without the other. We were there.

Response and Analysis

1. Hall often wonders whether Madeleine is merely imitating actions of her parents or if she is using her imagination. How might the ability to imitate versus to create make-believe situations reflect differences in cognitive development? According to developmental psychologists, at what age do children begin to imitate others? At what age do children begin engaging in make-believe?

2. Briefly describe the features of Piaget's sensorimotor period. What behaviors do you see in Madeleine, including her use of language, that correspond to this period?

3. Hall says that Madeleine, who was confronted constantly with her own powerlessness, used gestures and words like "Baby! Baby!" to exercise her right to make a choice. He also says that the choices she made, such as which cracker to eat, were insignificant. Yet he and Madeleine "pretended" that her choices were very important. Why might Hall act like Madeleine's choosing a cracker was important? How might small interactions such as this relate to Madeleine's growing sense of autonomy and power?

Personal Experience and Application

1. Do you think that some emotions are inborn while others are learned? Why or why not? What are the possible benefits for an infant being able to express certain emotions?

2. Suppose some friends ask you for a few recommendations on activities they might present to their three-month-old child to stimulate cognitive activity. What ideas might you offer? Why do you think the ideas would be effective?

Research

Conducting research involving infant participants is particularly challenging. For example, if you examine infants' ability to remember, how would you know if they actually remember something when you cannot ask them? Suppose that you want to investigate infants' facial expressions. You want to know if infants show common emotional reactions in their facial expressions (for example, surprise, happiness, fear). One of your first tasks is to design a procedure that will elicit emotional reactions and allow you to record facial expressions. What might you do to elicit emotional reactions in infants, such as a surprise response, a fear response, or a happy response? How would you know if an infant's response revealed surprise, fear, happiness, another emotion, or no emotion? What might you do to improve your accuracy in identifying and categorizing the responses?

SHAME

Dick Gregory

Psychological Concepts
cognitive development, emotional development,
environmental influences

How do impoverished surroundings and humiliating experiences affect a child's cognitive and emotional development? Comedian and civil rights activist Dick Gregory remembers that without a father or financial security he and his family lived in hunger and crowded living conditions. Handouts and pity embarrassed him; the identical coats given to poor children became badges of poverty for all to see. Gregory's teacher shamed him in front of his classmates, and that shame stayed with him for over twenty years. How might these events and conditions have affected his developing self-respect and his ability to learn in school?

I have never learned hate at home, or shame. I had to go to school for that. I was about seven years old when I got my first big lesson. I was in love with a little girl named Helene Tucker, a light-complected little girl with pigtails and nice manners. She was always clean and she was smart in school. I think I went to school then mostly to look at her. I brushed my hair and even got me a little old handkerchief. It was a lady's handkerchief, but I didn't want Helene to see me wipe my nose on my hand. The pipes were frozen again, there was no water in the house, but I washed my socks and shirt every night. I'd get a pot, and go over to Mister Ben's grocery store, and stick my pot down into his soda machine. Scoop out some chopped ice. By evening the ice melted to water for washing. I got sick a lot that winter because the fire would go out at night before the clothes were dry. In the morning I'd put them on, wet or dry, because they were the only clothes I had.

Everybody's got a Helene Tucker, a symbol of everything you want. I loved her for her goodness, her cleanness, her popularity. She'd walk down my street and my brothers and sisters would yell, "Here comes Helene," and I'd rub my tennis sneakers on the back of my pants and wish my hair wasn't so nappy and the white folks' shirt fit me better. I'd run out on the street. If I knew my place and didn't come too close, she'd wink at me and say hello. That was a good feeling. Sometimes I'd follow her all the way home, and shovel the snow off her walk and try to make friends with her Momma and her aunts. I'd drop money on her stoop late at night on my way back from shining shoes in the taverns. And she had a Daddy, and he had a good job. He was a paper hanger.

I guess I would have gotten over Helene by summertime, but something happened in that classroom that made her face hang in front of me for the next twenty-two years. When I played the drums in high school it was for Helene and when I broke track records in college it was for Helene and when I started standing behind microphones and heard applause I wished Helene would hear it, too. It wasn't until I was twenty-nine years old and married and making money that I finally got her out of my system. Helene was sitting in that classroom when I learned to be ashamed of myself.

It was on a Thursday. I was sitting in back of the room, in a seat with a chalk circle drawn around it. The idiot's seat, the troublemaker's seat.

The teacher thought I was stupid. Couldn't spell, couldn't read, couldn't do arithmetic. Just stupid. Teachers were never interested in finding out that you couldn't concentrate because you were so hungry, because you hadn't had any breakfast. All you could think about was noontime, would it ever come? Maybe you could sneak into the cloakroom and steal a bite of some kid's lunch out of a coat pocket. A bit of something. Paste. You can't really make a meal of paste, or put it on bread for a sandwich, but sometimes I'd scoop a few spoonfuls out of the paste jar in the back of the room. Pregnant people get strange tastes. I was pregnant with poverty. Pregnant with dirt and pregnant with smells that made people turn away, pregnant with cold and pregnant with shoes that were never bought for me, pregnant with five other people in my bed and no Daddy in the next room, and pregnant with hunger. Paste doesn't taste too bad when you're hungry.

The teacher thought I was a troublemaker. All she saw from the front of the room was a little black boy who squirmed in his idiot's seat and made noises and poked the kids around him. I guess she couldn't see a kid who made noises because he wanted someone to know he was there.

It was a Thursday, the day before the Negro payday. The Eagle always flew on Friday. The teacher was asking each student how much his father would give to the community chest. On Friday night, each kid would get the money from his father, and on Monday he would bring it to school. I decided I was going to buy me a Daddy right then. I had money in my pocket from shining shoes and selling papers, and whatever Helene Tucker pledged for her Daddy I was going to top it. And I'd hand the money right in. I wasn't going to wait until Monday to buy me a Daddy.

I was shaking, scared to death. The teacher opened her book and started calling out names alphabetically.

"Helene Tucker?"

"My Daddy said he'd give two dollars and fifty cents."

"That's very nice, Helene. Very, very nice indeed."

That made me feel pretty good. It wouldn't take too much to top that. I had almost three dollars in dimes and quarters in my pocket. I stuck my hand in my pocket and held onto the money, waiting for her to call my name. But the teacher closed her book after she called everybody else in the class.

I stood up and raised my hand.

"What is it now?"

"You forgot me."

She turned toward the blackboard. "I don't have time to be playing with you, Richard."

"My Daddy said he'd . . ."

"Sit down, Richard, you're disturbing the class."

"My Daddy said he'd give . . . fifteen dollars."

She turned around and looked mad. "We are collecting this money for you and your kind, Richard Gregory. If your Daddy can give fifteen dollars you have no business being on relief."

"I got it right now, I got it right now, my Daddy gave it to me to turn in today, my Daddy said . . ."

"And furthermore," she said, looking right at me, her nostrils getting big and her lips getting thin and her eyes opening wide, "we know you don't have a Daddy."

Helene Tucker turned around, her eyes full of tears. She felt sorry for me. Then I couldn't see her too well because I was crying too.

"Sit down, Richard."

And I always thought the teacher kind of liked me. She always picked me to wash the blackboard on Friday, after school. That was a big thrill, it made me feel important. If I didn't wash it, come Monday the school might not function right.

"Where are you going, Richard?"

I walked out of school that day and for a long time I didn't go back very often. There was shame there.

Now there was shame everywhere. It seemed like the whole world had been inside that classroom, everyone had heard what the teacher had said, everyone had turned around and felt sorry for me. There was shame in going to the Worthy Boys Annual Christmas Dinner for you and your kind because everybody knew what a worthy boy was. Why couldn't they just call it the Boys Annual Dinner, why'd they have to give it a name? There was shame in wearing the brown and orange and white plaid mackinaw the welfare gave to 3,000 boys. Why'd it have to be the same for everybody so when you walked down the street the people could see you were on relief? It was a nice warm mackinaw and it had a hood, and my Momma beat me and called me a little rat when she found out I stuffed it in the bottom of a pail full of garbage way over on Cottage Street. There was shame in running over to Mister Ben's at the end of the day and asking for his rotten peaches, there was shame in asking Mr. Simmons for a spoon full of sugar, there was shame in running out to meet the relief truck. I hated that truck, full of food for you and your kind. I ran into the house and hid when it came. And then I started to sneak through alleys, to take the long way home so the people going into White's Eat Stop wouldn't see me. Yeah, the whole world heard the teacher that day, we all know you don't have a Daddy.

Response and Analysis

1. What does Dick Gregory mean when he says he was "pregnant with poverty"? What were the physical and economic conditions that may have limited Gregory's ability to learn in school?

2. Gregory writes that "shame was everywhere." Where did Gregory find shame? Why? What messages discouraged him from developing self-respect?

Personal Experience and Application

1. Briefly describe two characteristics of the physical, social, or cultural environment in which you grew up. Do you think those characteristics positively or negatively influenced your cognitive or emotional development? Why?

2. Suppose that a parent group at a local after-school facility asks you to help develop a program for economically disadvantaged children between seven and nine years of age. List three objectives that you would want the program to achieve. How would you design the program to achieve the three objectives? Why do you think your program would be beneficial to children?

Research

Suppose you used a correlational design to examine the relationship between the economic conditions in which children are living and their academic abilities. Assume that you have conducted the study and have analyzed the data. Your analysis shows a correlation coefficient of +0.85 between economic conditions and academic ability. Does this finding indicate that the relationship is (1) positive or negative, and (2) strong or weak? Because you used a correlational design, why can't you conclude that the economic conditions caused the children's abilities? What other variables may influence the relationship between economic conditions and academic ability?

SHAPING UP ABSURD

Nora Ephron

Psychological Concepts
physical development, body image, conformity

Nora Ephron, author of *Sleepless in Seattle* and director of *You've Got Mail*, humorously describes her early adolescence when she was without breasts, a waist, or hips that could hold up a skirt. Ephron says that she was a late bloomer; embarrassed, she was driven to deceive others into thinking she had physically matured. At all stages of life, many people feel pressure to meet certain standards of attractiveness, but Ephron tells of the special pain for adolescents who believe they fail to meet those standards.

I have to begin with a few words about androgyny. In grammar school, in the fifth and sixth grades, we were all tyrannized by a rigid set of rules that supposedly determined whether we were boys or girls. The episode in *Huckleberry Finn* where Huck is disguised as a girl and gives himself away by the way he threads a needle and catches a ball—that kind of thing. We learned that the way you sat, crossed your legs, held a cigarette and looked at your nails, your wristwatch, the way you did these things instinctively was absolute proof of your sex. Now obviously most children did not take this literally, but I did. I thought that just one slip, just one incorrect cross of my legs or flick of an imaginary cigarette ash would turn me from whatever I was into the other thing; that would be all it took, really. Even though I was outwardly a girl and had many of the trappings generally associated with the field of girldom—a girl's name, for example, and dresses, my own telephone, an autograph book—I spent the early years of my adolescence absolutely certain that I might at any point gum it up. I did not feel at all like a girl. I was boyish. I was athletic, ambitious, outspoken, competitive, noisy, rambunctious. I had scabs on my knees and my socks slid into my loafers and I could throw a football. I wanted desperately not to be that way, not to be a mixture of both things but instead just one, a girl, a definite indisputable girl. As soft and as pink as a nursery. And nothing would do that for me, I felt, but breasts.

I was about six months younger than everyone in my class, and so for about six months after it began, for six months after my friends had begun to develop—that was the word we used, develop—I was not particularly worried. I would sit in the bathtub and look down at my breasts and know that any day now, any second now, they would start growing like everyone else's. They didn't. "I want to buy a bra," I said to my mother one night. "What for?" she said. My mother was really hateful

147

about bras, and by the time my third sister had gotten to that point where she was ready to want one, my mother had worked the whole business into a comedy routine. "Why not use a Band-Aid instead?" she would say. It was a source of great pride to my mother that she had never even had to wear a brassiere until she had her fourth child, and then only because her gynecologist made her. It was incomprehensible to me that anyone would ever be proud of something like that. . . .

I suppose that for most girls, breasts, brassieres, that entire thing, has more trauma, more to do with the coming of adolescence, of becoming a woman, than anything else. Certainly more than getting your period, although that too was traumatic, symbolic. But you could *see* breasts; they were there; they were visible. Whereas a girl could claim to have her period for months before she actually got it and nobody would ever know the difference. Which is exactly what I did. All you had to do was make a great fuss over having enough nickels for the Kotex machine and walk around clutching your stomach and moaning for three to five days a month about The Curse and you could convince anybody. There is a school of thought somewhere in the women's lib/women's mag/gynecology establishment that claims that menstrual cramps are purely psychological, and I lean toward it. Not that I didn't have them finally. Agonizing cramps, heating-pad cramps, go-down-to-the-school-nurse-and-lie-on-the-cot cramps. But unlike any pain I had ever suffered, I adored the pain of cramps, welcomed it, wallowed in it, bragged about it. "I can't go. I have cramps." "I can't do that. I have cramps." And most of all, gigglingly, blushingly: "I can't swim. I have cramps." Nobody ever used the hard-core word. Menstruation. God, what an awful word. Never that. "I have cramps."

The morning I first got my period, I went into my mother's bedroom to tell her. And my mother, my utterly-hateful-about-bras mother, burst into tears. It was really a lovely moment, and I remember it so clearly not just because it was one of the two times I ever saw my mother cry on my account (the other was when I was caught being a six-year-old kleptomaniac), but also because the incident did not mean to me what it meant to her. Her little girl, her firstborn, had finally become a woman. That was what she was crying about. My reaction to the event, however, was that I might well be a woman in some scientific, textbook sense (and could at least stop faking every month and stop wasting all those nickels). But in another sense—in a visible sense—I was as androgynous and as liable to tip over into boyhood as ever.

I started with a 28AA bra. I don't think they made them any smaller in those days, although I gather that now you can buy bras for five year olds that don't have any cups whatsoever in them; trainer bras they are called. My first brassiere came from Robinson's Department Store in Beverly Hills. I went there alone, shaking, positive they would look me over and smile and tell me to come back next year. An actual fitter took me into the dressing room and stood over me while I took off my blouse and tried the first one on. The little puffs stood out on my chest. "Lean over," said the fitter (to this day I am not sure what fitters in bra departments do except to tell you to lean over). I leaned over, with the fleeting hope that my breasts would miraculously fall out of my body and into the puffs. Nothing. . . .

My best friend in school was Diana Raskob. . . . Diana and I had been best friends since we were seven; we were about equally popular in school (which was to say, not particularly), we had about the same success with boys (extremely intermittent), and we looked much the same. Dark. Tall. Gangly.

It is September, just before school begins. I am eleven years old, about to enter the seventh grade, and Diana and I have not seen each other all summer. I have been to camp and she has been somewhere like Banff with her parents. We are meeting, as we often do, on the street midway between our two houses and we will walk back to Diana's and eat junk and talk about what has happened to each of us that summer. I am walking down Walden Drive in my jeans and my father's shirt hanging out and my old red loafers with the socks falling into them and coming toward me is . . . I take a deep breath . . . a young woman. Diana. Her hair is curled and she has a waist and hips and a bust and she is wearing a straight skirt, an article of clothing I have been repeatedly told I will be unable to wear until I have the hips to hold it up. My jaw drops, and suddenly I am crying, crying hysterically, can't catch my breath sobbing. My best friend has betrayed me. She has gone ahead without me and done it. She has shaped up.

Here are some things I did to help:

Bought a Mark Eden Bust Developer.

Slept on my back for four years.

Splashed cold water on them every night because some French actress said in *Life* magazine that that was what *she* did for her perfect bustline.

Ultimately, I resigned myself to a bad toss and began to wear padded bras. I think about them now, think about all those years in high school I went around in them, my three padded bras, every single one of them with different sized breasts. Each time I changed bras I changed sizes: one week nice perky but not too obtrusive breasts, the next medium-sized slightly pointed ones, the next week knockers, true knockers; all the time, whatever size I was, carrying around this rubberized appendage on my chest that occasionally crashed into a wall and was poked inward and had to be poked outward—I think about all that and wonder how anyone kept a straight face through it. My parents, who normally had no restraints about needling me—why did they say nothing as they watched my chest go up and down? My friends, who would periodically inspect my breasts for signs of growth and reassure me—why didn't they at least counsel consistency? . . .

Buster Klepper was the first boy who ever touched them. He was my boyfriend my senior year of high school. . . . Buster was really very sweet—which is, I know, damning with faint praise, but there it is. I was the editor of the front page of the high-school newspaper and he was editor of the back page; we had to work together, side by side, in the print shop, and that was how it started. On our first date, we went to see *April Love* starring Pat Boone. Then we started going together. Buster had a green coupe, a 1950 Ford with an engine he had handcromed until it shone, dazzled, reflected the image of anyone who looked into it, anyone usually being Buster polishing it or the gas-station attendants he constantly asked to check the oil in order for them to be overwhelmed by the sparkle on the valves. . . .

There was necking. Terrific necking. First in the car, overlooking Los Angeles from what is now the Trousdale Estates. Then on the bed of his parents' cabana at Ocean House. Incredibly wonderful, frustrating necking. I loved it, really, but no further than necking, please don't, please, because there I was absolutely terrified of . . . his finding out there was next to nothing there (which he knew, of course; he wasn't that dumb).

I broke up with him at one point. I think we were apart for about two weeks. At the end of that time I drove down to see a friend at a boarding school in Palos Verdes Estates and a disc jockey played *April Love* on the radio four times during the trip. I took it as a sign. I drove straight back to Griffith Park to a golf tournament Buster was playing in (he was the sixth-seeded teenage golf player in Southern California) and presented myself back to him on the green of the eighteenth hold. It was all very dramatic. That night we went to a drive-in and I let him get his hand under my protuberances and onto my breasts. He really didn't seem to mind at all. . . .

And even now, now that I have been countlessly reassured that my figure is a good one, now that I am grown up enough to understand that most of my feelings have very little to do with the reality of my shape, I am nonetheless obsessed by breasts. . . .

After I went into therapy, a process that made it possible for me to tell total strangers at cocktail parties that breasts were the hang-up of my life, I was often told that I was insane to have been bothered by my condition. I was also frequently told, by close friends, that I was extremely boring on the subject. And my girlfriends, the ones with nice big breasts, would go on endlessly about how their lives had been far more miserable than mine. Their bra straps were snapped in class. They couldn't sleep on their stomachs. They were stared at whenever the word "mountain" cropped up in geography. And *Evangeline*, good God what they went through every time someone had to stand up and recite the Prologue to Longfellow's *Evangeline*: "*. . . stand like druids of old . . . ! With beards that rest on their bosoms.*" It was much worse for them, they tell me. They had a terrible time of it, they assure me. I don't know how lucky I was, they say.

Response and Analysis

1. What did Nora Ephron think that breasts would do for her? Why do you think that adolescents are so concerned over the appearance of secondary sex characteristics during puberty? What societal influences promote such concerns? In general, what are the short-term and long-term psychological effects of late development for girls? For boys? What are the effects of early development for girls? For boys?

2. What is the relationship between body image and self-esteem in adolescence? Do you think this relationship is different for girls and boys? If so, how? Do you think that the relationship between body image and self-

esteem differs for various ethnic or cultural groups? If so, how?

Personal Experience and Application

1. Recall how you changed physically during adolescence. In what ways were you self-conscious about your body's changes? What do you think have been the long-term effects, if any, of how you and others reacted to those changes?

2. How are values concerning physical appearance conveyed to children, adolescents, and adults? What pressures do young men and women in American society experience if they do not conform to the idealized body image? How might these pressures affect self-esteem?

Research

Suppose you suspect that improved health care and diet may lead to children growing taller and stronger, and thus reaching sexual maturity more quickly. How could you test this theory by comparing children in more developed nations with children in less developed nations? What characteristics would be important in selecting comparison groups? What factors would you need to control? Could you conduct your study comparing children from different regions of the United States? Why or why not? Finally, what other influences might explain this trend?

THE SQUEEZED GENERATION

H. Michael Zal

Psychological Concepts
midlife transition, Erikson's generativity versus stagnation stage, midlife crisis, social clock

Around the age of forty, many people reappraise their lives and relationships. During the midlife transition, they may feel caught between the younger and the older generations.

What do people hope for when they become forty or fifty years old? What is unique about this stage? People have honed their careers and talents and hope to have some status and respect on the job and in the community. If they have families, their children are close to being independent. So, what now? H. Michael Zal tells us that "What now?" does not always bring what this group anticipated.

People in midlife may feel pressured to assist their children financially or to take care of their elderly parents. In addition, they may worry about their own health or job security. Husbands and wives may reflect on what they have not yet achieved and begin to feel a kind of desperation. Their marriages may be "old hat," and they may wonder how to rekindle love. Yet most people find solutions to these issues and find that this stage, like all the others, has great rewards. What suggestions does Zal offer the "sandwich generation"?

Nora was forty-nine. Something was wrong. It felt physical. She often had pressure in her chest and felt faint and short of breath. It felt emotional. She was often tense and moody. At times she thought that she would lose control and burst apart. She visited her family doctor. Except for moderate hypertension, the results of her physical exam were normal. All the lab test findings were within normal limits. Maybe it was menopause? A psychiatric opinion was sought. The clinical diagnosis was depression and anxiety. The real issue was the dilemma of middle age.

Nora's worries and complaints were not unique. As with many people in the sandwich generation she felt caught in the middle between generations, responsibilities, needs, and expectations. "I'm trying to sort out my obligations to my children, to my husband, to our aging parents, to my career, and to myself," she said. Nora felt stressed and driven by an intense emotional pressure which she did not fully understand.

"At this point in my life, I expected that I would be growing old gracefully and that everything would be OK. I always assumed that as I got older I would get wiser, mellow, and have the answers to some questions. I thought that I would know what to expect and what others expected of me. I felt that I would be a calm and cool person. Instead, I feel terrible inside. I'm not who I should be. I'm not in control." Her turmoil and confusion were influencing her work and her relationship with her husband, Don. Let's look at some of the people in her life and some of the problems fueling her anxiety and discontent.

The Children   Jose was nineteen and a college student living out of town. She called several times a week and dumped her problems concerning her boyfriend, school, and girlfriends on her parents. Nora worried for days only to find out when she called back that Jose had already forgotten the crisis and gone on to a new day and new issues.

Ben was twenty-three, married, and had two beautiful twin daughters. He and his wife, Dianne, had lived with Nora and Don for ten months after they married. They then moved to North Carolina. Ben was now unemployed and had gotten into a fight in a bar and been arrested. He and Dianne had separated three months ago, and Dianne and the babies were living with her mother. Nora worried about them all.

Henrietta, twenty-five, planned to marry in October. Fiancé Bob was a carpenter and worked sporadically. They had a fourteen-week-old baby son, Matthew.

Henrietta, Bob, and Matthew all lived with Nora and Don, while they saved to buy a house of their own. At a time when she expected her life to be her own, Nora was cooking and cleaning for five all over again. "The only comfort is that all my friends are going through the same thing. When I was young, you moved out and didn't go back. Things are different with the kids today."

The Parent Nora was concerned about her mother, Ethel, who was seventy-two and lived many miles away. She had had a mild stroke last year. She had been recently hospitalized due to lack of appetite, fatigue, and insomnia. No new physical diagnosis was made. She was told to seek counseling for depression. Nora described her mother as a wise, productive, intelligent, and religious woman who allowed no disagreement. Nora's father also had had a history of depression and hypertension. He had been a heavy drinker. Since her husband died ten years ago, Ethel had been self-sufficient and independent. When Nora visited her in the hospital, she could see a change. For the first time, Ethel looked frail and older. Uncharacteristically, she cried in her daughter's arms and shared her fear that she would have another stroke alone in her apartment and die. Nora realized that she too was aging. She began to think about her own health, her own future, and her own mortality.

Nora found it hard to be a caregiver at a distance. Her first instinct was to ask her mother to move to her home in Philadelphia. Somehow she knew that the offer would be rejected. She did talk to her brother and was very firm about what she felt her mother needed. She also called a local agency and was able to get someone to stay with her mother in the evenings several days a week.

The Spouse Don had taken a new hobby. He was fixing up the house and adding a new porch. Nora complained that it had become an obsession. "He spends 85 percent of his spare time on the house. I want to go out dancing. By the time we're done with the house, I'll be too old to enjoy myself. I'm getting older. I want to do some of the things that I want to do." In quiet moments, she wondered if Don still found her attractive and worried about gaining weight. His business commitments were also very time consuming. In spite of her resentment, she worried about his health. He smoked one-and-a-half packs of cigarettes a day and had had a heart attack four years ago. She wondered what would happen if he had another health crisis and what life would be like without him. "It seems that he and I are always faced with something. We don't have time for each other."

The In-law Don's father, Joseph, age seventy-eight, had been retired for many years. His wife, Camille, had died four years earlier after a long illness. Initially, Joe seemed to be making a good adjustment. Unlike many men his age, he had some hobbies and interests and played cards once a week. During the last year, his memory had been declining. Twice he had left the oven on overnight. His prostate had been removed, leaving him incontinent, and his vision was failing. Nora and Don constantly talked about the options that were available for Joe, including placement in a nursing home. They could never seem to make a decision.

The Job Nora was well respected at the office. She had worked hard for many years and was now a manager supervising twelve employees. She was taken aback at times when they called her "Ma'am" and complained that the "kids" were not as diligent about their work as she and her contemporaries were at their age. There had been some recent administrative changes which added to the turmoil at work. There was talk of further changes and possible layoffs. Nora handled the pressure by working harder and taking on more responsibility. She felt tense, insecure, and irritable. When told that she had high blood pressure, she responded that she had no time to be sick.

Job security was important to Nora. She had heard many stories about her parents suffering during the Depression. The recent upheaval at work also created tension for her because it threatened a hidden agenda in her life. "When I took this job, I thought that I had finally reached a pinnacle in my career. I've been in a fast track mode. I thought that this might finally be the end of the line employment-wise. I could stay here. It would be a nice way to end my career and eventually retire. I wanted to stop work at fifty-five. I would still have energy and still be young enough to enjoy the things we postponed all these years. They're messing up my life. If I have to start a new job at my age, it will shatter my plans." Even more confusing to her was the fact that she sometimes woke up at night and thought, "Maybe I'll give up my career and do some other kind of work."

As you can see, it is not surprising that Nora felt stressed and out of control. Her frustration was further fueled by her unfulfilled expectations. After early financial and marital struggles, the trials and tribulations of caring for children and attending to career goals, Nora, at forty-nine, expected to be able to coast for awhile. Instead, she was caught between demanding children, a frightened parent, a needy father-in-law, and her own needs and desires. Her marriage was drifting. At this stage in life, she expected that she would feel mellow and content. Instead, she felt conflicted and needy. Instead of a rest, she had new problems to solve. No wonder she was angry inside.

More traditionally oriented, like her mother, it had been difficult for Nora to cope with a grandchild born out of wedlock and a son who was not particularly goal-directed. She joked and called him a "free spirit," but was really quite disappointed in him. Prior to therapy, Nora had assumed that at her age she was done learning and changing. However, life is synonymous with change. This too was part of her frustration. Change was difficult for her. Middle age is a developmental stage where we can resolve old issues and continue to mature and grow. She had to accept these truths. Nora found that even in middle age she had conflicts to resolve, new feelings to understand, and new problems to solve. She started to see middle age as a challenge. She did well.

Medication helped improve her mood and calm her anxieties. In therapy, she became a little more introspective and gained new insight through her reflections. She was able to ventilate some of her anger and understand some of her other feelings. She got her younger brother to spend more time with Ethel. She started to set some limits on Henrietta and Bob and asked for more help around the house. The "kids" moved to their own house in November. Nora expressed some of her pent-up anger and disappointment at Ben and told me how she felt that he had let her down. She tried hard to encourage Jose to solve some of her own problems and to be more independent. Most of all, she tried not to feel guilty if she could not be everything to everyone. At work, she started to see herself in a new role as a consultant who had much experience and expertise to share but who no longer had to do it all herself. She started to delegate more.

Seventeen years earlier, she and Don had gone for marriage counseling. At the time, Nora had been depressed and unhappy. In a short course of outpatient therapy, she was able to come out of her depression and better communicate her needs. At this stage of her life, she again felt suddenly insecure and alone. She very much needed Don and felt resentful that he could not see this on his own and pay more attention to her instead of the house. Now, after twenty-eight years of marriage, she could be more insightful. "It's happening again," she said. Fortunately, with a little therapeutic encouragement, she was able to talk to Don. She told him what she wanted from him and how much she cared. They started to take walks together and even went dancing one Saturday night. Their relationship started to improve again.

In therapy, Nora reminisced about her father's love of music. He had often sung and played the guitar for his children. She remembered how relaxing it had been in her childhood home when her father played operatic music on their Victrola. She bought a compact disc player and started to enjoy music again. As she relaxed, a more creative side emerged. She worked in the garden more and talked about taking a course in flower arranging. She started to see the big picture and put things in perspective. "I can't get so crazy. I have to take one day at a time. I'll do what I can for others and take better care of me." Although still uptight at times, Nora started to feel more content and more in control. She even took her antihypertensive medication regularly. Life was not perfect but it was much improved.

Nora is representative of many of you in the sandwich generation. The fabric of her life is made up of relationships. Her children and the other members of her family are important to her. She also has her own needs and priorities and wants to continue to grow. Her worries about her health and her future are universal. She has certain expectations about life in middle age. Her dilemma is not unique. In spite of the current turmoil and the angry feelings, a special bond of love exists between Nora and her family which will endure forever.

Response and Analysis

1. Nora "felt caught in the middle between generations, responsibilities, needs, and expectations." Briefly describe the problems or issues that contributed to Nora's anxiety: her children, parents, spouse, in-laws, and job. How did she resolve her marital difficulties?

2. What are the characteristics of a midlife crisis? Who is most likely to experience such a crisis? Why? What are the main issues facing someone who is at Erikson's generativity versus stagnation stage of psychosocial development?

Personal Experience and Application

1. The social clock prescribes when certain social events and major life events should occur, such as marriage, children, and retirement. Think of someone you know who has felt pressured by a social clock. What did he or she feel pressured to do? Briefly discuss any pressures you have felt because of a social clock.

2. List at least five characteristics of a satisfying marriage. What factors lead people to divorce?

Research

Suppose you want to conduct a cross-cultural study to examine the social clock phenomenon. You want to know if college students in the United States, Brazil, South Africa, and Holland have similar expectations about when major life events such as marriage should occur. Write three questions that you might ask your participants. Will the questions be short answer or use a fixed-response scale (for example, strongly disagree, disagree, neither disagree nor agree, agree, strongly agree)? Why?

THE VIEW FROM EIGHTY

Malcolm Cowley

Psychological Concept
late adulthood

Martin Buber writes that "to be old is a glorious thing when one has not unlearned what it means to begin" (p. 6). Malcolm Cowley surely knew how to begin again: He published five books after he turned seventy. He died at the age of ninety-one. Cowley valued ceremonies, and when his friends and family celebrated his eightieth birthday with a party, he knew it was a rite of passage.

Aging, he said, is different from what any of us expect. When he discovers that other people see him as old, he is forced to redefine himself. He becomes aware of various messages he receives from his body that tell him he is aging.

Here Cowley shares his experiences, some challenging, some delightful, of becoming older. What he enjoys are moments of "simply sitting still, like a snake on a sun-warmed stone."

They gave me a party on my eightieth birthday in August 1978. First there were cards, letters, telegrams, even a cable of congratulation or condolence; then there were gifts, mostly bottles; there was catered food and finally a big cake with, for some reason, two candles (had I gone back to very early childhood?). I blew the candles out a little unsteadily. Amid the applause and clatter I thought about a former custom of the Northern Ojibwas when they lived on the shore of Lake Winnipeg. They were kind to their old people, who remembered and enforced the ancient customs of the tribe, but when an old person became decrepit, it was time for him to go. Sometimes he was simply abandoned, with a little food, on an island in the lake. If he deserved special honor, they held a tribal feast for him. The old man sang a death song and danced, if he could. While he was still singing, his son came from behind and brained him with a tomahawk.

That was quick, it was dignified, and I wonder whether it was any more cruel, essentially, than some of our civilized customs or inadvertencies in disposing of the aged. I believe in rites and ceremonies. I believe in big parties for special occasions such as an eightieth birthday. It is a sort of belated bar mitzvah, since the eighty-year-old, like a Jewish adolescent, is entering a new stage of life; let him (or her) undergo a *rite de passage*, with toasts and a cantor. Seventy-year-olds, or septuas, have the illusion of being middle-aged, even if they have been pushed back on a shelf. The eighty-year-old, the octo, looks at the double-dumpling figure and admits that he is old. That last act has begun, and it will be the test of the play.

He has joined a select minority that numbers, in this country, 4,842,000 persons (according to Census Bureau estimates for 1977), or about 2 percent of the American population. Two-thirds of the octos are women, who have retained the good habit of living longer than men. Someday you, the reader, will join that minority, if you escape hypertension and cancer, the two killers, and if you survive the dangerous years seventy-five to seventy-nine, when half the survivors till then are lost. With advances in medicine, the living space taken over by octos is growing larger year by year.

To enter the country of age is a new experience, different from what you supposed it to be. Nobody, man or woman, knows the country until he has lived in it and has taken out his citizenship papers. Here is my own report, submitted as a road map and guide to some of the principal monuments.

The new octogenarian feels as strong as ever when he is sitting back in a comfortable chair. He ruminates, he dreams, he remembers. He doesn't want to be disturbed by others. It seems to him that old age is only a costume assumed for those others; the true, the essential self is ageless. In a moment he will rise and go for a ramble in the woods, taking a gun along, or a fishing rod, if it is spring. Then he creaks to his feet, bending forward to keep his balance, and realizes that he will do nothing of the sort. The body and its surroundings have their messages for him, or only one message: "You are old." Here are some of the occasions on which he receives the message:

- when it becomes an achievement to do thoughtfully, step by step, what he once did instinctively

- when his bones ache
- when there are more and more little bottles in the medicine cabinet, with instructions for taking four times a day
- when he fumbles and drops his toothbrush (butterfingers)
- when his face has bumps and wrinkles, so that he cuts himself while shaving (blood on the towel)
- when year by year his feet seem farther from his hands
- when he can't stand on one leg and has trouble pulling on his pants
- when he hesitates on the landing before walking down a flight of stairs
- when he spends more time looking for things misplaced than he spends using them after he (or more often his wife) has found them
- when he falls asleep in the afternoon
- when it becomes harder to bear in mind two things at once
- when a pretty girl passes him in the street and he doesn't turn his head
- when he forgets names, even of people he saw last month ("Now I'm beginning to forget nouns," the poet Conrad Aiken said at eighty)
- when he listens hard to jokes and catches everything but the snapper
- when he decides not to drive at night anymore
- when everything takes longer to do—bathing, shaving, getting dressed or undressed—but when time passes quickly, as if he were gathering speed while coasting downhill. The year from seventy-nine to eighty is like a week when he was a boy.

Those are some of the intimate messages. "Put cotton in your ears and pebbles in your shoes," said a gerontologist, a member of that new profession dedicated to alleviating all maladies of old people except the passage of years. "Pull on rubber gloves. Smear Vaseline over your glasses, and there you have it: instant aging." Not quite. His formula omits the messages from the social world, which are louder, in most cases, than those from within. We start by growing old in other people's eyes, then slowly we come to share their judgment.

I remember a morning many years ago when I was backing out of the parking lot near the railroad station in Brewster, New York. There was a near collision. The driver of the other car jumped out and started to abuse me; he had his fists ready. Then he looked hard at me and said, "Why, you're an old man." He got back into his car, slammed the door, and drove away, while I stood there fuming. "I'm only sixty-five," I thought. "He wasn't driving carefully. I can still take care of myself in a car, or in a fight, for that matter." . . .

But there are also pleasures of the body, or the mind, that are enjoyed by a greater number of older persons.

Those pleasures include some that younger people find hard to appreciate. One of them is simply sitting still, like a snake on a sun-warmed stone, with a delicious feeling of indolence that was seldom attained in earlier years. A leaf flutters down; a cloud moves by inches across the horizon. At such moments the older person, completely relaxed, has become a part of nature—and a living part, with blood coursing through his veins. The future does not exist for him. He thinks, if he thinks at all, that life for younger persons is still a battle royal of each against each, but that now he has nothing more to win or lose. He is not so much above as outside the battle, as if he had assumed the uniform of some small neutral country, perhaps Liechtenstein or Andorra. From a distance he notes that some of the combatants, men or women, are jostling ahead—but why do they fight so hard when the most they can hope for is a longer obituary? He can watch the scrounging and gouging, he can hear the shouts of exultation, the moans of the gravely wounded, and meanwhile he feels secure; nobody will attack him from ambush.

Response and Analysis

1. What pleasures does Malcolm Cowley associate with old age? What messages about old age does he receive from society? Cowley suggests that "the aging person may undergo another identity crisis like that of adolescence." Briefly discuss the crisis.

2. Briefly summarize the physical, cognitive, social, and intellectual changes about which Cowley writes.

Personal Experience and Application

1. How do you feel when you are around senior citizens? What do you think is remarkable about senior citizens, including those who are in their eighties? What do you think may be rewarding and satisfying, as well as difficult, for those in this age group?

2. Suppose a local organization asks you to design a program to enhance the intellectual life of senior citizens. What types of activities might you suggest? Why?

Research

Suppose you wish to conduct an experiment to examine how senior citizens describe their personal identity. You ask a random sample of senior citizens to participate. You have to decide which of two assessment procedures to use. One procedure involves asking the participants to list as many words as they can that describe themselves. The other procedure involves presenting a list of one hundred traits to the participants and asking them to place a check next to each trait that describes themselves. List two advantages and two disadvantages of each approach. Which approach would you use? Why?

chapter *8*

MENTAL ABILITIES

*As I began to explain my ideas, [Einstein]
asked me to write the equations on the
blackboard so he could see how they
developed. Then came the staggering—and
altogether endearing—request: "Please go
slowly. I do not understand things quickly."
This from Einstein! He said it gently, and
I laughed. From then on, all vestiges of
fear were gone.*

Banesh Hoffman, "My Friend, Albert Einstein"

What is intelligence, and how do we work with the faculties we have been given? This chapter looks at the following concepts: giftedness, mental retardation, intelligence, and assessment.

Josh is a talented teenager who excels in all his subjects but whose passion is math. A concern for many bright adolescents is that their giftedness may make them seem like "completely weird" people. By participating in athletics and choosing friends unlike himself, Josh works at keeping others from thinking him strange. He also faces the dilemma of whether to choose a high-paying career or a less-well-paying one that will benefit humankind.

S. I. Hayakawa writes about his son Mark, who was born with Down syndrome. Hayakawa presents some of the challenges of raising his child at home, the relationship between Mark and his brother and sister, and the activities the family shares. He concludes: "It's a strange thing to say, and I am a little startled to find myself saying it, but often I feel that I wouldn't have had Mark any different."

Richard Vigil tells of his pain at being institutionalized as a child, of missing his family, and of his hopes to have a job and to marry. When he lived in institutions, Vigil would often run away; now at age twenty-nine he lives in a group home and likes it. Vigil shares how he feels about himself and what he would like in his future.

Many people excel in certain areas such as math but struggle with verbal skills. John Philo Dixon describes how his varied talents posed a problem not only for himself but also for his teachers and family. It was not until he was in the ninth grade that "the long depression of elementary school ended." Then he found his forte with algebra, higher mathematics, and later with physics. Dixon says that when he was a child he thought his problem was "personal" and "endured it in silence." Now he knows that children who have a special ability should not be made to feel inadequate just because they can't do everything.

Psychologist Jerome Sattler presents a case that raises important questions: What sources of information should guide decisions concerning a child? Does intelligence quotient change? Sattler also explores the benefits and limitations of intelligence tests and offers recommendations for assessing children.

TALENTED TEENAGERS

Mihaly Csikszentmihalyi, Kevin Rathunde, and Samuel Whalen

Psychological Concepts
giftedness, environmental influences on intelligence

How do talented teenagers spend their time? What attitudes do they have toward being talented? Josh, a bright high school student who loves math, does not want "to come across as brainy, or anything other than an average teenager." Josh experiences the conflict of many gifted teenagers. He wants to join his peers with their "'normal' interests and values"; yet, he also wants to meet his parents' expectations that he develop his talents. In spite of his desire to be a typical teen, he spends a great deal of time with computers, in playing chess, and in solving math problems alone and with others. What are Josh's dreams? Do they differ from his parents' aspirations?

In most respects Josh's preferences and interests resemble those of other males his age. A freshman at his school, he participates in a broad range of sports and looks forward to his first taste of high school athletic competition. His conversation turns easily to cars, rock groups, and his favorite foods. He can't wait until he is old enough to get a driver's license. But in at least one way Josh is quite an extraordinary fourteen-year-old. For Josh possesses a truly exceptional gift for mathematics. He combines this gift with formidable abilities in language and science as well as in most other academic subjects he has attempted thus far.

Meeting Josh in person, one would not suspect him of being a gifted type, an impression that would please him. Describing himself as shy and easygoing, Josh seems determined not to come across as brainy, or anything other than an average teenager. Like most adolescents, he does not want to be recognized as outstanding by adult standards, lest he alienate his peers. "I try not to let things like school take over my whole life," he says, adding that in general he tries "not to take everything too seriously."

Math, he admits, has always been easy and natural for him and has never demanded much hard work. Accelerated into advanced mathematics classes since the second grade, he was more than a year ahead of his peers by sixth grade and successfully competed in regional math tournaments. He began freshman year in high school in an advanced junior section, studying college algebra and trigonometry. By sophomore year he had exhausted the school's considerable offerings in mathematics.

Although he is aware of the magnitude of his talent, Josh's goals reflect a conventional pattern of "good grades, college, preferably in California, and a high-paying job." Asked why he wants a good job, he replies, "I want not to have to worry about where everything is coming from—have enough to be comfortable." When confronted with a hypothetical choice between a job that was enjoyable, and one that paid a lot of money, Josh answered, "I'd like to think I'd choose to do what I'd like to do, but you never know."

He knows that in these plans for a comfortable future, math figures as his "strongest suit." But rarely does Josh show enthusiasm for mathematics in itself. In his interview answers, math is a part of the generally uninteresting province of school, a typically boring place that nonetheless provides occasional opportunities for recognition and display. Of the things he admits enjoying about math, competition with the school's math team stands out because it provides a sense that he "knows what he is doing," that he is in control of a problem. He especially enjoys the satisfaction of cracking a problem for the first time, particularly one that is complex and interesting.

Compared with the guarded enthusiasm of the interview, the record of responses to the Experience Sampling Method (ESM)[1] shows a different picture. Despite his blasé protestations, there is no question that mathematics takes up a great deal of Josh's attention and that it provides some of the most rewarding experiences of his young life. Over 25 percent of his pager responses during the week of ESM experimentation involve mathematics in some form. Most of these instances involve computers: playing chess against a PC, reading an article about computer poetry, trying to write a program that will play a rock song, watching a program "completely blow up." The highest moods he reported all week were on a Monday afternoon working hard on a problem with the math team. It was a session that combined enjoyment of the company of his friends with real interest in the elusive solution to the problem. When he is thinking about math Josh always reports a level of skills above the average, sometimes much above. He also tends to report high challenges when working with math, and these are usually matched to the level of reported skills. Generally his moods when working with the computer are also appreciably above the mean—in other words, for Josh doing mathematics is usually a flow experience.

So even though Josh wishes to appear "cool" about his talent and does not want to seem too serious about it, the domain of mathematics has succeeded in providing sufficient intrinsic reward to sustain his investing attention over extended periods of time. This exclusive investment of psychic energy, which is very rare in adolescence—or, for that matter, in adulthood—is necessary to reach the higher levels of proficiency in any domain. As Newton replied when asked how he developed

---

[1]Experience Sampling Method: a technique that allows researchers to associate daily events with moods and behaviors. Participants carry a pager; when it sounds (at predetermined intervals), the participants record their activities and complete a questionnaire.

the universal theory of gravitation, he did it "by thinking about it constantly." One cannot think all the time productively about something one does not enjoy.

But the task of cultivating talent does not rest on Josh's shoulders alone. As is the case with most of the other teenagers we studied, Josh's entire family acts as a support system to help him concentrate. His mother, especially, clearly expresses high hopes for her gifted son. Seeing him as a potential "astronaut, physicist, or astronomer," she is emphatic that he "should use his extraordinary gifts . . . to make the world a better place." She expects that he will earn a "doctorate in something that interests him" and hopes that "he'll be driven more by his interests than by large amounts of money."

The only cloud on the horizon, as far as Josh's mother is concerned, is the potentially harmful effect of peers. She worries that Josh is too sensitive and therefore emotionally fragile, and that his friends are more callous and superficial. On this issue Josh disagrees. Intent on becoming more friendly and outgoing, he has chosen these friends precisely because they "aren't really the smart, smart type," thus helping him avoid acting like "a complete weird person." Recently he joined one of these friends on the water polo team, a sport he finds enjoyable but that conflicts with the practice schedule of the math team.

Josh's case illustrates several of the dilemmas confronting young people with exceptional intellectual gifts. On the one hand, there is the attraction of the peer group with its "normal" interests and values; on the other hand, there are parents who expect ascetic dedication to the cultivation of talent. There is the attraction of making a lot of money in the future, counterbalanced by the possibility of helping make the world a better place. There is the enjoyment of being with friends and of doing sports, counterbalanced by the solitary enjoyment of solving difficult problems on the computer. To a certain extent these options are not mutually exclusive, and Josh does a good job of trying to do justice to them all. But attention is a limited resource, and in a twenty-four-hour day he can concentrate on only so many things. How Josh allocates his attention in the four years of high school will determine to a large extent whether his outstanding mathematical talent will be realized or not.

Response and Analysis

1. Describe Josh's mathematical abilities and one of the challenges that face Josh and other intellectually gifted youth. Why is Josh's mother concerned that he might not use his intellectual gifts in the future?

2. How does Josh's home environment support the development of his academic abilities? Briefly discuss three environmental conditions that may be associated with high intelligence test scores.

Personal Experience and Application

1. Why might some teenagers make fun of other teenagers who have a passion for a scholarly subject and devote much time to the subject, but admire someone who works

hard at being a guitar player or a football player? Do you think that girls and boys hide their academic talents in order to be accepted by other teenagers? Why or why not?

2. Do you believe that schools may unknowingly discourage academically talented teenagers from using their talents? Why? How might the school staff and school policy motivate a student to use and enhance his or her talents?

Research

Suppose you want to identify variables that promote cognitive development in children. List the environmental conditions that you believe may promote cognitive development. Next, choose one variable on your list. How could you determine whether this variable promotes cognitive development?

OUR SON MARK

S. I. Hayakawa

and

I DON'T GET LOST VERY OFTEN

Richard Vigil

Psychological Concepts
Down syndrome, mental retardation

In the following two selections, S. I. Hayakawa and Richard Vigil write about mental retardation from two different perspectives. Hayakawa presents the view of a parent whose son has Down syndrome; Richard Vigil tells about his own life as a person with mental retardation. One striking difference is that Mark's family decided to keep him at home, whereas Richard's family placed him in an institution. Severity of retardation, family resources, and community pressures often affect the decision of whether to keep a child at home.

What are Mark and Richard capable of learning? What do others teach them by their attitudes and care? What do they teach others? Hayakawa says his son responds to how others measure him, and that, because he has been loved and accepted by his family, he has learned to feel good about himself and is a pleasure to live with.

Can either Mark or Richard hold jobs? What chores are they able to do? Both are impressive in what they have learned and are capable of doing, and both are able to hold deep affection for others.

It was a terrible blow for us to discover that we had brought a retarded child into the world. My wife and I had had no previous acquaintance with the problems of retardation—not even with the words to discuss it. Only such words as imbecile, idiot, and moron came to mind. And the prevailing opinion was that such a child must be "put away," to live out his life in an institution.

Mark was born with Down syndrome. The prognosis for his ever reaching anything approaching normality was hopeless. Medical authorities advised us that he would show some mental development, but the progress would be painfully slow and he would never reach an adolescent's mental age. We could do nothing about it, they said. They sympathetically but firmly advised us to find a private institution that would take him. To get him into a public institution, they said, would require a waiting period of five years. To keep him at home for this length of time, they warned, would have a disastrous effect on our family.

That was twenty-seven years ago. In that time, Mark has never been "put away." He has lived at home. The only institution he sees regularly is the workshop he attends, a special workshop for retarded adults. He is as much a part of the family as his mother, his older brother, his younger sister, his father, or our longtime housekeeper and friend, Daisy Rosebourgh.

Mark has contributed to our stability and serenity. His retardation has brought us grief, but we did not go on dwelling on what might have been, and we have been rewarded by finding much good in things the way they are. From the beginning, we have enjoyed Mark for his delightful self. He has never seemed like a burden. He was an "easy" baby, quiet, friendly, and passive; but he needed a baby's care for a long time. It was easy to be patient with him, although I must say that some of his stages, such as his love of making chaos, as we called it, by pulling all the books he could reach off the shelves, lasted much longer than normal children's.

Mark seems more capable of accepting things as they are than his immediate relatives; his mental limitation has given him a capacity for contentment, a focus on the present moment, which is often enviable. His world may be circumscribed, but it is a happy and bright one. His enjoyment of simple experiences—swimming, food, birthday candles, sports-car rides, and cuddly cats—has that directness and intensity so many philosophers recommend to all of us.

Mark's contentment has been a happy contribution to our family, and the challenge of communicating with him, of doing things we can all enjoy, has drawn the family together. And seeing Mark's communicative processes develop in slow motion has taught me much about the process in all children.

Fortunately Mark was born at a time when a whole generation of parents of retarded children had begun to question the accepted dogmas about retardation. Whatever they were told by their physicians about their children, parents began to ask: "Is that so? Let's see." For what is meant by "retarded child"? There are different kinds of retardation. Retarded child No. 1 is not retarded child No. 2, or 3, or 4. Down syndrome is one condition, while brain damage is something else. There are different degrees of retardation, just as there are different kinds of brain damage. No two retarded children are exactly alike in all respects. Institutional care *does* turn out to be the best answer for some kinds of retarded children or some family situations. The point is that one observes and reacts to the *specific* case and circumstances rather than to the generalization.

This sort of attitude has helped public understanding of the nature and problems of retardation to become much deeper and more widespread. It's hard to believe now that it was "definitely known" twenty years ago that institutionalization was the "only way." We were told that a retarded child could not be kept at home because "it would not be fair to the other children." The family would not be able to stand the stress. "Everybody" believed these things and repeated them, to comfort and guide the parents of the retarded.

We did not, of course, lightly disregard the well-meant advice of university neurologists and their social-worker teams, for they had had much experience and we were new at this shattering experience. But our general semantics, or our parental feelings, made us aware that their reaction to Mark was to a generalization, while to us he was an individual. They might have a valid generalization about statistical stresses on statistical families, but they knew virtually nothing about our particular family and its evaluative processes.

Mark was eight months old before we were told he was retarded. Of course we had known that he was slower than the average child in smiling, in sitting up, in responding to others around him. Having had one child who was extraordinarily ahead of such schedules, we simply thought that Mark was at the other end of the average range. . . .

It was parents who led the way: They organized into parents' groups; they pointed out the need for preschools, schools, diagnostic centers, work-training centers, and sheltered workshops to serve the children who were being cared for at home; they worked to get these services, which are now being provided in increasing numbers. But the needs are a long way from being fully met.

Yet even now the cost in money—not to mention the cost in human terms—is much less if the child is kept at home than if he is sent to the institutions in which children are put away. And many of the retarded are living useful and independent lives, which would never have been thought possible for them.

But for us at that time, as for other parents who were unknowingly pioneering new ways for the retarded, it was a matter of going along from day to day, learning, observing, and saying, "Let's see." . . .

Our daughter, Wynne, is now twenty-five. She started as Mark's baby sister, passed him in every way, and really helped bring him up. The fact that she had a retarded brother must have contributed at least something to the fact that she is at once delightfully playful and mature, observant, and understanding. She has a fine relationship with her two brothers.

Both Wynne and Alan, Mark's older brother, have participated, with patience and delight, in Mark's development. They have shown remarkable ingenuity in instructing and amusing him. On one occasion, when Mark was not drinking his milk, Alan called him to his place at the table and said, "I'm a service station. What kind of car are you?" Mark, quickly entering into the make-believe, said, "Pord."

Alan: "Shall I fill her up?"

Mark: "Yes."

Alan: "Ethyl or regular?"

Mark: "Reg'lar."

Alan (bringing the glass to Mark's mouth): "Here you are."

When Mark finished his glass of milk, Alan asked him, "Do you want your windshield cleaned?" Then, taking a napkin, he rubbed it briskly across Mark's face, while Mark grinned with delight. This routine became a regular game for many weeks.

Alan and Wynne interpret and explain Mark to their friends, but never once have I heard them apologize for him or deprecate him. It is almost as if they judge the quality of other people by how they react to Mark. They think he is "great," and expect their friends to think so too. . . .

What does [the] future hold for Mark?

He will never be able to be independent; he will always have to live in a protected environment. His below-50 IQ reflects the fact that he cannot cope with unfamiliar situations.

Like most parents of the retarded, we are concentrating on providing financial security for Mark in the future, and fortunately we expect to be able to achieve this. Alan and his wife and Wynne have all offered to be guardians for Mark. It is wonderful to know they feel this way. But we hope that Mark can find a happy place in one of the new residence homes for the retarded.

The residence home is something new and promising and it fills an enormous need. It is somewhat like a club, or a family, with a house-mother or manager. The residents share the work around the house, go out to work if they can, share in recreation and companionship. Away from their families, who may be overprotective and not aware of how much the retarded can do for themselves (are we not guilty of this, too!), they are able to live more fully as adults.

An indication that there is still much need for public education about the retarded here in California is that there has been difficulty in renting decent houses for this kind of home. Prospective neighbors have objected. In some ways the Dark Ages are still with us; there are still fear and hostility where the retarded are concerned.

Is Mark able to work? Perhaps. He thrives on routine and enjoys things others despise, like clearing the table and loading the dishwasher. To Mark, it's fun. It has been hard to develop in him the idea of work, which to so many of us is "doing what you don't want to do because you have to." We don't know yet if he could work in a restaurant loading a dishwasher. In school, he learned jobs like sorting and stacking scrap wood and operating a delightful machine that swoops the string around and ties up a bundle of wood to be sold in the supermarket. That's fun, too.

He is now in a sheltered workshop where he can get the kind—the one kind—of pleasure he doesn't have much chance for. That's the pleasure of contributing something productive and useful to the outside world. He does various kinds of assembling jobs, packaging, sorting, and simple machine operations. He enjoys getting a paycheck and cashing it at the bank. He cannot count, but he takes pride in reaching for the check in a restaurant and pulling out his wallet. And when we thank him for dinner, he glows with pleasure.

It's a strange thing to say, and I am a little startled to find myself saying it, but often I feel that I wouldn't have had Mark any different.

Note: This selection is written by Richard Vigil.

I'm twenty-nine years old now, and I like the place I live and I like my job. I have a girlfriend, and I love her very much. I hope that we can get married someday, but we have a lot of work to do first, mostly work about how to handle money and take care of an apartment.

I live in a group home, and I am learning a lot about those things now. I have to try things over and over and over again, but I don't remember ever trying to learn something and finding out that I couldn't learn it. Except playing the piano. I just couldn't do it, but I am going to try again someday. It takes a long time for me to learn something, but I just keep on trying.

When I was a little kid I lived in an institution. I hated it. I especially hated this one teacher in the school there who told me that I couldn't learn. I thought I was in the school to learn, and I thought the teacher should help me instead of telling me that I couldn't do it. I told my parents when they came to visit me, and they got angry with the teacher. After that I got a chance to show her that I could learn things.

But I hated living there, and I ran away when I was older. I ran away more than once. They can't make me stay there. I won't live there because I don't like it and I don't think I have to.

I feel free the way I live now. I go to work, I come back to the group home. I can go to see my girlfriend. Or I can go out to the movies. I get all around on the bus. I learned to ride the buses when I was in a sheltered workshop. They taught me. If I want to go someplace I've never been before I call the bus company offices and ask how to get there. Then I just try it out. Or I ask the bus drivers. Some are nice and some aren't. I don't get lost very often.

One of my favorite things to do is to go downtown at Christmas and see the parade and all the Christmas decorations. I know that they're for little kids, but I see a lot of grownups down there too. I really love Christmas. That was the happiest time I remember with my family. I don't see my family anymore. I miss them. I know that my mother didn't want to send me away, but I think that my brothers and sisters didn't want me around because they thought I couldn't learn anything.

I don't like to be called "retarded" because it means something bad to most people. I know it just means "slow-learning," but it doesn't mean anything to me in my own situation. What is M.R. anyway? It's just another word. We might be slow learners, but we're just as good as anybody.

I hope I have a kid someday. I really love kids, and I'd do anything to help them. If I had a retarded kid I'd love him and help him to learn things because I'd do anything in the world to help little kids. I think I would be a good father because I'd love my kid.

Response and Analysis

1. In what ways has Mark positively contributed to his family? How do Mark's siblings treat him? S. I. Hayakawa suggests that the public has had misconceptions about mental retardation. What are some of them?

2. People with IQ scores between 50 and 70 are considered mildly retarded, and those with scores between 35 and 49 are considered moderately retarded. People with IQ scores less than 70 may have difficulty communicating and performing tasks that are expected of people their age. Mark's IQ score is less than 50. Briefly discuss Mark's ability to perform tasks, communicate, and live on his own.

Personal Experience and Application

1. Were you ever chided or laughed at if you did not learn something fast enough to suit someone else? If so, how did that make you feel? Why do you think children, and even adults, sometimes make fun of people or deride them if they do not learn quickly?

2. Richard dreams of getting married and having a child of his own. What factors are important to consider in deciding about marriage? About having a child?

Research

Suppose you develop a test to assess verbal skills (for example, the ability to define words, the ability to understand and answer questions). You want to know if the test is reliable. You individually test twenty children who are six years old. Two weeks later, you readminister the same test to the same children. You find that the scores were higher for all of the children on the second test than on the first test. Why might this have occurred? How might it affect your judgment about the test's reliability?

THE SPATIAL CHILD

John Philo Dixon

Psychological Concepts
special abilities, verbal and quantitative ability

John Philo Dixon, now the research director for the American Shakespeare Theater, recalls how not being a good reader made him feel inadequate. His first grade teacher threatened to hold him back from second grade and children teased him about his reading ability. These experiences had a negative effect on his self-esteem. Although he became more comfortable with reading in later years, he had few academic successes during his elementary and middle school years. Finally, in ninth grade, Dixon realized that he had a special talent for math—a talent that for too long had gone unrecognized. To what extent did motivation and desire influence Dixon's ultimate achievements in school? How do various approaches to intelligence recognize special abilities in children?

It was a combination of mystification and depression that set in when Mrs. Wilson struggled at introducing me to reading in the first grade. As I looked around at my classmates, their ease at turning written words into the correct spoken words seemed to make them coconspirators. They possessed a secret wisdom to which I was not privy. Mrs. Wilson looked upon them with eyes of pleasure. They were her teacher's delight, her measure of success. She looked upon me with eyes of forlorn patience. I was the stumbling block in her attempt to deliver a class full of readers to the second grade teachers. I remember sitting bent low at my school desk, eyes downward, hoping not to be noticed as I bumbled over *Dick and Jane.*

Panic struck me when my mother had to visit school to talk about my difficulties. My mother had never had doubts about me. I could run, I could talk, I could play games, I could build things, I could sing—all those things that mark normalcy to a hopeful mother. Mrs. Wilson had found me defective, and I had become a problem child, even to those who were most dear to me. My mother's visit to Mrs. Wilson also caused terror in the confusion of my child's mind. I feared that my unused schemes to cheat on spelling tests—a strategic planning undertaken in the desire to avoid being lowest in the class—might have been found out. Perhaps Mrs. Wilson in her infinite wisdom could even read into the hearts of little boys. However, the conference had only to do with my incompetence. My mother sat beside Mrs. Wilson, and I sat at my desk across the otherwise empty room. My ears strained to hear bits and pieces of the litany of my problems. Mrs. Wilson concluded that I wasn't prepared to go on to second grade. Flunking was the ultimate stigma for a school child in rural Nebraska. It would have put my self-regard at the lowest of levels. To my everlasting gratitude, things weren't left at that. A deal was struck between Mrs. Wilson and my mother. I would only be allowed to enter second grade in the fall if my mother gave me special instruction in reading for the whole summer vacation. My mother's reading lessons had little more effect than those of Mrs. Wilson. I tried, but reading wasn't yet in me.

I entered second grade as much a nonreader as before, but thanked my lucky stars that I had made it, and braced for another year of being the uninformed outsider in a society of secret code decipherers. Sometime during the second grade I began to catch on to reading, and I don't remember being in serious threat of flunking after that. My school performance settled into the slow-poke category for most of elementary school. There were a few breaks in this eight-year stint of questionable reputation. There was the day the second grade teacher asked several students to make a line a yard long on the chalkboard without looking at the yard stick. Mine came closest to being the right length. The teacher hardly noticed this insignificant victory of one of her more unpromising students, but for me it was one of those rare triumphs that stands etched in my mind.

My third grade teacher told my mother there was a lot going on in my mind. How did she guess? In the small town in which I grew up, the "farmerish" wisdom of silence would occasionally be applied to me; more than a few times people would take note of my basically unspoken character and say, "Still water runs deep." I never did know how to take that. Was deep good or bad?

There was the week in Miss Reine's fourth grade class. I was allowed to help construct a model colonial village. I made houses, a stockade, and an intricate little spinning wheel. It was the most glorious week in elementary school. As far as I was concerned, it could have gone on forever. However, then it was necessary to move on to the "real" work of school. Miss Reine told me that I couldn't work on the model any more because I had spent too much time and gotten behind in my school work.

Throughout these eight years there was an interesting discrepancy. Although my reading never changed from a slow to halting pace, I nevertheless loved reading. Sometimes I would spend every minute possible devouring whole sets of books from the library bookcase in the back of the classroom; slowly, ruminatingly, but devouring. There was no way my reading could be rushed. Deep twinges of anguish accompanied speed reading drills. I would pretend to be reading faster than I could because I didn't want to be the last student to raise his hand to indicate being finished. Most of all I hated reading tests. If I didn't rush through tests much faster than I could possibly comprehend the material, I would find myself far from the end of the test when the time was called. Yet there were times when I spent all the time I could reading. Books were the entry way to the larger world. The ideas in books were marvelous even if my reading mechanics were tortuous. The ideas in books came to be an important focus of my life, and I would learn to put up with the difficulty for the sake of learning.

Crude drawing was something I did through my childhood, even though I don't remember ever having an art class or being encouraged in any way. In the early grades I would draw what I thought of as the structures of buildings; the beam patterns of skyscrapers and things like that. I was sort of embarrassed for doing these sketches because I didn't know why I wanted to. . . . I just did. Later I took up making crude architectural plans for buildings. I enjoyed music, sang in the chorus, and played different instruments in the band. Music was in me, and if I weren't so shy, I might have been a good musical performer, although I never learned to read music very well.

When I entered algebra class in the ninth grade, the long depression of elementary school ended. Algebra was fascinating to me from the moment I encountered it. In algebra I was the best in my class, and it wasn't just a momentary triumph like when I drew the most accurate length of a yard stick in second grade. My triumph in algebra stuck. In geometry and physics, I was even better. For the physics class in eleventh grade my school was participating in a statewide experiment to see whether instruction through a set of movies was better than regular instruction. My school had regular instruction and my teacher, Mr. Kasle, was good. As a part of the experiment, every other week we would take a special test, which would be sent to a university for scoring. When the scores came back, I would be several points above anyone else in the class. Having lived through the nightmare of the elementary school, I savored every moment of these victories, but savored them in trepidation that they were somehow a fluke, in fear that my incompetencies would descend upon me and I would once again fail. I live in fear of that to this day. It is not easy to free oneself of eight years of degradation when it is experienced at an age too young to have had a chance to know that success is also possible.

Sometime in the ninth grade my class was given a nonverbal IQ test. I don't know exactly how I scored on this test, but there were hints that I had done very well, and after the testing, I was accorded much more respect by my school teachers than before. Had the IQ test been a verbal one, the results, of course, would have been entirely opposite and I would have been seen as anything but brilliant.

There was no program for gifted children in the high school, but the teachers seemed to sense my need and arranged for me to take a correspondence course in advanced algebra. I received a text book in the mail along with my first assignment. I would do my assignments, send them off to the university, and receive them back corrected along with the next assignment. This solitary exercise in doing lists of algebra problems for a disembodied tutor did little to spark my imagination. Though I appreciate the good intention on my behalf in making this arrangement, I would most likely have been better off spending some extra time with Mr. Kasle, the local science teacher who seemed to have a good scientific mind.

The discrepancies in my abilities have persisted. When I took the Graduate Record Exams (GRE) at the completion of undergraduate school, my mathematics score was in the top 2 percent, while my verbal score was just barely in the top quarter. This difference has continually resulted in what to others may seem like an uneven performance. To the extent that tasks depend on a careful understanding of the spatial-mechanical world around me, I usually do quite well. To the extent that it depends on quick verbal analysis, my performance can seem debilitated.

As a child I thought of my problem as personal, and I endured it in silence. Now I cannot be so generous. I see no reason that children who have considerable ability of a distinct kind should be taught that they are inadequate, if not stupid.

Response and Analysis

1. Briefly summarize John Dixon's reading difficulties. What do his scores on the Graduate Record Exam suggest about his verbal and quantitative abilities? How did the validation of his mathematical and spatial ability affect his self-esteem? Why does Dixon fear that his success with mathematics and physics may be a "fluke"?

2. Which theoretical approach to intelligence argues for the presence of spatial intelligence? Briefly summarize this theoretical perspective.

Personal Experience and Application

1. What types of academic experiences in elementary or secondary school might cause some children to develop low self-esteem? How might these experiences affect an individual's sense of self when he or she becomes an adult?

2. What environmental factors do you think nourish or hinder intellectual development? Why?

Research

Suppose you want to know whether the gender of a test administrator influences a child's performance on an intelligence test. You hypothesize that children will receive higher IQ scores when the test is administered by someone of the same gender than by someone of the opposite gender. What is the research, or alternative, hypothesis? What is the null hypothesis? Imagine that you conduct the study and find that the children's scores are the same regardless of the test administrator's gender. Based on your finding, would you accept or reject the research hypothesis? Would you accept or reject the null hypothesis? Why or why not?

ASSESSMENT OF CHILDREN

Jerome M. Sattler

Psychological Concepts
intelligence, intelligence tests, assessment procedures

Psychologist Jerome Sattler, coauthor of the Stanford-Binet Intelligence Scale, fourth edition, discusses a case that shows how testing and psychological reports can affect people's lives. The case raises important questions. Does an individual's intelligence quotient (IQ) change? Should IQ be the only source of information to guide decisions concerning a child? In the second half of this selection, Sattler offers recommendations concerning the assessment of children, the use of labels, and the importance of considering ethnic and cultural diversity.

The case of *Daniel Hoffman* v. *the Board of Education of the City of New York* is instructive because it illustrates the important role that testing and psychological reports can play in people's lives. In this case, the report contained a recommendation that was ignored by the school administrators. Years later when the case was tried, the failure to follow the recommendations became a key issue.

Basis of Litigation

Daniel Hoffman, a twenty-six-year-old man, brought suit against the New York City Board of Education in 1978 to recover damages for injuries resulting from his placement in classes for the mentally retarded. The complaint alleged that (1) the Board was negligent in its original testing procedures and placement of Mr. Hoffman, causing or permitting him to be placed in an educational environment for mentally retarded children and consequently depriving him of adequate speech therapy that would have improved his only real handicap, a speech impediment; and (2) the Board was negligent in failing or refusing to follow adequate procedures for the recommended retesting of Mr. Hoffman's intelligence.

Board of Education's Position

The Board of Education took the position that Mr. Hoffman's IQ of 74, obtained on the Stanford-Binet Intelligence Scale when he was five years, nine months old, indicated that his placement in a class for the mentally retarded was appropriate. They contended that the test was proper, that it was administered by a competent and experienced psychologist, and that it was the unanimous professional judgment of Mr. Hoffman's teachers, based on their evaluation and his performance on standardized achievement tests, that a retest was not warranted. The Board made clear that at the time Mr. Hoffman was in school its policy was to retest only when retesting was recommended by teachers or requested by parents.

The psychological report was one of the key documents upon which the entire case rested. The psychologist had recommended that Mr. Hoffman be placed in a class for the mentally retarded on the basis of his IQ of 74. Mr. Hoffman entered special education classes and remained in them throughout his school years. However, the key sentence in the 1957 report was as follows: "*Also, his intelligence should be reevaluated within a two-year period so that a more accurate estimation of his abilities can be made*" (italics added).

The Board of Education argued that the psychologist did not literally mean "retesting" because he did not use this word in the report. Although a minority of the court concurred with this interpretation, the majority supported Mr. Hoffman's position that reevaluation meant only one thing—administration of another intelligence test.

Removal from Training Program

In a curious twist of fate, testing, which resulted in the assignment of Mr. Hoffman to special education, also played an important role in removing him from a special workshop program during his late teenage years. Mr. Hoffman had made poor progress during his school years, and there had been no significant change in his severe speech defect. At the age of seventeen years, he entered a sheltered workshop for retarded youths. After a few months in the program, he was given the Wechsler Adult Intelligence Scale and obtained a Verbal Scale IQ of 85, a Performance Scale IQ of 107, and a Full Scale IQ of 94. His overall functioning was in the Normal range. On the basis of these findings, Mr. Hoffman was not permitted to remain at the Occupational Training Center. On learning of this decision, he became depressed, often staying in his room at home with the door closed.

Mr. Hoffman then received assistance from the Division of Vocational Rehabilitation. At the age of twenty-one, he was trained to be a messenger, but he did not like this work. At the time of the trial, he had obtained no further training or education, had not made any advancement in his vocational life, and had not improved his social life.

Inadequate Assessment Procedures

During the trial it was shown that the psychologist who tested Mr. Hoffman in kindergarten had failed (1) to interview Mrs. Hoffman, (2) to obtain a social history, and (3) to discuss the results of the evaluation with her. If a history had been obtained, the psychologist would have learned that Mr. Hoffman had been tested ten months previously at the National Hospital for Speech Disorders and had obtained an IQ of 90 on the Merrill-Palmer Scale of Mental Tests.

Verdict and Appeals

The case was initially tried before a jury, which returned a verdict in favor of Mr. Hoffman, awarding him damages of $750,000. This decision was appealed to the Appellate Division of the New York State Supreme Court, which affirmed the jury verdict on November 6, 1978, but lowered damages to $500,000. The New York State Appeals Court overturned the Appellate Court's decision, including the original award, on December 17, 1979, finding that the court system was not the proper arena for testing the validity of educational decisions or for second guessing such decisions.

The Importance of the Case for the Practice of School and Clinical Psychology

The case of *Daniel Hoffman* v. *the Board of Education of the City of New York* is one of the first cases in which the courts carefully scrutinized psychological reports and the process of special education placement. The case touches on many important issues involved in the psychoeducational assessment process. Let us consider some of these issues.

1. *Psychological reports do count.* Psychological reports are key documents used by mental health professionals, teachers, administrators, physicians, courts, parents, and children.
2. *Words can be misinterpreted.* A pivotal point in the case was the meaning of the words "reevaluate" and "retest." Some participants in the case, as well as some justices, assigned these words different meanings. Therefore, careful attention must be given to the wording of reports. Reports must be written clearly, with findings and recommendations stated as precisely as possible.
3. *IQs change.* Children's IQs do not remain static. Although there is a certain stability after children reach six years of age, their IQs do change.
4. *Different tests may provide different IQs.* The three IQs obtained by Mr. Hoffman at five, six, and eighteen years of age may reflect differences in the content and standardization of the three tests rather than genuine changes in cognitive performance.
5. *Placement decisions must be based on more than one assessment approach.* A battery of psychological tests and procedures, along with interviews with parents and reports from teachers, should be used in the assessment process. All available information should be reviewed before placement recommendations are made.
6. *The instruments used must be appropriate.* A child who has a speech or language handicap may need to be assessed with performance tests in addition to, or in place of, verbal tests.
7. *Previous findings must be reviewed.* Before the formal assessment is carried out, the assessor must determine whether the child has been previously tested and, if so, review these findings.

Although many issues were involved in the case of Daniel Hoffman, the preceding points are particularly germane to the practice of school and clinical psychology. They illustrate that psychological evaluation, including the formulation of recommendations, requires a high level of competence. The case also demonstrates that it is incumbent on administrators to carry out the psychologist's recommendations.

Note: The citations for this case are 410 N.Y.S.2d 99 and 400 N.E.2d 317–49 N.Y.2d 121.

Guidelines for Assessment

The assessment process should never focus exclusively on a test score or a number. Each child has a range of competencies that can be evaluated by both quantitative and qualitative means. [The aim of a school psychologist] is to assess the competencies as well as the limitations of the child; the focus should not be on handicaps solely or on areas of weakness. The following principles form an important foundation for the clinical and psychoeducational use of tests.

- Tests are samples of behavior.
- Tests do not directly reveal traits or capacities, but may allow inferences to be made about the examinee.
- Tests should have adequate reliability and validity.
- Test scores and other test performances may be adversely affected by temporary states of fatigue, anxiety, or stress; by disturbances in temperament or personality; or by brain damage.
- Test results should be interpreted in light of the child's cultural background, primary language, and any handicapping conditions.
- Test results are dependent on the child's cooperation and motivation.
- Tests purporting to measure the same ability may produce different scores for that ability.
- Test results should be interpreted in relation to other behavioral data and to case history information, never in isolation.

Tests and other assessment procedures are powerful tools, but their effectiveness will depend on . . . skill and knowledge. When wisely and cautiously used, assessment procedures can assist . . . in helping children, parents, teachers, and other professionals obtain valuable insights. When used inappropriately, they can mislead those who must make important life decisions, thus causing harm and grief. As we saw in the case of Daniel Hoffman, . . . assessment results do have an impact on many people, directly affecting the lives of children and their parents. As a result of clinical and psychoeducational evaluations, actions are taken and critical decisions are made.

Labels and Classification

The study of intelligence . . . should leave [us] with a sense of wonder. We still know relatively little about how information is processed, stored, and retrieved; how differing environments affect learning; and how intellectual growth is best nourished. Consequently, . . . [we must] be mindful of the labels and classifications that [are] use[d] to categorize children, recognizing and respecting their resiliency. Do not expect children who receive the same label to perform in the same ways. Mentally retarded children, for example, differ in their abilities, learning styles, and temperaments. [We] may be surprised at their intelligence and humanity if you view these children without preconceptions. Although labels are important in the assessment process, you must not allow labels to regiment and restrict the ways you observe . . . each individual child.

The Need to Consider Ethnic and Cultural Diversity

However much we subscribe to the philosophy that well-normed standardized tests provide one of the most important means of assessment, we also must recognize the cultural diversity of children. Children come . . . from many different ethnic and cultural backgrounds, and these differing backgrounds must be considered in selection of tests and interpretation of norms. We have, on the one hand, forces that are continuously molding us into a more homogeneous society. On the other hand, subtle and not so subtle differences set apart the various ethnic groups in our country, including differences in language dialects and in patterns of family interaction. Such differences among blacks, whites, Hispanic-Americans, native Americans, and Asian Americans, for example, may affect the kinds of knowledge acquired by children. These ethnic differences must be considered in interpreting test results and in working with children and their families.

Response to the Attack on Tests

The past fifteen years have seen numerous attacks on the use of tests. Accusations have arisen from ethnic minority groups that standardized tests used to allocate limited educational resources penalized children whose family, socioeconomic status, and cultural experiences were different from those of white, middle-class normative groups. The very foundations of assessment practices have been questioned, including the tools that are used and the situations in which they are administered. Some critics maintain that intelligence tests and achievement tests are culturally biased and thus harmful to black children and other ethnic minority children. Others believe that many of the activities of school and clinical child psychologists are not in the best interests of the child. These activities include labeling children, testing children without their permission and without giving them full knowledge of the possible consequences of testing, and moving children from regular classrooms to potentially damaging special classes. Courts have issued decisions limiting the freedom of psychologists to use and select tests for evaluation and placement decisions.

Many critics fail to consider that tests have many valid uses. Tests allow for accountability, for measurement of change, and for evaluation of program effectiveness. As a result of testing, children gain access to special programs, which can contribute to their educational experiences. Tests are a standard for evaluating the extent to which children of all ethnic groups have learned the basic cognitive and academic skills necessary for survival in our culture. Few of the critics have proposed reasonable alternatives to present methods.

Although I believe that fundamentally the criticisms of testing have little merit because they are not based on research evidence and fail to consider current assessment practices, these attacks have uncovered some serious shortcomings in assessment practices. Labeling a Spanish-speaking child who does not speak English as mentally retarded, based on the results of an English-language verbal intelligence test, reflects incompetence on the part of the examiner. To keep poor records of parental permissions authorizing evaluations is shoddy practice, and to administer tests without seeking permission is entirely unethical. These and other such practices must not continue.

[Professionals] are accountable . . . to the children [they] serve, to their parents, to the schools, and to the larger community. We must not ignore the many valid criticisms of tests and test practices simply because we do not like them. We must continue to develop procedures and instruments that will better serve . . . clients. Procedures now available to protect . . . clients must be adhered to scrupulously. Although none of us like having our shortcomings pointed out, especially in public, we must listen to our critics and make sure that we are following the best scientific and clinical practices. I believe that the discord of the seventies and early eighties has had a cleansing and beneficial effect.

Response and Analysis

1. Why should the assessment process never rely solely on one test score or number? What guidelines should be followed when using intelligence and special ability tests? Which of these guidelines were followed in the case of *Daniel Hoffman* v. *the Board of Education of the City of New York?*

2. Why has testing been criticized? How has it been defended? Why should school psychologists consider ethnic and cultural diversity in the selection and interpretation of tests?

Personal Experience and Application

1. What do you think are the major strengths of intelligence tests? The major weaknesses?

What recommendations would you offer to improve these tests? Why?

2. Have you taken an intelligence test? Describe your experience. Do you think the results reflected your level of intelligence? Why or why not?

Research

Suppose you have developed a new subscale for an intelligence test. You want to know if it is reliable (i.e., if the test is repeated, would it have the same results?). How could you assess its reliability?

chapter 9

MOTIVATION AND EMOTION

Itzaak Perlman, born to an unmusical family in Israel, is said to have heard, at age three, a broadcast of a concerto being played by Jascha Heifetz. He kept pointing to the radio when the violin was heard, saying "I want that!" until his parents understood; they enrolled him with a private tutor to learn to play the instrument. Despite having become partly paralyzed, Perlman is considered one of the great virtuosi of his time.

MIHALY CSIKSZENTMIHALYI, *Talented Teenagers*

What motivates us? What is the connection between emotion and motivation? Several key concepts help us understand this connection: the desire to belong, hierarchy of needs, and personal tragedy.

In the first selection, Christopher Reeve tells of his life since he was thrown from his horse and suffered a spinal cord injury that left him a quadriplegic. Since the accident, Reeve has been admired for the heroic way he has continued to live. In spite of enormous obstacles, he is highly motivated to live as normal a life as possible. He exercises regularly to keep the muscles in his body from atrophying, and he continues to act in and direct films. Several factors motivate Reeve to work so hard—among them are the love of his wife and family and his hope that eventually surgery will enable him to walk again.

In the next selection, D. H. shows how an intense desire to belong can sometimes be harmful. He was eager to be admired by his high school classmates and was willing to take certain risks to gain that admiration. Believing that being a football

181

hero would quash his feelings of inferiority, D. H. was willing to take steroids to increase his muscularity. The drug, however, had serious consequences for him both psychologically and physically.

Sally, an attractive and successful businesswoman, tells her story of obsession with food and with being thin. She develops bulimia nervosa and tries to hide her condition from family and friends. Eventually, she is caught between her desire to be thin and her desire to restore her health.

Daniel Goleman shows how motivation and emotion are instrumental in being creative and in working at one's highest capacity. When people are excited about and completely absorbed in their work, they may be in a state of flow. The word *flow*, used by psychologist Mihaly Csikszentmihalyi, describes those times when people are at one with the task at hand and often experience moments of ecstasy.

STILL ME

Christopher Reeve

Psychological Concepts
sources of motivation, emotion

In the spring of 1995, while riding in a competition, actor Christopher Reeve was thrown from his horse. That fall caused a spinal cord injury and left him a quadriplegic. Through the determination of his wife and family, and especially through Reeve's own tenacity, he has continued a creative life. He received an Emmy nomination for his work as director on the film *In the Gloaming*, raises funds for research on spinal cord injuries, and gives inspiring talks to various groups throughout the country. In this selection, Reeve tells something of his daily routine (with the help of aides, it may take as long as three hours to get him dressed in the morning) and of his emotional reactions to what has happened. He also discusses what motivates him to continue living and to remain active. In Reeve, we discover the meaning of the word "heroic."

The door to our bedroom slides open, and Will comes in just as it's light enough to make out the trees above our skylight. He knows I can't speak to him because my trach has been inflated for the night, cutting off the air to my vocal cords. He waves to me, and I make a clicking sound in return as he passes by and jumps on Dana's bed, telling her it's time to get up and play floor hockey. They go out together, and soon I hear Will's play-by-play of the action as he and Dana go one-on-one with plastic golf clubs for sticks and a bottle top for a puck in the family room down the hall. It's just past six o'clock, too late to go back to sleep. Sometimes I try to doze, but mostly I watch the trees taking shape above me and prepare myself for the day.

Will continues playing hockey by himself while Dana makes him breakfast and the lunch he takes to school. At eight the nurse and aide on the morning shift come in. The nurse counts out my twenty pills, which I take in one swallow of cranberry juice: some are vitamins, some are to help control my spasms, the rest are to keep my bladder from shrinking and to maintain the proper functioning of my bowels. I treat myself to a single cup of coffee, which I drink all at once through a straw, and then we begin the painful process of moving my body from the position I've been in all night.

My joints and muscles are frozen, and I can barely turn my head because my neck is so stiff. Usually I have a tingling, burning sensation in both legs and pain behind my left knee where the blood clots were. I sleep with splints on both feet to prevent foot drop; if the tendons and ligaments are not flexed and are allowed to atrophy, it will never be possible to stand or walk. There are splints on my arms, too, which keep my fingers in a natural position. Otherwise they would clench into fists and ultimately never straighten out.

Once everything is removed I am rolled onto my back. But my body rebels no matter how gently they try to move me; my arms and legs flail wildly, and my chest tightens, making it difficult to breathe. The nurse turns on the oxygen that is always ready at the bedside. Because my muscles are still strong, it often takes the full weight of both the nurse and the aide to control these spasms and force my body to lie still. . . .

Even on days when I can stay at home, getting dressed takes time and, more important, the ability to accept not being able to do any of it by myself. When two people have to roll you back and forth in order to put on your underpants at age forty-five, it's a difficult lesson in patience and acceptance. I pick out my wardrobe, but I have no choice about one part of it: to promote better circulation in my legs, I always have to wear the hated T.E.D. hose. Finally I'm ready to be lifted into the chair. The entire ordeal of getting up can take as much as three hours. . . .

When I'm not on a tight schedule, I always do some kind of exercise as part of the morning ritual. We keep a chart of each day's activities so that every muscle group is worked equally. Apart from the physical benefits, I have found that exercising the body helps me focus on the future. No matter what kind of mood I'm in, I always make myself do something that will help prevent my physical condition from deteriorating. It's just like the first few months of 1977, when I was training for *Superman* and told my driver to take me to the gym even if I said I wanted to go home. Once I was there, there was nothing to do but change into my workout clothes and start lifting weights.

Now, facing muscle atrophy, loss of bone density, osteoporosis, and all the other side effects of a spinal cord injury, I use the same technique—only I'm the driver. There's no one standing over me cracking a whip, nothing to prevent me from lying in bed until late in the morning. I have to reply on self-discipline and faith, although my faith is based on science rather than religion. The very real possibility that an injured spinal cord can be repaired is a testimony to the dedication, perseverance, compassion, and skill of a few great minds. The least I can do is try to match their dedication as they achieve the seemingly impossible in the laboratory. I have faith that they will succeed, in spite of the fact that there is no certainty.

The morning routine of dressing and exercise is usually finished by eleven o'clock. I eat a light breakfast of cereal or a piece of toast with tea, and occasionally an omelet to keep my protein levels up. Sometimes I wish that I still couldn't stand food, because it's extremely difficult to stay thin. I often joke with Dana and the nurses about the weight I put on in the spring of '97. I remind them that in the pictures of me receiving my star on the Hollywood Walk of Fame I look like Marlon Brando—and not the Marlon Brando from *Streetcar* or *On the Waterfront*. . . .

People often ask me what it's like to have sustained a spinal cord injury and be confined to a wheelchair. Apart from all the medical complications, I would say the worst part of it is leaving the physical world—having had to make the transition from participant to observer long before I would have expected. I think most of us are prepared to give up cherished physical activities gradually as we age. I certainly wouldn't be competing in combined training events in my sixties or skiing nearly as fast as I used to. If I went sailing in my later years I wouldn't go single-handed. Stronger arms and more agile bodies would be needed to raise and trim the sails or steer in a heavy sea.

The difference is that I would have had time to prepare for other ways of enjoying the things I love to do most. But to have it all change and have most of it taken away at age forty-two is devastating. As much as I remind myself that being is more important than doing, that the quality of relationships is the key to happiness, I'm actually putting on a brave face. I do believe those things are true, but I miss freedom, spontaneity, action, and adventure more than I can say. Sometimes when we're up in Williamstown I sit out on the deck looking across our pastures to Mount Greylock, and I remember how I used to be a part of it. We hiked up the mountain, swam in the streams, rode our horses across the open fields, chopped our own Christmas tree from the woods above the house. Now it's just scenery—still beautiful, but almost as if cordoned off behind velvet ropes. I feel like a visitor at a spectacular outdoor museum. . . .

When the first Superman movie came out, I gave dozens of interviews to promote it. The most frequently asked question was: "What is a hero?" I remember how easily I'd talk about it, the glib response I repeated so many times. My answer was that a hero is someone who commits a courageous action without considering the consequences. A soldier who crawls out of a foxhole to drag an injured buddy back to safety, the prisoners of war who never stop trying to escape even though they know they may be executed if they're caught. And I also meant individuals who are slightly larger than life: Houdini and Lindbergh of course, John Wayne and JFK, and even sports figures who have taken on mythical proportions, such as Babe Ruth or Joe DiMaggio.

Now my definition is completely different. I think a hero is an ordinary individual who finds the strength to persevere and endure in spite of overwhelming obstacles. The fifteen-year-old boy down the hall at Kessler who had landed on his head while wrestling with his brother, leaving him paralyzed and barely able to swallow or speak. Travis Roy, paralyzed in the first eleven seconds of a hockey game in his freshman year at college. Henry Steifel, paralyzed from the chest down in a car accident at seventeen, completing his education and working on Wall Street at age thirty-two, but having missed so much of what life has to offer. These are real heroes, and so are the families and friends who have stood by them.

At UVA and at Kessler, I always kept the picture of the Pyramid of Quetzalcoatl in front of me. I would look at the hundreds of steps leading up to the clouds and imagine myself climbing slowly but surely to the top. That desire sustained me in the early days after my injury, but during the next couple of years I had to learn to face the reality: you manage to climb one or two steps, but then something happens and you fall back three. The worst of it is the unpredictability. Several times

I've made a commitment to appear at a function or give a speech, but the night before, or even that morning, a skin tear, or dysreflexia, or a lung infection suddenly developed and I had to go to the hospital instead.

Climbing up the steps, I've appeared at the Oscars, spoken at the Democratic Convention, directed a film, written this book, worked on political issues, and traveled more extensively than most high-level quadriplegics. But, falling backwards, I've been hospitalized eleven times for dysreflexia, pneumonia, a collapsed lung, a broken arm, two blood clots, a possible hip fracture, and the infection in my left ankle that nearly resulted in the partial amputation of my leg.

I was told by so many "experts"—doctors, psychologists, physical therapists, other patients, and well-meaning friends and family members—that as time went by not only would I become more stable physically but I would become well adjusted psychologically to my condition. I have found exactly the opposite to be true. The longer you sit in a wheelchair, the more the body breaks down and the harder you have to fight against it. Psychologically, I feel I have established a workable baseline: I have my down days, but I haven't been incapacitated by them. This doesn't mean, though, that I accept paralysis, or that I'm at peace with it.

The sensory deprivation hurts the most: I haven't been able to give Will a hug since he was two years old, and now he's five and a half. This is the reason Dana and I decided not to have another child; it would be too painful not to be able to hold and embrace this little creature the way I did with the others. The physical world is still very meaningful to me; I have not been able to detach myself from it and live entirely in my mind. While I believe it's true that we are not our bodies, that our bodies are like houses we live in while we're here on earth, that concept is more of an intellectual construct than a philosophy I can live by on a daily basis. I'm jealous when someone talks about a recent skiing vacation, when friends embrace each other, or even when Will plays hockey in the driveway with someone else.

If someone were to ask me what is the most difficult lesson I've learned from all this, I'm very clear about it: I know I have to give when sometimes I really want to take. I've realized instinctively that it's part of my job as a father now not to cause Will to worry about me. If I were to give in to self-pity or express my anger in front of him, it would place an unfair burden on this carefree five-year-old. If I were to turn inward and spend my time mourning the past, I couldn't be as close to Matthew and Alexandra, two teenagers who naturally need to turn to me for advice. And what kind of life would it be for Dana if I let myself go and became just a depressed hulk in a wheelchair? All of this takes effort on my part, because it's still very difficult to accept the turn my life has taken, simply because of one unlucky moment. . . .

At forty-two, still in my prime, I took it for granted that I could look forward to many peak experiences in every aspect of my life. I rarely if ever looked back, because the present was so rich and full of promise. But now, in spite of the pain it causes me, I can't help dwelling on the fact that so many wonderful moments are receding in the distance. . . .

I have to take the key to acting and apply it to my life. There is no other way to survive except to be in the moment. Just as my accident and its aftermath caused me to redefine what a hero is, I've had to take a hard look at what it means to live as fully as possible in the present.

Response and Analysis

1. How do you feel after reading this selection? Why do you feel this way? Where do you think Christopher Reeve's motivation comes from? From biological factors? Emotional factors? Cognitive factors? Social factors? Why?

2. How does Reeve demonstrate self-discipline? How is self-discipline bound to his motivation?

Personal Experience and Application

1. Reeve discusses his changing view of a hero. How would you define a hero or heroine? Make a list of people you consider heroes and heroines. What common thread makes all those on your list worthy of being called hero or heroine? What do you think motivates people to act in a heroic way?

2. Alcoholics Anonymous (AA) has a wise credo: "God grant me the serenity to accept that which I cannot change, the courage to change that which I can, and the wisdom to know the difference." Though Reeve does not refer to AA, in what ways is Reeve's approach similar to this philosophical view?

Research

Suppose you are interested in conducting a study to find out what motivates individuals to act in a way that others consider to be heroic. You ask students in your introductory psychology class to list two people they know that they consider to be heroes. You then contact each person. After securing their permission to participate, you send them a questionnaire asking them to discuss the factors that motivated them to act in "a heroic way." Would this approach be a good way to assess motivation? Would it be reliable? Why or why not? How else might you assess motivation?

DYING TO BE BIGGER

D. H.

Psychological Concepts
hormones, testosterone

What motivates a person to achieve a goal even at the risk of endangering his or her health? At fifteen years of age, D. H. is so determined to be a football star that he uses steroids to increase his size and prowess. Ignoring the prescribed dosage, he swallows five pills a day. Within weeks, D. H. notices unpleasant physical and emotional changes; he eventually becomes overly aggressive and, as his condition worsens, almost sterile. With the help of his parents, D. H. quits using steroids for a year. But what happens when he enters college and has as his roommate a six-foot-three, 250-pound linebacker? What adjustment problems does he experience after he quits taking steroids?

I was only fifteen years old when I first started maiming my body with the abuse of anabolic steroids. I was always trying to fit in with the "cool" crowd in junior high and high school. Willingly smoking or buying pot when offered, socially drinking in excess, displaying a macho image—and, of course, the infamous "kiss and tell" were essentials in completing my insecure mentality.

Being an immature, cocky kid from a somewhat wealthy family, I wasn't very well liked in general. In light of this, I got beat up a lot, especially in my first year of public high school.

I was one of only three sophomores to get a varsity letter in football. At five-foot-nine and 174 pounds, I was muscularly inferior to the guys on the same athletic level and quite conscious of the fact. So when I heard about this wonderful drug called steroids from a teammate, I didn't think twice about asking to buy some. I could hardly wait to take them and start getting bigger.

I bought three months' worth of Dianobol (an oral form of steroids and one of the most harmful). I paid fifty-five dollars. I was told to take maybe two or three per day. I totally ignored the directions and warnings and immediately started taking five per day. This is how eager I was to be bigger and possibly "cooler."

Within only a week, everything about me started to change. I was transforming mentally and physically. My attention span became almost nonexistent. Along with becoming extremely aggressive, I began to abandon nearly all academic and family responsibilities. In almost no time, I became flustered and agitated with simple everyday activities. My narcissistic ways brought me to engage in verbal as well as physical fights with family, friends, teachers, but mostly strangers.

My bodily transformations were clearly visible. In less than a month, I took the entire three-month supply. I gained nearly thirty pounds. Most of my weight was from water retention, although at the time I believed it to be muscle. Instead of having pimples like the average teenager, my acne took the form of grotesque, cystlike blood clots that would occasionally burst while I was lifting weights. My nipples became the size of grapes and hurt severely, which is common among male steroid users. My hormonal level was completely out of whack.

At first I had such an overload of testosterone that I would have to masturbate daily, at minimum, in order to prevent having "wet dreams." Obviously these factors enhanced my lust, which eventually led to acute perversion. My then almost-horrifying physique prevented me from having any sexual encounters.

All of these factors led to my classification as a wretched menace. My parents grew sick and tired of all the trouble I began to get in. They were scared of me, it seemed. They cared so much about my welfare, education, and state of mind that they sent me to a boarding school that summer.

I could not obtain any more steroids there, and for a couple of months it seemed I had subtle withdrawal symptoms and severe side effects. Most of the time that summer I was either depressed or filled with intense anger, both of which were uncontrollable unless I was in a state of intoxication from any mind-altering drug.

After a year of being steroid-free, things started to look promising for me, and I eventually gained control over myself. Just when I started getting letters from big-name colleges to play football for them, I suffered a herniated disc. I was unable to participate in any form of physical activity the entire school year.

In the fall, I attended a university in the Northeast, where I was on the football team but did not play due to my injury. I lifted weights with the team every day. I wasn't very big at the time, even after many weeks of working out. Once again I found myself to be physically inferior and insecure about my physique. And again came into contact with many teammates using steroids.

My roommate was a six-foot-three, 250-pound linebacker who played on the varsity squad as a freshman. As the weeks passed, I learned of my roommate's heavy steroid use. I was exposed to dozens of different steroids I had never even heard of. Living in the same room with him, I watched his almost daily injections. After months of enduring his drug offerings, I gave in.

By the spring of my freshman year, I had become drastically far from normal in every way. My body had stopped producing hormones due to the amount of synthetic testosterone I injected into my system. At five-foot-eleven, 225 pounds, disproportionately huge, acne-infested, outrageously aggressive, and nearing complete sterility, I was in a terrible state of body and mind. Normal thoughts of my future (not pertaining to football), friends, family, reputation, moral status, etc., were entirely beyond me. My whole entire essence had become one of a primitive barbarian. This was when I was taking something called Sustunon (prepackaged in a syringe labeled "For equine use only") containing four types of testosterone. I was "stacking" (a term used by steroid users which means mixing different types) to get well-cut definition along with mass.

It was around this time when I was arrested for threatening a security guard. When the campus police came to arrest me, they saw how aggressive and large my roommate and I were. So they searched our room and found dozens of bottles and hundreds of dollars' worth of steroids and syringes. We had a trial, and the outcome was that I could only return the next year if I got drug-tested on a monthly basis. I certainly had no will power or desire to quit my steroid abuse, so I transferred schools.

After a summer of even more heavy-duty abuse, I decided to attend a school that would cater to my instinctively backward ways. That fall I entered a large university in the South. Once again I simply lifted weights without being involved in competition or football. It was there that I finally realized how out of hand I'd become with my steroid problem.

Gradually I started to taper down my dosages. Accompanying my reduction, I began to drink more and more. My grades plummeted again. I began going to bars and keg parties on a nightly basis.

My celibacy, mental state, aggressiveness, lack of athletic competition, and alcohol problem brought me to enjoy passing my pain onto others by means of physical aggression. I got into a fight almost every time I drank. In the midst of my insane state, I was arrested for assault. I was in really deep this time. Finally I realized how different from everybody else I'd become, and I decided not to taper off but to quit completely.

The average person seems to think that steroids just make you bigger. But they are a drug, and an addictive one at that. This drug does not put you in a stupor or in a hallucinogenic state but rather gives you an up, all-around "bad-ass" mentality that far exceeds that of either normal life or any other narcotic I've tried when not taking steroids. Only lately are scientists and researchers discovering how addictive steroids are—only now, after hundreds of thousands may have done such extreme damage to their lives, bodies, and minds.

One of the main components of steroid addiction is how unsatisfied the user is with his overall appearance. Although I was massive and had dramatic muscular definition, I was never content with my body, despite frequent compliments. I was always changing types of steroids, places of injection, workouts, diet, etc. I always found myself saying, "This one oughta do it" or "I'll quit when I hit 230 pounds."

When someone is using steroids, he has psychological disorders that increase when usage stops. One disorder is anxiety from the loss of the superior feeling you get from the drug. Losing the muscle mass, high energy level, and superhuman sensation that you're so accustomed to is terrifying.

Another ramification of taking artificial testosterone over time is the effect on the natural testosterone level (thus the male sex drive). As a result of my steroid use, my natural testosterone level was ultimately depleted to the point where my sex drive was drastically reduced in comparison to the average twenty-one-year-old male. My testicles shriveled up, causing physical pain as well as extreme mental anguish. Thus I desired girls less. This however did lead me to treat them as people, not as objects of my desires. It was a beginning step on the way to a more sane and civil mentality.

The worst symptoms of my withdrawal after many months of drug abuse were emotional. My emotions fluctuated dramatically, and I rapidly became more sensitive. My hope is that this feeling of being trailed by isolation and aloneness will diminish and leave me free of its constant haunting.

Response and Analysis

1. Why did D. H. begin and then continue using anabolic steroids even when he knew they were harmful? D. H. writes that he was in a "terrible state of body and mind" when using steroids. What psychological problems did he experience? What physical problems?

2. How did excessive use of steroids affect D. H.'s sexual interest and behavior? Why? How do sex hormones (androgens and estrogens) affect sexual behavior after puberty? How can lack of testosterone production in males influence sexual interest and behavior?

Personal Experience and Application

1. What pressures to conform to a particular group's style of appearance and behavior did you feel in high school? Did you give in to any of these pressures? Why? When might conformity be harmful? When might conformity be helpful?

2. D. H. reported that his school would only let him return if he had a drug test every month. What penalties do you believe should be brought against athletes at your school who use anabolic steroids? Do you think penalties can deter the use of steroids? Why?

Research

Suppose you want to know if people who use anabolic steroids have low self-esteem and tend to be depressed. You must decide whether you want to develop a questionnaire to assess self-esteem and depression or to use existing questionnaires with known reliability and validity. What are the advantages and disadvantages of using existing questionnaires or developing your own questionnaire?

NEW HOPE FOR BINGE EATERS

Harrison G. Pope Jr. and James I. Hudson

Psychological Concepts
eating disorders, anorexia nervosa, bulimia nervosa

Harrison Pope and James Hudson tell the story of Sally, whose story is similar to that of many others, often women, who suffer from bulimia nervosa. While a senior in college, Sally suffered for a time from depression and became increasingly preoccupied with food. Soon she was binge eating and desperate to find ways to take off the weight she had just gained. As her bulimia nervosa progressed, Sally began to withdraw from social life. Why would an attractive, young woman go on food binges, gain weight, vomit to lose the weight, and then repeat the cycle? How does she attempt to break the cycle?

[Sally's] story was familiar. As far back as her sophomore year, while a student at a prestigious women's college in Massachusetts, she had already noticed that she seemed unusually preoccupied with food. In the cafeteria line, she often stopped to study the labels on bottles of salad dressing, cans of juice, and containers of yogurt, to see how many calories each contained, often calculating and recalculating the total number of calories that she had consumed during the day. She was not at all overweight then—although at times, in the privacy of her room, she critically examined herself in the mirror and wished that she had the self-discipline to be thinner. But these feelings seemed little different from those of her friends. Perhaps, during those early years, she had been a bit more depressed than average—particularly so, she remembered, during the days just prior to her menstrual periods—but on the whole her life in the dormitory, her dates with the boys from a nearby college, her grades, her summers in Maine with her family, seemed much the same as those of everyone else.

It was in her senior year that the eating binges began. During the early fall of that year, she felt despondent and unhappy with herself. With this depression came a rise in her preoccupation with food and her thoughts about wanting to lose weight. She paid more attention to her diet. But then one night, alone in her room, she suddenly found herself compulsively devouring chocolate cookies until the entire package of sixty cookies was gone. But the craving for food continued. She rushed to the corner store to buy more supplies. Minutes later, back in her room with an entire gallon of chocolate chip ice cream, abandoning any last pretense of restraint, Sally began eating it with a tablespoon, straight from the carton. Incredibly, it was gone in twenty minutes. Feeling sick, sedated, and disgusted with herself, she collapsed into her bed and slept for twelve hours.

The next morning she discovered to her horror that she had gained seven pounds. Only a strict diet, if not an outright fast, could erase what she had done. Slowly, painstakingly, over the next eight days she lost all of the dreadful weight. But toward the end of that time a strange, uneasy feeling built up inside her—and on the eighth night, it all happened again.

The second binge started a new cycle of fasting, but this time, before she had quite lost all the weight she had gained, a third binge erupted. Soon the binges settled down into a regular pattern, occurring every fourth or fifth night, with rigorous diets in between. Sally quickly learned to recognize the vague tension that heralded the approach of the next episode; she found herself making elaborate plans to be alone on that evening, to stockpile the food in advance in her room, and to guard against any possible interruption.

The cycle of binging and fasting developed its own inexorable momentum. Whatever her attempts to control it, whatever schemes she tried to interrupt it, it continued. She did not dare to confide in other girls at the school or in her boyfriend, although she was convinced that he must have guessed her secret from watching her sharp fluctuations of weight. When he broke up with her that winter, it seemed to confirm that he knew.

Her depression mounted. Within six months she had gained thirteen pounds; each new binge left guilt and hopelessness in its wake. She recalled a dark morning in February, when she awakened in her room after a binge the previous night, overcome with shame and loneliness, and thought seriously, for the first time, of suicide. She even fumbled through the medicines on her bureau—aspirin, decongestants, cough medicine—wondering if enough of them could be painlessly fatal. The feeling dissipated within a few hours, but it was to return many times in the following years.

That spring came a blessing and a curse: Sally discovered how to use laxatives. At first they were an immense relief; she could purge some of the food that she ate, and no longer was forced to fast between binges. She even managed to lose ten pounds before her graduation. But before long, she had to take twenty, then fifty, and sometimes even a hundred times the usual dose to achieve an effect—and felt wasted and drained for the next twenty-four hours.

After graduating, she began her first job as a public relations consultant for a firm in Boston, and found an apartment of her own in a quiet suburb west of the city. Even though her job proved rewarding, the work atmosphere inviting, and her associates friendly, her work offered only scant relief from the tyranny of her chronic preoccupation with food. The binges occurred almost nightly, as soon as she got home from work. Soon she found herself spending eighty to a hundred dollars a week on food, and another twenty or thirty on laxatives. Her social life dissolved. She no longer had a boyfriend, but it didn't matter; food seemed to occupy all of her thoughts. She developed a repertoire of excuses to extricate herself from evening social obligations so as to be free to go home and binge. Arriving at her local supermarket, she often felt compelled to explain as she was checking out that she was throwing a party, in order to justify a shopping cart filled with ice cream, cookies, and other carbohydrate-rich foods. Then she usually drove several miles to a large pharmacy in a neighboring town; the clerk in the local drugstore had noticed her too many times buying laxatives.

"There was no one to whom I could talk about it," she said. "I didn't know anyone else who ever had these experiences, or at least admitted to them. I thought I must just be weird; I'd never heard the word *bulimia*. There wasn't any publicity about it in those days."

From time to time, Sally resolved to fight her affliction, forcing herself to go without binging. But within two or three days, intolerable tension and anxiety would begin to build, her resolve would collapse, and the cycle would begin again.

After countless attempts, Sally eventually learned to make herself vomit. Vomiting was difficult at first, but it liberated her from her dependence on laxatives, and made it easier for her to lose weight. In fact, she soon lost another fifteen pounds, to the point where she dipped several pounds below the lowest weight she had attained in college. Even then, she still found herself wondering, many times a day, if she looked fat. Often she would forgo breakfast and eat only sparingly at lunch—but this only increased the ferocity of the nightly binges. Recognizing this, she tried deliberately to eat more during the day, but could not bring herself to do so; the thought of consuming even a few hundred calories, without the option of vomiting, aroused too much anxiety.

Despite this, she managed to advance at work, fulfill her few social obligations, and maintain an unblemished exterior. She even began dating, but her sexual drive, she recalled, was almost nil; ninety-nine percent of her thoughts revolved around food.

It was nearly five years after the onset of the bulimic symptoms that Sally finally sought out counseling.

"I would have seen someone sooner," she said, "but I didn't know where I could find someone who could possibly understand my problem. Then I learned the name of a psychologist who had seen a friend of mine at work, and I decided to give it a try.

"At first, I was embarrassed even to describe my problem to him. But he proved to be a very warm and understanding person, and he quickly put me at ease. After I had seen him only a few times, I learned a number of things about myself—that I had constantly tried to be perfect in my family, in my schoolwork, and in my appearance. It seemed to make a lot of sense. But I still binged. The therapist tried hard to work with me, but I was never able to gain much control. I felt like a failure."

Sally continued seeing him once a week, sometimes twice, for more than a year. Finally she stopped, not because she questioned the value of the sessions, but because the expense seemed too great for her to manage. Little did she realize the new expense that awaited her: a dentist discovered that the enamel on her teeth was seriously eroded as a result of her vomiting. He estimated that the work required would cost a minimum of two thousand dollars. The news stunned her, but it did not stop the binges.

A few months later, she experienced a period of new and unfamiliar symptoms: strange attacks of anxiety began to strike her, seemingly at random, several times a week. She described one such episode that occurred while she was riding to work on the train: A sudden feeling of dread came over her; her heart raced, her hands tingled, and she gasped for air. Something horrible seemed about to happen—as if she were about to have a heart attack, or suddenly go crazy. Her only thought was to find some escape, someplace to hide. The attack faded over the course of half an hour; she hastily got off the train in Boston, shaken but able to get to work. For months afterward she drove her car to work, fearing that another trip on the train might trigger a similar experience. But the attacks continued; more and more she sought the safety of her apartment when not at work. Finally, she decided to consult a psychiatrist.

"I never got the feeling that he really understood my problems. After only two sessions, he prescribed some large orange pills that made me feel like a zombie even when I took only half the prescribed amount. He called them 'major tranquilizers.' I could barely get out of bed in the morning, and I walked around feeling dazed and uninterested in everything going on around me."

"The pills did nothing for the anxiety attacks, and they seemed to make the eating binges worse. I complained to the doctor, but he felt that I should continue to take them, even though I could not understand his explanation of what they were supposed to do. I finally stopped taking them on my own, and stopped seeing him soon afterward."

Sally's medication had probably been one of the phenothiazines—a family of drugs designed to treat psychotic symptoms such as delusions and hallucinations. Although Sally had displayed none of these symptoms, it was not surprising to hear that someone had prescribed a phenothiazine for her; these powerful drugs, with numerous side effects, are sometimes prescribed for syndromes in which they are valueless, based on the questionable assumption that they are effective for ordinary anxiety or depression.

But after her unfortunate encounter with the psychiatrist something good finally happened. Sally heard of a self-help organization dedicated to the problem of eating disorders. She found the organization filled with women who told stories very much like her own. Soon she joined a group workshop. Talking with the other group members gave her immense relief and new resolve, for the first time in years. Her self-esteem improved; no longer did she feel quite so ashamed. In a bold move, she even described the binges—at least in part—to her boyfriend. He seemed to understand, and, contrary to her fears, did not seem alienated by her confession. In fact, they grew closer, and six months later they became engaged.

But despite her release from shame and isolation, Sally found that the binges stubbornly persisted—and the morning depressions that followed them remained devastating. Most of the other women in her group admitted that they still binged as well; only one seemed to have freed herself from the symptoms. Like Sally, some wondered aloud if they would ever be liberated from their compulsion; they spoke of successive experiences with three, four, or five different courses of treatment, with many different sorts of therapists. Several of the group members described positive and rewarding experiences in therapy—but they were still binging.

Sally concluded her story:

"I've got to keep trying. Cliff and I plan to get married in September. It's been nine years now, and I'm still binging three or four times a week—never less than once a week even during the best periods. I can't stand it anymore; I'm tired of spending my life constantly obsessed with food; I'm tired of making myself throw up; I'm tired of wrecking my body."

With each passing month, more and more patients like Sally come to our offices, and to the offices of other professionals around the country. They tell stories of years of uncontrollable binge eating—sometimes unknown to even their closest friends—accompanied by depression, anxiety, and suicidal feelings. Often their occupational, social, and sexual lives have been eroded as a result of their all-consuming preoccupation with food. With growing desperation, as one treatment after another has failed, they come, as Sally did, torn between hope and skepticism, afraid to believe that any treatment could possibly be successful. Some are well informed about bulimia; others are the victims of fanciful ideas or frank misinformation. Many never reach the offices at all. For every Sally who seeks professional help, there may be five, ten, or even twenty others who covertly suffer from uncontrollable eating binges—perhaps not even knowing that their syndrome is a recognized illness, for which effective treatments are now being developed. It appears that bulimia is reaching epidemic proportions in this country, and probably around the world. But it is a secret epidemic, and we in our offices see only a tiny portion of those who suffer from it.

Fortunately, new research suggests that bulimia, unlike some other epidemic illnesses, can now often be treated rapidly. Thus, it becomes all the more tragic that so many people—numbering into the millions in the United States alone—may suffer unnecessarily, unaware that improved treatment is available.

Response and Analysis

1. What factors may have influenced Sally to develop an eating disorder? How did she attempt to control her weight? Briefly describe her "binge-purge" cycle. What physical and psychological problems did she experience as a result of binging and purging?

2. What are anorexia nervosa and bulimia nervosa? What are the typical characteristics—such as age, gender, and personality traits—of people who suffer from an eating disorder,

such as anorexia nervosa or bulimia nervosa? How do biological and nonbiological factors regulate or influence eating?

Personal Experience and Application

1. Do you think that American society overemphasizes physical appearance and thinness? Why or why not? If so, how are these values conveyed to children, adolescents, and adults? What pressures might young men and women experience if they do not conform to the idealized image? What pressures do you feel to conform to the idealized image? How do these pressures affect your self-esteem?

2. Do you know someone who has an eating disorder? If so, how has it affected his or her life, including self-esteem and relationships? How has it affected your relationship with the person? Has the person overcome the problem? If so, how?

Research

Suppose you conduct a study to investigate the relationship between self-esteem and anorexia nervosa. You have one hundred female and male students at your college or university complete an eating disorder questionnaire and a self-esteem questionnaire. The results show that there is a moderately strong positive correlation ($r = 0.55$) between anorexia nervosa and self-esteem. What are the *three* possible explanations for this relationship? Based on the results, why is it not possible to determine which explanation is correct?

FLOW

Daniel Goleman

Psychological Concepts
flow, creativity

Motivation and emotion are intrinsically bound to our ability to be creative and absorbed in our work. In this selection, Daniel Goleman refers to an artist, an athlete, and a surgeon who are completely engrossed in some aspect of their work. Each experiences a kind of ecstasy, a state described by Mihaly Csikszentmihalyi as *flow.* Goleman defines flow and discusses what brings it about. Perhaps you can think of times in your life when you have been completely engrossed in an activity and were excited as much about the process as the end result.

A composer describes those moments when his work is at its best:

> You yourself are in an ecstatic state to such a point that you feel as though you almost don't exist. I've experienced this time and again. My hand seems devoid of myself, and I have nothing to do with what is happening. I just sit there watching in a state of awe and wonderment. And it just flows out by itself.

His description is remarkably similar to those of hundreds of diverse men and women—rock climbers, chess champions, surgeons, basketball players, engineers, managers, even filing clerks—when they tell of a time they outdid themselves in some favored activity. The state they describe is called "flow" by Mihaly Csikszent-mihalyi, the University of Chicago psychologist who has collected such accounts of peak performance during two decades of research. Athletes know this state of grace as "the zone," where excellence becomes effortless, crowd and competitors disappearing into a blissful, steady absorption in the moment. Diane Roffe-Steinrotter, who captured a gold medal in skiing at the 1994 Winter Olympics, said after she finished her turn at ski racing that she remembered nothing about it but being immersed in relaxation: "I felt like a waterfall." . . .

Flow represents perhaps the ultimate in harnessing the emotions in the service of performance and learning. In flow the emotions are not just contained and channeled, but positive, energized, and aligned with the task at hand. To be caught in the ennui of depression or the agitation of anxiety is to be barred from flow. Yet flow (or a milder microflow) is an experience almost everyone enters from time to time, particularly when performing at their peak or stretching beyond their former limits. . . .

That experience is a glorious one: the hallmark of flow is a feeling of spontaneous joy, even rapture. Because flow feels so good, it is intrinsically rewarding. It is a state in which people become utterly absorbed in what they are doing, paying undivided attention to the task, their awareness merged with their actions. Indeed, it interrupts flow to reflect too much on what is happening—the very thought "I'm doing this wonderfully" can break the feeling of flow. Attention becomes so focused that people are aware only of the narrow range of perception related to the immediate task, losing track of time and space. A surgeon, for example, recalled a challenging operation during which he was in flow; when he completed the surgery he noticed some rubble on the floor of the operating room and asked what had happened. He was amazed to hear that while he was so intent on the surgery part of the ceiling had caved in—he hadn't noticed at all. . . .

There are several ways to enter flow. One is to intentionally focus a sharp attention on the task at hand; a highly concentrated state is the essence of flow. There seems to be a feedback loop at the gateway to this zone: it can require considerable effort to get calm and focused enough to begin the task—this first step takes some discipline. But once focus starts to lock in, it takes on a force of its own, both offering relief from emotional turbulence and making the task effortless.

Entry to this zone can also occur when people find a task they are skilled at, and engage in it at a level that slightly taxes their ability. As Csikszentmihalyi told me, "People seem to concentrate best when the demands on them are a bit greater than usual, and they are able to give more than usual. If there is too little demand on them, people are bored. If there is too much for them to handle, they get anxious. Flow occurs in that delicate zone between boredom and anxiety." . . .

Watching someone in flow gives the impression that the difficult is easy; peak performance appears natural and ordinary. This impression parallels what is going on within the brain, where a similar paradox is repeated: the most challenging tasks are done with a minimum expenditure of mental energy. In flow the brain is in a "cool" state, its arousal and inhibition of neural circuitry attuned to the demand of the moment. When people are engaged in activities that effortlessly capture and hold their attention, their brain "quiets down" in the sense that there is a lessening of cortical arousal. That discovery is remarkable, given that flow allows people to tackle the most challenging tasks in a given domain, whether playing against a chess master or solving a complex mathematical problem. The expectation would be that such challenging tasks would require *more* cortical activity, not less. But a key to flow is that it occurs only within reach of the summit of ability, where skills are well-rehearsed and neural circuits are most efficient.

A strained concentration—a focus fueled by worry—produces increased cortical activation. But the zone of flow and optimal performance seems to be an oasis of cortical efficiency, with a bare minimum of mental energy expended. That makes sense, perhaps, in terms of the skilled practice that allows people to get into flow: having mastered the moves of a task, whether a physical one such as rock climbing or a mental one such as computer programming, means that the brain can be more efficient in performing them. Well-practiced moves require much less brain effort than do ones just being learned, or those that are still too hard. Likewise, when the brain is working less efficiently because of fatigue or nervousness, as happens at the end of a long, stressful day, there is a blurring of the precision of cortical effort, with too many superfluous areas being activated—a neural state experienced as being highly distracted. The same happens in boredom. But when the brain is operating at peak efficiency, as in flow, there is a precise relation between the active areas and the demands of the task. In this state even hard work can seem refreshing or replenishing rather than draining. Because flow emerges in the zone in which an activity challenges people to the fullest of their capacities, as their skills increase it takes a heightened challenge to get into flow. If a task is too simple, it is boring; if too challenging, the result is anxiety rather than flow. It can be argued that mastery in a craft or skill is spurred on by the experience of flow—that the motivation to get better and better at something, be it playing the violin, dancing, or gene-splicing, is at least in part to stay in flow while doing it. Indeed, in a study of two hundred artists eighteen years after they left art school, Csikszentmihalyi found that it was those who in their student days had savored the sheer joy of painting itself who had become serious painters. Those who had been motivated in art school by dreams of fame and wealth for the most part drifted away from art after graduating.

Csikszentmihalyi concludes: "Painters must want to paint above all else. If the artist in front of the canvas begins to wonder how much he will sell it for, or what the critics will think of it, he won't be able to pursue original avenues. Creative achievements depend on single-minded immersion."

Response and Analysis

1. What are the main features of flow? How do people enter flow, or "the zone"?

2. Why is performance enhanced when people are in a state of flow? How do most people feel when they are in a state of flow? Why?

Personal Experience and Application

1. Have you ever been in a state of flow? If so, what was the activity? What were you doing that allowed you to enter flow? How well were you performing your activity while in this state? How did it feel to be in "the zone"? When you were absorbed in the activity, were you concerned with a successful outcome (that is, was the activity itself as satisfying as the result)? Why or why not?

2. Assume that students who experience flow during an activity will be more motivated to improve their performance in that activity. What do you think teachers might do to help students experience flow?

Research

Suppose you want to conduct a study to examine the conditions in which people enter a state of flow. You ask one hundred students on your campus to participate. You give them a questionnaire with the following questions: "Have you ever been in a state of flow? If so, during what activity did you enter the state of flow? What were you doing that allowed you to enter flow?" What problems do you think students might have in answering these questions? What can you do to help clarify the questions? Why is it important that all students have a similar understanding of what the questions are asking?

chapter 10

PERSONALITY

*The child in the womb is already created as a
uniqueness to be developed, and this fact is
decisive: the origin of personality is the origin
of the potential personality: uniqueness.*

MARTIN BUBER, in MAURICE FRIEDMAN,
Martin Buber's Life and Work: The Later Years

What shapes our personality? The selections in this chapter illustrate the development of self-identity, the relationship between self-concept and the social environment, personality traits, and growth orientation.

Born in America of Japanese immigrants, Kesaya Noda has so many conflicting images of who she should be that she struggles to understand who she is and who she would like to be. Noda confronts not only historical and cultural identities but also what it means to be a woman here and now.

Joyce Lee astutely points to the challenge many immigrant children face in elementary school. How does a child make herself understood when she doesn't know the language of her new land? One way is to demonstrate skills: Lee had a talent for origami that impressed both her teacher and the children in her class. Her early experiences of coming to America are powerful memories for Lee. How might such experiences influence personality?

Writing about the importance of reputation, tennis star Arthur Ashe reveals several of his personality traits. Honesty, fairness, and kindness are all qualities he tries to cultivate. Ashe sees a strong connection between the personal and the interpersonal. How he behaves affects others, and if he disappoints his father, his mother, or his community, they would let him know. Highly conscientious, he wants to be an honorable man.

When Annie Dillard receives her first microscope, she is eager to see wildlife. What she wants most is to see the amoeba, but it does not turn up readily. When she finally gets puddle water and finds the amoeba under the microscope, she is elated. Dillard wants to share her discovery with her parents, but they decide not to join her. How does Dillard react when she is left alone with no one to share her excitement?

ASIAN IN AMERICA

Kesaya E. Noda

Psychological Concepts
self-concept, positive regard

What shapes our personality? How do we begin to understand who we are? Kesaya Noda struggled with the differences between her Asian heritage and the American world in which she lived. As a Japanese-American born in California and raised in New Hampshire, she faced cultural and gender issues that complicated her personal identity. In what way, she asked herself, was she Japanese? In what way was she Japanese-American? Was there any conflict between the ways these two cultures viewed women? In this selection, she offers answers that helped define her identity.

Sometimes when I was growing up, my identity seemed to hurtle toward me and paste itself right to my face. I felt that way, encountering the stereotypes of my race perpetuated by non-Japanese people (primarily white) who may or may not have had contact with other Japanese in America. "You don't like cheese, do you?" someone would ask. "I know your people don't like cheese." Sometimes questions came making allusions to history. That was another aspect of the identity. Events that had happened quite apart from the me who stood silent in that moment connected my face with an incomprehensible past. "Your parents were in California? Were they in those camps during the war?" And sometimes there were phrases or nicknames: "Lotus Blossom." I was sometimes addressed or referred to as racially Japanese, sometimes as Japanese-American, and sometimes as an Asian woman. Confusions and distortions abounded.

How is one to know and define oneself? From the inside—within a context that is self-defined, from a grounding in community and a connection with culture and history that are comfortably accepted? Or from the outside—in terms of messages received from the media and people who are often ignorant? Even as an adult I can still see two sides of my face and past. I can see from the inside out, in freedom. And I can see from the outside in, driven by the old voices of childhood and lost in anger and fear.

I Am Racially Japanese

A voice from my childhood says: "You are other. You are less than. You are unalterably alien." This voice has its own history. We have indeed been seen as other and alien since the early years of our arrival in the United States. The very first immigrants were welcomed and sought as laborers to replace the dwindling numbers of Chinese, whose influx had been cut off by the Chinese Exclusion Act of 1882. The Japanese fell natural heir to the same anti-Asian prejudice that had arisen against the Chinese. As soon as they began striking for better wages, they were no longer welcomed.

I can see myself today as a person historically defined by law and custom as being forever alien. Being neither "free white" nor "African," our people in California were deemed "aliens, ineligible for citizenship," no matter how long they intended to stay here. Aliens ineligible for citizenship were prohibited from owning, buying, or leasing land. They did not and could not belong here. The voice in me remembers that I am always a *Japanese*-American in the eyes of many. A third-generation German-American is an American. A third-generation Japanese-American is a Japanese-American. Being Japanese means being a danger to the country during the war and knowing how to use chopsticks. I wear this history on my face.

I move to the other side. I see a different light and claim a different context. My race is a line that stretches across ocean and time to link me to the shrine where my grandmother was raised. Two high, white banners lift in the wind at the top of the stone steps leading to the shrine. It is time for the summer festival. Black characters are written against the sky as boldly as the clouds, as lightly as kites, as sharply as the big black crows I used to see above the fields in New Hampshire. At festival time there is liquor and food, ritual, discipline, and abandonment. There is music and drunkenness and invocation. There is hope. Another season has come. Another season has gone.

I am racially Japanese. I have a certain claim to this crazy place where the prayers intoned by a neighboring Shinto priest (standing in for my grandmother's nephew who is sick) are drowned out by the rehearsals for the pop singing contest in which most of the villagers will compete later that night. The village elders, the priest, and I stand respectfully upon the immaculate, shining wooden floor of the outer shrine, bowing our heads before the hidden powers. . . .

Our family has served this shrine for generations. The family's need to protect this claim to identity and place outweighs any individual claim to any individual hope. I am Japanese.

I Am a Japanese-American

"Weak." I hear the voice from my childhood years. "Passive," I hear. Our parents and grandparents were the ones who were put into those camps. They went without resistance; they offered cooperation as proof of loyalty to America. "Victim," I hear. And, "Silent."

Our parents are painted as hard workers who were socially uncomfortable and had difficulty expressing even the smallest opinion. Clean, quiet, motivated, and determined to match the American way; that is us, and that is the story of our time here.

"Why did you go into those camps?" I raged at my parents, frightened by my own inner silence and timidity. "Why didn't you do anything to resist? Why didn't you name it the injustice it was?" Couldn't our parents even think? Couldn't they? Why were we so passive?

During the several years that follow I learn about the people and the place, and much more about what has happened in this California village where my parents grew up. The *issei*, our grandparents, made this settlement in the desert. Their first crops were eaten by rabbits and ravaged by insects. The land was so barren that men walking from house to house sometimes got lost. Women came here too. They bore children in 114-degree heat, then carried the babies with them into the fields to nurse when they reached the end of each row of grapes or other truck-farm crops.

I had had no idea what it meant to buy this kind of land and make it grow green. Or how, when the war came, there was no space at all for the subtlety of being who we were—Japanese-Americans. Either/or was the way. I hadn't understood that people were literally afraid for their lives then, that their money had been frozen in banks; that there was a five-mile travel limit; that when the early evening curfew came and they were inside their houses, some of them watched helplessly as people they knew went into their barns to steal their belongings. The police were patrolling the road, interested only in violators of curfew. There was no help for them in the face of thievery. I had not been able to imagine before what it must have felt like to be an American—to know absolutely that one is an American—and yet to have almost everyone else deny it. Not only deny it, but challenge that identity with machine guns and troops of white American soldiers. In those circumstances it was difficult to say, "I'm a Japanese-American." "American" had to do.

But now I can say that I am a Japanese-American. It means I have a place here in this country, too. I have a place here on the East Coast, where our neighbor is so much a part of our family that my mother never passes her house at night without glancing at the lights to see if she is home and safe; where my parents have hauled hundreds of pounds of rocks from fields and arduously planted Christmas trees and blueberries, lilacs, asparagus, and crab apples; where my father still dreams of angling a stream to a new bed so that he can dig a pond in the field and fill it with water and fish. "The neighbors already came for their Christmas tree?" he asks in December. "Did they like it? Did they like it?"

I have a place on the West Coast where my relatives still farm, where I heard the stories of feuds and backbiting, and where I saw that people survived and flourished because fundamentally they trusted and relied upon one another. A death in the family is not just a death in a family; it is a death in the community. I saw people help each other with money, materials, labor, attention, and time. I saw men gather once a year, without fail, to clean the grounds of a ninety-year-old woman who had helped the community before, during, and after the war. I saw her remembering them with birthday cards sent to each of their children.

I come from a people with a long memory and a distinctive grace. We live our thanks. And we are Americans. Japanese-Americans.

I Am a Japanese-American Woman

Woman. The last piece of my identity. It has been easier by far for me to know myself in Japan and to see my place in America than it has been to accept my line of connection with my own mother. She was my dark self, a figure in whom I thought I saw all that I feared most in myself. Growing into womanhood and looking for some model of strength, I turned away from her. Of course, I could not find what I sought. I was looking for a black feminist or a white feminist. My mother is neither white nor black.

My mother is a woman who speaks with her life as much as with her tongue. I think of her with her own mother. Grandmother had Parkinson's disease and it had frozen her gait and set her fingers, tongue, and feet jerking and trembling in a terrible dance. My aunts and uncles wanted her to be able to live in her own home. They fed her, bathed her, dressed her, awoke at midnight to take her for one last trip to the bathroom. My aunts (her daughters-in-law) did most of the care, but my mother went from New Hampshire to California each summer to spend a month living with Grandmother, because she wanted to and because she wanted to give my aunts at least a small rest. During those hot summer days, mother lay on the couch watching the television or reading, cooking foods that Grandmother liked, and speaking little. Grandmother thrived under her care.

The time finally came when it was too dangerous for Grandmother to live alone. My relatives kept finding her on the floor beside her bed when they went to wake her in the mornings. My mother flew to California to help clean the house and make arrangements for Grandmother to enter a local nursing home. On her last day at home, while Grandmother was sitting in her big, overstuffed armchair, hair combed and wearing a green summer dress, my mother went to her and knelt at her feet. "Here, Mamma," she said. "I've polished your shoes." She lifted Grandmother's legs and helped her into the shiny black shoes. My Grandmother looked down and smiled slightly. She left her house walking, supported by her children, carrying her pocket book, and wearing her polished black shoes. "Look, Mamma," my mom had said, kneeling. "I've polished your shoes."

Just the other day, my mother came to Boston to visit. She had recently lost a lot of weight and was pleased with her new shape and her feeling of good health. "Look at me, Kes," she exclaimed, turning toward me, front and back, as naked as the day she was born. I saw her small breasts and the wide, brown scar, belly button to pubic hair, that marked her because my brother and I were both born by Caesarean section. Her hips were small. I was not a large baby, but there was so little room for me in her that when she was carrying me she could not even begin to bend over toward the floor. She hated it, she said.

"Don't I look good? Don't you think I look good?"

I looked at my mother, smiling and as happy as she, thinking of all the times I have seen her naked. I have seen both my parents naked throughout my life, as they have seen me.

I know this to be Japanese, this ease with the physical, and it makes me think of an old Japanese folk song. A young nursemaid, sent far from her home to be a servant, is singing a lullaby to a baby who is strapped to her back.

> If I should drop dead,
> bury me by the roadside!
> I'll give a flower
> to everyone who passes.
>
> What kind of flower?
> The cam-cam-camellia [tsun-tsun-tsubaki]
> watered by Heaven:
> alms water.

The nursemaid is the intersection of the human, the natural world, the body and the soul. In this song, she looks steadily at life, which is sometimes so terribly sad. I think of her while looking at my mother. . . .

I recently heard a man from West Africa share some memories of his child-hood. He was raised Muslim, but when he was a young man, he found himself deeply drawn to Christianity. He struggled against his inner impulse for years, try-ing to avoid the church yet feeling pushed to return to it again and again. "I would have done *anything* to avoid the change," he said. At last he became Christian. After-wards he was afraid to go home, fearing that he would not be accepted. The fear was groundless, he discovered, when at last he returned—he had separated himself, but his family and friends (all Muslim) had not separated themselves from him.

The man, who is now a professor of religion, said that in the Africa he knew as a child and a young man, pluralism was embraced rather than feared. There was "a kind of tolerance that did not deny your particularity," he said. He alluded to zest-ful, spontaneous debates that would sometimes loudly erupt between Muslims and Christians in the village's public spaces. His memories of an atheist who harangued the villagers when he came to visit them once a week moved me deeply. Perhaps the man was an agricultural advisor or inspector. He harassed the women. He would say: "Don't go to the fields! Don't even bother to go to the fields. Let God take care of you. He'll send you the food. If you believe in God, why do you need to work? You don't need to work! Let God put the seeds in the ground. Stay home."

The professor said, "The women laughed, you know? They just laughed. Their attitude was, 'Here is a child of God. When will he come home?'"

The storyteller, the professor of religion, smiled a most fantastic tender smile as he told this story. "In my country, there is a deep affirmation of the oneness of God," he said. "The atheist and the women were having quite different experiences in their encounter, though the atheist did not know this. He saw himself as quite separate from the women. But the women did not see themselves as being separate from him. 'Here is a child of God,' they said. 'When will he come home?'"

Response and Analysis

1. Kesaya Noda asks, "How is one to know and define oneself?" Briefly describe Noda's three identities: racially Japanese, Japanese-American, and Japanese-American woman. What factors shape each of these identities?

2. According to Carl Rogers, what is self-concept and positive regard? How might the evaluations by others, such as parents and teachers, and a child's need for approval, influence the child's personality?

Personal Experience and Application

1. Write a brief essay in response to the following question: Who am I?

2. Do you believe that people are basically good? Why or why not?

Research

Suppose you want to examine how personality characteristics change over time. You decide to conduct a longitudinal study with one hundred psychology students. Your plan is to administer the Minnesota Multiphasic Personality Inventory (MMPI) every year for ten years. However, because of scheduling difficulties, you are unable to administer the MMPI at the same time each year. During the first five years, the participants complete the MMPI in mid-December; during the second five years, they complete it in mid-June. How might the time of year influence your findings? Why?

RACISM DOESN'T GROW UP

Joyce Lee

Psychological Concepts
reciprocal influences, self-efficacy, self-esteem

Many children experience at some time feeling isolated from a group. To belong and to be like others is a powerful desire, especially for the young. Joyce Lee, who moved to Portland, Oregon, from Hong Kong when she was a child, faced the challenges that many newcomers face—learning to communicate, being accepted, and making friends. Here, Lee shares how her experiences brought forth certain qualities in her personality.

I came to Portland, Oregon, in 1969 from Hong Kong. I came with my mother and my two brothers. I was placed at an elementary school in a working class neighborhood almost immediately after I arrived in America. I was five years old when I experienced, for the first time in my life, that being "different" was not something to strive for. Acting different could alienate you, looking different could make you feel inferior.

I remember in kindergarten standing next to the bathroom, in front of the children's coat rack, immobile, for one schoolyear. I had no friends, I didn't talk with anyone, including the teachers. After a few months, it seemed that teachers didn't talk to me either. We just co-existed in the room, me with the coat rack, the other children with the teachers. If a classmate gave me any attention, I stood as still as possible, wanting them to think I wasn't a real person. I pretended to be an inanimate object. Eventually the classmate would lose their interest. It got to be an understanding between myself and the class. They would treat me like a statue and I would behave like one. Actually, they treated me better than a statue; I didn't get vandalized. And, because I was a statue tucked away in the corner, I was never in anyone's way. I didn't make noise, I tried not to blink or move. I was actually content with the arrangement. I was even more content to stay home, but ended up in school everyday for no reason I could see.

I don't remember what happened at the end of the day. I think my mother must have come by to pick me up. When I saw her, I was human again.

If I had to use the bathroom, I waited until I thought no one was looking, used it as fast as I could, and returned to my corner.

It must have been frustrating for kindergarten teachers to have me in their class. They were probably at a loss as to what to do since I didn't respond or participate. They decided that I was mentally retarded.

My mother, who spoke no English, was told that I would be enrolled in a school for retarded children. She was horrified, but she couldn't convince my teachers that I was normal. My aunt, who did speak English, couldn't convince them either.

Out of ingenuity and desperation, my mother told me to fold lots of paper boats and birds in school. She taught me every paper boat she knew, every bird, frog, pig, and so on. (I already knew how to fold some boats, paper boat races are common among little children in Hong Kong.) When I displayed my origami skills at school, I was no longer categorized as a "special child." What happened after this time is a little fuzzy. I remember that the teachers had a different attitude toward me. The other kids didn't think I was dumb anymore. I still didn't talk, but eventually, a special effort was made to integrate me into activities, an effort to which I responded.

There was also a special effort to teach me English, which I had not understood before. When I understood some of the language, I started to excel.

Looking back, I try to understand why I refused to budge from my spot. I suspect that I distrusted everyone. With the exception of one American-born Chinese girl who spoke English, no one else looked like me. I also didn't understand the language and the interactions between teacher and student. In Hong Kong, corporal punishment and mental abuse were common methods of discipline at my school. To write the Chinese character "father" wrong meant a couple of slaps on the hand and face. If you persisted in writing the character wrong, you would lose bathroom privileges or lunch privileges. That was in nursery school. The Oregon kindergarten teachers, by contrast, didn't discipline the children. I didn't trust them.

Whoopi Goldberg has a standup routine in which she plays a little Black girl who wears a mop on her head and pretends to be White. As I was growing up, I wanted to be White, too. After third grade, the kids became meaner. When kids made fun of me in second or first grade, I didn't know enough of the language to be offended or hurt. After third grade, I knew a lot of English. The treatment seemed to get worse. "Chink," "slanty eyes," "jap," "Hong Kong phooey," were names I grew up with. When I wasn't called those names, I was sometimes beaten up after school by one or two kids waiting for me. Surprisingly, I was beaten up not just by White kids but also Black kids. In fact, the Black kids were worse than the White ones. The White ones would take me on singularly, but the Black kids were often in groups. When I reached high school, the name calling continued—although I didn't get beaten up anymore.

By high school, White kids and Black kids segregated, they had little to do with each other, except in school sports. The racial hatred I experienced was from the football jocks, not the jocks who were from educated middle class families, but primarily jocks from poor blue-collar families. There were quite a few of these guys. Some of the girls on the cheerleading team, girls from middle class families, also showed contempt for non-Whites.

My school had huge racial and economic class gaps. We had a program for Asian refugees from Cambodia, Vietnam, and Laos. We also had a program for juvenile delinquents, who had a choice of attending institutions or attending my high school. On the other side of the spectrum, we had programs for young scholars who were too advanced in certain subjects to continue high school and had the option of attending Reed College for a few courses on scholarship. With this ethnic, academic, and class diversity, one might have expected a little more sophistication, more tolerance from the students. Unfortunately, this was not the case.

The refugees were hated and often targets of racial violence. Sometimes, I would see other Chinese students get threatened and harassed. I felt sorry for them but at the same time, relieved that, for the moment, it wasn't me. I hated myself for a long time and was ashamed of being Chinese, was ashamed of being an immigrant with uneducated parents, was ashamed of being poor. For thirteen years, I endured the constant barrage of racial slurs.

I remember one incident that was particularly harrowing. During one of our annual picnics in the park, the varsity football rednecks decided that the picnic was being "invaded by gooks," and started bashing heads for recreation. The Asian refugees, probably tired of being picked on day after day, fought back for a change. The fight turned into a race riot involving two hundred students. I avoided a pummeling that day by running out of the park as fast as I could.

Even though I was on the school paper and art staff, I was still regarded as a "gook." I had hoped that all the years I had endured of these rednecks had built me some kind of immunity. I was an active student, a student that had something to contribute on *their* terms. I was a senior at that time and had distinguished myself from the refugees, primarily to show that I wasn't like them. I was really "American."

My high school isn't too different from any other high school in America, nor my experiences particularly special. I know I had it better than many immigrants coming to this country.

What I found incredible after all these years is not so much the racism I encountered, or even the violence and hatred against my people, but the institutional blind eye to that racism. The educators, school administrators, and parents of those jocks did NOTHING about the racial problems at our school. Instead, the race riot in the park was hushed up. There was no discussion of what happened. After the riot, it was just another day. However, *I* will never forget that day. I will never forget how fast my heart raced, and the looks of hatred and fear around me. I still feel repercussions from those years in Oregon.

Today, in San Francisco, I run into an occasional racial slur—although not to the extent I did when I was younger. In the late 80's and early 90's, the phrase "Asian Invasion" was a label stamped on groups of Asians who accomplished the same goals as Euro-immigrants. I encountered a few paranoid and resentful Whites who feared our growing economic strength. However, most of the damage from my childhood manifests itself in more internal ways.

Feelings of insignificance, of low self-esteem, are qualities acquired from a childhood in the United States. Feelings of inadequacy creep up when I happen to date a White guy; guilt accompanies us to a movie or restaurant. I'm paranoid that White women secretly resent me; some have shown that they do. I feel inadequate around educated White middle class people in a social setting. I compensate by putting on a confidence mask. "Oh yes, I'm educated, too, and I grew up in a mainstream family. Oh, yes, we celebrate Christmas, of course—my family lives in the suburbs." I feel stupid when this happens because my conformity is transparent. The confidence mask is thin.

I would be kidding myself if I didn't acknowledge some Westernization and assimilation into American culture. My family calls me "banana," yellow outside, white inside. English is now my "first language" and I don't get to speak Cantonese that often. This doesn't mean that I'm not proud of my heritage and that I've embraced Western values 100 percent. I'm part of that culture that has rejected mainstream options like marriage, kids, house, security, suburbia—options available in both of my cultures: American and Chinese.

To totally embrace Chinese values is very similar to a total embrace of American values: marriage, kids, steady income, a house in suburbia, a set of "practical" goals. The obligation that is not part of the Western model is lifelong duty and allegiance to elders at the price of personal will and freedom. No thank you.

The greatest agony for me, even after those years in Oregon, is discovering how little things have changed. It's been approximately fifteen years since I was last enmeshed in the Portland Public School System. Five years ago, my little eleven-year-old cousin, who had arrived from China two years before, took me aside and revealed to me the shame she was facing in school. "There are things I don't tell my parents," she said. Reluctantly, she told me how the White kids at school picked on her, said mean racist things to her, pushed her around. Since she barely spoke English, she had a hard time making friends; she dreaded school.

What consoling words did I have for her? All I could say to her was: "It's not you, it's never you, it's their stupidity and ignorance. Unfortunately, there's a lot of them, and only one of you. Just remember, I'll be there if you need to talk to me anytime." I didn't have the heart to tell her what to expect in high school. I did tell her that I went through the same things she did. I felt helpless; I couldn't offer her anymore than those few scant sentences.

Response and Analysis

1. In what way was being an immigrant difficult for Joyce Lee? What makes a child feel isolated from his or her peers? How might that isolation affect personality?

2. How did the following factors influence Lee when she was in kindergarten: her personality, thinking patterns, behavior, and the kindergarten classroom (including the other children and the teacher)? How might Albert Bandura's concept of reciprocal influences (or reciprocal determinism) and self-efficacy explain Lee's experiences?

Personal Experience and Application

1. Were children ever mean to you or treat you badly when you were in elementary school? What did they do? How did you react? How did you feel? Were you ever mean to or treat badly another child when you were in grade school? If so what did you do? How did the child react? How do you feel today about the way you treated the child?

2. Do you think that events in your childhood helped shape the kind of person you are today? Briefly describe a few of these events and the impact they have had on your personality.

Research

Suppose you want to design a correlational study to examine the relationship between self-efficacy and self-esteem. Write a hypothesis for your study. Whom might you ask to participate? Why?

A REPUTATION DESERVED

Arthur Ashe and Arnold Rampersad

Psychological Concepts
Eysenck's personality dimensions, five-factor model, honesty, integrity

What is the value of reputation? What personality traits make for a good reputation? Tennis champion Arthur Ashe writes that "if one's reputation is a possession, then of all my possessions, my reputation means most to me." By reputation, however, he does not mean behavior fabricated to impress others. Ashe wants to develop qualities that will be valued by others: kindness, integrity, and honesty. When he contracted the AIDS virus, it was especially painful for him to publicly acknowledge his condition because he feared that some people would think that he contracted the virus through drug use or sexual promiscuity—neither of which was true.

If one's reputation is a possession, then of all my possessions, my reputation means most to me. Nothing comes even close to it in importance. Now and then, I have wondered whether my reputation matters too much to me; but I can no more easily renounce my concern with what other people think of me than I can will myself to stop breathing. No matter what I do, or where or when I do it, I feel the eyes of others on me, judging me.

Needless to say, I know that a fine line exists between caring about one's reputation and hypocrisy. When I speak of the importance to me of my reputation, I am referring to a reputation that is deserved, not an image cultivated for the public in spite of the facts. I know that I haven't always lived without error or sin, but I also know that I have tried hard to be honest and good at all times. When I fail, my conscience comes alive. I have never sinned or erred without knowing I was being watched.

Who is watching me? The living and the dead. My mother, Mattie Cordell Cunningham Ashe, watches me. She died when I was not quite seven. I remember little about her, except for two images. My last sight of her alive: I was finishing breakfast and she was standing in the side doorway looking lovingly at me. She was dressed in her blue corduroy dressing gown. The day was cool and cloudy, and when I went outside I heard birds singing in the small oak tree outside our house. And then I remember the last time I saw her, in a coffin at home. She was wearing her best dress, made of pink satin. In her right hand was a single red rose. Roses were her favorite flower, and my daddy had planted them all around the house; big, deep-hued red roses.

Every day since then I have thought about her. I would give anything to stand once again before her, to feel her arms about me, to touch and taste her skin. She is with me every day, watching me in everything I do. Whenever I speak to young persons about the morality of the decisions they make in life, I usually tell them, "Don't do anything you couldn't tell your mother about."

My father is watching me, too. My father, whose mouth dropped open when he first saw Jeanne, my wife. She looked so much like my mother, he said. He is still a force in my life. Some years ago, before he died of a stroke in 1989, I was being interviewed by the television journalist Charlayne Hunter-Gault in her home.

"Tell me, Arthur," she said, laughter in her voice, "how is it that I have never heard anyone say anything bad about you? How is it that you have never cursed an umpire, or punched an opponent, or gotten a little drunk and disorderly? Why are you such a goody-goody?"

I laughed in turn, and told the truth.

"I guess I have never misbehaved because I'm afraid that if I did anything like that, my father would come straight up from Virginia, find me wherever I happen to be, and kick my ass."

When I told that story not long ago on Men's Day at the Westwood Baptist Church in Richmond, Virginia, everyone smiled and some folks even laughed. They knew what I was talking about, even those few living in that little enclave of blacks surrounded by whites in Richmond who had never met my father. They knew fathers (and mothers) exactly like him, who in times past would come up and find you wherever you were and remind you exactly who you were and don't you forget it. You were their child, that's who.

My father was a strong, dutiful, providing man. He lived and died semi-literate, but he owned his own home and held jobs that were important to him and to people in the community where we lived. His love and his caring were real to me from that Sunday morning in 1950 when he sat on the bottom bunk bed between my brother Johnnie and me and told us between wrenching sobs that our mother had died during the night. From that time on he was father and mother to us. And the lesson he taught above all was about reputation.

"What people think of you, Arthur Junior, your reputation, is all that counts." Or, as I heard from so many older people as I grew up, "A good name is worth more than diamonds and gold."

What others think of me is important, and what I think of others is important. What else do I have to go by? Of course, I cannot make decisions based solely on what other people would think. There are moments when the individual must stand alone. Nevertheless, it is crucial to me that people think of me as honest and principled. In turn, to ensure that they do, I must always act in an honest and principled fashion, no matter the cost.

One day, in Dallas, Texas, in 1973, I was playing in the singles final of a World Championship Tennis (WCT) tournament. My opponent was Stan Smith, a brilliant tennis player but an even more impressive human being in his integrity. On one crucial point, I watched Smith storm forward, racing to intercept a ball about to bounce a second time on his side of the net. When the point was over, I was sure the ball had bounced twice before he hit it and that the point was mine. Smith said he had reached the ball in time. The umpire was baffled. The crowd was buzzing.

I called Smith up to the net.

"Stan, did you get to that ball?"

"I did. I got it."

I conceded the point. Later, after the match—which I lost—a reporter approached me. Was I so naïve? How could I have taken Smith's word on such an important point?

"Believe me," I assured him, "I am not a fool. I wouldn't take just anybody's word for it. But if Stan Smith says he got to the ball, he got to it. I trust his character."

When I was not quite eighteen years old, I played a tournament in Wheeling, West Virginia, the Middle Atlantic Junior Championships. As happened much of the time when I was growing up, I was the only black kid in the tournament, at least in the under-eighteen age section. One night, some of the other kids trashed a cabin; they absolutely destroyed it. And then they decided to say that I was responsible, although I had nothing to do with it. The incident even got into the papers. As much as I denied and protested, those white boys would not change their story.

I rode to Washington from West Virginia with the parents of Dickie Dell, another one of the players. They tried to reassure me, but it was an uncomfortable ride because I was silently worrying about what my father would do and say to me. When I reached Washington, where I was to play in another tournament, I telephoned him in Richmond. As I was aware, he already knew about the incident. When he spoke, he was grim. But he had one question only.

"Arthur Junior, all I want to know is, were you mixed up in that mess?"

"No, Daddy, I wasn't."

He never asked about it again. He trusted me. With my father, my reputation was solid.

I have tried to live so that people would trust my character, as I had trusted Stan Smith's. Sometimes I think it is almost a weakness in me, but I want to be seen as fair and honest, trustworthy, kind, calm, and polite. I want no stain on my character, no blemish on my reputation. And that was why what happened to me early in April 1992 hit me as hard as it did.

The night before I met Jimmy Connors in the men's singles final at Wimbledon in the summer of 1975, I went to bed and slept soundly. That match was the biggest of my life. It was also one that just about everybody was sure I would lose, because Connors was then the finest tennis player in the world, virtually invincible. In fact, the match was supposed to be a slaughter, and I was to be the sacrificial lamb. Before going to bed I had talked and talked with various friends about strategy and tactics, but when it was time to go to sleep, I shrugged off all the nervousness and the worrying, as I usually do, and slept peacefully—as peacefully as that proverbial lamb.

The night of Tuesday, April 7, 1992, was another matter altogether. Try as I could, I was not able to deliver myself to sleep. Once again I had talked and talked, this time mainly with my wife at home but also with friends on the telephone. Once again we discussed strategy and tactics as I tried to make myself ready for another ordeal, but one far more threatening to me than four sets in the final at Wimbledon against Connors. This time I could not bring myself to sleep, except in fits and starts. From my windows on the fourteenth floor of my apartment building in Manhattan I saw the lights of the city and watched for the sun to come up through the murk and mist of Brooklyn and Queens to the east. Before six o'clock, with the sky still dark, I was dressed and ready to go, ready to hunt for a newspaper, to discover if my secret was out, exposed to the world. I knew that once that happened, my life and the lives of my family would be changed forever, and almost certainly for the worse.

In a shop across the avenue I found the newspaper I was waiting for, *USA Today*. I scanned the front page, then flipped back to the sports section. There was not a word about me. I felt a great relief. And then I knew that the relief was only temporary, that it was now up to me to take the matter into my own hands and break the news to whatever part of the world wanted to hear it. And I would have to do it that day, Wednesday, because the days—maybe the hours—of my secret were definitely numbered. I had to announce to the world that I, Arthur Ashe, had AIDS.

Response and Analysis

1. Why did Arthur Ashe believe that he "must always act in an honest and principled fashion, no matter the cost"? Why were honesty, integrity, and reputation so important to Ashe? How did Ashe define reputation?

2. What are the similarities and differences of Eysenck's approach and the five-factor model approach? Briefly describe a few features of Ashe's personality using either Eysenck's major personality dimensions or the five-factor model of personality.

Personal Experience and Application

1. What is your reaction to the value Ashe places on reputation? Do you believe that he is too concerned with how others view him? Why or why not? What value do you place on your reputation? Why?

2. Briefly describe a few of your personality traits using either Eysenck's major personality dimensions or the five-factor model of personality.

Research

Suppose you want to conduct a study examining how unconscious conflicts and motives influence personality. You decide to use a projective test and ask the participants what they see in a picture. How might you determine the test's reliability? Do you think projective tests provide a valid measure of personality? Why or why not?

HANDED MY OWN LIFE

Annie Dillard

Psychological Concepts
phenomenological approach, growth orientation

One Christmas, Annie Dillard's parents give her what she had longed for: a microscope. By spring, she is able to gather some warm puddle water that she hopes will yield an amoeba for her to see. Placing the drop of water on the slide under the lens, Dillard is elated: "I would have known him anywhere," she writes, "blobby and grainy as his picture." Excited, she runs to her parents. They must come and see her find. But they would rather sit in the dining room drinking coffee! Why don't they go with her? What is young Annie Dillard's reaction and what does it reveal about her personality?

After I read *The Field Book of Ponds and Streams* several times, I longed for a microscope. Everybody needed a microscope. Detectives used microscopes, both for the FBI and at Scotland Yard. Although usually I had to save my tiny allowance for things I wanted, that year for Christmas my parents gave me a microscope kit.

In a dark basement corner, on a white enamel table, I set up the microscope kit. I supplied a chair, a lamp, a batch of jars, a candle, and a pile of library books. The microscope kit supplied a blunt black three-speed microscope, a booklet, a scalpel, a dropper, an ingenious device for cutting thin segments of fragile tissue, a pile of clean slides and cover slips, and a dandy array of corked test tubes.

One of the test tubes contained "hay infusion." Hay infusion was a wee brown chip of grass blade. You added water to it, and after a week it became a jungle in a drop, full of one-celled animals. This did not work for me. All I saw in the microscope after a week was a wet chip of dried grass, much enlarged.

Another test tube contained "diatomaceous earth." This was, I believed, an actual pinch of the white cliffs of Dover. On my palm it was an airy, friable chalk. The booklet said it was composed of the silicaceous bodies of diatoms—one-celled creatures that lived in, as it were, small glass jewelry boxes with fitted lids. Diatoms, I read, come in a variety of transparent geometrical shapes. Broken and dead and dug out of geological deposits, they made chalk, and a fine abrasive used in silver polish and toothpaste. What I saw in the microscope must have been the fine abrasive—grit enlarged. It was years before I saw a recognizable, whole diatom. The kit's diatomaceous earth was a bust.

All that winter I played with the microscope. I prepared slides from things at hand, as the books suggested. I looked at the transparent membrane inside an onion's skin and saw the cells. I looked at a section of cork and saw the cells, and at scrapings from the inside of my cheek, ditto. I looked at my blood and saw not much; I looked at my urine and saw long iridescent crystals, for the drop had dried.

All this was very well, but I wanted to see the wildlife I had read about. I wanted especially to see the famous amoeba, who had eluded me. He was supposed to live in the hay infusion, but I hadn't found him there. He lived outside in warm ponds and streams, too, but I lived in Pittsburgh, and it had been a cold winter.

Finally late that spring I saw an amoeba. The week before, I had gathered puddle water from Frick Park; it had been festering in a jar in the basement. This June night after dinner I figured I had waited long enough. In the basement at my microscope table I spread a scummy drop of Frick Park puddle water on a slide, peeked in, and lo, there was the famous amoeba. He was as blobby and grainy as his picture; I would have known him anywhere.

Before I had watched him at all, I ran upstairs. My parents were still at the table, drinking coffee. They, too, could see the famous amoeba. I told them, bursting, that he was all set up, that they should hurry before his water dried. It was the chance of a lifetime.

Father had stretched out his long legs and was tilting back in his chair. Mother sat with her knees crossed, in blue slacks, smoking a Chesterfield. The dessert dishes were still on the table. My sisters were nowhere in evidence. It was a warm evening; the big dining-room windows gave onto blooming rhododendrons.

Mother regarded me warmly. She gave me to understand that she was glad I had found what I had been looking for, but that she and Father were happy to sit with their coffee, and would not be coming down.

She did not say, but I understood at once, that they had their pursuits (coffee?) and I had mine. She did not say, but I began to understand then, that you do what you do out of your private passion for the thing itself.

I had essentially been handed my own life. In subsequent years my parents would praise my drawings and poems, and supply me with books, art supplies, and sports equipment, and listen to my troubles and enthusiasms, and supervise my hours, and discuss and inform, but they would not get involved with my detective work, nor hear about my reading, nor inquire about my homework or term papers or exams, nor visit the salamanders I caught, nor listen to me play the piano, nor attend my field hockey games, nor fuss over my insect collection with me, or my poetry collection or stamp collection or rock collection. My days and nights were my own to plan and fill.

When I left the dining room that evening and started down the dark basement stairs, I had a life. I sat [next] to my wonderful amoeba, and there he was, rolling his grains more slowly now, extending an arc of his edge for a foot and drawing himself along by that foot, and absorbing it again and rolling on. I gave him some more pond water.

I had hit pay dirt. For all I knew, there were paramecia, too, in that pond water, or daphniae, or stentors, or any of the many other creatures I had read about and never seen: volvox, the spherical algal colony; euglena with its one red eye; the elusive, glassy diatom; hydra, rotifers, water bears, worms. Anything was possible. The sky was the limit.

Response and Analysis

1. How does Annie Dillard respond to her parents' refusal to see the amoeba? Why do you think she responds this way? Dillard writes, "I began to understand then, that you do what you do out of your private passion for the thing itself." What does she mean by this?

2. How does Dillard's story illustrate the phenomenological approach to personality? Abraham Maslow's idea of growth orientation? How might experiences like the one Dillard presents here influence personality?

Personal Experience and Application

1. How was young Annie handed her own life? Do you remember an incident with your parents, guardian, or a teacher in which you realized that you had been handed your own life? Describe the incident.

2. Do you think most people possess a growth orientation? Why or why not?

Research

Suppose you want to conduct a study to determine how many people have "peak experiences." According to Maslow, when people have a peak experience, they feel joy simply because they are alive and believe that they are using their fullest potential. Write ten questions that you would ask your participants in order to assess whether they have had a peak experience. Would participants answer your questions with an open response scale or a fixed response scale (for example, 1 = not at all to 5 = very much)? Why? What are two advantages and two disadvantages to using an open response scale? A fixed response scale?

chapter *11*

PSYCHOLOGICAL DISORDERS AND TREATMENT

A night flowing with birds, a ragged moon,
And in broad day the midnight come again!
A man goes far to find out what he is—
Death of the self in a long tearless night,
All natural shapes blazing unnatural light.

THEODORE ROETHKE, "In a Dark Time"

What is it like to feel the "death of the self" about which the poet Theodore Roethke writes? What might people with a psychological disorder experience when "in broad day" they feel dark as midnight? In this chapter we present narratives by people who live with obsessive-compulsive disorder, dissociative identity disorder, depression, and schizophrenia. We also present two selections, written by therapists, that offer insights into therapeutic approaches.

Obsessive-compulsive disorder (OCD) is characterized by repeated intrusions of unwanted thoughts (obsessions) or behaviors (compulsions). If you were at work and suddenly wondered whether you had locked your house, unplugged the iron, or turned off the oven, would you drive back home to find out? Once you determined that you had indeed safeguarded your house, would you then feel compelled to return, say, twenty minutes later to check again? People who suffer from OCD may do just that. They are unable to turn their attention away from a particular thought, and, overcome with anxiety, they perform some ritual or dwell on some special thought to pacify their concerns. In the first reading, Dr. S. tells of his frustration with having to meet the demands of OCD. For instance, on one occasion, he had to check repeatedly to see if he had run over someone with his car. Eventually worn down by this disorder, he sought help. Interestingly, he recognized signs of this disorder not only in his young son but in his grandfather, father, and brothers.

The next selection, written by Quiet Storm (a pseudonym), is one of several works published by persons diagnosed with dissociative identity disorder and who, through treatment, have begun to recognize and address the painful dissociations of identity. A victim of child abuse, Storm adopted several personalities for protection from beatings, humiliation, and isolation. Speaking of herself in first-person plural, she recounts the torture "we" endured. In her "internal house" live several persons who struggle to heal their many wounds.

Tracy Thompson, a reporter for the *Washington Post,* considers the effects of depression and how it threatens her ability to enjoy life. When she was in her teens, Thompson discovered that writing about her feelings brought relief, and eventually she dared to go public and discuss her disorder, even though she feared it might affect how her employers saw her. She expresses some apprehensions about the use of Prozac, but it has, along with therapy, enabled her to live a relatively normal life.

When Allan Davis was a junior at Princeton University, he began to believe that people on television were talking to and about him. Over time, he developed a delusional belief system focused on sexuality, secret codes, and organized crime. Davis, now in his forties, lived several chaotic years before he found a treatment program that helped him. Here he details his experiences with schizophrenia and the treatment program.

Psychotherapy refers to any formal, systematic treatment designed to help persons who are experiencing psychological problems. It normally involves a dialogue between one or more clients and a therapist or team of therapists, who must rely on a theoretical framework to understand and treat problems. Therapist David D. Burns shows how the cognitive techniques he teaches clients can also assist him in coping with the stresses of being a therapist, which, at times, can be considerable. In the final selection, psychologist Lauren Slater describes her struggle to understand the world of her schizophrenic clients as she tries to help them connect with each other through group therapy. These selections show that providing treatment for people suffering from psychological disorders can be challenging and rewarding.

THE ACCIDENT THAT
DIDN'T HAPPEN

Judith L. Rapoport

Psychological Concept
obsessive-compulsive disorder

Dr. S., a clinical psychologist, recalls driving down the highway and thinking, "What if I hit someone on the road?" Once that thought entered his mind, he felt compelled to drive back to the place of the mythical mishap and check the area for a body. Dr. S. says that it is impossible to describe the anguish an obsessive-compulsive attack can bring. The sufferer becomes hostage to the disorder. For example, between the ages of twenty-two and thirty-three, Dr. S. experienced repeated incidents like the one described here. Dr. S.'s family relations were made even more difficult because his young son suffered from the disorder as well. What behavior does his son, Jeffrey, engage in, and what conclusions does Dr. S. draw about OCD?

I'm driving down the highway doing 55 MPH. I'm on my way to take a final exam. My seat belt is buckled and I'm vigilantly following all the rules of the road. No one is on the highway—not a living soul.

Out of nowhere an obsessive-compulsive disorder (OCD) attack strikes. It's almost magical the way it distorts my perception of reality. While in reality no one is on the road, I'm intruded with the heinous thought that I *might* have hit someone . . . a human being! God knows where such a fantasy comes from.

I think about this for a second, and then say to myself, "That's ridiculous. I didn't hit anybody." Nonetheless, a gnawing anxiety is born. An anxiety I will ultimately not be able to put away until an enormous emotional price has been paid.

I try to make reality chase away this fantasy. I reason, "Well, if I hit someone while driving, I would have *felt* it." This brief trip into reality helps the pain dissipate . . . but only for a second. Why? Because the gnawing anxiety that I really did commit the illusionary accident is growing larger—so is the pain.

The pain is a terrible guilt that I have committed an unthinkable, negligent act. At one level, I know this is ridiculous, but there's a terrible pain in my stomach telling me something quite different.

Again, I try putting to rest this insane thought and that ugly feeling of guilt. "Come on," I think to myself, "this is *really* insane!"

But the awful feeling persists. The anxious pain says to me, *"You Really Did Hit Someone."* The attack is now in full control. Reality no longer has meaning. My sensory system is distorted. I have to get rid of the pain. Checking out this fantasy is the only way I know how.

I start ruminating, "Maybe I did hit someone and didn't realize it . . . Oh my God! I might have killed somebody! I have to go back and check." Checking is the only way to calm the anxiety. It brings me closer to truth somehow. I can't live with the thought that I actually may have killed someone—I have to check it out.

Now I'm sweating . . . literally. I pray this outrageous act of negligence never happened. My fantasies run wild. I desperately hope the jury will be merciful. I'm particularly concerned about whether my parents will be understanding. After all, I'm now a criminal. I must control the anxiety by checking it out. Did it really happen? There's always an infinitesimally small kernel of truth (or potential truth) in all my OC fantasies.

I think to myself, "Rush to check it out. Get rid of the hurt by checking it out. Hurry back to check it out. God, I'll be late for my final exam if I check it out. But I have no choice. Someone could be lying on the road, bloody, close to death." Fantasy is now my only reality. So is my pain.

I've driven five miles farther down the road since the attack's onset. I turn the car around and head back to the scene of the mythical mishap. I return to the spot on the road where I "think" it "might" have occurred. Naturally, nothing is there. No police car and no bloodied body. Relieved, I turn around again to get to my exam on time.

Feeling better, I drive for about twenty seconds and then the lingering thoughts and pain start gnawing away again. Only this time they're even more intense. I think, "Maybe I should have pulled *off* the road and checked the side brush where the injured body was thrown and now lies? Maybe I didn't go *far enough* back on the road and the accident occurred a mile farther back."

The pain of my possibly having hurt someone is now so intense that I have no choice—I really see it this way.

I turn the car around a second time and head an extra mile farther down the road to find the corpse. I drive by quickly. Assured that this time I've gone far enough I head back to school to take my exam. But I'm not through yet.

"My God," my attack relentlessly continues, "I didn't get *out* of the car to actually *look* on the side of the road!"

So I turn back a third time. I drive to the part of the highway where I think the accident happened. I park the car on the highway's shoulder. I get out and begin rummaging around in the brush. A police car comes up. I feel like I'm going out of my mind.

The policeman, seeing me thrash through the brush, asks, "What are you doing? Maybe I can help you?"

Well, I'm in a dilemma. I can't say, "Officer, please don't worry. You see, I've got obsessive-compulsive disorder, along with four million other Americans. I'm simply acting out a compulsion with obsessive qualities." I can't even say, "I'm really sick. Please help me." The disease is so insidious and embarrassing that it cannot be admitted to anyone. Anyway, so few really understand it, including myself.

So I tell the officer I was nervous about my exam and pulled off to the roadside to throw up. The policeman gives me a sincere and knowing smile and wishes me well.

But I start thinking again: "Maybe an accident did happen and the body has been cleared off the road. The policeman's here to see if I came back to the scene of the crime. God, maybe I really did hit someone . . . why else would a police car be in the area?" Then I realize he would have asked me about it. But would he, if he was trying to catch me?

I'm so caught up in the anxiety and these awful thoughts that I momentarily forget why I am standing on the side of the road. I'm back on the road again. The anxiety is peaking. Maybe the policeman didn't know about the accident? I should go back and conduct my search more *thoroughly*.

I want to go back and check more . . . but I can't. You see, the police car is tailing me on the highway. I'm now close to hysteria because I honestly believe someone is lying in the brush bleeding to death. Yes . . . the pain makes me believe this. "After all," I reason, "why would the pain be there in the first place?"

I arrive at school late for the exam. I have trouble taking the exam because I can't stop obsessing on the fantasy. The thoughts of the mythical accident keep intruding. Somehow I get through it.

The moment I get out of the exam I'm back on the road checking again. But now I'm checking two things. First that I didn't kill or maim someone and second, that the policeman doesn't catch me checking. After all, if I should be spotted on the roadside rummaging around the brush a second time, how in the world can I possibly explain such an incriminating and aimless action? I'm totally exhausted, but that awful anxiety keeps me checking, though a part of my psyche keeps telling me that this checking behavior is ridiculous, that it serves absolutely no purpose. But, with OCD, there is no other way.

Finally, after repeated checks, I'm able to break the ritual. I head home, dead tired. I know that if I can sleep it off, I'll feel better. Sometimes the pain dissipates through an escape into sleep.

I manage to lie down on my bed—hoping for sleep. But the incident has not totally left me—nor has the anxiety. I think, "If I really did hit someone, there would be a dent in the car's fender."

What I now do is no mystery to anyone. I haul myself up from bed and run out to the garage to check the fenders on the car. First I check the front two fenders, see no damage, and head back to bed. But . . . *did I check it well enough?*

I get up from bed again and now find myself checking the *whole body* of the car. I know this is absurd, but I can't help myself. Finally . . . finally, I disengage and head off to my room to sleep. Before I nod off, my last thought is, "I wonder what I'll check next?"

Let me tell you about myself. I'm thirty-six years old and have had obsessions, at least in mild form, since I was six years old. My son Jeffrey, age five, has had the illness since at least age two. My two brothers most probably have the disease, though less severely. There is a good chance my nephew, age eight, has OCD as well as my father and his father also. I can write this here, but families with OCD almost never tell each other about it if they can help it. I am the one who broke the silence. My brother has had a remarkable response to imipramine [which occasionally helps

OCD]. He said, "I never thought I would live my life without the pain and anxiety of all my 'dread' thoughts." Perhaps my other brother and nephew will consider treatment also.

I cannot really describe the torturous pain of the anxiety brought on by an obsessive-compulsive disorder attack. The checking incident I just relayed to you used to happen to me often. Between the ages of twenty-two and thirty-three (save for one or two brief remissions) this kind of an attack occurred every day. Many times it stayed with me all day long and, if it disappeared, a new attack, spawned from the old one, would quickly replace it. Later, other forms of checking began. I have stayed till midnight at my laboratory compelled to check my computer's simplest calculations by hand. The work is unpublished because I can never be certain that the numbers were averaged correctly.

I do not intend to sound dramatic, nor am I soliciting sympathy or pity. It's simply a fact of life that it's the pain—the deep, searing, never-ending pain—that makes this illness so unbearable. I know the pain. So do all the other OCs out there who share this illness with me and my family members. . . .

While there were indications from early childhood that I had the disease, it didn't clearly manifest itself until I was twenty-two years old. My symptoms were typical of obsessive-compulsives. I would check the gas oven and door locks, sometimes twenty times before I could go to bed at night. I would worry about poisoning myself and others with insecticides or cleaning fluids I may have touched. I would drive home from work, thinking that I left the light on in my office and drive all the way back to see if it was off: "It could start a fire." Sometimes I did this more than once in a day.

Many of the obsessions and compulsions were based in an extraordinary fear that my aggressive impulses, my anger, would, without me knowing it, leak out. I always thought I would start a fire by being negligent with cigarettes or kill someone by being a reckless driver. My vigilance was ongoing . . . and exhausting.

Each obsessive incident was accompanied by the fantasy that if I *didn't* act on it, something terrible would happen to me or someone else. Losing my job, being sent to prison, or hurting someone else were average catastrophic fantasies. Making *sure* these outcomes would not occur drove my compulsive behaviors.

The energy and time I would exert toward a hundred aimless acts has me shaking my head in disgust right now. I look back and wonder how I lived this way for over ten years. It was unbearable.

I hid my disease. I was like an alcoholic hiding his drink. My greatest fear was to be discovered. At times, my wife hated me for the illness. I hated myself. But I couldn't help it. The disease controls you, not the reverse.

In 1973, one year after the first onset, I went into therapy. The psychiatrist was very good. Over the next three years I made some excellent progress. I learned ways to cope and adapt. If there was an emotional source to the illness, the psychiatrist did as much as could be done to eliminate it.

Shortly thereafter, I went into remission and was okay for about a year or so. Not perfect, but substantially improved. After five years in therapy, it became clear that normal life-stress events seemed to trigger obsessive-compulsive episodes. After the birth of my first child, the disease struck again. This time it was worse than ever before.

My Son's Story

I went to father's night at my Jeffrey's pre-school. He was playing with a Fisher-Price toy, a schoolhouse, but his play was strange. He stood before the toy, jumped up and down, and flapped his arms as if excited by it. (We later labeled this behavior "flapping.") His muscles from head to toe contracted and relaxed over and over again. He would grunt and contort his face as if he was exerting great effort. When the jumping stopped, he would put his arms together and wiggle his fingers just above eye level (we later labeled this behavior "wormies"). The finger movement was a form of self-stimulation; the grunting and muscle contraction, relaxation sequence would continue during "wormies" as well. He did this nonstop for thirty-five minutes. I could not disengage him. No matter what I tried, he simply wouldn't stop.

Occasionally he would bring a person, toy, chair, or desk into the play, but these self-stimulating behaviors and the self-induced muscle contractions continued. When I tried to disengage him I was met with repeated and rigid resistance. He *had to do* this bizarre behavior. He also had to play with the toy "his" way. Any change I introduced was vehemently rejected.

That night I spoke with my wife. We had a strong hunch that something wasn't right.

We carefully reviewed his behavior over the past year. We noted his excitability and extremely low attention span. He could not sit still, nor could he focus on a task. It would literally take him fifteen minutes to put his socks on because he was so distracted by other things. We discussed how he would wiggle his fingers or dangle strings in front of his eyes for long periods of time (labeled "stringing") while doing muscle contractions and grunting. His resistance to change and new experiences were all too easy to identify. His obsessions with counting, serializing, and the repetition of questions to which he already had heard the answers a hundred times before were also recalled. At age two he would throw a fit if an object was not in its "proper" location on his night table and when he would get upset, he would cry, "Mommy, calm me down!"

We couldn't engage him in activity that was right for his age. When we did get him involved in some normal play—say, block building—he would bring "stringing," "wormies," and "flapping," along with the muscle contractions, into the play.

As we began to identify all the puzzle's pieces, we knew we could no longer chalk all this up to developmental lag or immaturity. We desperately wanted to, but we couldn't. Something was fundamentally wrong. And he was getting worse.

Often we look back and ask ourselves, how could we have waited so long to get help? The question is really a variation of another one: "How could we have been so negligent?" The answers can be found in several places.

Denial is one. What parent wants to face the fact that his or her child is handicapped? Jeffrey was so young—just four years old—that it was easy to rationalize away much of his aberrant behavior: "He'll grow out of it." "It's only temporary." "He's a boy and boys mature slower than girls."

Moreover, he had so many healthy positive attributes. His intelligence was apparent. His language skills were consistently improving. His attitude was generally good and he expressed a wide range of feelings—sadness, joy, silliness, boredom, and he loved to laugh. A strong need to please his parents, especially Mommy, was developing. He was insatiably curious about spatial locations: "Kroger's is next to Wendy's? Right, Mommy?" He was gentle and kind, perhaps to a fault, and affectionate—he would hug and kiss and snuggle with us.

Yet when a child dangles strings in front of his eyes four hours a day and tells you he can't help himself, or asks, "Mommy, why do I play with strings?", rationalizations soon wear painfully thin. Our child was very sick. We could no longer pretend, and we also knew that we had to do something about it.

A parent of an obsessive-compulsive child must understand the pain of the anxiety and also its control over one's behavior. Your child has absolutely *no control* over what he or she is doing . . . NONE. Your child's rituals may be totally aimless. They will make no sense to you. You cannot intellectually understand why your child does what he or she does. Don't try to understand in this way because all it will do is frustrate you; normal human reasoning and logic does not exist with this disease. The only logic is your child's relentless pain, his enormous need to stop this pain, and his involuntary behavior geared to this end.

Response and Analysis

1. What is the difference between an obsession and a compulsion? Describe the obsession(s) and compulsion(s) experienced by Dr. S. and his son. How does OCD affect Dr. S.'s daily activities?

2. What did Dr. S. learn in therapy about the events that trigger his episodes? How might cognitive or behavioral therapists treat persons with OCD?

Personal Experience and Application

1. Most of us have checked to see if we locked a door, even though we are almost certain that we did. On occasion, we may have even driven back home to make certain that we unplugged an iron. Imagine if thoughts to check the door and the iron haunted us dozens or hundreds of times a day. What might you do to try to control your urge to recheck every previous action you had taken? How might your repetitive behavior affect your daily routines? Your relationships with others?

Research

Suppose you want to investigate the therapeutic effects of support groups for sufferers of OCD. Your first task is to contact support groups and obtain their cooperation. What ethical issues might be involved in conducting research with participants who suffer from OCD? How might you solve these ethical problems?

I HAVE DISSOCIATIVE IDENTITY DISORDER

Quiet Storm

Psychological Concept
dissociative identity disorder (formerly called multiple personality disorder)

Quiet Storm, a pseudonym the writer gave herself to symbolize the quiet surface that covers an inner storm, writes of the several people who she believes live within her. Each has a separate identity, career, and "memories, talents, dreams, and fears." She describes several of the women who are a part of her, and tells how they evolved as defenders against child abuse. Storm's interior world is vast, filled with children, adolescents, and adults. People often notice great changes in her and remark that she often seems like a completely different person. All of her selves are gradually healing, but integration is not an issue she is ready to confront.

Some readers may find portions of Storm's article disturbing because of the abusive ordeals she presents as causes of her illness.

Elaina is a licensed clinical therapist. Connie is a nurse. Sydney is a delightful little girl who likes to collect bugs in an old mayonnaise jar. Lynn is shy and has trouble saying her l's, and Heather—Heather is a teenager trying hard to be grown-up. We are many different people, but we have one very important thing in common: We share a single body.

We have Multiple Personality Disorder (MPD). We have dozens of different people living inside us, each with our own memories, talents, dreams, and fears. Some of us "come out" to work or play or cook or sleep. Some of us only watch from inside. Some of us are still lost in the past, a tortured past full of incest and abuse. And there are many who were so damaged by this past and who have fled so deep inside, we fear we may never reach them.

Imagine a little girl walking with her parents through a bookstore. She's only four, but she already knows how to read. She sees a book she really wants, and asks her parents if she can have it. They tell her no, and a single tear of disappointment rolls down her cheek. A single tear, but it is one tear too many.

The little girl's parents don't say anything in the store, but when they get home they take off her panties and beat her until her bottom is raw and bleeding. The panties are replaced with a diaper that is fastened to her skin with silver duct tape. She is locked in a closet for three days. She is fed laxative mixed with milk in a baby bottle; her diaper is never changed. Her parents tell her again and again that she is a dirty little baby and will never grow up. They are right.

There is more, worse, but the little girl does not remember it. It's too painful to remember more. If she stays in that closet and refuses to acknowledge the passing of time, then maybe those awful things didn't really happen. Maybe there can be some other ending to her story.

In a way that little girl never left that closet. Another little girl did, one who shared the same body but whose existence began the moment the closet door opened. Where there was one, now there were two—one who understood that she must never ever cry to her parents for any reason and another who huddled forever in a dark inner closet, because to remember what happened next, when her parents finally came to get her, would be too much for a single young mind to bear.

Many of our Alter personalities were born of abuse. Some came because they were needed, others came to protect.

Leah came whenever she heard our father say "Come lay awhile with me." If she came, none of our other Alters would have to do those things he wanted. She could do them for us, and protect us from that part of our childhood.

Halfcup came when we were left at home for days on end with nothing to eat. She cooked meals for us. She cleaned up afterward so our parents wouldn't know we'd found a way to unlock our bedroom door. Halfcup still loves to cook. Last Christmas we bought her a new set of pots and pans.

Connie came when the body was beaten so badly that somebody had to come who didn't feel the pain, who could comfort the Alters who hurt, who could tell the doctor we'd fallen off our bike. We couldn't let anyone tell him what really happened. That would have made our parents even madder.

Unlike many of our Alters, Connie grew up into an adult as our body did. She was created to be a healer, so it was only natural that when she was old enough, she would enroll in nursing school.

Connie didn't know that at the same time she was in nursing school, Elaina was in grad school working on her social work degree. Nor did Elaina know about Connie. All they knew was that, even with only three hours of sleep each night, there never was enough time to get things done.

MPD is not a disease. It is not a sickness. It is a highly developed coping mechanism that allows the young mind to compartmentalize, or "dissociate," repeated and traumatic abuse. The six-year-old who smiles at her teacher at school cannot hold back the tears when her father enters her room in the middle of the night. Somebody else has to come, somebody who can do those things without crying because crying isn't ever allowed. And the little girl whose mother tucks her in at night and calls her Peaches will never understand why that same mother ties her to the bed when she has a fever and beats her and tells her only bad little girls get sick. Somebody else has to come—somebody whose nose isn't stuffy and who doesn't have a fever.

Being able to create Alter personalities to cope with the abuse is the only thing that allowed us to survive our childhood alive. MPD was never a disease—it was a gift, the gift of life we gave to ourselves.

Once we were grown up and had escaped from our abusive parents, the system that protected us for so many years became unnecessary. But still our internal system of multiple personalities survived, and the longer we went untreated the worse things became for us. We lost time, as Alters unknown to us took control of the body. Sometimes they went shopping. Sometimes they haunted libraries. Sometimes they cowered on the floor in the closet because one of our Alters saw a little girl walking hand in hand with her father and the very sight of it terrified her. Often an innocent remark from a friend would trigger old memories of abuse, and for the Alter who held those memories it was as if the abuse were still going on. We couldn't stand to be touched, or to have anyone tell us they cared for us. We felt worthless and alone.

It took five years and as many therapists before we found someone who recognized our MPD. It was another year before we fully accepted the diagnosis. Only then did we truly begin to know ourselves.

The more we learn about ourselves and the abuse that created us, the stronger our system becomes. We've become one another's friends. We form alliances, accept responsibilities. We take care of each other.

Elaina and Connie work for our living. Elaina is a respected therapist who is building an extensive private practice. Connie works weekends at one of the local emergency rooms. Heather drives the car, and watches out for all the children we still have inside of us. Sydney sits with the tiniest ones when they are crying, and Lynn holds the stuffed polar bear while we sleep and pesters Heather to make sure we have plenty of crayons on hand for when she and her inside friends want to color.

Like many Multiples, we have constructed a large internal house where we go to live when we are not occupying the body. It's several stories high, with crystal chandeliers and big picture windows, and there's an inner yard filled with rainbows where the little ones go to play while Elaina and Connie are busy at work. The little ones are never allowed out when the adults are at their jobs. We have enough trouble hiding our MPD from people as it is. We have to wear tinted contacts because our eye color changes every time a different Alter comes out, and if we had a dollar for every time somebody has said to us, "Jeez, it's like you're a completely different person," we wouldn't have to worry so much about paying the $7,000 a year we have to spend on therapy because our medical insurance doesn't cover MPD.

We each have our own rooms in our internal house. We can decorate them the way we want, and lock the door and be absolutely safe from harm. But it's sad to know there are many doors in this house of ours that have never been opened. Late at night we hear the sobs and screams of those who live behind these doors, Alters who are still imprisoned by their abusive pasts and for whom there is yet no peace.

One of our Alters named Molly recently told our therapist that the very first thing she can remember was being locked in a closet. There was someone in there with her, a little girl dressed only in a diaper that was taped to her skin. Molly remembered leaving the closet, but didn't know what became of that other little girl.

Our therapist tried hard to reach Molly's companion, but she wouldn't talk to him. She was too afraid to come out, terrified of the devastating memories that loomed just beyond her closet door.

That was the day of the tremendous thunderstorm. There were high winds, pelting sheets of rain, lightning, hail, and thunder. We seem to gather a lot of internal energy from storms. We feel electric inside and sometimes seem to feel a part of the storm itself. We think of ourselves as a storm, a quiet storm where outside everything may appear calm and peaceful but inside violent tornadoes rage.

Anyway, as soon as the storm began, we went driving in Heather's car. All around us the storm was swirling and howling. We could see, we could practically feel, the rain pelting down on us through the glass T-top roof.

While Heather drove, Molly led many of us to the place deep inside where that little girl still cowered in her closet. She opened the door and went inside. She held the little girl in her arms, and told her about all of us and how we were waiting outside to love her and take care of her. All she had to do was remember the past and by remembering, free herself from it.

Bravely, the little girl took Molly's hand and walked with her out of that closet. Everything appeared misty to her at first, but then the memories coalesced and we all looked on as she remembered what happened more than a quarter of a century ago so vividly that it all seemed to be happening to her again, right then and there. She remembered the baths, the boiling hot water, the acrid lye soap, the wire brush with the rounded wooden handle. She remembered the pain, the blood, the searing violation of her private parts.

"You won't be a bad little girl anymore, will you?"

"No, Mama! No, Daddy!"

We remembered too. We wept, we screamed, we shared the pain while Heather drove us through streets full of water that sloshed against the wheel rims, through bolts of lightning that lit up the sky and through thunder that shook the car.

We named the little girl Misty, and when she was through remembering, Molly took her to her room where she removed her soiled diaper and bathed her ever so gently, and then helped her into a pink night dress and a pair of big-girl panties. The two curled up on fluffy pillows.

Outside, the storm was still raging, but inside, for a time, all was quiet in the eye of our storm.

Little by little we were healing ourselves and freeing ourselves from the tyranny of our past. Our therapist tells us that when we have remembered everything and worked through the pain associated with these memories, we will no longer need Alter personalities to protect us, and then and only then we can begin the process of integration into a single, cohesive personality. But that will be our decision—whether or not we will even want to turn from many back into one.

Integration isn't something we even think about right now. Right now we're far too busy working to heal all the wounded children inside us, the frightened adolescents and angry adults. Together we will continue to reclaim what was stolen from us by the perpetrators of our abuse. We cannot recapture the lost years, the shattered innocence, but we will not let our past destroy our future. We are survivors of our abuse, not its victims. We know that the loudest cries are often very, very quiet. We will listen to these cries, and we will honor each part of us that endured the pain in silence.

For us, the silence is broken.

Response and Analysis

1. What tragic events does the author suggest led to her developing dissociative identity disorder (formerly called multiple personality disorder)? Why does she believe the personalities were needed? What does the author mean when she writes, "We think of ourselves as a storm, a quiet storm where outside everything may appear calm and peaceful but inside violent tornadoes rage"?

2. Briefly describe the personality named Molly. What did Molly tell the therapist? When did the other personalities remember the terrible events that occurred when the author was a little girl? According to the psychodynamic perspective and the behavioral perspective, how do dissociative disorders such as dissociative identity disorder develop?

Personal Experience and Application

1. Suppose the office of psychological services at your college or university asks you to help create a public service announcement discussing the causes of child abuse. List three factors that are associated with child abuse. What recommendations might you offer to reduce its incidence?

Research

Suppose you conducted a research project examining the worldwide prevalence of dissociative identity disorder. Imagine that your results show that the prevalence of dissociative identity disorder varies considerably across cultures. In what ways could you explain this finding?

THE BEAST: A RECKONING WITH DEPRESSION

Tracy Thompson

Psychological Concept
depression

Journalist Tracy Thompson describes how depression has been like a beast, hounding her and changing the course of her life. Depression has affected her close personal relationships and caused her anxiety about her job. At times she would be listless and have thoughts of suicide. She wonders if her career would be in jeopardy if others discovered she had a mood disorder. Although Prozac has helped, she expresses concerns with its possible side effects. Yet medication, while not a cure, has allowed Thompson to benefit from therapy and to lead a reasonably normal life.

My body aches intermittently, in waves, as if I had malaria. I eat with no appetite, simply because the taste of food is one of my dwindling number of pleasures. I am tired, so tired. Last night I lay like a pile of old clothes, and when David came to bed I did not stir. Sex is a foreign notion. At work today I am forgetful; I have trouble forming sentences, I lose track of them halfway through, and my words keep getting tangled. I look at my list of things to do today, and keep on looking at it; nothing seems to be happening. Things seem sad to me. . . .

At least that's how it seems. Sitting in the subway station, waiting for the train, I realize I am not thinking straight, so I do what I've done before in this situation: I get out a pen and paper and start writing down what I call my "dysfunctional thoughts." Just between the car and the subway station escalator, I accumulate these: "Everybody but me is in shape. I am fat." Then: "My career is going nowhere. I'm never going to get a promotion at work. They think I'm second-rate." And: "My relationship with David is not working. I'm getting irritable and withdrawn, finding fault. More proof that I can't handle intimacy."

I take it on faith that I am thinking in distorted ways at the moment. But I'm never really sure of that when it would most help to know. I don't even know when this current siege began—a week ago? A month ago? The onset is so gradual, and these things are hard to tell. All I know is, the Beast is back.

It is called depression, and my experiences with it have shaped my life—altered my personality, affected my most intimate relationships, changed the course of my career—in ways I will probably never be fully aware of. These days, however, the Beast has been cornered—which is to say that he escapes from time to time, but I have some control over him. I have an array of new antidepressant drugs at my disposal—far more powerful than traditional antidepressants, faster-acting and with fewer side effects—and a psychiatrist with whom I have developed trust and a good working relationship. After many years of pretending the Beast did not exist, I now have deep respect for my adversary.

I call him "Beast" because it suits him—though I imagine "him" not as a creature but as a force, something that has slipped outside the bounds of natural existence, a psychic freight train of roaring despair. For most of my life, the Beast has been my implacable and unpredictable enemy, disappearing for months or years, then returning in strength. He appeared in the most benign of guises, hiding in plain view behind a word I thought I understood, but didn't. I was using the word "depression" as early as fourteen in my diary, but I did so in the nonmedical sense of the word—the ordinary, transient despair of being a teenager. Yet, even in grammar school, there were long stretches—weeks, maybe months, it is impossible now to say—when every morning I counted the hours that had to pass before I could crawl into bed again, times when I escaped to the shower and turned on the water full blast to disguise the sound of my weeping, unhappy over something I could not name. I suspected something was wrong with me, that this flat and colorless world I lived in was different from the one most other people lived in, and I wanted desperately to be "normal." . . .

I started taking Prozac after more than a year of a debilitating depression only partially relieved by traditional antidepressants. Within weeks, that mental hurricane had stopped dead in its tracks. I offer no proof; first X happened, and then Y. But it is hard not to attribute that miracle to the little green-and-white pills, difficult not to give them credit for the fact that since then, I've lived something like a normal life. It's been a gift.

Maybe even a miracle. Prozac seems to offer a shortcut on that old American journey, the pursuit of happiness. It promises social assertiveness, relief from pesky personality quirks, a cheerful disposition for the terminally cranky—but at what cost? On the filing cabinet in my study I have a *New Yorker* cartoon that explores what great thinkers of the nineteenth century might have been like on Prozac. My favorite is Edgar Allan Poe, greeting a raven with a sprightly "Hello, birdie!" It sums up our ambivalence.

I'm ambivalent sometimes too. Will I pay a price for this normal life sometime, somewhere—a cancerous tumor, a learning-disabled child? I don't know. Nobody knows. I have rolled the dice, I have made a gambler's bargain. To some, this seems a reckless venture into a Brave New World of personality enhancement. People tell me I'm foolish, that I've donated my brain to science before I'm even dead, that I've opted for an artificial life instead of the authentic one I could have had. . . .

I'm closing in on forty, the point at which youth stops being taken for granted and becomes a relative term. It's too early for grand summary statements—but even so, I find myself weighing conclusions about how much this illness has come to define me, and how much I have imprinted my personality on it. I'm casting about for some rule, some unifying principle, by which this puzzle of my life can be seen as a whole. And it seems to me that my illness has been the product of three forces: genetics, culture, and chance.

I was born with a predisposition to suffer from depression. I was also fated to grow up in a culture filled with anxiety—some the product of the times I lived in, some the product of the religious sensibilities imposed on me by my parents, who were themselves transmitting the culture they were born into. Part of it was the residual fearfulness I sensed from my mother, who could not escape her own past. And then there was a childhood accident which marred my face just as I was entering adolescence—a chance event, a unique stressor, which forever altered my trajectory.

Over time, all these things worked together—and, in doing so, they permanently altered the "wiring" in my brain, which was not perfectly "wired" to begin with. This is a way of thinking about depression which scientists are exploring, which is known informally as "kindling." It makes sense to me. It describes the way my brain works in other spheres—mastering an algebra problem in eighth grade, learning to serve a tennis ball: a bombardment of stimuli, a repeated reaction, the spark of comprehension, the eventual effortlessness of what had once seemed foreign and impossible. Emotions, I believe, are also partly learned. And can be relearned—with help.

For me, help began with psychoactive drugs. Drugs were not a miracle cure or a replacement for therapy; they were what enabled me to derive the maximum benefit from therapy, which was hard work. Drugs are tools, nothing more—but that is no small thing. To a person scaling a cliff, a grappling hook is the difference between life and death.

I make no summary statement, then; I only say that at one crucial point, I chose life. It was an arduous choice, and I tried my best to avoid it. When I could avoid it no longer, it came down to the realization that I owned a moral responsibility for my life. The question then became: how do I live now? And then, having faced that question, I realized something else: every day, the question is asked again.

Response and Analysis

1.   What symptoms of depression does Tracy Thompson experience? How does having depression affect her work and interactions with others? Why was she apprehensive about disclosing her depression?

2.   Thompson describes Prozac and therapy as important parts of her treatment. What are the most common means of treating depression? How effective are they?

Personal Experience and Application

1.   How is depression different from the blues, sadness, or grief? Do you think that depression differs from these other states physiologically? Why or why not?

2.   Do you think that differences in prevalence for depression and bipolar disorder might be the result of social expectations, clinicians' interpretations, or women's

greater willingness than men to report distress? Why or why not?

Research

Suppose you suspect that a client's income level affects the quality of treatment she or he receives. You hypothesize that persons with higher incomes have better treatment outcomes because they have access to higher-quality treatment than those with lower incomes. You conduct a study examining how treatment outcomes are affected by the following variables: client's income, client's education level, therapist's training, therapist's years of experience, and therapist's fees. Which among these variables do you suspect would correlate most strongly with successful treatment rates? Why? How else might the results be explained?

I FEEL CHEATED BY HAVING THIS ILLNESS

Allan Davis

Psychological Concept
schizophrenia

Allan Davis had to cope with being homeless and schizophrenic. After he had completed a degree in English Language and Literature at Princeton University, Davis's life deteriorated as his schizophrenia progressed. His symptoms improved when he received antipsychotic medication during his first hospitalization, but they returned when he discontinued the medication. He was constantly beset with anxiety and fear, so he began using illegal drugs to blunt his feelings. Eventually, his behavior brought him into contact with the courts, and from there he was transferred to a hospital where he received treatment.

My schizophrenia sneaked up on me and filled my life with danger. When my schizophrenia became obvious in 1977, I was twenty-three, an African American junior at Princeton University, and a drug abuser.

 The first abnormal thing I remember was my perception that people on television were talking to me and about me. Later, I became convinced that everybody at

Princeton was gay, and I became frightened by the prospect of flunking out if I didn't match that standard, which I did not. I also believed I learned a color code known only to members of organized crime or the intelligence community.

Then, Memorial Day weekend of 1977, my girlfriend's brother was killed in a car accident. That was the beginning of a major delusion in my life: that people don't really die. I convinced myself that the body in the casket was a dummy. My girlfriend didn't understand that I was becoming ill with schizophrenia, but she had her own problem. She was devastated by her brother's death and spent her time crying in my arms or angrily physically attacking me for not doing anything to make her feel better. We finally separated.

By 1982, at twenty-eight, I had constructed a fantasy world where I was the only male capable of having sex and where people didn't really die, they just became other people, always female. Occasionally I would doubt my fantasy and become depressed, but eventually I would simply take more illegal drugs until I was high enough to convince myself again.

I came home to Topeka in late 1982. A psychiatrist diagnosed my problem as schizophrenia, but no medication was prescribed. I didn't know what schizophrenia was and neither did my parents. Even now I don't think they fully understand. My parents thought my problem behavior was a result of my drug use, but, in truth, my schizophrenic delusion was the cause of my problems. Even when I didn't use drugs, my delusions remained.

Within a few months, Mr. Davis began treatment at the Menninger Community Service Office, a Topeka outpatient clinic.[1] *He first saw a psychiatrist and later was in psychotherapy with a social worker. He recalls that he was not invested in treatment at that time and eventually dropped out. Because he was too ill to hold a job, he received a monthly disability check that made it possible for him to move from his parents' home to a place of his own. It also supported his drug habit.*

Today I know for sure that I have schizophrenia, because I had visual and auditory disturbances. But for a long time I refused to believe the diagnosis of schizophrenia meant anything was seriously wrong with me. I still believed in my fantasy world, and I thought the diagnosis of schizophrenia was just a convenient way to get a disability check.

In 1986 I began to experience severe, unexplained physical problems which I now attribute to anxiety. I would be asleep but aware and unable to breathe or move for what seemed like a minute. I had this problem occasionally as a child, but now it occurred with regularity. I also had heart palpitations, which scared me so much that my fantasy world collapsed. I was afraid I was dying, and I was afraid to die. I stopped using drugs because they made me more anxious.

---

[1] The italicized portions were added by the editors of *Menninger Perspective* and offer important information about Mr. Davis's illness and treatment.

These palpitations led Mr. Davis to see his general physician, who suggested that his symptoms might be related to a mental illness.

I followed my physician's advice and checked into the psychiatric ward at a local general hospital. I came out with a prescription for an antipsychotic medication.

With the medication, Mr. Davis's thought disturbances abated, but he was extremely depressed and withdrawn. He stayed in bed until late in the morning, then went to his parents' home to eat, watch television, and nap. Returning to his home by 8 P.M., he would take his medication and be in bed by 8:30 P.M. With no friends, his only social contacts occurred when he attended the church where his father is pastor.

I gained sixty pounds, I stopped shaving, and my appearance basically became much worse. In truth, I was depressed because of the eventuality of death. Nobody noticed my depression; they just thought I was withdrawn.

I took the antipsychotic drug until 1988, when the prescribing psychiatrist discontinued it because he thought I was exhibiting symptoms of tardive dyskinesia.

Tardive dyskinesia is a serious side effect of some antipsychotic medications. It is marked by involuntary movements, frequently involving the mouth and tongue and sometimes the limbs and trunk. Symptoms may remit in some patients who quit taking the offending drug, but they may be permanent for others.

From 1986 to 1989, Mr. Davis also returned to the Menninger Community Service Office, but he frequently was unable to talk to the therapist about his feelings and could not participate in the treatment process.

After the medication was discontinued, my delusion eventually returned. I also began using drugs again. My visual disturbances returned and were more numerous. I would see after-images of people where people no longer were, I would see lights in the night sky traveling between the stars, and more commonly I would see streaks of light or darkness in the daytime.

Escalating Problems

The years from 1989 to 1991 were especially turbulent for Mr. Davis and for members of his family. He lived with his parents, but disagreements with them led him to leave for extended periods. Once, he traveled to Texas, New York, Boston, and, finally, Seattle, where he lived in a shelter and briefly worked at a fast food restaurant. After six months, he returned to Topeka.

Later in 1991, I moved from Topeka to Los Angeles because marijuana was cheaper and more plentiful there. I obtained an apartment in a building for the homeless mentally ill, but then I started using daily a product sold to me as crack. I thought when I got high everybody and everything got high, so even though I was not impressed with the product, I would still use it and marijuana to—as I believed—bring peace and avoid earthquakes. I was deep into my delusion and terribly unaware that I lived in a dangerous world.

When my drug usage got me evicted from my apartment, I became officially homeless. I had been a Boy Scout as a kid, so I was neatly efficient at urban camping. I began spending much of my days in a park frequented by drug dealers and users. While there I found labels, still with legible lot numbers on them, from local anesthetics such as lidocaine, a novocaine substitute. I became convinced that the crack I was buying was nothing more than a drug from a dentist's office. I sought assistance from, in my opinion, the proper drug authority: the police who permitted the drug sales. Twice, when the police stopped while driving through the drug park I gave them the labels.

I never understood why one person who bought drugs in the park called me a snitch and threatened my life, but my deluded beliefs and lack of awareness of danger were getting me into trouble. I began to have more and more disagreements with the park residents who hung around and mooched off of the drug salesmen.

Because I believed I was a special drug user and deserved to be treated in a special way, I would say things that got me into altercations, but I almost always ran. One time I was being chased and a bystander blocked my path. I evaded him but stumbled and fell. When I got up, he hit me. I suffered a fractured jaw, because I was breathing through my open mouth when I was hit.

I was on the operating table having my jaw wired shut when I began to bleed from the nose and choke. The anesthesiologist didn't know that one sinus was smaller than the other, so I bled when the tubes were removed from my nose. The wires on my teeth shredded the insides of both lips as I struggled to breathe. I awoke in severe pain.

With my jaw wired shut, I returned to the drug park certain in my delusion that I was safe. My visual disturbances continued, and I began to experience mild auditory disturbances. The voices usually said "here" or "me."

One morning while I was in the park, I heard an auditory disturbance say, "Here's where he gets hurt." I guess I burned my finger on a marijuana cigarette. Then, as I was going somewhere, I looked behind me and saw a park resident who had never really threatened me following me. I tried to evade him, but I heard another voice in front of me—another auditory disturbance—say, "Here." By then I knew better than to do anything the voices said to do, so I stopped, because the voice was in front of me.

I felt a thud on my left shoulder and saw that my pursuer had kept running past me when I stopped. He was looking back at me, and he was holding a five-inch folding knife. I had been stabbed less than an inch from my spine. The wound was three or four inches deep, but no major blood vessels or organs were damaged.

Because of my delusional condition, because I referred to my visual disturbances as antipersonnel radar, and because one police officer considered me a troublemaker, I could not get the police to find and arrest my attacker when I returned to the park several days after being stabbed. It took a lot to get me to stay away from the drug park. In my fantasy world I was safe, but I had a knife wound that said I wasn't safe.

I finally left Los Angeles and came home after two years. One day I was arrested at the local mall.

One of the mall merchants accused Mr. Davis of creating a disturbance in her store. He left the store when asked, but the store manager called mall security anyway. The mall security chief told Mr. Davis he was banned from the entire mall and could not return. Mr. Davis went back inside to call the mall manager to verify that he could be banned from the entire mall and was arrested. Another shopper had observed his arrest, and she volunteered to testify at his trial.

When I got to court I was shocked to find that my court-appointed attorney had not prepared a defense for me or interviewed the witness, and the witness did not appear. I was convicted. When I complained to my attorney, he lost his temper, threatened to kick my "——— —," and chased me from the courtroom.

The judge didn't see what happened, and I guess he assumed that the mentally ill person was at fault, because he called me back into the courtroom and found me in contempt of court. My protestations that I hadn't done anything and my inability to follow the judge's order to be quiet landed me in jail.

The jail psychiatrist found me incompetent to be sentenced and recommended that I go to the Menninger hospital or stay in jail. I went to the Menninger hospital after almost a month in jail.

The Menninger Hospital

Menninger operates a spectrum of clinical programs for persons with chronic mental illnesses and has earned a reputation as a center of excellence for the treatment of persons like Mr. Davis. Central to these programs is the HOPE Unit of the C. F. Menninger Memorial Hospital. This unit, whose acronym stands for Health Opportunities and Psychological Enhancement, provides extended inpatient treatment for persons with severe mental illnesses.

The HOPE Unit was particularly appropriate for Mr. Davis because of the comprehensive treatment it provides. Primary symptoms of schizophrenia, such as delusions, disturbances of association, and excessive ambivalence, seem to be of biological origin and can often be treated with psychotropic drugs. However, the negative symptoms, such as apathy and deterioration of healthy daily living habits, are, at least in part, actually psychological reactions to the biological disorder. They must be treated using approaches such as individual psychotherapy, group psychotherapy, and psychosocial treatment. The HOPE unit provides all of these.

Nevertheless, Mr. Davis remained reluctant to participate in treatment. In his state of delusion, he continued to believe that the street drugs that he had been taking would be most beneficial for him. Fearing that medications would cause serious side effects, he refused to take the antipsychotic medications prescribed by his psychiatrist.

Thus, the first task for staff was to develop a trusting relationship with Mr. Davis. Through daily contact, psychiatrist Katherine Weyrens and members of the nursing team addressed his fears. Without pressuring or pushing too hard, they encouraged him to relax and talk, as he was able. Knowing his fears about medications, they provided sound, accurate information about psychotropic drugs and what he might expect from them.

In addition, Mr. Davis participated in individual and group psychotherapy. His parents and brothers joined him in a meeting with his treatment team. Through this meeting, they came to better understand and accept his illness and were able to provide ongoing support for him.

Three months into his hospitalization, Mr. Davis agreed to take an antipsychotic medication.

After three months of refusing medication, which I regarded as virtually poison, I relented, really because I had no choice, and tried an antipsychotic drug. My understanding was that if I did not try the drug, the law would send me to a state facility where I would be forced to take it.

With no access to illegal drugs to reinforce the delusion and my back in a corner, it took me only two days to accept what is real: people do die, sex does occur, and so does violence. I was out of the fantasy for the final time, never more to return.

During his fourth and final month in the hospital, as his antipsychotic drug regimen was refined, Mr. Davis continued to improve. Working with staff and participating with other patients in therapy groups, he earned more privileges and was able to go unescorted to prescribed activities including the gym. He began working with an art therapist.

Leaving the Hospital

To sustain their gains, patients with serious, chronic mental illnesses like schizophrenia need a stable, supportive environment in which to continue treatment following hospitalization. Menninger Partial Hospitalization Services are designed to meet those needs by providing ongoing group therapy, opportunities for socialization, help in reentering society through volunteer work, school, or employment, and the monitoring of medications. As their condition allows, patients live in group homes, with family members, or on their own. It was to this program that Mr. Davis transferred, and he returned to his parents' home.

After moving home, I asked my prescribing psychiatrist for an antidepressant, and two weeks after beginning to take it I was pleasantly surprised that I was feeling better. Encouraged by that success, I then asked for an anti-anxiety agent, and a very small dosage was prescribed for me. That also helped.

The antipsychotic medication has eliminated the visual and auditory disturbances. I regret the years I spent in my nonmedicated condition. Now I need all three of my prescriptions.

Mr. Davis has been in the partial hospital program for eighteen months. He spends a portion of each day five days a week at Menninger, participating in a variety of meetings and activities including yoga classes, a relapse prevention group, and a medications group in which patients learn about the medications they are taking and the effects—both good and bad—that they may produce. He writes for the patients' newsletter and attends classes at Washburn University in Topeka.

He meets weekly with his case coordinator, social worker Kay Kelly, to assess how his life is going and to get help with any problems, and he continues to see his psychiatrist.

Twice weekly he participates in a therapy group. "I know that social isolation is a symptom of both schizophrenia and depression," Mr. Davis said. "I'm not very talkative in groups, but I think I am benefiting from attending." Ms. Kelly said Mr. Davis also helps other group members through his understanding of their experiences and how they are feeling. Although it is difficult for him, with encouragement he has been able to reach out to others.

Mr. Davis also has made strides in developing a circle of friends through the Sunshine Connection, a drop-in center for consumers of mental health services. He is president of the center's board of directors. Funded by Kansas Social and Rehabilitation Services and located on the grounds of Topeka State Hospital, the Sunshine Connection provides activities for mental health patients on Friday nights and Saturday afternoons when most other outpatient programs are closed. Up to fifty people visit the center on Saturday to enjoy table tennis and other games, television, movie videos, live music, and snacks.

Looking to the Future

I keep myself neat and exercise regularly. I am studying journalism at Washburn University. My GPA (grade point average) is 3.5, and I optimistically expect it to go higher. I expect to have a real job someday. Maybe I'll write my autobiography, because there is a lot more to my story than can be told in this brief account and, besides, not many people come back from where I was.

Although his future is uncertain, Mr. Davis expects to complete his degree in mass media and likely will attend the University of Kansas to get a master's degree in a journalism-related field. He is interested in teaching at the college level.

Having come to grips with his own illness, he also has thought of working in the mental health field. One possibility, he said, would be to work as a case manager in a community mental health center, where he could apply what he has learned through his own struggle with schizophrenia to helping others with mental illnesses. "Based on my own experience, I know how difficult it is to convince consumers (patients) of things," he said.

Despite the progress he has made and his hard-earned understanding and acceptance of his illness and what life is like for a person with a chronic mental illness, Mr. Davis continues to face challenges. He feels cheated by having his illness and wonders why he couldn't have lived a "normal life like everybody else."

I am convinced that I have schizophrenia, and I am pretty sure I will be taking medications for the rest of my life. I'm forty-two years old. I've never been married and I have no children. I have no love in my life. I have no relatives in the Midwest except my parents. I am very concerned about growing old alone. One of my major concerns is the inevitability of death, but there is nothing I can do about it.

I think about being stabbed, and it scares me. I am embarrassed by some of the things I did. I don't have any ill feelings about my arrest or the events in the court-room, because that led to my recovery. I feel cheated by having this illness.

Response and Analysis

1. What symptoms of schizophrenia does Allan Davis display? Give examples of visual, auditory, and emotional disturbances, and of his difficulties interacting with people.

2. What reasons does Davis give for his using illegal drugs? How did his delusional beliefs concerning drug use get him into trouble? What treatment did Davis finally receive? What helped him?

Personal Experience and Application

1. Briefly summarize Davis's conflicts with the courts, his attorney, and other persons who are homeless. Why do you think he had these conflicts? Do you think he has felt cheated by society as well as by schizophrenia? Why or why not?

2. Three to four million Americans with schizophrenia are permanently unemployed, and many are unemployable. About half of all patients in mental hospitals are diagnosed with schizophrenia. Considering these statistics, how should society care for people with schizophrenia? Where should people with schizophrenia live? Who do you think should assist people with schizophrenia and other psychological disorders when they cannot work and cannot pay for living expenses or for mental health treatment?

Research

Suppose you conduct a twenty-year longitudinal study to investigate the degree to which symptoms associated with schizophrenia improve over time. The participants are fifty people who are twenty years old and meet the DSM-IV criteria for schizophrenia. Your objective is to assess the participants at the same time each year for twenty years. Unfortunately, you have increasing difficulty locating the participants over the years. By the twentieth year, you are able to contact only 40 percent of the original fifty participants. How might the loss of participants affect your conclusions?

FEELING GOOD

David D. Burns

Psychological Concept

applying cognitive therapy techniques to work-related
stress

In therapy, difficult clients can make unreasonable demands, show hostility, and violate many of the social norms that lubricate most interactions. As a result, psychotherapists and other mental health workers may feel overwhelmed, unappreciated, and even abused. Some therapists may come to expect this—it is part of the job—but expecting it does not necessarily make it easy.

As a cognitive therapist, David Burns helps clients look at the way they think about their world, and especially at what they expect from themselves and others. Certain thoughts and expectations may lead to negative emotions and negative behavior. Using himself as an example, Burns shows that challenging one's thoughts can lead to more reasonable expectations for oneself and others and, in turn, to more positive emotions and behaviors.

A recent study of stress has indicated that one of the world's most demanding jobs—in terms of the emotional tension and the incidence of heart attacks—is that of an air-traffic controller in an airport tower. The work involves precision, and the traffic controller must be constantly alert—a blunder could result in tragedy. I wonder however if that job is more taxing than mine. After all, the pilots are cooperative and intend to take off or land safely. But the ships I guide are sometimes on an intentional crash course.

Here's what happened during one thirty-minute period last Thursday morning. At 10:25 I received the mail, and skimmed a long, rambling, angry letter from a patient named Felix just prior to the beginning of my 10:30 session. Felix announced his plans to carry out a "blood bath," in which he would murder three doctors, including two psychiatrists who had treated him in the past! In his letter Felix stated, "I'm just waiting until I get enough energy to drive to the store and purchase the pistol and the bullets." I was unable to reach Felix by phone, so I began my 10:30 session with Harry. Harry was emaciated and looked like a concentration camp victim. He was unwilling to eat because of a delusion that his bowels had "closed off," and he had lost seventy pounds. As I was discussing the unwelcome option of hospitalizing Harry for forced tube feeding to prevent his death from starvation, I received an emergency telephone call from a patient named Jerome, which interrupted the session. Jerome informed me he had placed a noose around his neck and was seriously considering hanging himself before his wife came home from work. He announced his unwillingness to continue outpatient treatment and insisted that hospitalization would be pointless.

I straightened out these three emergencies by the end of the day, and went home to unwind. At just about bedtime I received a call from a new referral—a well-known woman VIP referred by another patient of mine. She indicated she'd been depressed for several months, and that earlier in the evening she'd been standing in front of a mirror practicing slitting her throat with a razor blade. She explained she was calling me only to pacify the friend who referred her to me, but was unwilling to schedule an appointment because she was convinced her case was "hopeless."

Every day is not as nerve-racking as that one! But at times it does seem like I'm living in a pressure cooker. This gives me a wealth of opportunities to learn to cope with intense uncertainty, worry, frustration, irritation, disappointment, and guilt. It affords me the chance to put my cognitive techniques to work on myself and see firsthand if they're actually effective. There are many sublime and joyous moments too.

If you have ever gone to a psychotherapist or counselor, the chances are that the therapist did nearly all the listening and expected you to do most of the talking. This is because many therapists are trained to be relatively passive and nondirective—a kind of "human mirror" who simply reflects what you are saying.[1] This one-way style of communication may have seemed unproductive and frustrating to you. You may have wondered—"What is my psychiatrist really like? What kinds of feelings does he have? How does he deal with them? What pressures does he feel in dealing with me or with other patients?"

Many patients have asked me directly, "Dr. Burns, do you actually practice what you preach?" The fact is, I often do pull out a sheet of paper on the train ride home in the evening, and draw a line down the center from top to bottom so I can utilize the double-column technique[2] to cope with any nagging emotional hangovers from the day. If you are curious to take a look behind the scenes, I'll be glad to share some of my self-help homework with you. This is your chance to sit back and listen while the *psychiatrist* does the talking! At the same time, you can get an idea of how the cognitive techniques [used] to overcome clinical depression can be applied to all sorts of daily frustrations and tensions that are an inevitable part of living for all of us.

---

[1][According to David Burns] some of the newer forms of psychiatric treatment, such as cognitive therapy, allow for a natural fifty-fifty dialogue between the client and therapist, who work together as equal members of a team.

[2]Double-column technique: a listing of negative self-statements on one side of a column and positive self-statements on the other side of the column.

Coping with Hostility: The Man Who Fired Twenty Doctors

One high-pressure situation I often face involves dealing with angry, demanding, unreasonable individuals. I suspect I have treated a few of the East Coast's top anger champions. These people often take their resentment out on the people who care the most about them, and sometimes this includes me.

Hank was an angry young man. He had fired twenty doctors before he was referred to me. Hank complained of episodic back pain, and was convinced he suffered from some severe medical disorder. Because no evidence for any physical abnormality had ever surfaced, in spite of lengthy, elaborate medical evaluations, numerous physicians told him that his aches and pains were in all likelihood the result of emotional tension, much like a headache. Hank had difficulty accepting this, and he felt his doctors were writing him off and just didn't give a damn about him. Over and over he'd explode in a fury, fire his doctor, and seek out someone new. Finally, he consented to see a psychiatrist. He resented this referral, and, after making no progress for about a year, he fired his psychiatrist and sought treatment at our Mood Clinic.

Hank was quite depressed, and I began to train him in cognitive techniques. At night when his back pain flared up, Hank would work himself up into a frustrated rage and impulsively call me at home (he had persuaded me to give him my home number so he wouldn't have to go through the answering service). He would begin by swearing and accusing me of misdiagnosing his illness. He'd insist he had a medical, not a psychiatric problem. Then he'd deliver some unreasonable demand in the form of an ultimatum: "Dr. Burns, either you arrange for me to get shock treatments tomorrow or I'll go out and commit suicide tonight." It was usually difficult, if not impossible, for me to comply with most of his demands. For example, I don't give shock treatments, and furthermore I didn't feel this type of treatment was indicated for Hank. When I would try to explain this diplomatically, he would explode and threaten some impulsive destructive action.

During our psychotherapy sessions Hank had the habit of pointing out each of my imperfections (which are real enough). He'd often storm around the office, pound on the furniture, heaping insults and abuse on me. What used to get me in particular was Hank's accusation that I didn't care about him. He said that all I cared about was money and maintaining a high therapy success rate. This put me in a dilemma, because there was a grain of truth in his criticism—he was often several months behind in making payments for his therapy, and I was concerned that he might drop out of treatment prematurely and end up even more disillusioned. Furthermore, I *was* eager to add him to my list of successfully treated individuals. Because there was some truth in Hank's haranguing attacks, I felt guilty and defensive when he would zero in on me. He, of course, would sense this, and consequently the volume of his criticism would increase.

I sought some guidance from my associates at the Mood Clinic as to how I might handle Hank's outbursts and my own feelings of frustration more effectively.

The advice I received from Dr. Beck was especially useful. First, he emphasized that I was "unusually fortunate" because Hank was giving me a golden opportunity to learn to cope with criticism and anger effectively. This came as a complete surprise to me; I hadn't realized what good fortune I had. In addition to urging me to use cognitive techniques to reduce and eliminate my own sense of irritation, Dr. Beck proposed I try out an unusual strategy for interacting with Hank when he was in an angry mood. The essence of this method was (1) Don't turn Hank off by defending yourself. Instead, do the opposite—urge him to say all the worst things he can say about you. (2) Try to find a grain of truth in all his criticisms and then agree with him. (3) After this, point out any areas of disagreement in a straightforward, tactful, nonargumentative manner. (4) Emphasize the importance of sticking together, in spite of these occasional disagreements. I could remind Hank that frustration and fighting might slow down our therapy at times, but this need not destroy the relationship or prevent our work from ultimately becoming fruitful.

I applied this strategy the next time Hank started storming around the office screaming at me. Just as I had planned, I urged Hank to keep it up and say all the worst things he could think of about me. The result was immediate and dramatic. Within a few moments, all the wind went out of his sails—all his vengeance seemed to melt away. He began communicating sensibly and calmly, and sat down. In fact, when I agreed with some of his criticisms, he suddenly began to defend me and say some nice things about me! I was so impressed with this result that I began using the same approach with other angry, explosive individuals, and I actually did begin to enjoy his hostile outbursts because I had an effective way to handle them.

I also used the double-column technique for recording and talking back to my automatic thoughts after one of Hank's midnight calls (see Figure 1). As my associates suggested, I tried to see the world through Hank's eyes in order to gain a certain degree of empathy. This was a specific antidote that in part dissolved my own frustration and anger, and I felt much less defensive and upset. It helped me to see his outbursts more as a defense of his own self-esteem than as an attack on me, and I was able to comprehend his feelings of futility and desperation. I reminded myself that much of the time he was damn hard working and cooperative, and how foolish it was for me to demand he be totally cooperative at all times. As I began to feel more calm and confident in my work with Hank, our relationship continually improved.

Eventually, Hank's depression and pain subsided, and he terminated his work with me. I hadn't seen him for many months when I received a message from my answering service that Hank wanted me to call him. I suddenly felt apprehensive; memories of his turbulent tirades flooded my mind, and my stomach muscles tensed up. With some hesitation and mixed feelings, I dialed his number. It was a sunny Saturday afternoon, and I'd been looking forward to a much needed rest after an especially taxing week. Hank answered the phone: "Dr. Burns, this is Hank. Do you remember me? There's something I've been meaning to tell you for some time . . ." He paused, and I braced for the impending explosion. "I've been essen-

Figure 1. Coping with Hostility

Automatic Thoughts	*Rational Responses*
1. I've put more energy into working with Hank than nearly anyone, and this is what I get—abuse!	1. Stop complaining. You sould like Hank! He's frightened and frustrated, and he's trapped in his resentment. Just because you work hard for someone, it doesn't necessarily follow that they'll feel appreciative. Maybe he will some day.
2. Why doesn't he trust me about his diagnosis and treatment?	2. Because he's in a panic, he's extremely uncomfortable and in pain, and he hasn't yet gotten any substantial results. He'll believe you once he starts getting well.
3. But in the meantime, he should at least treat me with respect!	3. Do you expect him to show respect *all* the time or *part* of the time? In general, he exerts tremendous effort in his self-help program and does treat you with respect. He's determined to get well—if you don't expect perfection, you won't have to feel frustrated.
4. But is it fair for him to call me so often at home at night? And does he have to be so abusive?	4. Talk it over with him when you're both feeling more relaxed. Suggest that he supplement his individual therapy by joining a self-help group in which the various patients call each other for moral support. This will make it easier for him to cut down on calls to you. But for now, remember that he doesn't *plan* these emergencies, and they are very terrifying and real to him.

tially free of pain and depression since we finished up a year ago. I went off disability and I've gotten a job. I'm also the leader of a self-help group in my own hometown."

This wasn't the Hank I remembered! I felt a wave of relief and delight as he went on to explain, "But that's not why I'm calling. What I want to say to you is . . ." There was another moment of silence—"I'm grateful for your efforts, and I now know you were right all along. There was nothing dreadfully wrong with me, I was just upsetting myself with my irrational thinking. I just couldn't admit it until I knew for sure. Now, I feel like a whole man, and I had to call you up and let you know where I stood . . . It was hard for me to do this, and I'm sorry it took so long for me to get around to telling you."

Thank you, Hank! I want you to know that some tears of joy and pride in you come to my eyes as I write this. It was worth the anguish we both went through a hundred times over!

Response and Analysis

1. What cognitive therapy techniques does David Burns use? What situations other than those he describes might benefit from these techniques? Why?

2. How did Burns come to understand and then respond to Hank's angry outbursts?

Personal Experience and Application

1. Burns's article raises an interesting question: If a therapist seeks psychological treatment, what features does he or she look for in a therapist? Do you think most therapists seek treatment from therapists with the same orientation as themselves? Why or why not? What other factors do you think a therapist would be interested in when looking for a therapist? Why?

2. Burns says that he seeks advice from colleagues on certain cases. What is your reaction to this? How does this affect your view of him as a therapist?

Research

Suppose you want to study the effectiveness of cognitive techniques for treating depression. Before beginning the study, you identify several variables that might influence the results: (1) therapist's years of practice, (2) severity of client's symptoms, and (3) level of rapport between therapist and client. How do you think each of these variables might affect the results?

GROUP THERAPY WITH PERSONS WITH SCHIZOPHRENIA

Lauren Slater

Psychological Concept
group therapy

Psychologist Lauren Slater began her professional career working in an institution with persons diagnosed with schizophrenia. The patients were often lost in worlds of their own; they showed marked delusions, hallucinations, and bizarre associations. They often spoke in incoherent sentences and were unable to have meaningful relationships with other people. Slater finds herself exhausted by constantly directing their attention to objective reality and to basic living skills. She decides to experiment and use unconventional techniques. Her attempts to help clients overcome their isolation and make connections with each other show that creativity has a place in therapy.

My first group. Six men, all of whose charts I've read prior to actually meeting them. I watch as they file into the group room. They say their names one by one when I ask, and as they do I match up names and faces with the information I've gleaned from records.

There is Tran, nicknamed Moxi, a small, cocoa-colored Vietnamese who came to this country after the war, and who bows to invisible Buddhas all day in the corridors. There is Joseph, with a mangy beard, a green-and-khaki combat helmet he puts on the pillow next to him when he sleeps. Charles is forty-two years old and dying of AIDS. Lenny once stood naked in Harvard Yard and recited poetry. Robert believes fruits none of us can see are exploding all around him. And then there is Oscar, 366 pounds, and claiming constant blow jobs from such diverse females as the Queen of England and Chrissy, the Shih Tzu dog next door.

Oscar slogs into the group room, groans, lowers himself onto the floor, and lies there with his hairy belly bloating up.

"I am," I say, my voice cracking from fear (for I have never done this kind of work before; all my other patients have been violent or sad or scared but not . . . not . . . *this*), "your new group therapist. We'll be meeting once a week to talk things over, see how your lives are going, confront problems, think up solutions, play some games, even. How does that sound?"

Silence. Oscar, on the floor, appears to be asleep. Surprisingly delicate snores issue from his thick lips. The other men sit pressed against the walls or staring into their own squares of space as though they are strangers riding a train. And yet some of them have been living together in this institution for as long as seven years. As I get more acquainted with these people, I will come to understand how they almost always dwell in such silence. At mealtimes, or in the common room, they sit rocking, tracing imaginary figures in the air, lecturing on astrophysics to an invisible audience of esteemed colleagues, while in some place I cannot get to, comets explode and suns warp into white dwarves. The men's worlds are so far away from me and from one another that only occasionally will they reach out to filch a cigarette from someone next to them, moments later hunching back into themselves and collapsing into private giggles.

But I don't know any of this yet. I'm still brand new. I look around at my drooling patients. My mind charges over techniques, hovers, herds—how can I get them to interact? The silence thickens and I can hear, coming from outside, the dry gratings of insects in the summer heat.

Finally Joseph clears his throat, takes off his combat helmet, and stares deeply into its hollow. "What's in there, Joseph?" I ask. "What's in your helmet?"

"Blood be gone and hell swell saboooose," he says. "A girl curve feminine adventure."

I struggle to think of what to say. What part of this do I understand? What part can I, or any of the other group members, connect to? A girl curve? An adventure? I decide to let it go. "And, Charlie," I say, "can you tell me something about yourself?"

"Charl*es*," he cries. "No not Charlie but Charl*es* Charl*es* Charl*es*." He bites into his lip and swings his head so violently I am reminded of a long time ago, when I went to the aquarium and saw a shark with a fish in the barbs of its teeth, the shark's flat silver head whipping back and forth as its prey's body burst. "Charl*es* Charl*es* Charl*es*," he keeps repeating.

"Charl*es*," Lenny, a black man, sings from the other side of the room. Lenny has skin the color of deep coal, his limbs long with rippled muscles rooted in them. Lenny looks so healthy, his body speaking the bones and sinews that stretch inside it. Surely, I think, this man will make some sense.

"Oh, Charl*es*," Lenny says, looking not at Charles but resolutely up at the ceiling, "you need a protegé like Henry Collins. I have my protegé, Henry Collins, and if I don't go to Chelsea he stays with me and helps me not to be a pimp. I was once a pimp but before that my name is Cuppy."

"Cuppy?" I say to Lenny, squinting. "Your name is Cuppy?"

"Sometimes," Lenny says. "That depends on the fog."

It is useless, I think to myself during the first few weeks of the group, to try to get these men to connect with one another or myself, because connections between human beings depend at least partly on words, and the words of the schizophrenic are terribly skewed. The schizophrenic speaks a mumbo-jumbo language psychologists call a "word salad," nouns and verbs, fragments from the past, snippets of dreams all tossed into the lush wet mess. Sometimes beautiful sparks of sense do fly out, and other times bizarre but poetic hallucinations—the man with the blue ears who sleeps on the ceiling, miraculous cures that curl from test tubes foaming inside someone's head. You look for these swaths of sense and rhythm and, as you would any good wave, you try to ride it, but too often it fizzles into foam and you find yourself washed up in a tangle of mental kelp. . . .

It is late August now, and I've been leading the group for two months. . . .

I am tired of the bizarreness of my patients, more tired still of trying to ignore their hallucinations and to focus, instead, on money and meds and keeping the shirt stain-free. When Lenny tells me in group he is communing with a woman who is also a paintbrush, I say to him, as I've been trained, "No, Lenny. There are no women who are also paintbrushes in this group. Why don't you tell all of us what you actually mean? Why don't you stop slumping, sit up, and button your shirt?" When Joseph tells the group he has shot seven soldiers in World War I, I say, "You have never been in World War I. You are here in this room. With all of us now. Tell us what your plans for the weekend are and why you have overslept three days in a row." Doing this work is like being the goalie in a soccer game; over and over again the swift kicks of craziness come at you, and over and over again you try to deflect them, or better yet, take the air right out of the ball. . . .

And that may be why, when, a few days later, Oscar announces a spaceship has landed on his enormous belly, I break down. "All right," I say, looking around the room, eyeing the door and hoping it's closed so none of the other staff can hear, "why don't we go for a ride in it, then? Let's go."

"Let's go!" the irrepressible Lenny shouts, jumping up and down.

"Where?" I say, and indeed I mean it. I am thinking of the diced-up apples of desire, the green leaves of love. What about these things I hear in the schizophrenic's dream talk? . . .

Lenny strides across the room and eases down on the floor right next to Oscar. He takes his deep-black hand and lays it on top of Oscar's swollen white stomach. The hand sits there like a black star in a white sky, some sort of weird reversal.

"Move in," I say, looking around to the rest of my group members. "Charles," I say, "move in, right up next to Oscar. You too, Moxi," I say to the little man who, week after week, sits hunched and rocking in a corner, who won't move, won't speak, ever. Moxi is the most closed-off of all. He is missing three fingers and one testicle because the voice of Mother Mary told him to cut them off. The most he will do in group is mumble a yes or a no. "You too, Moxi," I say a little louder.

The men all eye me, something alert in their usually slack faces; they edge forward on their seats. I edge out of my own seat and sit on the floor, so close I can see the rise and fall of Oscar's belly, on his face the bubbles of sweat that seep from large red pores.

"A spaceship," I repeat to Oscar. "On your belly right now. To take us into your world." The rest of the men creep forward, sit Indian-style in a circle around him. It's the closest I've ever seen any of them get to one another. "We are going into the spaceship," I say, "and we're all riding up. What do we see, Oscar? Where are we?"

Lenny still has his hand on Oscar's belly, and now he is moving it back and forth, rubbing. Oscar, his voice flat and thick, begins to speak.

"Sheba," he says. "We are going to see Sheba. She lives up there, my girl does, in the sky. She is a star. She eats leg of lamb without the skin. And octopus."

"Octopus," Joseph says. "Freaky."

"Sheba is your girl," I say.

"I have hundreds of girls," Oscar replies, "all over the sky. Definitely they are albinos. They keep me company. They love me."

"They love you," I say and, thinking of the overweight unloved-by-girls Oscar, something sad rises up in me. I feel my own voice grow low, whispery. The room seems darker, even though the summer sun burns like an ember in the white sky outside. Shadows, sexy shadows, ripple and sway on the walls. . . .

One day, a week before Charles finally dies, I bring a rubber ball into group. "OK," I say. "Everyone up. Stand in a circle."

"Not unless Robert comes," Lenny mumbles.

"Robert can come," I say, looking over toward Robert, who has his hands jammed over his ears. "Take your hands away from your ears, Robert," I shout, "and join our circle."

We make a circle, even Moxi.

"Whoever has the ball," I explain, "cannot toss it to someone else unless he asks a question of that person first. And whoever receives the ball has to answer the question and cannot throw the ball without asking a new question. In this way, we will reestablish our friendships and continue to get to know one another better."

The men stare at me, flat-eyed. I throw the ball to Joseph. "Joseph," I say, "what are you most afraid of?"

Joseph catches the ball. "Chips," he says. "Chips the CIA have planted in my brain." He throws the ball to Oscar. "Oscar," he says, "are you—?" but then he splutters into panicked giggles and can't finish the question. Oscar doesn't even bother catching the ball. It bounces off his blubbery chest and dribbles into the center of the circle.

"OK!" I say, all fake enthusiasm. "Let's start again!" I trot into the center of the circle, pick the ball back up. But I feel ridiculous.

I bounce the ball, thinking. "Robert," I say, tossing it again. "Who do you most love?" Robert catches the ball, cradles it, and won't let go. "Throw the ball, Robert," I say. "Go on." He throws the ball then, but backward, over his head, so it swerves outside the circle, and we're all left looking at one another, looking at nothing.

I sigh. "It's hard for everyone," I say at last. "Maybe you are all too upset about Charles."

"Nuh-uh," says Oscar. He slinks back into his customary slump on the floor. "We're not upset about Charles. We're all like Charles. None of us can die, because we're already dead."

And then each member of the circle, as though on cue, slumps to the floor. Only Moxi is left standing.

Moxi's eyes tick around the room, tick back and forth over the fallen bodies. His little broom of a mustache quivers. "No," he says. It is maybe the first word he has ever said in group. "No!" he says again. "Not true! Not true!" His English is laden with a heavy Vietnamese accent. "No no no," he chants. "I come here all the way from Vietnam. I have family. Family!"

"Who's in your family?" I ask, thinking of the chart I read on Moxi, in which it was reported his father and three sisters were bombed to death in his village during the war.

"Here!" he says, his eyes still swinging around the room, lighting on me and then on the other slumped men. "Here, here. In America! My family is in this place, this room. Now!" he shouts. "Here!"

And then Moxi bursts forth. He splits his separate sphere. I don't know why Moxi once put a knife to his penis but perhaps it had to do as much with the imagined voice of Mother Mary as with the need to cut away the thick skin of madness and maleness that prevents unions from happening with any ease.

And Moxi bursts forth. He unzips his fly, and with his hips shrugs off his pants. . . .

And the little man, half-naked, begins to dance. The rest of the men come together, draw in. They hum and clap in time to a rhythm and we are all a part of it, some sacred strip dance of death and life and the links between bodies—my fingers, your toes, my cut, your crying. Moxi sways. He rolls up his shirt sleeve and, crooning, points to more charred spots on his skin. "Here," he says. "And here too." He points with precision, insists that we see his hurts, insists, yes, that we see *him*, and some love gets built around his bared body.

Still naked, Moxi kneels and begins to draw a female figure.

"Who is she?" Robert whispers.

"She is a lady," Moxi answers. "A lady from Vietnam who I want to marry but who is already married."

He looks like he is going to cry now as he scurries about the room rolling down his shirt sleeves, pulling back on his pants. Then he does cry, standing in the center of the group room. He puts his hand over his heart and starts to sing in Vietnamese. His voice and the ballad have a mournful, ancient feel, each word with some weeping inside.

"Moxi, that was beautiful," I say. "What does the song mean?"

"I love a lady who doesn't love me; I am lost, oh, so lost," Moxi says. "That's what the song means." And then he sings it again, louder, his voice lovely and quavering.

"You are so lonely, aren't you, Moxi," I say.

"Yes, and I am so sad because Oscar won't shake my hand."

Oscar, leaning back against the wall, hands folded on the bubble of his belly, opens one eye as slowly as a lizard in the sun. "Huh?" he says.

"You won't shake my hand," Moxi repeats, agitated now.

"Don't always feel like it, Moxi," Oscar says. "Sometimes I'm just too tired."

"But you want Oscar to shake your hand, Moxi," I say.

"Everyone to shake my hand," Moxi says.

"Can we shake Moxi's hand?" I ask the group.

"Yeah," says Lenny. "And then we go to a whorehouse."

"OK," I say to Moxi. "Go on. We want to shake your hand."

Moxi skips around the room, nimble, hopeful. He cavorts and bows. He shakes each man's hand with pride. "Welcome to my country," he says to each person as he clasps him in a handshake. "Welcome to my country."

"Welcome," each one of us says back.

What country does he mean? I wonder. For sure there is something a little crazy about all of this, but also so appropriate. I think of the empty skull Oscar once drew and how we are, in this group, trying to learn to go through bone and enter those private sockets where our separate brains sit. And I think, Dr. Maslow, no matter how sick we are, how strained we are, we never stop wanting such closeness. We never lose the language altogether.

Response and Analysis

1. As a group therapist, Lauren Slater uses some creative techniques to try to get the group members to interact with her and with each other. What techniques does she use? What do you think are the benefits and risks of her approach? Why?

2. Slater implies that she was taught to emphasize reality testing, self-help skills, and social skills with the clients. How effective is social-skills training in improving the functioning of clients with schizophrenia? How do you think its effectiveness compares with that of insight-oriented or exploratory therapies such as cognitive, psychoanalytic, or humanistic psychotherapy?

Personal Experience and Application

1. Group therapy with persons with schizophrenia might have quite different goals than group therapy with people from other populations. How do you think the group goals and the therapist's behavior might differ between this group and (1) a support group for victims of abuse or (2) a group of juvenile delinquents?

2. List three disorders for which group therapy would be helpful. What do you believe are the benefits of group therapy for these disorders? The disadvantages?

Research

Imagine you want to compare three methods of treating schizophrenia: (1) medication alone, (2) group therapy alone, and (3) medication in conjunction with group therapy. The independent variable is type of treatment. The dependent variable is schizophrenic behavior. Which type of treatment do you think would be most effective? State your prediction as a hypothesis (include all three levels of the independent variable). How long would you conduct the study? Why? How would you measure the effectiveness of the treatments?

chapter *12*

HEALTH, STRESS, AND COPING

Humans cannot exist if everything that
is unpleasant is eliminated instead of
understood.

MARLO MORGAN, *Mutant Message Down Under*

Is our physical and mental health endangered when we suffer great stress? What resources do we have to cope with misfortune? Health psychology looks at the relationships among stress, health, and coping. This chapter presents illustrations of several key concepts: coping and social support, posttraumatic stress disorder (PTSD), stress and the immune system, biofeedback, and stress management.

Tennis professional Arthur Ashe was at the peak of his life when he learned that he had acquired immunodeficiency syndrome (AIDS). He drew on personal discipline and training to help sustain him. In the final years before his death, Ashe, writing about his life and how he coped with AIDS, says that he never asked why it was he who had to suffer this tragic illness because then he would have had to ask why it was he who had also been so fortunate.

Sometimes it may take a person a long time to overcome a traumatic experience. After devastating experiences during the Vietnam War, John returned home and found some Americans not proud of him for fighting for his country; instead, they called him "baby killer" and "rapist." John, who was diagnosed with PTSD and who finds it difficult to trust people, shows why certain forms of stress may be difficult to overcome.

Psychologist James Pennebaker presents compelling evidence to show that writing about stress not only may provide insights and understanding but also may help our immune system. Pennebaker's research demonstrates that communication, whether written or spoken, may help us face and possibly overcome significantly disturbing events in our lives.

Psychologist Shelley Taylor shows how a positive attitude can help us when we are ill or under stress. She became curious about why some people who suffer crippling illnesses or extreme hardships do not become depressed and submissive. What Taylor discovers is that hope and "positive illusions" give people energy that help them cope with their misfortunes.

Biofeedback therapist Aleene Friedman describes how she helped Joyce relieve her almost constant headaches. Joyce was diagnosed as having migraine and tension headaches, and when she suffered an attack, she was unable to do more than stay in bed. Biofeedback therapy offered Joyce new strategies to deal with her pain, and she gained substantial relief.

DAYS OF GRACE

Arthur Ashe and Arnold Rampersad

Psychological Concepts
coping, social support, AIDS

Tennis champion Arthur Ashe was only thirty-eight years old when he suffered a heart attack. Four years later, he had double-bypass heart surgery and received a blood transfusion to help him heal faster. That transfusion cost him his life: The blood was tainted with the human immunodeficiency virus (HIV). In February 1993, at the age of forty-nine, Ashe died of AIDS.

In his autobiography, Ashe says that the qualities that helped him cope with his illnesses were those that had shaped his character: respect for reputation, honor, discipline, and dignity. These he learned from his parents. Later, his tennis coaches taught him sportsmanship: to behave with grace, to keep anger in control, and not to let despair take over. He knew that to give in to anxiety or fear—even for a second—could lose a game.

Ashe lived with hardship from birth. When he was asked by a reporter if having AIDS was the heaviest burden of his life, he hesitated but a second and then replied: "No, it isn't. It's a burden all right . . . but being black is the greatest burden I've had to bear" (p. 126).

No one in my hospital room that day had to ask the question I knew would be on many people's minds, perhaps on most people's minds. But the rest of the world would ask: How had Arthur Ashe become infected?

To almost all Americans, AIDS meant one of two conditions: intravenous drug use or homosexuality. They had good reason to think so. Of the 210,000 reported cases of Americans, male and female, afflicted with AIDS by February 1992, 60 percent were men who had been sexually active with another man; about 23 percent had been intravenous illicit drug users; at least 6 percent more had been both homosexual and drug abusers; another 6 percent or so had been heterosexual; 2 percent had contracted the disease from blood transfusions; and 1 percent were persons with hemophilia or other blood-coagulant disorders.

The link between individual behavior and infection is crucial to AIDS. Indeed, AIDS was "discovered" in North America in 1980, when doctors in New York and Los Angeles noticed that an unusually high number of young male homosexuals had contracted *Pneumocystis carinii* pneumonia without the usual precondition, an immune system depressed by prescribed medicine. At about the same time, a normally quite rare disease, Kaposi's sarcoma, also began to spread; and once more the victims were young male homosexuals. Later that year, Dr. Michael Gottlieb at UCLA, a federally funded clinical investigator, was the first to notify the Centers for Disease Control about the puzzling outbreak of infections.

By the middle of the following year, the evidence was conclusive and alarming that a new disease was with us, and that it was becoming a nationwide epidemic. The search then began for its cause. After much hard work, HIV was isolated and identified in 1983. An individual tested positive for HIV when a blood test determined the presence in the blood of antibodies fighting the attack by the human immunodeficiency virus, or HIV. Then AIDS was finally defined as a combination in any person of HIV and one or more of over two dozen opportunistic diseases. The search for a cure continued—and continues. . . .

So how, the public would want to know, did Arthur Ashe contract AIDS? Had I been quietly shooting up heroin over the years? Or was I a closet homosexual or bisexual, hiding behind a marriage but pursuing and bedding men on the sly? . . .

The facts of the case are simple. Recovering from double-bypass heart surgery in 1983, I felt miserable even though I had experienced post-operative pain before. I can remember a conversation I had with a doctor in which I complained about feeling unbelievably low, and he laid out my options for me.

"You can wait it out, Arthur, and you'll feel better after a while," he said. "Or we can give you a couple of units of blood. That would be no problem at all."

"I would like the blood," I replied. I don't think I hesitated for a moment. Why feel miserable when a palliative is at hand? Surely there was nothing to be feared from the blood bank of a major American hospital, one of the most respected medical facilities in New York City. In fact, less than a month later, in July 1983, Margaret Heckler, President Reagan's Secretary of Health and Human Services, confidently made an announcement to the people of the United States: "The nation's blood supply is safe." Her words are etched in my memory. . . .

The news that I had AIDS hit me hard but did not knock me down. I had read of people committing suicide because of despair caused by infection with HIV. Indeed, in the preceding year, 1987, men suffering from AIDS were 10.5 times more likely to commit suicide than non-HIV-infected people who were otherwise similar to them.

In 1988, the AIDS suicide rate fell, but only to 7.4 times the expected rate. In 1990, it was 6 times the expected rate. The drop continued, but the far greater likelihood of suicide among AIDS patients persists, according to a 1992 issue of the *Journal of the American Medical Association.* (Incidentally, most of the HIV-infected men who kill themselves use prescription drugs to do so, instead of the guns that most male suicides use.) The main reason for the decline in this suicide rate, according to the report, was the general improvement in treatment, including the development of drugs that gave AIDS patients more hope. By 1992, however, the suicide rate was starting to rise again, as many of the therapies for AIDS, including those I was dependent on, began to show their limitations.

For me, suicide is out of the question. Despair is a state of mind to which I refuse to surrender. I resist moods of despondency because I know how they feed upon themselves and upon the despondent. I fight vigorously at the first sign of depression. I know that some depression can be physically induced, generated by the body rather than the mind. Such depression is obviously hard to contain. But depression caused by brooding on circumstances, especially circumstances one cannot avoid or over which one has no control, is another matter. I refuse to surrender myself to such a depression and have never suffered from it in my life.

Here is an area in which there are very close parallels between ordinary life and world-class athletic competition. The most important factor determining success in athletic competition is often the ability to control mood swings that result from unfavorable changes in the score. A close look at any athletic competition, and especially at facial expressions and body language, reveals that many individuals or even entire teams go into momentary lapses of confidence that often prove disastrous within a game or match. The ever-threatening danger, which I know well from experience, is that a momentary lapse will begin to deepen almost of its own accord. Once it is set in motion, it seems to gather enough momentum on its own to run its course. A few falling pebbles build into an avalanche. The initiative goes to one's opponent, who seems to be impossibly "hot" or "on a roll"; soon, victory is utterly out of one's reach. I've seen it happen to others on the tennis court; it has sometimes happened to me. In life-threatening situations, such as the one in which I now found myself, I knew that I had to do everything possible to keep this avalanche of deadly emotion from starting. One simply must not despair, even for a moment.

I cannot say that even the news that I have AIDS devastated me, or drove me into bitter reflection and depression even for a short time. I do not remember any night, from that first moment until now, when the thought of my AIDS condition and its fatality kept me from sleeping soundly. The physical discomfort may keep me up now and then, but not the psychological or philosophical discomfort.

I have been able to stay calm in part because my heart condition is a sufficient source of danger, were I to be terrified by illness. My first heart attack, in 1979, could have ended my life in a few chest-ravaging seconds. Both of my heart operations were major surgeries, with the risks attendant on all major surgery. And surely no brain operation is routine. Mainly because I have been through these battles with death, I have lost much of my fear of it.

I was not always that way. I had been a sickly child, but for most of the first thirty-six years of my life, until 1979, I nurtured a sense of myself as indestructible, if not actually immortal. This feeling persisted even after my heel surgery in 1977. For nine years since my first heart attack, however, I had been living with a powerful sense of my own mortality. And I have had many other signs, in the deaths of others, that have led me to think of my own end as something that could be imminent. So AIDS did not devastate me. AIDS was little more than something new to deal with, something new to understand and respond to, something to accept as a challenge, as if I might defeat it.

One can ready oneself for death. I see death as more of a dynamic than a static event. The actual physical manifestation of the absence of life is simply the ultimate step of a process that leads inevitably to that stage. In the interim, before the absolute end, one can do much to make life as meaningful as possible.

What would have devastated me was to discover that I had infected my wife, Jeanne, and my daughter, Camera. I do not think it would make any difference, on this score, whether I had contracted AIDS "innocently" from a blood transfusion or in one of the ways that most of society disapproves of, such as homosexual contacts or drug addiction. The overwhelming sense of guilt and shame would be the same in either case, if I had infected another human being.

A friend of mine has ventured the opinion that much as I love Jeanne, I am truly crazy about Camera. Well, Jeanne loves me, but I think she, too, is truly crazy about Camera. The thought that this beautiful child, not yet two years old, who has brought more pure joy into our lives than we had ever known before we laid eyes on her, could be infected with this horrible disease, because of me, was almost too much even to think about.

Both Jeanne and Camera were quickly tested. Both, thank God, were found to be free of any trace of HIV. Their testing has continued, and they remain free of infection. . . .

With AIDS, I have good days and bad days. The good days, thank goodness, greatly outnumber the bad. And the bad days are not unendurable. Mainly my stomach lets me down and I suffer from diarrhea. I take my pills, and I am disciplined enough to stick to my schedule. Sometimes I become a little tired, but I have learned anew to pace myself, to take short rests that invigorate me. In this matter of AIDS, as in so many aspects of my life, I am a lucky man.

I believe that there are five essential pillars to support the health and well-being of every individual. The first is unhindered access to physicians who will render primary care, listen to and advise the patient, and follow up with treatments in a professional manner. The second is the availability of medicines, treatments, and other therapies. The third is the support of family and friends. The fourth is the determination of the patient to make himself or herself better, to take charge of his or her well-being in cooperation with others. The fifth essential pillar is health insurance, because few people can bear the cost of a serious illness without falling irretrievably into debt. Take away any of these five pillars, I believe, and the structure of individual health and welfare starts to collapse.

I have been fortunate to have all five pillars solidly in place: excellent physicians, perhaps the best that can be had; the most efficacious medicines, no matter what the cost; the loving support of a skilled, intelligent spouse and the most loyal and resourceful group of friends anyone could have; self-reliance taught from my boyhood by my father but reinforced by decades of rigorous training in a sport based on individualism; and no fewer than three generous health-insurance policies.

AIDS does not make me despair, but unquestionably it often makes me somber. For some time I have wrestled with certain of Susan Sontag's ideas or insights in her remarkable books *Illness as Metaphor* and *AIDS and Its Metaphors.* In the former, inspired by her battle against cancer, Sontag writes about "the punitive or sentimental fantasies concocted about" illness, especially illnesses such as leprosy, tuberculosis, and cancer. "My point is that illness is *not* a metaphor, and that the most truthful way of regarding illness—and the healthiest way of being ill—is one purified of, most resistant to, metaphoric thinking." AIDS is not a metaphor for me, but a fact; and yet I find it hard to avoid its metaphoric energy, which is almost irresistible. I reject the notion that it is God's retribution for the sins of homosexuals and drug abusers, as some people argue, but on occasion I find its elements and properties peculiarly appropriate to our age.

I live in undeniable comfort—some would say luxury—in a spacious, lovely apartment high above Manhattan. When I venture out to walk the streets below, I see how others live who have not been dealt as generous a hand. I see poverty, usually with a face as dark as mine or darker, sitting on a box in front of my bank with a cup in her hand; or trudging wearily along the sidewalks; or fallen down into foul gutters. Around the corner, huddled on chilly stoops near the Greek Orthodox church, I see loneliness gnawing at human beings who surely deserve a far better fate. I hear madness crying out in the indifferent streets.

Sometimes, gloomily, I wonder about a connection between AIDS and where we in the United States are headed as a people and a nation as this century moves to a close. Too many people seem determined to forget that although we are of different colors and beliefs, we are all members of the same human race, united by much more than the factors and forces that separate us. Sometimes I wonder what is becoming of our vaunted American society, or even Western civilization, as an unmistakable darkness seems to settle over our lives and our history, blocking out the sun. Our national destiny, which at times seems as bright as in the past, sometimes also appears tragically foreshortened, even doomed, as the fabric of our society is threatened by endless waves of crime, by the weakening of our family structures, by the deterioration of our schools, and by the decline of religion and spiritual values. AIDS then takes on a specially ominous cast, as if in its savagery and mystery it mirrors our fate.

Surely we need to resist surrendering to such a fatalistic analogy. Some people profess to see little purpose to the struggle for life. And yet that is precisely the task to which, in my fight against the ravages of AIDS, I devote myself every day: the struggle for life, aided by science in my fight with this disease. I know that we are all, as human beings, going to our death, and that I may be called, because of AIDS, to go faster than most others. Still, I resolutely do battle with this opponent, as I boldly did battle with my opponents on the tennis court. True, this fight is different. The biggest difference is that I now fight not so much to win as not to lose. This enemy is different, too—dark and mysterious, springing on civilization just when civilization was sure that it had almost rid itself of mysterious beasts forever. But it must be fought with science, and with calm, clear thinking.

I know that I must govern that part of my imagination that endows AIDS with properties it does not intrinsically possess. I must be as resolute and poised as I can be in the face of its threat. I tell myself that I must never surrender to its power to terrify, even under its constant threat of death.

Response and Analysis

1. Arthur Ashe applied lessons that he learned through his professional tennis career and through other illnesses to help him cope with AIDS. Describe an emotion-focused and problem-focused coping strategy he used. Why was social support important to Ashe? How might social support reduce the effects of stress, emotional distress, and vulnerability to illness?

2. Ashe presented "five essential pillars to support the health and well-being of every individual." What are the five pillars? Does psychological research suggest that any of these "pillars" positively promote health and well-being?

Personal Experience and Application

1. Describe a lesson that you learned through one of your interests or hobbies that has helped you cope with a stressful situation. Why was this coping strategy effective?

2. Suppose you are invited to give a five-minute presentation on AIDS to a psychology class at your college or university. Write a speech in which you discuss (1) what causes AIDS, (2) four risk factors for HIV, (3) three common myths about how AIDS can be contracted, and (4) three ways to minimize exposure to HIV.

Research

Arthur Ashe believed that the support of family and friends is important to our health and well-being. Suppose you want to design a study to test this idea. State Ashe's idea in the form of a hypothesis. How might you measure social support? How might you assess health and well-being?

FROM VIETNAM TO HELL

Shirley Dicks

Psychological Concepts
posttraumatic stress disorder, general adaptation
syndrome stress model

The Vietnam War left in its wake many men who were unable to return to the life they had known, and many of these veterans suffered from posttraumatic stress disorder (PTSD). Some became abusive, alcoholic, and unable to find satisfying work. Many of their marriages ended in divorce.

Shirley Dicks, whose former husband was a Vietnam veteran, interviewed several men diagnosed with PTSD. These veterans speak of suffering from depression, emotional paralysis, headaches, isolation, and nightmares about Vietnam. When young men become "screaming military fanatics" who are taught to kill, then we can't, says one veteran, "bring them home unbriefed, untrained, and expect them to be normal" (p. 57).

Here is the story of John, who reveals his anger and suffering as he speaks about his experiences: "I became so unfeeling at nineteen years old that, after a fight . . . I would pick up the dead and throw them in bags, and then we'd eat lunch." What other experiences does John describe that may have contributed to his developing PTSD? For a man so injured, what strengths does John appear to have? Why is it important that he tell his story?

My name is John and I'd prefer not to use my last name. I don't trust many people anymore, but the story of Vietnam needs to be told. I've been through hell since the Vietnam War. My life was ruined and no one cared. I'm outraged at the whole thing. I went to war at the age of nineteen to fight for this country, and when I came home they were upset with me. I feel like a time bomb, that I could go to jail at any time because I might do something stupid. I can't handle authority or someone telling me what to do. Right now I'm out in the woods by myself.

When I first went to Vietnam, I was scared like all the others. We were young and knew we were going to war to be killed, wounded or whatever and it was scary. When we landed in the country, we didn't know what to do. The people who had been there awhile didn't want anything to do with us because we didn't know anything, and they felt their lives would be jeopardized. The jungle itself was beautiful, green, blue vegetation, and the water in the mountain streams was crystal clear. I was a rifleman during the Tet Offensive in nineteen sixty-eight. I stayed basically in the jungle, so my contact was mostly with the NVA[1] soldiers.

The NVA were trained soldiers, and we would fight face to face. They usually outnumbered us. The United States would tell the people back home how many we had killed. In reality they were hitting us hard, and that's where the Agent Orange came in. They decided that they would kill the foliage so we could see the NVA. They sprayed chemicals over the jungles, and it killed the foliage, but it also sprayed on the men and later caused cancer.

We never got much sleep in the jungles. Even the days we didn't see the NVA, at least three men would be shot in the head by snipers. You never knew if it would be you that day or if you were one of the lucky ones. I was eating lunch one day with my buddy, and we were talking about his girl back in the States. A round hit him in the head, and I had his brains in my lunch and all over me. He never felt a thing, but I did: I've never gotten over it and I don't think I ever will.

They would tell us that we had to stay up at night, that this was the night the NVA would come in and we needed to be ready. Can you imagine thinking that all night long? We were all so tired, but we didn't sleep. Nothing happened that night. I became so unfeeling at nineteen years old that, after a fight, I would pack up the wounded and send them off. I would pick up the dead and throw them in bags, and then we'd eat lunch. We'd sit down and eat lunch. We had to be hard; we were Marines and you couldn't let anyone see that it bothered you. You had to be a man and take it. I opened up my lima beans and ate them. Do you know why we ate the lima beans after a fight? We hated them but after seeing the death and destruction, you didn't taste them. That's why we ate them at that time.

I had been in the country about six weeks when we had to go out on patrol one night. I had dysentery and asked the sergeant if I could miss that one patrol. I was sick and didn't think I could make it, or be of help to anyone else. He said in no uncertain terms that I was going if I was dying. So I went down the trail with them. I was so sick, and it was uncomfortable. I wasn't trying to get out of going into the bush, I was just plain sick. My temperature was going up as the day wore on. The medic said that I should go back, that I was too sick to go on, but the sergeant said I would go on or die. They were not going to send a chopper in to take me out. I drank all of my water because I was so hot and feverish. Then I traded my fruit cocktail for a couple of swigs of water from the guy in front of me. I didn't have any more valuables on me, so I didn't get any more water. These guys didn't want to have anything to do with me because I was new in the country. They thought I couldn't take it, getting sick and all. We didn't make contact all day with the enemy. We reached our destination and got some water to drink. It was Thanksgiving Day, and they were cooking turkey and instant potatoes. I wanted to eat so badly, but I was so sick that I couldn't. The sergeant came over and asked me if I was going to

---

[1]NVA: North Vietnamese Army.

eat. I told him that I was too sick, so he just left me there and went down to eat. Finally I was put on a chopper and sent to the hospital. I woke up and the nurses were cleaning me. I smelled so bad and had sores all over my body. Two weeks later, I was back in the bush again.

One day on patrol three of our men disappeared. We didn't know what had happened to them until the second day. We came upon their bodies on the trail. The NVA had defaced them, cut off their penises and stuck them in their mouths. We were uptight now. We were scared because they might do this to us if they got a chance.

I remember it was Christmas, and I felt tears in my eyes. I said to myself that I was in some serious trouble. My nerves were getting bad, guys were dying like flies all around me, and it was kill or be killed. We were fighting in their backyards, and we stood out like sore thumbs, ready to be ambushed. They would use snakes to get us, put them about face height so we'd walk into them. They called them the five step snake. You couldn't go five steps after being bitten before you died. They had all kinds of booby traps. Sometimes they used poison gas, but the greatest fear we had was to be a POW.

When I came back to the United States, I couldn't believe the people would be mad at us. We thought we were heroes for laying our lives down for our country. We were warriors and had fought our war. They called me "baby killer" and "rapist," and I couldn't understand it. I hadn't done any of that over there, but the people here didn't understand the war. All they could do was place the blame.

I couldn't hold on to a job because of the PTSD. At first I thought it was normal for me to have hallucinations and dreams about Vietnam. I thought the flashbacks and the tiredness were normal, too, but they weren't. It was a symptom of post-traumatic stress disorder. I would take sleeping pills to get some sleep at night. The pills kept me drugged, but the VA wanted me to take them. I needed outside help since the VA wasn't doing anything but giving me sleeping pills. I went to a psychiatrist who treated me for the PTSD. I tried to get money from the government because of the PTSD, but the government refused. I think the veterans have a real problem and should be helped for their safety as well as for the safety of other people. We went to war to fight for our country. They send us out here with no money and some of us are unable to work because of the mental and physical stresses. If you can't work and support your family and it's because you fought for the government, then they should help us. They should have deprogrammed us as soon as we reached the U.S. I think it would have helped a lot of us if they had had some sort of programs for us.

For years after Vietnam, I lived out in the woods. I would wash in the stream, eat cold food, and go to the bathroom in the woods. Finally I got a little heater and would heat some of the canned food that I ate. I was getting modern then.

I've been diagnosed as having severe PTSD. I went to the veterans' centers and they helped. I couldn't hold a job for very long, and I couldn't sleep. I began to smoke a little marijuana; then I needed something to wake me up. It was a merry-go-round. I keep on having nightmares and flashbacks about Vietnam. I get into fights all the time because I can't stand somebody telling me what to do. I find myself on the edge of life all the time. Vietnam did that to me.

I used to sleep with a gun all the time until one night I was having a flashback and found myself shooting at some trees. I decided not to take a chance on that happening again. My wife could have come walking down the path and been killed.

I don't believe we belonged in Vietnam. They told us in training we were going over there because they didn't want the Vietnamese over here fighting on our backdoor and raping our women. They said it was necessary to go over and fight the war. I didn't see any necessity in it. We went over there with the good intentions of cleaning up these bad guys and coming home as heroes. That was a joke. The other wars were necessary, but not this one. My child isn't going to war for this country.

I can remember the happiest day in Vietnam. We were on the jet on our way back home, so high that the Vietnamese couldn't fire at us and that was a very happy feeling. We knew that now the only way we were going to die was if the jet were to crash. We were almost home with all our arms and legs. We weren't going home in a basket; we were going home in one piece. Little did we know, most of us were eaten up with Agent Orange, PTSD, and traumas. We thought we were all set; we were going back. We got home and found out differently.

I've driven eighteen wheelers all over the country but can't seem to last very long at any one place. Vietnam haunts me today; I hear the groans of the dying. Everyone yells out to God when they know they're dying, and I used to wonder if I would do the same.

A man can't kill another man and be the same as he was when he was a child. You can cover it up and pretend, and try to forget it, but it never goes away. It poisons you, robs you, and changes you from what you once were. What I once was I can never be again because I fought for my country. A child went to war, and a crazy man came home. I don't know of any other way to put it.

Response and Analysis

1. What stressors and traumatic events did John experience during the Vietnam War? How did his behavioral, cognitive, and emotional reactions change during his tour of duty in Vietnam? What physical, behavioral, cognitive, and emotional problems did he experience upon returning to the United States?

2. According to the general adaptation syndrome stress model, what physical reactions occur at the alarm, resistance, and exhaustion stages? How did John cope with PTSD?

Personal Experience and Application

1. Do you know someone who has experienced a traumatic event, such as a war, a violent crime, or a natural disaster? Describe the event. What physical, behavioral, cognitive, and emotional reactions did the person experience in the weeks and months following

the event? Did the person believe that he or she had control over the situation? How might feelings of control affect the degree of stress a person experiences?

2. If you find yourself in an extremely stressful situation and are experiencing prolonged stress, what three actions might you take to minimize the likelihood of your becoming ill?

Research

John and other Vietnam War veterans participated in an open interview in which they were asked similar questions and allowed to respond in whatever way they wished. List two advantages and two disadvantages of an open interview. Do the advantages outweigh the disadvantages, or vice versa? Why? Describe another way to study how the Vietnam War affected veterans.

OPENING UP

James W. Pennebaker

Psychological Concepts

social support, coping, traumatic experiences, immune system

Could writing about or sharing our confidential or traumatic experiences activate our immune system and promote better health? Psychologist James Pennebaker investigates the relationship between people's health and their sharing of secret or upsetting thoughts or experiences with others. Because some people find it difficult to reveal private matters to others, Pennebaker also considered whether writing in a journal would offer the same health benefits as talking with another person. Pennebaker presents provocative results from his research.

The medical and science writer for the *Dallas Morning News*, Rita Rubin, had heard a rumor that we had found that writing about upsetting experiences was good for your health. She had recently moved from Ohio, where she had followed an up-and-coming research team that was investigating the links between psychological stress and immune-system function. Rita was the first to suggest that I contact them and, perhaps, join forces.

The research team was Janice K. Kiecolt-Glaser, a clinical psychologist, and her husband Ronald Glaser, an immunologist, both with the Ohio State University College of Medicine. Together, they were blazing a trail by showing that overwhelming experiences such as divorce, major exams in college, and even strong feelings of loneliness adversely affected immune function. Their most recent finding was that relaxation therapy among the elderly could improve the action of the immune system. The work by Jan and Ron was groundbreaking because it relied on precise state-of-the-art techniques to measure the action of t-lymphocytes, natural killer cells, and other immune markers in the blood. Further, unlike most researchers in immunology, Jan and Ron were sophisticated about psychology.

By a wonderful coincidence, Jan and I were invited to a small conference in New Orleans soon after Rita Rubin's introduction. The first night of the conference, before we had finished our first can of Dixie beer, Jan and I had outlined an experiment to see if writing about traumas could directly affect the action of the immune system. Three months later, the study was under way.

The experiment was similar to the first confession study.[1] Fifty students wrote for twenty minutes a day for four consecutive days about one of two topics. Half wrote about their deepest thoughts and feelings concerning a trauma. The remaining twenty-five students were expected to write about superficial topics. Unlike in the first confession study, however, the students consented to have their blood drawn the day before writing, after the last writing session, and again six weeks later.

The week of running the study was frenzied. I had a staff of almost a dozen people helping me with the experiment in Dallas. As before, the experimental volunteers poured out their hearts in their writing. The tragedies they disclosed were comparable to those in the first experiment. Instances of rape, child abuse, suicide attempts, death, and intense family conflict were common. Again, those who wrote about traumas reported feeling sadder and more upset each day relative to those who wrote about superficial topics.

Collecting the blood and measuring immune function was a novel experience that added to the frenzy. As soon as the blood was drawn, we'd pack it and drive like hell to get to the airport so we wouldn't miss the last plane for Columbus, Ohio. Once the blood samples arrived, the people in the immunology lab would work around the clock, in an assembly-line manner. The procedure involved separating the blood cells and placing a predetermined number of white cells in small dishes. Each dish contained differing amounts of various foreign substances, called mitogens. The dishes were then incubated for two days to allow the white blood cells time to divide and proliferate in the presence of the mitogens.

---

[1]First confession study: one of Pennebaker's first studies on writing about trauma.

The logic of this procedure is fascinating. In the body, there are a number of different kinds of white cells, or lymphocytes, that control immune function. T-lymphocytes, for example, can stimulate other lymphocytes to make antibodies. Antibodies, along with parts of the body's defense system, can retard and kill bacteria and viruses foreign to the body. The immune measures that we used mimicked this bodily process in the dishes. Just as viruses and bacteria can stimulate the proliferation of t-lymphocytes in the body, the mitogens did the same in the laboratory dishes. If the lymphocytes divide at a fast rate in response to the mitogens, we can infer that at least part of the immune system is working quickly and efficiently.

So what did we find? People who wrote about their deepest thoughts and feelings surrounding traumatic experiences evidenced heightened immune function compared with those who wrote about superficial topics. Although this effect was most pronounced after the last day of writing, it tended to persist six weeks after the study. In addition, health-center visits for illness dropped for the people who wrote about traumas compared to those who wrote on the trivial topics.

There was another important finding as well. Every day, after writing, we asked people who had written about traumas to respond to the questionnaire item "To what degree did you write about something that you have previously held back from telling others?" As you can see, the question was intended to get at people's previous attempts at inhibition. That is, the more they had held back, the more they had inhibited talking about the topic. Overall, we found that those who showed the greatest improvement in immune function were the same ones who had held back in telling others about the things they had written. In other words, those who had been silently living with their upsetting experiences benefited the most from writing.

We had now completed two experiments that showed similar things. Taken together, the studies indicated that writing about traumatic experiences was beneficial depending on how people wrote about them. All indications suggested that the effects were not due to simple catharsis or the venting of pent-up emotions. Indeed, the first confession study demonstrated that writing only about emotions surrounding a trauma did not produce long-term health benefits. Further, both experiments indicated that writing about feelings associated with traumatic experiences was painful. Virtually no one felt excited, on top of the world, or even mildly cheerful immediately after writing about the worst experiences of his or her life.

In the surveys that we sent out several months after the experiments, we asked people to describe in their own words what long-term effects, if any, the writing experiment had on them. Everyone who wrote about traumas described the study in positive terms. More important, approximately 80 percent explained the value of the study in terms of insight. Rather than explaining that it felt good to get negative emotions off their chests, the respondents noted how they understood themselves better. Some examples:

It helped me think about what I felt during those times. I never realized how it affected me before.

I had to think and resolve past experiences. . . . One result of the experiment is peace of mind, and a method to relieve emotional experiences. To have to write emotions and feelings helped me understand how I felt and why.

Although I have not talked with anyone about what I wrote, I was finally able to deal with it, work through the pain instead of trying to block it out. Now it doesn't hurt to think about it.

The observations of these people, and everyone else who participated in these studies, are almost breathtaking. They are telling us that our thought processes can heal.

These studies were just the beginning of a research project that has been expanding in several directions. Several variations of the writing experiments have now been conducted by us and by researchers in other laboratories. I now trust the effects that we have gotten. In each study that has been conducted, we have discovered some limits to the writing technique as well as methods that boost its effectiveness.

In the meantime, I want to share with you some of the main points about the writing method that I have found to be related to health. Keep in mind that I am speaking as a researcher and not a therapist. My recommendations about confronting upsetting events are based on experiments, occasional case studies, and my own experiences. It is very possible that your writing about your own traumas or upsetting feelings may not be helpful. If this happens, you should be your own researcher. Experiment with different topics and approaches. Something may work for you in resolving your own conflicts that may not work for anyone else. With these warnings in mind, here are some questions commonly asked about the writing method.

What should your writing topic be?   It is not necessary to write about the most traumatic experience of your life. It is more important to focus on the issues that you are currently living with. If you find yourself thinking or dreaming about an event or experience too much of the time, writing about it can help resolve it in your mind. By the same token, if there has been something you would like to tell others but you can't for fear of embarrassment or punishment, express it on paper.

Whatever your topic, it is critical to explore both the objective experience (i.e., what happened) and your feelings about it. Really let go and write about your very deepest emotions. *What* do you feel about it and *why* do you feel that way?

Write continuously. Don't worry about grammar, spelling, or sentence structure. If you run out of things to say or reach a mental block, just repeat what you have already written.

When and where should you write? Write whenever you want or whenever you feel you need to. I am not convinced that writing about significant experiences needs to be done that frequently. Although many people write every day in diaries, most of the entries do not grapple with fundamental psychological issues. Also be attentive to too much writing. Don't use writing as a substitute for action or as some other type of avoidance strategy. Moderation in all things includes transcribing your thoughts and feelings.

Where you write depends on your circumstances. Our studies suggest that the more unique the setting, the better. Try to find a room where you will not be interrupted or bothered by unwanted sounds, sights, or smells.

What should you do with what you have written? Anonymity is important in our experiments. In many cases, it is wise to keep what you have written to yourself. You might even destroy it when you're finished (although many people find this hard to do). Planning to show your writing to someone can affect your mind-set while writing. For example, if you would secretly like your lover to read your deepest thoughts and feelings, you will orient your writing to your lover rather than to yourself. From a health perspective, you will be better off making yourself the audience. In that way, you don't have to rationalize or justify yourself to suit the perspective of another person.

What if you hate to write—is there a substitute? We have conducted several studies comparing writing with talking into a tape recorder. Among college students, writing appears to be slightly more efficient in getting people to let go and divulge their thoughts and feelings. This probably reflects, in part, the fact that college students are practiced at writing. Some of the people I work with who are not in school find writing to be quite aversive. For these people, I recommend their talking about their deepest thoughts and feelings into a tape recorder. As with writing, I urge them to talk continuously for fifteen minutes a day.

Whether writing or talking is a more comfortable medium for you, remember that letting go and disclosing intimate parts of yourself may take some practice. If you have never written or talked about your thoughts and feelings, you may find doing so particularly awkward at first. If so, just relax and practice. Write or talk continuously for a set amount of time. No one is evaluating you.

What can you expect to feel during and after writing? As we have found in all of our studies, you may feel sad or depressed immediately after writing. These negative feelings usually dissipate within an hour or so. In rare cases, they may last for a day or two. The overwhelming majority of our volunteers, however, report feelings of relief, happiness, and contentment soon after the writing studies are concluded.

Exploring your deepest thoughts and feelings is not a panacea. If you are coping with death, divorce, or other tragedy, you will not feel instantly better after writing. You should, however, have a better understanding of your feelings and emotions as well as the objective situation that you are in. In other words, writing should give you a little distance and perspective on your life.

Response and Analysis

1. James Pennebaker offers several recommendations for writing about traumatic experiences and upsetting events. Briefly discuss them. Why might these recommendations reduce stress?

2. According to Pennebaker, how might disclosing pent-up thoughts and emotions affect the immune system?

Personal Experience and Application

1. Have you written about a traumatic experience or an upsetting event? If so, how often did you write about it? How did you feel after writing about the experience? What are some of the similarities and differences between writing in a personal journal or diary and doing the type of writing described by Pennebaker?

2. How often do you talk with others about important problems or issues in your life? With whom do you talk? Do you believe talking with others about your problems is helpful? Why or why not?

Research

Suppose you wish to conduct an experiment that involves having students in introduction to psychology courses write about a distressing or traumatic event they have experienced. Before conducting the study, you must secure approval from the human participants' Institutional Review Board at your college or university. Two of the purposes of the Review Board are to ensure

that your procedures are ethical and to protect the rights and dignity of the participants.

Most Review Boards require the researcher to submit a form describing, among other things, the activities in which the students will participate. Suppose the procedures are as follows. When the participants arrive at your lab, you escort them to individual cubicles where they cannot see the other participants or the experimenter. You then ask the participants to read and sign a consent form, and allow students who do not wish to participate to leave. Next, you ask half of the participants to write for thirty minutes about a distressing or traumatic event that they have experienced. You ask the other half to write for thirty minutes about their favorite summer vacation. You tell all participants that their essays are anonymous and that they should not put their names on their essay. At the end of the thirty-minute period, you ask the participants to place their essays in an unmarked envelope. Finally, you ask each participant to complete a brief survey indicating whether they gained new insights about themselves by participating in the study.

In addition to a description of procedures, most Institutional Review Boards ask the researcher to list the potential benefits and risks of the study to the participants. Based on the description of procedures, make a list of the potential benefits and risks to students who will participate in your study. Do you believe the risks outweigh the benefits, or vice versa? Why? Why is it important to allow students to leave if they do not want to participate at any time during the experiment? Why is it important to debrief participants at the end of the session?

POSITIVE ILLUSIONS

Shelley E. Taylor

Psychological Concepts
coping (emotional, cognitive, behavioral), cognitive restructuring

Are we powerless when we suffer from severe illness or trauma, or can we react positively? What determines whether we respond with desperation and resignation or with hope and fortitude?

As a graduate student in psychology, Shelley Taylor became interested in how people confront unbearable burdens, such as the loss of a job, loss of income, illness, or the death of a family member or friend. In looking for answers, Taylor discovers the value of what she calls "positive illusions." She found that people are more optimistic when they think they have control over their stress or illness. Why might believing in a "positive illusion" contribute to good health or a sense of well-being?

As a college student, I worked in a mental hospital for several months. When I took the job, I assumed that those who are confined to such institutions had been driven by the pain of life into madness. I expected to find people suffering intolerable stress—the death of a loved one, the destruction of home and property by a natural disaster, a divorce or other wrenching separation. This, I assumed, must be what leads to mental illness. I was quickly disabused of this belief. Indeed, as I soon learned, victims of disasters—personal ones such as assault or rape, or natural catastrophes such as a fire or flood—rarely develop the signs of mental illness. When interviewed some months after what would seem to be devastating losses, these people often report that their lives are at least as happy and satisfying as they were before these disastrous events.

These facts so intrigued me that, following my graduate training, I determined to study the processes whereby recovery from a tragic or near-tragic event takes place. Such problems are not to be studied lightly. Conducting interviews with rape victims, cancer patients, and men vulnerable to sudden death—the groups that would constitute our first investigations—is a wrenching way to make a living. People who are facing death or who have recently faced it have much to say and a lot of it is hard to hear. Yet there were also remarkable stories of recovery.

Originally, I had thought of adjustment to trauma and recovery from devastation as a homeostatic process, that is, as a mental regulatory system whose function it is to maintain psychological balance and stability. I suspected that there might be mechanisms within the mind that help restore people's emotional and cognitive balance to the levels experienced before a victimizing event. A homeostatic hypothesis is a logical choice, for it applies quite well to many biological problems. The gastric system, for example, has five different methods by which hydrochloric acid can be produced, and if one or more of them is disrupted, then the others can take over, maintaining gastric functioning at approximately its previous level. Homeostasis seemed on the surface to be an apt description of the recovery processes of the mind.

In fact, what we soon uncovered was a different process altogether. Rather than being restored to their previous level of functioning, many of the people we interviewed seemed actually to have achieved a higher level of functioning than they had experienced prior to the victimizing event. Many of these victims said that their lives prior to the victimizing events had simply rolled along as a life will when one makes no particular effort to intervene actively in its course. The threatening events to which they were exposed, however, forced them to rethink their priorities and values, and many victims indicated that their lives were now self-consciously lived a moment at a time, in order to extract as much enjoyment and meaning from life as possible. They thought about the reasons behind what they did as they had never before, put value on what truly mattered to them, and in some cases, undertook new activities that left them feeling more fulfilled. As one of the cancer patients we interviewed put it, "The trick, of course, is to do this without getting cancer."

My life was changed by contact with these people. After listening to hours of interviews in which victims thoughtfully appraised their lives and their accomplishments and explained how they had restructured their activities and thinking in order to make their lives more rewarding and meaningful, one feels almost embarrassed by the lack of similar attention to one's own life. Consequently, this work has the effect of forcing a rigorous scrutiny of one's own values and a questioning of the intrinsic merit of its activities, sometimes prompting as well an unwelcome contemplation of death. At these moments, my husband comments, "You and Woody Allen . . ." and sets off to find lighter diversions. Despite these risks, I have watched with pleasure as successive waves of students who have worked with me have also found their lives enriched by contact with people who have been forced to confront the meaning and value in their lives. After four or five interviews my students come back as changed people, and years later will write letters about how important the experiences were to their development as scientists and as mature adults.

A curious picture began to emerge in our research findings. Many of the psychological recoveries recounted by these victims seemed to depend on certain distortions of their situations, especially overly optimistic perceptions concerning chances of recovery from a disease, or the belief that they could actively control the likelihood of a repeat victimization in the future. It was surprising and disturbing to listen to a cancer patient recount the meaning that the experience had brought to her life, and to hear her state with confidence that she would never get cancer again, knowing from the chart records that she would almost certainly develop a recurrence and ultimately die of the disease. But what was more surprising was the discovery that those people who maintained these overly optimistic assessments of their situations and the beliefs that they could control the victimizing events were actually better adjusted to their circumstances and not more poorly adjusted. We came to call these adaptive fictions *illusions*, and although they did not exist in every account of recovery from victimization, they were nonetheless prevalent.

Puzzled by this unanticipated role of creative imagination in recovery, we looked for a context in which to explore it further. We turned first to the mental health literature, but although it was interesting in its own right, it was not especially helpful for understanding the illusions we observed among our victims of *life*-threatening events. We turned next to the research on cognition and social cognition, new and fast-growing subspecialties of psychology that have attracted many of the brightest scientists in the field. And it was here that we began to find clues. First, a brief digression is required.

At different points in their histories, most of the sciences have had frameworks that, once articulated, attracted the majority of scientists and advanced the field suddenly and abruptly in an all-new direction. Cognitive psychology has represented such a development for psychology. The cognitive perspective, which focuses on how the mind is organized and how it functions, has become a dominant framework for developmental psychologists, who study the lives of children and adults across the lifespan; social psychologists, who examine how people think about social activities and interact with others; and clinicians, who attempt to understand mental health and illness. These fields have been so overwhelmed by the cognitive perspective in recent years that, in many respects, social psychologists, clinicians, and developmental psychologists are often cognitive psychologists as well.

What is the cognitive perspective? It is an understanding of how people think about themselves and the world. The cognitive perspective focuses on the person's interpretations. It examines how ordinary people think about people and how they think they think about people and why they think that way. To a cognitive psychologist, for example, it is less important to know whether someone failed a test than to know whether he or she regards failure as a setback or as a learning experience. It is less important to know if a person is Protestant, Catholic, or Jewish than to understand what purpose religion serves in the person's life. It is less important to know if a person makes a lot of money and has an exciting job than it is to know if he or she is contented with those circumstances. Interpretation is the key element in the cognitive analysis.

Ironically, this literature helped us to understand better the kinds of adaptive fictions we saw in our victims, for cognitive research documents similar perceptions in normal, everyday thought. That is, rather than being firmly in touch with reality, the normal human mind distorts incoming information in a positive direction. In particular, people think of themselves, their future, and their ability to have an impact on what goes on around them in a more positive manner than reality can sustain. Just as victims of life-threatening events seem to be motivated to recover from victimization and actively restructure victimizing events in a positive manner, so people who are confronted with the normal rebuffs of everyday life seem to construe their experience so as to develop and maintain an exaggeratedly positive view of their own attributes, an unrealistic optimism about the future, and a distorted faith in their ability to control what goes on around them.

These labors and investigations have culminated in the perspective on mental health set forth in this book. I argue that the normal human mind is oriented toward mental health and that at every turn it construes events in a manner that promotes benign fictions about the self, the world, and the future. The mind is, with some significant exceptions, intrinsically adaptive, oriented toward overcoming rather than succumbing to the adverse events of life. In many ways, the healthy mind is a self-deceptive one, as I will attempt to show. At one level, it constructs beneficent interpretations of threatening events that raise self-esteem and promote motivation; yet at another level, it recognizes the threat or challenge that is posed by these events.

The viewpoint that people need to distort reality in order to adjust successfully to it would seem to be quite cynical on the surface. I hope to convey exactly the opposite sentiment. The ability of the mind to construe benefit from tragedy and to prevent a person from becoming overwhelmed by the stress and pain of life is a remarkable achievement. To a scientist, it makes the mind infinitely more interesting to study. If all our minds did was to take in information as it actually exists and represent it faithfully, the chief task of a psychologist would be to function as a historian of mundane mental activity. Exploring how the mind imposes structure and meaning on events and how it does so systematically in adaptive ways is truly an adventure. Moreover, one emerges from the exploration, not with cynical disdain for the petty ways in which people must cover up their faults and distort their tragedies, but with a huge respect for an organism that has evolved to the point that it can triumph over adversity through sheer mental effort. The mind's resources are exceptional and impressive, and their ability to help people overcome adversity is testimony to the resilience of the human spirit.

Response and Analysis

1. Why might believing in a "positive illusion" contribute to good health and/or a sense of well-being? Why would a cognitive psychologist be less interested in "whether someone failed a test than . . . whether he or she regards failure as a setback or as a learning experience"?

2. People may use one or more coping strategies to deal with stressful situations. Describe and give an example of an emotional, a cognitive, and a behavioral coping strategy.

Personal Experience and Application

1. Describe a stressful situation in which either you or someone you know had optimistic perceptions or "positive illusions" about the outcome. What were the positive illusions? How did they help you or the person you

know cope with the situation? When might positive illusions be an ineffective strategy?

2. List the stressors in your life, including daily pressures, life strains, and life changes. Which stressors create the most and the least stress? What can you do to reduce the amount of stress in your life?

Research

One of the first steps in the research process is developing an interesting idea to test. How did Shelley Taylor's interviews with victims of personal and natural disasters lead to new ideas and hypotheses? How have those interviews affected Taylor and her graduate students?

TREATING CHRONIC PAIN

Aleene Friedman

Psychological Concepts
biofeedback, stress management

How effective is biofeedback in helping patients find relief from their pain? What techniques do biofeedback therapists use to treat their patients?

Biofeedback therapist Aleene Friedman tells the story of Joyce, one of her patients who suffered from persistent headaches. Joyce underwent extensive psychological and physiological diagnostic tests, none of which revealed any abnormalities. Because she was a computer programmer, Joyce and her physicians considered whether eye strain or poor posture might be the cause of her headaches. After determining that these were unlikely causes, Joyce and her physicians at Scripps Clinic decided that she would be an excellent candidate for the biofeedback program.

In the following selection, Dr. Friedman discusses some of the biofeedback techniques she used to help Joyce. About a year after treatment, Joyce reported that she continued to monitor herself at home, and that she seldom suffered from headaches. What did biofeedback offer Joyce? What self-help procedures did Joyce learn to reduce her pain?

J oyce was self-referred for headaches. She had a mixed headache pattern of both muscle contraction and vascular (migraine) headaches. She had been medically treated without satisfactory results and stated that she had decided "to give biofeedback a try." When asked about her symptoms, she stated:

> I seldom have a day without a headache, but the symptoms vary in intensity. The migraines are the worst, and they generally occur about every four or five weeks, and really knock me out. The other headaches occur almost everyday, but there isn't an exact pattern. They do tend to occur more often in the late afternoon, but sometimes I wake up with a headache or get one in the evening. I seldom miss work because of a headache, but I am tired of having headaches and tired of trying to control them with medications.

During this first session I learned that Joyce's migraine headaches had started during her late teens but were not directly connected to her menses. She was now thirty-two years old, unmarried, lived alone, was not close to her family, and liked her work as a computer programmer. She earned an excellent income, enjoyed time with her friends, and liked the company of her dog and two cats. When asked how long she had been suffering from the muscle contraction headaches, she stated:

> Up until ten years ago I would sometimes have an occasional tension (muscle-contraction) headache, but I could take something like aspirin and decrease the symptoms within an hour. The headaches crept up on me over the past ten years, and I kept trying to ignore them, but now it is impossible. The funny thing is that the migraine headaches have remained about the same in frequency and intensity, and now I am more concerned about the tension headaches than the migraines—except, of course, when I have a migraine headache.

During our initial conversation I learned that Joyce often worked overtime, and did not exercise on a regular basis, but did like to camp and hike during her vacations. She was pleasant and did not appear to be in any distress during this first meeting. When asked about her condition, she stated that she had a very slight headache but did not have any other symptoms. She described herself as calm, energetic, perfectionistic, and sometimes driven. Joyce did not drink colas, she had one or two cups of coffee a day, did not smoke, and seldom drank alcohol. She was currently stressed by her parents (if they contacted her), her work (she tended to work long hours), her symptoms, and her finances (she was earning more money than she had ever expected to earn, and her affluence was a source of stress).

For several sessions I utilized the electromyograph (EMG) to help Joyce to reduce her upper-body tension levels. When the muscles exhibit elevated levels of tension during rest, it indicates a source of chronic tension. I monitored her upper-back muscles, neck and shoulder areas, forehead (frontalis), and the muscles of her jaw. We discussed ways to decrease eye tension and to utilize breathing techniques to reduce upper-body tension levels. On a scale of one to ten Joyce's highest levels of tension were over the frontalis and registered between 3.0 and 3.5. When she learned to reduce her jaw tension and to relax her eye tension, she brought this level down to a low of 1.5. I explained to her that it would not be normal to maintain a relaxed state throughout the day, but that the same is true of maintaining high levels of tension throughout the day. Ordinarily, a level of tension between 2.0 and 2.5 is considered a moderately low level of tension, and a tension level below 2.0 is considered a low level of tension. But this is not a standard that is accepted by all biofeedback therapists.

The EMG measures the electrical current that is produced by the muscle that is being monitored. During a time of rest the output should be low. But when a muscle or muscle group becomes chronically tense, the output is high, and the work load is inappropriate for the amount of work being done. This is a waste of one's resources, and it also contributes to chronic stress and chronic pain. The rhythm of the body is one of tense–relax, and when this rhythm is broken it exerts a stress that is communicated within the body as a whole.

Sometimes a patient will experience a dramatic reduction in his or her symptoms after only one or two sessions of biofeedback therapy. For a lasting effect the patient needs to incorporate what is being learned during the session into everyday life, and to generalize his or her ability to decrease the tension levels over one particular muscle group. EMG electrodes monitor surface muscle tension, and the ability to elicit a generalized relaxation response is important.

Joyce did not experience an immediate decrease in her symptoms, but she was becoming more aware of her habitual patterns of holding tension in the neck, shoulders, and facial area. When a pattern of tension becomes habitualized, it is not recognized and/or associated with the pain or discomfort that eventually surfaces. Then, too, some pain is referred pain, and it may be difficult to recognize the relationship between the pain itself and the actual source of the pain. This is especially true of back injuries, but temporomandibular joint (TMJ) disorders may also cause pain and/or discomfort that will appear to be unrelated to the primary source of the problem. Headaches, dizziness, ringing in the ears, facial pain, and other problems are often related to this common disorder.

I asked Joyce to practice "mini-exercises" off and on throughout the day so that she would begin to reduce her upper-body tension levels. These mini-exercises included using her breathing to reduce facial tension, short tense–relax exercises for the neck and shoulders, consciously relaxing the eyes and masseter muscles from time to time, and moving and stretching whenever she had the chance to do so. I encouraged her to take time for lunch and a short walk everyday. Joyce worked a fifty- to sixty-hour work week. It is difficult to reduce symptoms if a connection with nature and diversity is lacking. We discussed the fact that she had other options and that it would be possible for her to plan short weekend trips. This would provide an opportunity for hiking and a total break from her work.

Joyce was beginning to have a decrease in her muscle-contraction headaches, and she had not yet had a vascular headache. I continued to monitor her upper-body tension levels, but I also introduced the blood-flow (temperature) feedback.[1]

---

[1]Blood-flow (temperature) feedback: a type of feedback that measures peripheral blood flow, especially of the hands and feet.

This is a standard treatment modality for migraine headaches, but it is also a primary tool for general relaxation and to combat various other disorders. Except for the hands and feet, internal and external body temperatures remain about the same unless there is a traumatic injury or illness. The core temperature is usually about 99° F, and the external body temperature is slightly cooler. I have seen many patients who are chronically stressed, and their hand temperature is often in the low eighties. This is especially true of female patients. Migraine headaches are vascular headaches, and a drop in hand temperature is a warning sign that indicates the vascular tension that usually precipitates a migraine headache is occurring. I do not emphasize learning to warm the hands to abort a headache, but rather to utilize warming techniques to prevent migraine headaches.

It was not easy for Joyce to warm her hands so I covered her with a light blanket. She had become accustomed to her cool hands, and I wanted her to experience what it felt like to have warm extremities. Her pre-session finger temperature readings were in the low eighties and her post-session readings were in the low nineties. We worked on exercises that emphasized feelings of being heavy and warm, and I also introduced relaxing images. It takes time to relax the smooth muscles of the vascular system, but this is an excellent way to attain a deep state of relaxation.

Within five weeks Joyce's pre-session EMG levels were decreased, and she was able to maintain a low tension level throughout the session. She reported that she was having decreased tension headache symptoms but that she had suffered a migraine headache that had occurred over the weekend. It is not unusual for a vascular headache to occur after a week of hard work. Some patients feel punished for relaxing but it is often part of the "let down" phenomenon of the migraine headache pattern. With Joyce, as well as other patients, there is a need to explore one's own patterns. Diet, specific triggers, muscle tension, vascular tension, head injuries, extreme stress, and numerous other factors may contribute to an individual's headache pattern.

During the next month I continued to emphasize upper-body relaxation, temperature training, and the development of imagery skills. I gave Joyce some home practice tapes and some finger sensors that indicated changes in her hand temperature. This was still another way to help her to tune into the subtle body changes that contributed to her headache symptoms. Eventually, Joyce developed her own personal relaxation image. She was able to close her eyes, take a deep breath, exhale her chronic tension, and imagine her own personal relaxation image while she maintained relaxed breathing. This was a short exercise that provided a moment of deep relaxation. Joyce was beginning to understand her symptoms, and she was pleased by her progress. She was having fewer muscle-contraction headaches, and the intensity and duration of her migraine headaches had decreased. She had gone six weeks without having had a vascular headache, and she was now much more aware of the contributing factors. Joyce decided when it was time for her to continue working by herself, but we did schedule two follow-up sessions. She knew that she was not "cured," but she was aware of her own resources and her capacity for self-regulation. Joyce called me about a year after her final biofeedback session.

She had purchased a house in a semi-rural area and she was able to do most of her work in her home computer center. She was taking daily walks, pacing herself, and enjoying her "almost headache-free existence."

Response and Analysis

1. What stressors did Joyce report to the biofeedback therapist? How did the electromyograph (EMG) help Joyce recognize muscle tension?

2. The therapist suggested several "mini-exercises" to reduce upper-body tension levels. Describe a few of them. How did the therapist use temperature feedback to help Joyce reduce muscle tension?

Personal Experience and Application

1. How do you know when you are tense or stressed? In the past three months, when were you most tense and when were you most relaxed? What activities bring on tension? How do you relieve tension?

2. Which of the following stress-management techniques do you believe would help you manage stress: a relaxation program, improved nutrition, increase in exercise. Why?

Research

Suppose you want to conduct a study to determine which biofeedback training technique most effectively reduces heart rate. The independent variable, training technique, has three levels or conditions: (1) present a tone and a light when heart rate decreases, (2) present a constant digital display of the heart rate, and (3) do not present any feedback about heart rate. Your study has one dependent variable: heart rate.

You must now choose whether the participants should participate in all three conditions or in only one condition. If they participate in all three conditions, in what order should you present them? For example, should the participants first see the tone and light when their heart rate decreases, then see a constant digital display of their heart rate, and then receive no feedback about their heart rate? Or should you vary the order in which you present the stimuli? Why?

List one advantage and one disadvantage to having the participants take part in all three conditions and in only one condition. Which approach would you choose? Why?

chapter *13*

SOCIAL THOUGHT
AND SOCIAL BEHAVIOR

*Let us now imagine two men, whose life is
dominated by appearance, sitting and
talking together. Call them Peter and Paul.
Let us list the different configurations
which are involved. First, there is Peter as
he wishes to appear to Paul, and Paul as he
wishes to appear to Peter. Then there is
Peter as he really appears to Paul, that is,
Paul's image of Peter, which in general does
not in the least coincide with what Peter
wishes Paul to see; and similarly there is
the reverse situation. Further, there is
Peter as he appears to himself, and Paul as
he appears to himself. Lastly, there are the
bodily Peter and the bodily Paul. Two
living beings and six ghostly appearances,
which mingle in many ways in the conversation between the two. Where is there
room for any genuine interhuman life?*

MARTIN BUBER, *Elements of the Interhuman*

Do we, as Martin Buber illustrates, try to create certain impressions of ourselves for
others? How do our impressions of others affect how we respond to them? In
addition to asking these questions, social psychologists also want to know how we
form our opinions and attitudes and what makes interpersonal relations succeed or

fail. This chapter illustrates several key concepts related to social thought and social behavior: attitude formation and change, the power of persuasion, stereotypes, prejudice, competition, group dynamics, and altruism.

C. P. Ellis, former member of the Ku Klux Klan, explains his long-standing attitude against African Americans. Eventually, however, Ellis's experiences cause him to reverse his opinion, and he begins working with African Americans in his community. Can his attitude change be permanent?

Social psychologist Robert B. Cialdini confesses that he can easily succumb to effective persuasion. Wondering why some people can so readily sell an idea or a product and others so readily snap up their wares, Cialdini studies what he calls "weapons of influence." Certain principles, he finds, are at work. Cialdini looks at the power of scarcity and the tendency of the mind to take shortcuts, and he shows how these can be exploited in the name of influence.

What attitudes do we have toward people different from ourselves—different in race, citizenship, age, gender, or economic status? Fear is one reaction that Brent Staples evokes in some people who are not African American like himself. To counter their fear, Staples finds that the only protection he has is to create a safer stereotype of himself for others to perceive.

Why are we sometimes kind, sometimes violent, sometimes competitive, sometimes cooperative? Alfie Kohn argues that "competition by its very nature is harmful." Too often one person ends up winning at the expense of another person who loses. Kohn believes that competition may foster destructive personality traits and injure human relationships.

World-renown mountain climber and nature photographer Galen Rowell was a member of an American expedition to summit K2, one of the world's most difficult ascents. That team experienced tremendous hurdles in its attempt to climb the mountain, including growing friction among the group members, dissatisfaction with the leaders, and difficult negotiations with the porters who carried most of the team's gear. How might leadership styles interact with the situation in which the group members find themselves? What can the group members do to promote group harmony?

When and why are we helpful toward strangers? The editors of *Random Acts of Kindness* asked people to describe when they had been the recipient of thoughtfulness or when they had helped strangers themselves. The altruistic acts these people experienced appear to have increased, at least temporarily, their sense of happiness and well-being.

C. P. ELLIS

Studs Terkel

Psychological Concepts
attitudes, attitude change, cognitive dissonance, prejudice

Is it possible to change an attitude that is held for nearly half a century? Do attitudes influence behavior? Can behavior influence attitudes?

What follows is an interview between the well-known oral historian and writer Studs Terkel and former Ku Klux Klan member C. P. Ellis. Born into extreme poverty, Ellis and his father succumbed to bitterness as they struggled to survive. "I began to blame it on black people. I had to hate somebody," Ellis explains. Ellis became a leader in the Klan, a group his father considered "the savior of the white people." Yet Ellis accepted an invitation from the American Federation of Labor and Congress of Industrial Organizations (AFL-CIO) union to work with African Americans in his community. That decision dramatically changed his life and his attitudes toward African Americans. In this selection, Ellis uses pejorative language toward African Americans, though he asks Terkel to "pardon the expression" and says he doesn't speak that way often. What enables a man who held strong prejudicial attitudes toward people of another race to cooperate with, understand, and accept them?

My father worked in a textile mill in Durham. He died at forty-eight years old. It was probably from cotton dust. Back then, we never heard of brown lung. I was about seventeen years old and had a mother and sister depending on somebody to make a livin'. It was just barely enough insurance to cover his burial. I had to quit school and go to work. I was about eighth grade when I quit.

My father worked hard but never had enough money to buy decent clothes. When I went to school, I never seemed to have adequate clothes to wear. I always left school late afternoon with a sense of inferiority. The other kids had nice clothes, and I just had what Daddy could buy. I still got some of those inferiority feelin's now that I have to overcome once in a while.

I loved my father. He would go with me to ball games. We'd go fishin' together. I was really ashamed of the way he'd dress. He would take this money and give it to me instead of putting it on himself. I always had the feeling about somebody looking at him and makin' fun of him and makin' fun of me. I think it had to do somethin' with my life.

My father and I were very close, but we didn't talk about too many intimate things. He did have a drinking problem. During the week, he would work every day, but weekends he was ready to get plastered. I can understand when a guy looks at his paycheck and looks at his bills, and he's worked hard all the week, and his bills are larger than his paycheck. He'd done the best he could the entire week, and there seemed to be no hope. It's an illness thing. Finally you just say: "The heck with it. I'll just get drunk and forget it." . . .

My father never seemed to be happy. It was a constant struggle with him just like it was for me. It's very seldom I'd see him laugh. He was just tryin' to figure out what he could do from one day to the next.

After several years pumping gas at a service station, I got married. We had to have children. Four. One child was born blind and retarded, which was a real additional expense to us. He's never spoken a word. He doesn't know me when I go to see him. But I see him, I hug his neck. I talk to him, tell him I love him. I don't know whether he knows me or not, but I know he's well taken care of. All my life, I had work, never a day without work, worked all the overtime I could get and still could not survive financially. I began to say there's somethin' wrong with this country. I worked my butt off and just never seemed to break even. . . .

I was workin' a bread route. The highest I made one week was seventy-five dollars. The rent on our house was about twelve dollars a week. . . .

I left the bread route with fifty dollars in my pocket. I went to the bank and borrowed four thousand dollars to buy the service station. I worked seven days a week, open and close, and finally had a heart attack. Just about two months before the last payments of that loan. My wife had done the best she could to keep it runnin'. Tryin' to come out of that hole, I just couldn't do it.

I really began to get bitter. I didn't know who to blame. I tried to find somebody. I began to blame it on black people. I had to hate somebody. Hatin' America is hard to do because you can't see it to hate it. You gotta have somethin' to look at to hate. (Laughs.) The natural person for me to hate would be black people, because my father before me was a member of the Klan. As far as he was concerned, it was the savior of the white people. It was the only organization in the world that would take care of the white people. So I began to admire the Klan.

I got active in the Klan while I was at the service station. Every Monday night, a group of men would come by and buy a Coca-Cola, go back to the car, take a few drinks, and come back and stand around talkin'. I couldn't help but wonder: Why are these dudes comin' out every Monday? They said they were with the Klan and have meetings close-by. Would I be interested? Boy, that was an opportunity I really looked forward to! To be part of somethin'. I joined the Klan, went from member to chaplain, from chaplain to vice-president, from vice-president to president. The title is exalted cyclops.

The first night I went with the fellas, they knocked on the door and gave the signal. They sent some robed Klansmen to talk to me and give me some instructions. I was led into a large meeting room, and this was the time of my life! It was thrilling. Here's a guy who's worked all his life and struggled all his life to be something, and here's the moment to be something. I will never forget it. Four robed Klansmen led me into the hall. The lights were dim, and the only thing you could see was an illuminated cross. I knelt before the cross. I had to make certain vows and promises. We promised to uphold the purity of the white race, fight communism, and protect white womanhood.

After I had taken my oath, there was loud applause goin' throughout the building, musta been at least four hundred people. For this one little ol' person. It was a thrilling moment for C. P. Ellis.

It disturbs me when people who do not really know what it's all about are so very critical of individual Klansmen. The majority of 'em are low-income whites, people who really don't have a part in something. They have been shut out as well as the blacks. Some are not very well educated either. Just like myself. We had a lot of support from doctors and lawyers and police officers.

Maybe they've had bitter experiences in this life and they had to hate somebody. So the natural person to hate would be the black person. He's beginnin' to come up, he's beginnin' to learn to read and start votin' and run for political office. Here are white people who are supposed to be superior to them, and we're shut out.

I can understand why people join extreme right-wing or left-wing groups. They're in the same boat I was. Shut out. Deep down inside, we want to be part of this great society. Nobody listens, so we join these groups. . . .

This was the time when the civil rights movement was really beginnin' to peak. The blacks were beginnin' to demonstrate and picket downtown stores. I never will forget some black lady I hated with a purple passion. Ann Atwater. Every time I'd go downtown, she'd be leadin' a boycott. How I hated—pardon the expression, I don't use it much now—how I just hated the black nigger. (Laughs.) Big, fat, heavy woman. She'd pull about eight demonstrations, and first thing you know they had two, three blacks at the checkout counter. Her and I have had some pretty close confrontations.

I felt very big, yeah. (Laughs.) We're more or less a secret organization. We didn't want anybody to know who we were, and I began to do some thinkin'. What am I hidin' for? I've never been convicted of anything in my life. I don't have any court record. What am I, C. P. Ellis, as a citizen and a member of the United Klansmen of America? Why can't I go to the city council meeting and say: "This is the way we feel about the matter? We don't want you to purchase mobile units to set in our schoolyards. We don't want niggers in our schools."

We began to come out in the open. We would go to the meetings, and the blacks would be there and we'd be there. It was a confrontation every time. I didn't hold back anything. We began to make some inroads with the city councilmen and county commissioners. They began to call us friend. Call us at night on the telephone: "C. P., glad you came to that meeting last night." They didn't want integration either, but they did it secretively, in order to get elected. They couldn't stand up openly and say it, but they were glad somebody was sayin' it. We visited some of the city leaders in their home and talk to 'em privately. It wasn't long before councilmen would call me up: "The blacks are comin' up tonight and makin' outrageous demands. How about some of you people showin' up and have a little balance?" I'd get on the telephone. "The niggers is comin' to the council meeting tonight. Persons in the city's called me and asked us to be there."

We'd load up our cars and we'd fill up half the council chambers, and the blacks the other half. During these times, I carried weapons to the meetings, outside my belt. We'd go there armed. We would wind up just hollerin' and fussin' at each other. What happened? As a result of our fightin' one another, the city council still had their way. They didn't want to give up control to the blacks nor the Klan. They were usin' us.

I began to realize this later down the road. One day I was walkin' downtown and a certain city council member saw me comin'. I expected him to shake my hand because he was talkin' to me at night on the telephone. I had been in his home and visited with him. He crossed the street. Oh shit, I began to think, somethin's wrong here. Most of 'em are merchants or maybe an attorney, an insurance agent, people like that. As long as they kept low-income whites and low-income blacks fightin', they're gonna maintain control.

I began to get that feeling after I was ignored in public. I thought: Bullshit, you're not gonna use me any more. That's when I began to do some real serious thinkin'. . . .

I spent a lot of sleepless nights. I still didn't like blacks. I didn't want to associate with 'em. Blacks, Jews, or Catholics. My father said: "don't have anything to do with 'em." I didn't until I met a black person and talked with him, eyeball to eyeball, and met a Jewish person and talked to him, eyeball to eyeball. I found out they're people just like me. They cried, they cussed, they prayed, they had desires. Just like myself. Thank God, I got to the point where I can look past labels. But at that time, my mind was closed. . . .

Then something happened. The state AFL–CIO received a grant from the Department of HEW,[1] a $78,000 grant: how to solve racial problems in the school system. I got a telephone call from the president of the state AFL–CIO. "We'd like to get some people together from all walks of life." I said: "All walks of life? Who you talkin' about?" He said: "Blacks, whites, liberals, conservatives, Klansmen, NAACP[2] people."

I said: "No way am I comin' with all those niggers. I'm not gonna be associated with those type of people." A White Citizens Council guy said: "Let's go up there and see what's goin' on. It's tax money bein' spent." I walk in the door, and there was a large number of blacks and white liberals. I knew most of 'em by face 'cause I seen 'em demonstratin' around town. Ann Atwater was there. (Laughs.) I just forced myself to go in and sit down.

The meeting was moderated by a great big black guy who was bushy-headed. (Laughs.) That turned me off. He acted very nice. He said: "I want you all to feel free to say anything you want to say." Some of the blacks stand up and say it's white racism. I took all I could take. I asked for the floor and cut loose. I said: "No, sir, it's black racism. If we didn't have niggers in the schools, we wouldn't have the problems we got today."

---

[1]HEW: Department of Health, Education, and Welfare.
[2]NAACP: National Association for the Advancement of Colored People.

I will never forget. Howard Clements, a black guy, stood up. He said: "I'm certainly glad C. P. Ellis come because he's the most honest man here tonight." I said: "What's that nigger tryin' to do?" (Laughs.) At the end of that meeting, some blacks tried to come up shake my hand, but I wouldn't do it. I walked off.

Second night, same group was there. I felt a little more easy because I got some things off my chest. The third night, after they elected all the committees, they want to elect a chairman. Howard Clements stood up and said: "I suggest we elect two co-chairpersons." Joe Beckton, executive director of the Human Relations Commission, just as black as he can be, he nominated me. There was a reaction from some blacks. Nooo. And, of all things, they nominated Ann Atwater, that big old fat black gal that I had just hated with a purple passion, as co-chairman. I thought to myself: Hey, ain't no way I can work with that gal. Finally, I agreed to accept it, 'cause at this point, I was tired of fightin', either for survival or against black people or against Jews or against Catholics.

A Klansman and a militant black woman, co-chairmen of the school committee. It was impossible. How could I work with her? But after about two or three days, it was in our hands. We had to make it a success. This give me another sense of belongin', a sense of pride. This helped this inferiority feelin' I had. A man who has stood up publicly and said he despised black people, all of a sudden he was willin' to work with 'em. Here's a chance for a low-income white man to be somethin'. In spite of all my hatred for blacks and Jews and liberals, I accepted the job. Her and I began to reluctantly work together. (Laughs.) She had as many problems workin' with me as I had workin' with her.

One night, I called her: "Ann, you and I should have a lot of differences and we got 'em now. But there's somethin' laid out here before us, and if it's gonna be a success, you and I are gonna have to make it one. Can we lay aside some of these feelin's?" She said: "I'm willing if you are." I said: "Let's do it." . . .

I said: "If we're gonna make this thing a success, I've got to get to my kind of people." The low-income whites. We walked the streets of Durham, and we knocked on doors and invited people. Ann was goin' into the black community. They just wasn't respondin' to us when we made these house calls. Some of 'em were cussin' us out. "You're sellin' us out, Ellis, get out of my door. I don't want to talk to you." Ann was gettin' the same response from blacks. "What are you doin' messin' with that Klansman?"

One day, Ann and I went back to the school and we sat down. We began to talk and just reflect. Ann said: "My daughter came home cryin' every day. She said her teacher was makin' fun of me in front of the other kids." I said "Boy, the same thing happened to my kid. White liberal teacher was makin' fun of Tim Ellis's father, the Klansman. In front of other peoples. He came home cryin'." At this point—(he pauses, swallows hard, stifles a sob)—I begin to see, here we are, two people from the far ends of the fence, havin' identical problems, except hers bein' black and me bein' white. From that moment on, I tell ya, that gal and I worked together good. I begin to love the girl, really. (He weeps.)

The amazing thing about it, her and I, up to that point, had cussed each other, bawled each other, we hated each other. Up to that point, we didn't know each other. We didn't know we had things in common.

We worked at it, with the people who came to these meetings. They talked about racism, sex education, about teachers not bein' qualified. After seven, eight nights of real intense discussion, these people, who'd never talked to each other before, all of a sudden came up with resolutions. It was really somethin', you had to be there to get the tone and feelin' of it. . . .

I tell people there's a tremendous possibility in this country to stop wars, the battles, the struggles, the fights between people. People say: "That's an impossible dream. You sound like Martin Luther King." An ex-Klansman who sounds like Martin Luther King. (Laughs.) I don't think it's an impossible dream. It's happened in my life. It's happened in other people's lives in America. . . .

Since I changed, I've set down and listened to tapes of Martin Luther King. I listen to it and tears come to my eyes 'cause I know what he's sayin' now. I know what's happenin'.

Response and Analysis

1. Describe C. P. Ellis's feelings, thoughts, and behaviors toward African Americans before and after he accepted the AFL-CIO's invitation to work with African Americans. What factors contributed to his anti-African American attitude?

2. Why do you think Ellis changed his attitude toward African Americans? How might cognitive dissonance explain the change in Ellis's attitude after he accepted the AFL-CIO's invitation to work with African Americans?

Personal Experience and Application

1. Have you ever acted in a way that was inconsistent with a strong attitude that you had? If so, what was the attitude and what was your behavior? How did you feel after acting in a way that was inconsistent with your attitude? Did your attitude or behavior change? Why or why not?

2. Suppose a professor asks you to join a task force whose mission is to improve race relations at your college or university. Discuss two activities that you would propose. Why do you think these activities would promote positive race relations?

Research

Suppose you want to investigate attitudes about race relations in America. You decide to randomly select Americans to participate in a telephone survey. First you need to write the questions for the survey. Write six questions that will assess the participants' feelings, thoughts, and actions concerning race relations. The participants should be able to answer the questions using the following scale: strongly disagree, disagree, neither disagree nor agree, agree, strongly agree. Some might provide socially desirable responses rather than honest responses to your questions. How might you construct the questionnaire to increase the likelihood that the participants will provide honest answers?

INFLUENCE

Robert B. Cialdini

Psychological Concepts
persuasion, compliance, scarcity principle,
psychological reactance

Social psychologist Robert B. Cialdini has long been interested in why some people are so successful at persuasion. Why are some people good fundraisers? Why are some people more easily swayed by sales pitches than others? What strategies seem to work most effectively when one wants to influence others? Cialdini presents several techniques that seem to work, and he offers explanations for their effectiveness. In one example, he tells of a woman who rushes to the copying machine where a long line of people wait to use it. She asks: "May I use the Xerox machine because I have to make some copies?" Would this request persuade you to let her in ahead of you? You may be surprised at how people reacted to her request.

I got a phone call one day from a friend who had recently opened an Indian jewelry store in Arizona. She was giddy with a curious piece of news. Something fascinating had just happened, and she thought that, as a psychologist, I might be able to explain it to her. The story involved a certain allotment of turquoise jewelry she had been having trouble selling. It was the peak of the tourist season, the store was unusually full of customers, the turquoise pieces were of good quality for the prices she was asking; yet they had not sold. My friend had attempted a couple of standard sales tricks to get them moving. She tried calling attention to them by shifting their location to a more central display area; no luck. She even told her sales staff to "push" the items hard, again without success.

Finally, the night before leaving on an out-of-town buying trip, she scribbled an exasperated note to her head saleswoman, "Everything in this display case, price × ½," hoping just to be rid of the offending pieces, even if at a loss. When she returned a few days later, she was not surprised to find that every article had been sold. She was shocked, though, to discover that, because the employee had read the "½" in her scrawled message as a "2," the entire allotment had sold out at twice the original price!

That's when she called me. I thought I knew what had happened but told her that, if I were to explain things properly, she would have to listen to a story of mine. Actually, it isn't my story; it's about mother turkeys, and it belongs to the relatively new science of ethology—the study of animals in their natural settings. Turkey mothers are good mothers—loving, watchful, and protective. They spend much of their time tending, warming, cleaning, and huddling the young beneath them. But there *is* something odd about their method. Virtually all of this mothering is triggered by one thing: the "cheep-cheep" sound of young turkey chicks. Other identifying features of the chicks, such as their smell, touch, or appearance, seem to play minor roles in the mothering process. If a chick makes the "cheep-cheep" noise, its mother will care for it; if not, the mother will ignore or sometimes kill it. . . .

Before we enjoy too smugly the ease with which lower animals can be tricked by trigger features into reacting in ways wholly inappropriate to the situation, we might realize two things. First, the automatic, fixed-action patterns of these animals work very well the great majority of the time. For example, because only healthy, normal turkey chicks make the peculiar sound of baby turkeys, it makes sense for mother turkeys to respond maternally to that single "cheep-cheep" noise. By reacting to just that one stimulus, the average mother turkey will nearly always behave correctly. It takes a trickster like a scientist to make her tapelike response seem silly. The second important thing to understand is that we, too, have our preprogrammed tapes; and, although they usually work to our advantage, the trigger features that activate them can be used to dupe *us* into playing them at the wrong times.

This parallel form of human automatic action is aptly demonstrated in an experiment by Harvard social psychologist Ellen Langer. A well-known principle of human behavior says that when we ask someone to do us a favor we will be more successful if we provide a reason. People simply like to have reasons for what they do. Langer demonstrated this unsurprising fact by asking a small favor of people waiting in line to use a library copying machine: *Excuse me, I have five pages. May I use the Xerox machine because I'm in a rush?* The effectiveness of this request-plus-reason was nearly total: 94 percent of those asked let her skip ahead of them in line. Compare this success rate to the results when she made the request only: *Excuse me, I have five pages. May I use the Xerox machine?* Under those circumstances only 60 percent of those asked complied. At first glance, it appears that the crucial difference between the two requests was the additional information provided by the words "because I'm in a rush." But a third type of request tried by Langer showed that this was not the case. It seems that it was not the whole series of words, but the first one, "because," that made the difference. Instead of including a real reason for compliance, Langer's third type of request used the word "because" and then, adding nothing new, merely restated the obvious: *Excuse me, I have five pages. May I use the Xerox machine because I have to make some copies?* The result was that once again nearly all (93 percent) agreed, even though no real reason, no new information was added to justify their compliance. . . . The word "because" triggered an automatic compliance response from Langer's subjects, even when they were given no subsequent reason to comply. . . .

Although some of Langer's additional findings show that there are many situations in which human behavior does not work in a mechanical, tape-activated way, what is astonishing is how often it does. For instance, consider the strange behavior of those jewelry store customers who swooped down on an allotment of turquoise pieces only after the items had been mistakenly offered at double their original price. . . .

The customers, mostly well-to-do vacationers with little knowledge of turquoise, were using a standard principle—a stereotype—to guide their buying: "expensive = good." Thus the vacationers, who wanted "good" jewelry, saw the turquoise pieces as decidedly more valuable and desirable when nothing about them was enhanced but the price. Price alone had become a trigger feature for quality; and a dramatic increase in price alone had led to a dramatic increase in sales among the quality-hungry buyers. . . .

It is easy to fault the tourists for their foolish purchase decisions. But a close look offers a kinder view. These were people who had been brought up on the rule "You get what you pay for" and who had seen that rule borne out over and over in their lives. Before long, they had translated the rule to mean "expensive = good." The "expensive = good" stereotype had worked quite well for them in the past, since normally the price of an item increases along with its worth; a higher price typically reflects higher quality. So when they found themselves in the position of wanting good turquoise jewelry without much knowledge of turquoise, they understandably relied on the old standby feature of cost to determine the jewelry's merits. . . .

In fact, automatic, stereotyped behavior is prevalent in much of human action because in many cases it is the most efficient form of behaving, and in other cases it is simply necessary. You and I exist in an extraordinarily complicated stimulus environment, easily the most rapidly moving and complex that has ever existed on this planet. To deal with it, we *need* shortcuts. We can't be expected to recognize and analyze all the aspects in each person, event, and situation we encounter in even one day. We haven't the time, energy, or capacity for it. Instead, we must very often use our stereotypes, our rules of thumb to classify things according to a few key features and then to respond mindlessly when one or another of these trigger features is present. . . .

It is odd that despite their current widespread use and looming future importance, most of us know very little about our automatic behavior patterns. Perhaps that is so precisely because of the mechanistic, unthinking manner in which they occur. Whatever the reason, it is vital that we clearly recognize one of their properties: They make us terribly vulnerable to anyone who does know how they work. . . .

Scarcity: The Rule of the Few

The city of Mesa, Arizona, is a suburb in the Phoenix area where I live. Perhaps the most notable features of Mesa are its sizable Mormon population—next to that of Salt Lake City, the largest in the world—and a huge Mormon temple located on exquisitely kept grounds in the center of the city. Although I had appreciated the landscaping and architecture from a distance, I had never been interested enough in the temple to go inside until the day I read a newspaper article. It told of a special inner sector of Mormon temples to which no one has access but faithful members of the

Church. Even potential converts must not see it. There is one exception to the rule, however. For a few days immediately after a temple is newly constructed, nonmembers are allowed to tour the entire structure, including the otherwise restricted section.

The newspaper story reported that the Mesa temple had recently been refurbished and that the renovations had been extensive enough to classify it as "new" by Church standards. Thus, for the next several days only, non-Mormon visitors could see the temple area traditionally banned to them. I remember quite well the effect of the article on me: I immediately resolved to take a tour. But when I phoned a friend to ask if he wanted to come along, I came to understand something that changed my decision just as quickly.

After declining the invitation, my friend wondered why *I* seemed so intent on a visit. I was forced to admit that, no, I had never been inclined toward the idea of a temple tour before, that I had no questions about the Mormon religion I wanted answered, that I had no general interest in architecture of houses of worship, and that I expected to find nothing more spectacular or stirring than I might see at a number of other temples, churches, or cathedrals in the area. It became clear as I spoke that the special lure of the temple had a sole cause: If I did not experience the restricted sector shortly, I would never again have the chance. Something that, on its own merits, held little appeal for me had become decidedly more attractive merely because it would soon become unavailable.

Since that encounter with the scarcity principle—that opportunities seem more valuable to us when their availability is limited—I have begun to notice its influence over a whole range of my actions. For instance, I routinely will interrupt an interesting face-to-face conversation to answer the ring of an unknown caller. In such a situation, the caller has a compelling feature that my face-to-face partner does not: potential unavailability. If I don't take the call, I might miss it (and the information it carries) for good. Never mind that the ongoing conversation may be highly engaging or important—much more than I could reasonably expect an average phone call to be. With each unanswered ring, the phone interaction becomes less retrievable. For that reason and for that moment, I want it more than the other.

I count myself far from alone in this weakness. Almost everyone is vulnerable to the scarcity principle in some form. Take as evidence what happens at singles bars as closing time approaches and as chances to meet suitable members of the opposite sex become scarcer. At three separate times during the evening—three and a half hours, two hours, and a half hour before closing—researchers in Virginia randomly selected customers at several bars and asked them to rate the attractiveness of the opposite-sex individuals present. Contrary to what one might expect, the romantic possibilities still remaining only a half hour before closing were judged as the best-looking by far. How might we account for this surprising finding? It could be argued, for example, that the influence of greater amounts of alcohol causes everybody and everything to seem more pleasant-looking by night's end. Or it might be that the truly beautiful people don't come out until late; if so, the study's results were not drink-distorted but accurate.

Although possible, these explanations do not stand up well under close scrutiny. For example, the researchers found that the women who were present at the bars just before closing looked best only to the male patrons; similarly, the late-staying men looked best only to the female customers. Thus it was not true that people *generally* were more attractive or seemed more attractive late in the evening. Instead, only those who were potential romantic partners grew "better-looking" as the night wore on.

A more satisfying explanation of the patrons' ratings can be found in the scarcity principle: Opposite-sex individuals look better near closing time because the chances to meet them are rapidly dwindling. And anything that is becoming less available seems more attractive. . . .

With the scarcity principle operating so powerfully on the worth we assign things, it is natural that compliance professionals will do some related operating of their own. Probably the most straightforward use of the scarcity principle occurs in the "limited-number" tactic, when the customer is informed that a certain product is in short supply that cannot be guaranteed to last long. During the time I was researching compliance strategies by infiltrating various organizations, I saw the limited-number tactic employed repeatedly in a range of situations: "There aren't more than five convertibles with this engine left in the state. And when they're gone, that's it, 'cause we're not making 'em anymore." "This is one of only two unsold corner lots in the entire development. You wouldn't want the other one; it's got a nasty east-west exposure." "You may want to think seriously about buying more than one case today because production is backed way up and there's no telling when we'll get any more in."

Sometimes the limited-number information was true, sometimes it was wholly false. But in each instance, the intent was to convince customers of an item's scarcity and thereby increase its immediate value in their eyes. I admit to developing a grudging admiration for the practitioners who made this simple device work in a multitude of ways and styles. I was most impressed, however, with a particular version that extended the basic approach to its logical extreme by selling a piece of merchandise at its scarcest point—when it seemingly could no longer be had. The tactic was played to perfection in one appliance store I investigated, where 30 to 50 percent of the stock was regularly listed as on sale. Suppose a couple in the store seemed from a distance to be moderately interested in a certain sale item. There are all sorts of cues that tip off such interest—closer-than-normal examination of the appliance, a casual look at any instruction booklets associated with the appliance, discussions held in front of the appliance, but no attempt to seek out a salesperson for further information. After observing the couple so engaged, a salesperson might approach and say, "I see you're interested in this model here, and I can understand why; it's a great machine at a great price. But, unfortunately, I sold it to another couple not more than twenty minutes ago. And, if I'm not mistaken, it was the last one we had."

The customers' disappointment registers unmistakably. Because of its lost availability, the appliance jumps suddenly in attractiveness. Typically, one of the customers asks if there is any chance that an unsold model still exists in the store's back room, or warehouse, or other location. "Well," the salesperson allows, "that is possible, and I'd be willing to check. But do I understand that this is the model you want and if I can get it for you at this price, you'll take it?" Therein lies the beauty of the technique. In accord with the scarcity principle, the customers are asked to commit to buying the appliance when it looks least available—and therefore most desirable. Many customers do agree to a purchase at this singularly vulnerable time. Thus, when the salesperson (invariably) returns with the news that an additional supply of the appliance has been found, it is also with a pen and sales contract in hand. The information that the desired model is in good supply may actually make some customers find it less attractive again. But by then, the business transaction has progressed too far for most people to renege. The purchase decision made and committed to publicly at an earlier, crucial point still holds. They buy.

Related to the limited-number technique is the "deadline" tactic in which some official time limit is placed on the customer's opportunity to get what the compliance professional is offering. Much like my experience with the Mormon temple's inner sanctum, people frequently find themselves doing what they wouldn't particularly care to do, simply because the time to do so is shrinking. The adept merchandiser makes this tendency pay off by arranging and publicizing customer deadlines . . . that generate interest where none may have existed before.

A variant of the deadline tactic is much favored by some face-to-face, high-pressure sellers because it carries the purest form of decision deadline: right now. Customers are often told that unless they make an immediate decision to buy, they will have to purchase the item at a higher price or they will be unable to purchase it at all. A prospective health-club member or automobile buyer might learn that the deal offered by the salesperson is good only for that one time; should the customer leave the premises, the deal is off. One large child-portrait photography company urges parents to buy as many poses and copies as they can afford because "stocking limitations force us to burn the unsold pictures of your children within twenty-four hours." A door-to-door magazine solicitor might say that salespeople are in the customer's area for just a day; after that, they—and the customer's chance to buy their magazine package—will be long gone. A home vacuum-cleaner operation I infiltrated instructed its sales trainees to claim, "I have so many other people to see that I have the time to visit a family only once. It's company policy that even if you decide later that you want this machine, I can't come back and sell it to you." This, of course, is nonsense; the company and its representatives are in the business of making sales, and any customer who called for another visit would be accommodated gladly. As the company sales manager impressed on his trainees, the true purpose of the can't-come-back claim has nothing to do with reducing overburdened sales schedules. It is to "keep the prospects from taking the time to think the deal over by scaring them into believing they can't have it later, which makes them want it now."

Psychological Reactance

The evidence, then, is clear. Compliance practitioners' reliance on scarcity as a weapon of influence is frequent, wide-ranging, systematic, and diverse. Whenever such is the case with a weapon of influence, we can feel assured that the principle involved has notable power in directing human action. In the instance of the scarcity principle, that power comes from two major sources. The first is familiar. Like the other weapons of influence, the scarcity principle trades on our weakness for short-cuts. The weakness is, as before, an *enlightened* one. In this case, because we know that the things that are difficult to possess are typically better than those that are easy to possess, we can often use an item's availability to help us quickly and correctly decide on its quality. Thus, one reason for the potency of the scarcity principle is that, by following it, we are usually and efficiently right.

In addition, there is a unique, secondary source of power within the scarcity principle: As opportunities become less available, we lose freedoms; and we *hate* to lose the freedoms we already have.

Response and Analysis

1. Why does Robert Cialdini believe that people respond in certain situations with an automatic compliance response?

2. What is the scarcity principle? Briefly describe the "limited-number" tactic and the "deadline" tactic. Why are the scarcity principle, limited number tactic, and the deadline tactic effective forms of influence?

Personal Experience and Application

1. Describe a situation in which an "automatic behavior pattern" led you to do something that, given more thought, you might not have done. What evoked the automatic behavior pattern?

2. Have you ever fallen prey to someone using principles of scarcity to try to sell you something? Briefly describe the situation.

What do you notice now about the situation that you did not notice at the time? How might your new awareness about subtle influence practices affect your behavior in the future?

Research

Suppose you want to conduct a study to examine how scarcity influences perceptions of value. You will show participants various items and tell them that the items are either becoming scarce or are in plentiful supply. You then will ask the participants to indicate how much they think the items are worth. How would you carry out the study? For example, what items would you use? Would you show the items to each participant alone or together in a group? Why? Would you personally present the items to each participant, or would you show the items on a computer screen or in some other way? Why? What other procedures would you include in your study?

BLACK MEN AND PUBLIC SPACE

Brent Staples

Psychological Concepts
stereotypes, prejudice, discrimination, impression
formation

Brent Staples, now on the editorial staff of the *New York Times,* writes about being
prejudged because he is African American. When he was a graduate student at the
University of Chicago, he often took long walks at night because of his insomnia.
He then became aware of the fear he instilled: Women hurried across streets,
running to get away from him; drivers quickly locked their car doors. One time as
he rushed to a deadline at a magazine office, he was mistaken for a burglar and
was pursued by the security officer. False charges against him were common. "Over
the years," writes Staples, "I learned to smother the rage I felt at so often being
taken for a criminal. Not to do so would surely have led to madness." What criteria
did people use to assume the worst about Staples? How did other people's
stereotypes affect his self-image?

My first victim was a woman—white, well dressed, probably in her early twenties. I came upon her late one evening on a deserted street in Hyde Park, a relatively affluent neighborhood in an otherwise mean, impoverished section of
Chicago. As I swung onto the avenue behind her, there seemed to be a discreet,
uninflammatory distance between us. Not so. She cast back a worried glance.
To her, the youngish black man—a broad six feet two inches with a beard and
billowing hair, both hands shoved into the pockets of a bulky military jacket—
seemed menacingly close. After a few more quick glimpses, she picked up her
pace and was soon running in earnest. Within seconds she disappeared into a cross
street.

That was more than a decade ago, I was twenty-two years old, a graduate student newly arrived at the University of Chicago. It was in the echo of that terrified
woman's footfalls that I first began to know the unwieldy inheritance I'd come
into—the ability to alter public space in ugly ways. It was clear that she thought herself the quarry of a mugger, a rapist, or worse. Suffering a bout of insomnia, however, I was stalking sleep, not defenseless wayfarers. As a softy who is scarcely able
to take a knife to a raw chicken—let alone hold one to a person's throat—I was surprised, embarrassed, and dismayed all at once. Her flight made me feel like an ac-
complice in tyranny. It also made it clear that I was indistinguishable from the
muggers who occasionally seeped into the area from the surrounding ghetto. That

first encounter, and those that followed, signified that a vast, unnerving gulf lay between nighttime pedestrians—particularly women—and me. And I soon gathered that being perceived as dangerous is a hazard in itself. I only needed to turn a corner into a dicey situation, or crowd some frightened, armed person in a foyer somewhere, or make an errant move after being pulled over by a policeman. Where fear and weapons meet—and they often do in urban America—there is always the possibility of death.

In that first year, my first away from my hometown, I was to become thoroughly familiar with the language of fear. At dark, shadowy intersections, I could cross in front of a car stopped at a traffic light and elicit the *thunk, thunk, thunk, thunk* of the driver—black, white, male, or female—hammering the door locks. On less traveled streets after dark, I grew accustomed to but never comfortable with people crossing to the other side of the street rather than pass me. Then there were the standard unpleasantries with policemen, doormen, bouncers, cabdrivers, and others whose business it is to screen out troublesome individuals *before* there is any nastiness.

I moved to New York nearly two years ago and I have remained an avid night walker. In central Manhattan, the near-constant crowd cover minimizes tense one-on-one street encounters. Elsewhere—in SoHo, for example, where sidewalks are narrow and tightly spaced buildings shut out the sky—things can get very taut indeed.

After dark, on the warrenlike streets of Brooklyn where I live, I often see women who fear the worst from me. They seem to have set their faces on neutral, and with their purse straps strung across their chests bandolier-style, they forge ahead as though bracing themselves against being tackled. I understand, of course, that the danger they perceive is not a hallucination. Women are particularly vulnerable to street violence, and young black males are drastically overrepresented among the perpetrators of that violence. Yet these truths are no solace against the kind of alienation that comes of being ever the suspect, a fearsome entity with whom pedestrians avoid making eye contact.

It is not altogether clear to me how I reached the ripe old age of twenty-two without being conscious of the lethality nighttime pedestrians attributed to me. Perhaps it was because in Chester, Pennsylvania, the small, angry industrial town where I came of age in the 1960s, I was scarcely noticeable against a backdrop of gang warfare, street knifings, and murders. I grew up one of the good boys, had perhaps a half-dozen fistfights. In retrospect, my shyness of combat has clear sources.

As a boy, I saw countless tough guys locked away; I have since buried several, too. They were babies, really—a teenage cousin, a brother of twenty-two, a childhood friend in his mid-twenties—all gone down in episodes of bravado played out in the streets. I came to doubt the virtues of intimidation early on. I chose, perhaps unconsciously, to remain a shadow—timid, but a survivor.

The fearsomeness mistakenly attributed to me in public places often has a perilous flavor. The most frightening of these confusions occurred in the late 1970s and early 1980s, when I worked as a journalist in Chicago. One day, rushing into the office of a magazine I was writing for with a deadline story in hand, I was mistaken for a burglar. The office manager called security and, with an ad hoc posse, pursued me through the labyrinthine halls, nearly to my editor's door. I had no way of proving who I was. I could only move briskly toward the company of someone who knew me.

Another time I was on assignment for a local paper and killing time before an interview. I entered a jewelry store on the city's affluent Near North Side. The proprietor excused herself and returned with an enormous red Doberman pinscher straining at the end of a leash. She stood, the dog extended toward me, silent to my questions, her eyes bulging nearly out of her head. I took a cursory look around, nodded, and bade her good night.

Relatively speaking, however, I never fared as badly as another black male journalist. He went to nearby Waukegan, Illinois, a couple of summers ago to work on a story about a murderer who was born there. Mistaking the reporter for the killer, police officers hauled him from his car at gunpoint and but for his press credentials would probably have tried to book him. Such episodes are not uncommon. Black men trade tales like this all the time.

Over the years, I learned to smother the rage I felt at so often being taken for a criminal. Not to do so would surely have led to madness. I now take precautions to make myself less threatening. I move about with care, particularly late in the evening. I give a wide berth to nervous people on subway platforms during the wee hours, particularly when I have exchanged business clothes for jeans. If I happen to be entering a building behind some people who appear skittish, I may walk by, letting them clear the lobby before I return, so as not to seem to be following them. I have been calm and extremely congenial on those rare occasions when I've been pulled over by the police.

And on late-evening constitutionals I employ what has proved to be an excellent tension-reducing measure: I whistle melodies from Beethoven and Vivaldi and the more popular classical composers. Even steely New Yorkers hunching toward nighttime destinations seem to relax, and occasionally they even join in the tune. Virtually everybody seems to sense that a mugger wouldn't be warbling bright, sunny selections from Vivaldi's *Four Seasons*. It is my equivalent of the cowbell that hikers wear when they know they are in bear country.

Response and Analysis

1. Give an example of prejudice and of discrimination in Brent Staples's story. How did Staples use stereotypes to make others perceive him as less threatening? Why was this effective?

2. What criteria did people use to assume the worst about Staples? How did other people's stereotypes affect his self-image?

Personal Experience and Application

1. Have you ever treated someone differently because of his or her ethnicity or age? What did you do? How did your actions make you feel? How do you think your actions made the other person feel?

2. Can people be prejudiced without being aware of it? Why or why not?

Research

Suppose you wish to conduct an experiment to examine first impressions. You want to know whether a person's name influences how she or he is perceived. You will have all participants read the same newspaper article, but you will tell one-third of the participants that the article was written by a person with an Irish surname, one-third that it was written by a person with an Asian surname, and one-third that it was written by a person with a Latin surname. After reading the article, the participants will rate the quality of the writing and grammar using the following scale: poor, fair, good, very good, excellent. Do you believe that the participants will rate the article differently on the basis of the surname? If so, which author will receive the highest rating and which will receive the lowest? Is this an adequate way to study how stereotypes influence how people are perceived? Why or why not? Finally, how might the participants' ethnicity influence the results?

WHY COMPETITION?

Alfie Kohn

Psychological Concepts
competition, cooperation, interpersonal relations

Alfie Kohn challenges us to consider the ramifications of competition and cooperation. His points are thought-provoking: competition may be unhealthy because it
means that one person sets out to defeat another person (one has to be brighter
than, faster than, or prettier than the other); it injures community ("those on the
other side are excluded"); and it fosters deception (some may cheat and lie to win).
In short, one person's success and self-worth hinge on another person's defeat and
failure. Is competition unhealthy? Is it detrimental to individuals and groups?

"W-H-I-T-E! White Team is the team for me!" The cheer is repeated, becoming
increasingly frenzied as scores of campers, bedecked in the appropriate color, try to
outshout their Blue opponents. The rope stretched over the lake is taut now, as determined tuggers give it their all. It looks as if a few will be yanked into the cold
water, but a whistle pierces the air. "All right, we'll call this a draw." Sighs of disappointment follow, but children are soon scrambling off to the Marathon. Here,
competitors will try to win for their side by completing such tasks as standing up-
side-down in a bucket of shampoo or forcing down great quantities of food in a few
seconds before tagging a teammate.

   As a counselor in this camp over a period of several years, I witnessed a number of Color Wars, and what constantly amazed me was the abrupt and total transformation that took place each time one began. As campers are read their assignments, children who not ten minutes before were known as "David" or "Margie"
suddenly have a new identity; they have been arbitrarily designated as members of a
team. The unspoken command is understood by even the youngest among them:
Do everything possible to win for your side. Strain every muscle to prove how superior *we* are to the hostile Blues.

   And so they will. Children who had wandered aimlessly about the camp are
suddenly driven with a Purpose. Children who had tired of the regular routine are
instantly provided with Adventure. Children who had trouble making friends are
unexpectedly part of a new Crowd. In the dining hall, every camper sits with his or
her team. Strategy is planned for the next battle; troops are taught the next cheer.
There is a coldness bordering on suspicion when passing someone with a blue T-
shirt—irrespective of any friendship B.C. (Before Colors). If anyone has reserva-

tions about participating in an activity, he needs only to be reminded that the other team is just a few points behind.

"Why Sport?" asks Ed Cowan (*The Humanist*, November/December 1979). When the sports are competitive ones, I cannot find a single reason to answer his rhetorical query. Mr. Cowan's discussion of the pure—almost mystical—aesthetic pleasure that is derived from athletics only directs attention away from what is, in actuality, the primary impetus of any competitive activity: winning.

I would not make such a fuss over Color War, or even complain about the absurd spectacle of grown men shrieking and cursing on Sunday afternoons were it not for the significance of the role played by competition in our culture. It is bad enough that Americans actually regard fighting as a sport: it is worse that the outcome of even the gentlest of competitions—baseball—can induce fans to hysteria and outright violence. But sports is only the tip of the proverbial iceberg. Our entire society is affected by—even structured upon—the need to be "better than."

My thesis is admittedly extreme; it is, simply put, that *competition by its very nature is always unhealthy.* This is true, to begin with, because competition and cooperation are mutually exclusive orientations. I say this fully aware of the famed camaraderie that is supposed to develop among players—or soldiers—on the same side. First, I have doubts, based on personal experience, concerning the depth and fullness of relationships that result from the need to become more effective against a common enemy.

Second, the "realm of the interhuman," to use Martin Buber's phrase, is severely curtailed when those on the other side are excluded from any possible community. Worse, they are generally regarded with suspicion and contempt in any competitive enterprise. (This is not to say that we cannot remain on good terms with, say, tennis opponents, but that whatever cooperation and meaningful relationship is in evidence exists in spite of the competitiveness.) Finally, the sweaty fellowship of the lockerroom (or, to draw the inescapable parallel again, the trenches) simply does not compensate for the inherent evils of competition.

The desire to win has a not very surprising (but too rarely remarked upon) characteristic: It tends to edge out other goals and values in the context of any given competitive activity. When I was in high school, I was a very successful debater for a school that boasted one of the country's better teams. After hundreds and hundreds of rounds of competition over three years, I can assert in no uncertain terms that the purpose of debate is not to seek the truth or resolve an issue. No argument, however compelling, is ever conceded; veracity is never attributed to the other side. The only reason debaters sacrifice their free time collecting thousands of pieces of evidence, analyzing arguments, and practicing speeches, is to win. Truth thereby suffers in at least two ways.

In any debate, neither team is concerned with arriving at a fuller understanding of the topic. The debaters concentrate on "covering" arguments, tying logical knots, and, above all, sounding convincing. Beyond this, though, there exists a tremendous temptation to fabricate and distort evidence. Words are left out, phrases added, sources modified in order to lend credibility to the position. One extremely successful debater on my team used to invent names of magazines which ostensibly printed substantiation for crucial arguments he wanted to use.

With respect to this last phenomenon, it is fruitless—and a kind of self-deception, ultimately—to shake our heads and deplore this sort of thing. Similarly, we have no business condemning "overly rough" football players or the excesses of "overzealous" campaign aides or even, perhaps, violations of the Geneva Convention in time of war (which is essentially a treatise on How to Kill Human Beings Without Doing Anything *Really* Unethical). We are engaging in a massive (albeit implicit) exercise of hypocrisy to decry these activities while continuing to condone, and even encourage, the competitive orientation of which they are only the logical conclusion.

The cost of any kind of competition in human terms is incalculable. When my success depends on other people's failure, the prospects for a real human community are considerably diminished. This consequence speaks to the profoundly anti-humanistic quality of competitive activity, and it is abundantly evident in American society. Moreover, when my success depends on my being *better than*, I am caught on a treadmill, destined never to enjoy real satisfaction. Someone is always one step higher, and even the summit is a precarious position in light of the hordes waiting to occupy it in my stead. I am thus perpetually insecure and, as psychologist Rollo May points out, perpetually anxious.

> . . . Individual competitive success is both the dominant goal in our culture and the most pervasive occasion for anxiety . . . [This] anxiety arises out of the interpersonal isolation and alienation from others that inheres in a pattern in which self-validation depends on triumphing over others. (*The Meaning of Anxiety*, rev. ed.)

I begin to see my self-worth as conditional—that is to say, my goodness or value becomes contingent on how much better I am than so many others in so many activities. If you believe, as I do, that unconditional self-esteem is a singularly important requirement for (and indicator of) mental health, then the destructiveness of competition will clearly outweigh any putative benefit, whether it be a greater effort at tug-of-war or a higher gross national product.

From the time we are quite small, the ethic of competitiveness is drummed into us. The goal in school is not to grow as a human being or even, in practice, to reach a satisfactory level of intellectual competence. We are pushed instead to become brighter than, quicker than, better achievers than our classmates, and the endless array of scores and grades lets us know at any given instant how we stand on that ladder of academic success.

If our schools are failing at their explicit tasks, we may rest assured of their overwhelming success regarding this hidden agenda. We are well trained to enter the marketplace and compete frantically for more money, more prestige, more of all the "good things" in life. An economy such as ours, understand, does not merely permit competition: *it demands it*. Ever greater profits becomes the watchword of private enterprise, and an inequitable distribution of wealth (a polite codeword for human suffering) follows naturally from such an arrangement.

Moreover, one must be constantly vigilant lest one's competitors attract more customers or conceive some innovation that gives them the edge. To become outraged at deceptive and unethical business practices is folly; it is the competitiveness of the system that promotes these phenomena. Whenever people are defined as opponents, doing everything possible to triumph must be seen not as an aberration from the structure but as its very consummation. (I recognize, of course, that I have raised a plethora of difficult issues across many disciplines that cry out for a more detailed consideration. I hope, however, to at least have opened up some provocative, and largely neglected, lines of inquiry.)

This orientation finds its way into our personal relationships as well. We bring our yardstick along to judge potential candidates for lover, trying to determine who is most attractive, most intelligent, and . . . the best lover. At the same time, of course, *we* are being similarly reduced to the status of competitor. The human costs are immense.

"Why Sport?", then, is a good question to begin with. It leads us to inquire, "Why Miss Universe contests?" "Why the arms race?" and—dare we say it—"Why capitalism?" Whether a competition-free society can actually be constructed is another issue altogether, and I readily concede that this mentality has so permeated our lives that we find it difficult even to imagine alternatives in many settings. The first step, though, consists in understanding that rivalry of any kind is both psychologically disastrous and philosophically unjustifiable, that the phrase "healthy competition" is a contradiction in terms. Only then can we begin to develop saner, richer lifestyles for ourselves as individuals, and explore more humanistic possibilities for our society.

Response and Analysis

1. When Alfie Kohn worked as a camp counselor, he was surprised by how easily the campers formed group identities based solely on their arbitrary assignment to a team. The "children who not ten minutes before were known as 'David' or 'Margie' suddenly [had] a new identity" and did everything possible to prove the superiority of their team. How might group identity promote competition? How might it promote cooperation?

2. Do you believe students have to compete with each other in order to learn? Why or why not? Why does Kohn believe that "competition by its very nature is always unhealthy"? List two situations in which competition may promote learning and self-worth. List two in which competition may hinder learning and promote self-doubt.

Personal Experience and Application

1. Do you agree or disagree with Kohn's view of competition? Why?

2. Suppose you are a counselor at a summer camp and are responsible for selecting a game every Friday afternoon in which

thirty fourth-grade campers will participate. Would you select a game that requires the campers to cooperate or compete, or both? Why?

Research

Suppose you want to examine the effects of communication on competition and cooperation. In the communication condition, the participants "talk" to each other using a computer. In the no-communication condition, the participants do not talk to each other. You randomly decide who will be in the communication and no-communication conditions when the participants arrive for the study.

Four psychology students participate in each session and when the participants arrive, you escort them to individual cubicles where they cannot see the other participants or the experimenter. Each cubicle is equipped with a computer, video monitor, and keyboard. You then ask the partici-

pants to read and sign a consent form. Each cubicle has a color code—red, blue, green, or brown. During the session, the participants use only their color code to identify themselves; they never reveal their name or identity to the other participants.

Participants in the communication condition use the computer to "talk" with the other group members for fifteen minutes. Participants in the no-communication condition write an essay describing themselves on the computer for fifteen minutes.

After the fifteen-minute period, you ask each participant to play a game with the other three members in their session. During the game, each participant will have an opportunity to cooperate or compete with the other group members. Do you think that the participants in the "talk" or "no-talk" group will be more competitive? Why? Will your findings generalize to adults who are not college students? Why or why not?

THE REVOLT ON K2

Galen Rowell

Psychological Concepts
group dynamics, leadership, fundamental attribution
error

To reach the summit of the world's highest peaks, climbers must not only have experience, wisdom, and physical strength, but also must be able to function well as a group. As a member of an American expedition to summit K2 (elevation 28,741 feet), one of the world's most difficult ascents, world-renown climber and nature photographer Galen Rowell and his teammates kept journals describing their adventures. To make a successful summit attempt, the team negotiated with and hired 650 porters to carry tons of equipment and food over one hundred miles to the base of the mountain. As they neared the mountain, many porters demanded additional pay and clothing. Once the team leaders accommodated the requests, the porters made new demands. It was a difficult situation for the team leaders, who had to keep on schedule, stay within their budget, and maintain harmony among the porters and the climbers.

In this selection, we are introduced to the team after many porters have quit the expedition and as the climbers are attempting to move higher up the mountain. Friction among the climbers has been growing, and many feel that the primary leaders are self-interested, do not plan to let the other climbers attempt a summit bid, and consider the other climbers less skilled. Consider how each climber perceives the situation and the leadership styles of the main leaders. How do the leaders perceive the situation? Might a different style of leadership have been more successful in keeping the team unified?

This selection includes excerpts from the journals of some of the climbers. The key figures are Lou and Jim Whittaker, twin brothers; Jim Wickwire (referred to as Wick); Rob Schaller, the team physician; Leif Patterson; Galen Rowell; and two men named Fred—Fred Stanley and Fred Dunham—who are feeling excluded from the rest of the group and have considered leaving the expedition. Lou and Jim Whittaker and Jim Wickwire were instrumental in forming the climbing team and leading the trip.

On June 16, I climbed to Camp II with Lou, Wick, Rob, and Steve. . . . The two Freds [Fred Stanley and Fred Dunham] were in base camp with Leif, both very subdued after a wild confrontation with the rest of the team. I sympathized fully with their emotions about the expedition, but not with their threats to go home. During the approach, both Freds had been more upset than anyone about the porters' failure to honor their contract when the going got rough. Now, to my way of thinking, they were doing exactly the same thing. We owed it to each other, even if we were no longer friends, to stick together long enough to make a serious attempt on the mountain. Otherwise, many man-years of effort and hope would have been spent in vain.

The Freds believed that the Whittakers and Wickwire formed a conspiracy in Seattle to place themselves on the summit to the exclusion of others. I didn't believe it. The kinds of partnerships that are often called conspiracies are usually nothing more than expressions of mutual self-interest. Wick [Wickwire] and Lou *seemed* as if they were involved in a conspiracy because each was individually motivated toward the same goal: being first on the summit. Jim recognized them as the winners of a self-styled competition. But if an agreement on the summit team existed beforehand, why had Wick and Lou pushed so hard to prove themselves? If a conspiracy had really existed, why didn't they just take it easy, waiting for Jim to pull them out of a hat after we prepared the lower camps?

Each of us had a slightly different interpretation of the Freds' revolt. Unfortunately, Fred Dunham did not keep a diary, but what follows are the descriptions that the other team members recorded at the time.

Lou Whittaker

Big crisis today! Last night the Freds talked til midnight and today [Fred] Stanley says he has *quit* the expedition. Feels he has no say in anything and that Jim and Wick and myself are running the expedition without letting anyone else have a vote. They were both very quiet yesterday after a ribbing that they got when they laughed because Wick and I were turned back from Camp II because of snow. Jim said usually when someone tries to do what we all want, like try to climb the mountain, failure would not be something to delight in. . . . The Freds have been so negative on everything . . . and now the rest of the team. I think a fear of the mountain may have them both stymied.

[Fred] Dunham said he would carry tomorrow but [Fred] Stanley may not. . . . He is really in a pout right now like a five-year-old—hard to sympathize with. . . . I didn't think I was being too strong with the Freds, but Wick said we (Jim and I) can tend to bulldoze through problems and can come on very strong.

Rob Schaller

Two days ago we had a real crisis with the two Freds, both suddenly admitting to being alienated by the Big Three [Lou Whittaker, Jim Whittaker, and Jim Wickwire] and not feeling a part of the expedition. [Fred] Stanley believes there is a conspiracy to get the Big Three on the top and we are only coolies to accomplish that purpose. He seems to have transferred his hostilities toward the Baltis to the rest of us. . . . Stanley talks seriously of leaving and I talk with him for hours but to little avail. . . .

Jim Whittaker

[Fred] Stanley is really running off at the mouth. Claims he is going to quit the expedition—that Lou, Wick, and I have a pact, made in Seattle, that the three of us are going to reach the summit of K2 and he is just going to carry for us. Claims no one else will get a chance. He says that I am a dictator, Wick [Wickwire] is ignoring everyone else but Lou and I and to hell with everyone. . . .

Leif Patterson

My lungs are not clear. . . . This is such a messed-up trip: My own sickness would mean little in a good team of first-rate friends. But the team is an unhappy one. It is nearly split apart from inner tensions. It is my lot to help pull together, unify, and without sufficient health I cannot succeed in that. I believe that you do not remedy a disastrous confidence crisis merely by talking it over. That is a first step. But the crisis was precipitated by cumulative *actions* in the first place, and actions cannot be eradicated by words, only by other actions. I believe we can still overcome difficulties and unify our team by actions which will allow each individual recognition for his efforts, and by honesty. The Wick-Lou summit consideration should be dissolved. Wick should do his job as deputy leader, which would first and foremost be to mend his relations with his close friends: the two Freds and Rob. The summit must be there to tempt all of us, not only a couple of gung-hos. The illness afflicting us as a team is already dangerously far advanced.

Jim Wickwire [Wick]

A major new crisis has hit the expedition: the possible defection of the two Freds. The problem has been brooding for some time. Both have felt they have had little involvement in expedition decision-making, that any ideas or comments they have about what should be done are not listened to or are rejected out of hand. Fred Dunham has been in deep gloom since the Manzoor radio incident of the tenth. Last night after dinner Fred D. unloaded to Galen and Steve how unhappy he was that "his friend Jim Wickwire had been distant," and that he was fed up with constantly being put down by Jim [Whittaker]. Last night, I could hear both of them talking in subdued voices far into the night. Something serious was up and was confirmed by Galen's relation of his discussion the previous evening with [Fred] Dunham. Apparently, [Fred] Stanley felt the same way and there was talk of their leaving the expedition. . . .

After breakfast, Jim [Whittaker] and I went to their [the Freds'] tent to talk with them. Jim led off, saying that his principal objective was to get up the mountain and that everything he had done had been directed toward that end. That to reach the summit every person on the team was important and if he stepped on their toes he was sorry. Fred S. remarkably responded: "Nice pep talk, but I don't believe a word you said." I angrily interjected, "That's completely unfair." And so it went, in a very unsatisfactory way, for a few minutes with Jim there and then for another half hour with them alone. . . . Finally I walked away. Just before leaving for Camp I, [I] talked briefly to Fred Dunham, who said he would continue to work for the expedition because of what he felt was an obligation to those persons who had made contributions at his behest. During the discussion with both Freds, I conceded I wanted to get to the top of K2, that was why I was here, and if I didn't make it to the top, I wanted to leave here with no regrets and knowing that I had given everything to the effort of getting there. Curiously, Fred Stanley said that the reason he came on the expedition was because of Fred's [Dunham] and my presence. That's nice, but not a sufficient reason for coming all the way to Pakistan and K2. . . .

Fred Stanley

Last evening when I got to camp with Steve, the porters and Manzoor welcomed us, untying our rope and carrying our packs to our tents. A kind of warm glow came over me. I got into my sweater and down vest and wind shirt, got my cup out, and headed for the cook tent. . . . Dinner was ready. I was feeling pretty good and somewhere into the conversation I mentioned that Fred [Dunham] and I could hardly contain ourselves at the irony of Wick and Lou starting out for Camp II the previous *afternoon* and then returning fifteen minutes later (in a snowstorm) after all their noise and valorous talk. That is, I started to mention it and Jim [Whittaker] jumped on me, shouting me out, saying how the two Freds were happy about their failures . . . how we're always happy when something goes wrong, how we were happy when he didn't make Camp I from base camp in forty-five minutes as he had bragged he would (this I knew nothing of), etc. I just shut up and slowly finished my dinner. . . .

I am really at a low ebb. I have lost all enthusiasm for the expedition, wishing there was some way out without leaving the rest in the lurch. Each person in this small group counts a lot. . . .

Galen has struck up a psychoanalysis session with the rest of the group this morning, discussing Fred and me and himself, also. I believe he's found it an opportunity to bring out his problems with the Whittakers and air them—a good catharsis for him. Lou, Wick, and everyone are getting into the act now, psychoanalyzing us. I can't hear it all, actually only a phrase or two, but I sure have to chuckle. It sounds to me like Galen's good intentions of trying to get us treated better, listened to, respected for our positions, not put down every time we open our mouths, are being shouted down.

Wick [Wickwire] is talking vehemently. I hear noises about fragile egos, losing a few on Himalayan expeditions, crying in the tent. . . . Fred came back saying the

Jims [Whittaker and Wickwire] wanted to talk to us. I finally got them to under-stand I didn't really care to talk about it other than to say I was unhappy with per-sonal relationships and was ready to bail out. Fred said he was ready to stay and do as he was told. . . . Jim [Whittaker] made a pep talk and plea that he was doing things as he thought they ought to be done and was only interested in getting the expedition to the summit, and unless I was willing to talk about it there wasn't much he could do. What it boiled down to was he was begging for bodies to stay on; otherwise the expedition had had it. He finally left and Fred talked a little more with Wick, who tried to explain his position and actions, talking about safety, our supposed preoccupation with safety, technique, technical competence. . . . All I could think of was what does this have to do with the Whittakers treating people like shit? . . .

I woke at seven this morning, my mind immediately in high gear—one of those situations when everything is spread before one with perfect clarity. . . . Everything I would have liked to have said to Wick and Jim the previous morning is completely sorted out in my mind now. I am looking forward to the radio contact and tell the others I would like to make it. I also prepared to do a thing I was less than proud of—recording a conversation with others when they didn't know it. Something I wanted as a personal reference . . . something I can present to Wick or [the] Whittakers [Jim and Lou] if things are said which there is going to be a ques-tion about.

Response and Analysis

1. The two men named Fred—Fred Stanley and Fred Dunham—were the climbers who staged "the revolt." What were their primary concerns with the way the expedition was being conducted? With the leaders? How did the main leaders (Jim and Lou Whittaker and Jim Wickwire) respond to the Freds' concerns? Do you think the leaders' re-sponse was appropriate? Why or why not? Next, define fundamental attribution error. Do you think that some of the climbers were making the fundamental attribution error? Why or why not?

2. Do you think the effectiveness of the leaders was influenced by their determination to personally reach the summit of K2, the stresses involved with managing the expedi-tion (including negotiating with the porters), and the daily physical demands? Why or why not? What style of leadership do you think would have been most appropriate? Why?

Personal Experience and Application

1. Suppose the leaders of a climbing expedition to a high-altitude mountain in the Himalaya ask you to offer a few recommendations to promote group cohesiveness and harmony among the climbers. They would like you to offer specific activities for the group to per-form at the beginning of the expedition as well as ideas on how to solve problems like those that occurred during the ascent of K2. List your recommendations and reasons why you believe they would be effective.

2. Have you been in a group that experienced conflict? What created the conflict? How did

the group members perceive the situation? How was the conflict resolved? What might have been done to avoid or minimize the conflict?

Research

Suppose you want to examine how role titles influence expectations. For example, might people expect a group leader to act in her or his self-interest or in the interest of the group? What would people expect of a clerk? Of a group member? To find out, you write a scenario describing the work activities of Taylor, a member of a six-person work crew. Taylor is to perform the same activities as the other crew members but also has an additional task to perform. The scenario also

indicates that Taylor is not working as hard as the other crew members on the group activity.

One-third of the participants who read the scenario are told that Taylor is the group leader, one-third that Taylor is the clerk, and one-third that Taylor is a group member. After reading the scenario, the participants rank reasons to explain why Taylor did not work as hard as the other group members, such as tired, self-interested, had a sense of privilege, had other responsibilities to perform. In this study, what is the independent variable? What are the levels or conditions of the independent variable? What is the dependent variable? How would you determine which participants read which of the three scenarios? Why?

RANDOM ACTS OF KINDNESS

Editors

Psychological Concepts
helping behavior, altruism

When and why do we unselfishly help other people? Here are three charming stories that tell about people who moved beyond their daily obligations and responsibilities and unselfishly helped other people. What might motivate people to commit random acts of kindness? What effects might helping others or bringing whimsical joy to others have on both giver and receiver?

My girlfriend and I are avid backpackers. I can't even describe the feeling I get after we lock up the car and hit the trail, and every step is one step farther into the hills and one step farther away from all the crazy stuff that goes on in the world. In my mind it is such a different reality once we are on the trail, and I guess that is why I always put all my "worldly" things in a small green zip-up bag and stuff it away in a corner of my backpack. I mean everything—wallet, with all my ID, credit cards, license, etc., all my money, my keys—everything you need to survive in the modern world and everything that is irrelevant back in the woods.

This particular trip was a five-day trek through some of the most beautiful parts of the Cascades. As we headed back down toward the parking area where we had left the car, I was really sad to be leaving what to me was such a simple and beautiful way of living. I could just feel the tension and anxiety beginning to creep back into my body as we got closer and closer to civilization. When we finally got to the car there was a small piece of paper tucked under the windshield-wiper blade that read, "left rear tire." I walked back and looked at the left rear tire but it was fine. The note made no sense to me at all—three seconds back into the world and already lunacy. Then I started fishing through my backpack for my green bag. It wasn't there. I look back at the left rear tire—there was the bag. I have no idea when I lost it, I have no idea who found it, or how they ever found my car amid all the possible parking places in that part of the Cascades. My keys, my wallet, nearly $100 in cash, all neatly tucked in my zip-up green bag sitting on top of my left rear tire. Thank you, whoever you are, you gave me back much more than you know.

*   *   *   *   *

I have been going to the same bagel/coffee shop every Sunday for years. One morning in the middle of a great dreary drizzly weekend, I trudged in dripping wet with my newspaper carefully tucked under my overcoat and ordered my usual bagel with lox and cream cheese and an espresso. I was casually informed that my coffee had already been paid for. I looked around expecting to see some friends sitting somewhere but didn't, and when I asked, the young woman at the register just smiled and said someone paid for twenty coffees and you are number eight. I sat there for almost an hour, reading my paper, and watching more surprised people come in to find their morning coffee pre-paid. There we all were, furtively at first and then with big funny smiles on our faces, looking at everyone else in the restaurant trying to figure out who had done this incredible thing, but mostly just enjoying the experience as a group. It was a beautiful blast of sunshine on an otherwise overcast winter day.

*   *   *   *   *

We were on vacation in Florida, with four kids all under the age of ten. The weather had been very hot and humid so this particular day we decided to pack a cooler full of sandwiches and soft drinks and drive out along the coast until we found a nice beach. It was sort of an adventure since we didn't really know where we were going, but after a while we found a really beautiful beach that was pretty isolated. We parked and unloaded ourselves onto the sand. It was really great, except that, after a few hours, it just got too hot for the kids and they were starting to whine and complain. So we decided to head back to the air-conditioned hotel. When we got back to the car, however, there were the keys, dangling from the ignition with all the windows rolled up and all the doors locked. In frustration, I screamed, "Who locked the doors?" to which Beth, my five-year-old, responded, "You tell us always to lock the doors." I felt totally defeated. At first I was just going to smash the window in, but after Beth's evenhanded comment, I thought that would be a bit too violent. So I walked up the road about a half mile to a house along the beach. When I got there, this elderly couple invited me in, let me use their telephone to call roadside service, then packed me into their car and drove back to pick up the rest of my family. They brought us all back to their home, and within a few minutes the kids were swimming in their pool while my wife and I sat on an air-conditioned veranda sipping a cool drink and swapping vacation stories. Roadside service came and went and three hours later we headed back to our motel, much refreshed and glowing from the surprising and wonderful experience.

Response and Analysis

1. What effects might helping others or bringing whimsical joy to others have on both giver and receiver? Summarize two theories that attempt to explain why people unselfishly help others.

2. Discuss how the following characteristics influenced helping behavior in each story: recognition of need for help, attractiveness of person in need, familiarity with surroundings, presence of others.

Personal Experience and Application

1. Make a list of five altruistic deeds that you could do. Make another list of five altruistic deeds that other people have performed to help you.

2. Describe a situation in which you unselfishly helped someone. Now describe a situation in which you knew someone needed assistance but you did not provide help. What features of each situation influenced your decision to provide assistance?

Research

Suppose you want to examine how physical proximity influences liking. You randomly assign participants to one of two conditions. In the close condition, you seat four participants in a circle so that they can touch one another with their arms extended. In the far condition, you seat one participant against each of the four walls. You ask the participants to talk for five minutes and get acquainted. Then you ask them to privately rate how much they like the other members in their group. You debrief the participants and excuse them.

To your surprise, the participants in both the close and far conditions rated the members of their group as equally likable. List three reasons that may explain why there was no difference in likable ratings between the two groups. Is it possible that your procedure did not effectively manipulate proximity? Why or why not? Can you think of another way to manipulate proximity?

References

pp. 120–121: Anderson, R. C., Reynolds, R. E., Schallert, D. L., & Goetz, E. T. (1977). Frameworks for comprehending discourse. *American Education Research Journal, 14,* 367–382.

p. 39: Brody, J. E. (1982, November 16). Noise poses a growing threat, affecting hearing and behavior. *New York Times.*

p. 156: Buber, M. (1952). *Eclipse of God: Studies in the relation between religion and philosophy.* New York: Harper.

p. 99: Loftus, E. F., & Palmer, J. C. (1974). Reconstruction of automobile destruction: An example of the interaction between language and memory. *Journal of Verbal Learning and Behavior, 13,* 585–589.

Credits

Chapter 1 Physiological Bases of Behavior

p. 3: Excerpt from *Carnal Acts* by Nancy Mairs. Copyright © 1990 by Nancy Mairs. Reprinted by permission of Beacon Press, Boston. **p. 7:** Excerpted with permission from *Show Me the Way to Go Home* by Larry Rose. Copyright © 1996 by Elder Books. Available from Elder Books, PO Box 490, Forest Knolls, CA 94933 (1-800-909-COPE). **p. 13:** Text from Sidney Dorros, *Parkinson's: A Patient's View.* Copyright © 1981 by Sidney Dorros. Excerpted by permission of Seven Locks Press, Inc. **p. 19:** K. H. Lipsitz, "I Refused to Be Sick . . . and It Almost Killed Me," from *Mademoiselle*, April 1994. **p. 24:** Excerpt from William H. Bergquist, R. McLean, and B. A. Kobylinski, *Stroke Survivors.* Copyright © 1994 by Jossey-Bass Inc., Publishers. Reprinted by permission.

Chapter 2 Sensation and Perception

p. 30: Excerpt from *Moving Violations: War Zones, Wheelchairs, and Declarations of Independence* by John Hockenberry. Copyright © 1995 by John Hockenberry. Reprinted with permission of Hyperion. **p. 35:** Reprinted by permission of Sterling Lord Literistic, Inc. from *Deafness: An Autobiography* by David Wright. Copyright © 1969. **p. 40:** Excerpt from *An Anthropologist on Mars* by Oliver Sacks. Copyright © 1995 by Oliver Sacks. Reprinted by permission of Alfred A. Knopf, Inc. **p. 44:** From *A Natural History of the Senses* by Diane Ackerman. Copyright © 1994 by Diane Ackerman. Reprinted by permission of Random House, Inc.

Chapter 3 Consciousness

p. 50: Excerpt from *Asleep in the Fast Lane: The Impact of Sleep on Work* by Lydia Dotto. Copyright © 1990 by Stoddart Publishing Co., Ltd. Reprinted by permission of Lydia Dotto. **p. 55:** Excerpted from *Always Running, La Vida Loca: Gang Days in L.A.* Copyright © 1993 by Luis J. Rodriguez. Used by permission of Curbstone Press. **p. 59:** "Bob Welch" from *The Courage to Change* by Dennis Wholey. Copyright © 1984 by Dennis Wholey. Reprinted by permission of Houghton Mifflin Company. All rights reserved. **p. 64:** Reprinted with the author's permission from Robert G. Meyer, *Practical Clinical Hypnosis: Technique and Application.* Copyright © 1992 by Jossey-Bass Inc., Publishers. First published by Lexington Books.

Chapter 4 Learning

p. 74: David N. Sattler and Chuck Tompkins. "Positive Reinforcement in Animal Training: An Interview with Chuck Tompkins." Reprinted by permission. **p. 78:** From *Voices from the Future* by Susan Goodwillie. Copyright © 1993 by Susan Goodwillie. Reprinted by permission of Crown Publishers, Inc. **p. 83:** Jaime Escalante and Jack Dirmann, *The Jaime Escalante Math Program.* Copyright © 1990 by the National Education Association. Reprinted by permission.

Chapter 5   Memory

pp. 88 and 94: Copyright © 1991 by Dr. Elizabeth Loftus and Katherine Ketcham. From *Witness for the Defense: The Accused, the Eyewitness, and the Expert Who Puts Memory on Trial* by Dr. Elizabeth Loftus and Katherine Ketcham. Reprinted by permission of St. Martin's Press, L.L.C. **p. 100:** Tony Dajer/copyright © 1991 by The Walt Disney Co. Reprinted with permission of *Discover* magazine. **p. 104:** Excerpt from A. R. Luria, *The Mind of a Mnemonist*. Copyright © 1968 by Basic Books. Reprinted by permission.

Chapter 6   Thought and Language

p. 113: Five-page excerpt from *You Just Don't Understand* by Deborah Tannen, Ph.D. Copyright © 1990 by Deborah Tannen, Ph.D. Reprinted by permission of William Morrow & Company, Inc. **p. 117:** Nancy Masterson Sakamoto, "Conversational Ballgames." Excerpt from *Polite Fictions*, Copyright © 1982. Reprinted by permission. **p. 121:** From *Hunger of Memory* by Richard Rodriguez. Reprinted by permission of David R. Godine, Publisher, Inc. Copyright © 1982 by Richard Rodriguez. **p. 126:** From Daniel M. Wegner, *White Bears and Other Unwanted Thoughts: Suppression, Obsession, and the Psychology of Mental Control*. Copyright © 1994 by Guilford Press. Reprinted by permission. **p. 132:** Michele Mitchell, "Fear" from *Women's Sports and Fitness*, January 1986, Volume 8, Number 1. Reprinted by permission.

Chapter 7   Human Development

p. 137: Excerpts from *Madeleine's World: A Child's Journey from Birth to Age Three* by Brian Hall. Copyright © 1997 by Brian Hall. Reprinted by permission of Houghton Mifflin Company. All rights reserved. **p. 143:** "Shame," copyright © 1964 by Dick Gregory Enterprises, Inc., from *Nigger: An Autobiography* by Dick Gregory. Used by permission of Dutton, a division of Penguin Putnam, Inc. **p. 147:** Copyright © 1972 by Nora Ephron. Reprinted by permission of International Creative Management (ICM). **p. 151:** Reprinted by permission of the author from *The Sandwich Generation: Caught Between Growing Children and Aging Parents*. H. Michael Zal, D.O., is a board certified psychiatrist with a private practice in Bala Cynwyd, PA. He is a clinical professor, Department of Psychiatry, Philadelphia College of Osteopathic Medicine. **p. 156:** From *The View from 80* by Malcolm Cowley. Copyright © 1976, 1978, 1980 by Malcolm Cowley. Used by permission of Viking Penguin, a division of Penguin Putnam, Inc.

Chapter 8   Mental Abilities

p. 162: Excerpts from *Talented Teenagers: The Roots of Success and Failure* by Mihaly Csikszentmihalyi, Kevin Rathunde, and Samuel Whalen. Copyright © 1993 by Cambridge University Press. Reprinted with the permission of Cambridge University Press. **p. 165:** From *Through the Communication Barrier: On Speaking, Listening, and Understanding* by S. I. Hayakawa, edited by Arthur Chandler. Copyright © 1979 by Harper & Row. Reprinted by permission of the Estate of S. I. Hayakawa. **p. 169:** Excerpt from *We Have Been There* by Terrell Dougan, Lyn Isbell, and Patricia Vyas. Copyright © 1979, 1983 by Dougan, Isbell, & Vyas Associates. Reprinted by permission of the publisher, Abingdon Press. **p. 171:** From Dixon, *The Spatial Child*. Copyright © 1983. Courtesy of Charles C. Thomas, Publisher, Springfield, Illinois. **p. 175:** Excerpt from *Assessment of Children* by Jerome M. Sattler. Copyright © 1988 by Jerome M. Sattler, Publisher. Reprinted by permission.

Chapter 9   Motivation and Emotion

p. 183: From *Still Me* by Christopher Reeve. Copyright © 1998 by Cambria Productions, Inc. Reprinted by permission of Random House, Inc. **p. 188:** "Dying To Be Bigger" by D. H.

Originally published in the December 1991 issue of *Seventeen* magazine. Reprinted by permission. **p. 192:** Pages 1–7 from *New Hope for Binge Eaters* by Harrison G. Pope, M.D. and James I. Hudson, M.D. Copyright © by Harrison G. Pope, M.D. and James I. Hudson, M.D. Used by permission of HarperCollins Publishers, Inc. **p. 197:** From *Emotional Intelligence* by Daniel Goleman. Copyright © 1995 by Daniel Goleman. Used by permission of Bantam Books, a division of Random House, Inc.

Chapter 10   Personality

p. 202: Reprinted by permission of the author, Kesaya E. Noda, from *Making Waves* by Asian Women United. Copyright © 1989 by Asian Women United. **p. 207:** Joyce Lee, "Racism Doesn't Grow Up," from Elena Featherston (Ed.), *Skin Deep: Women Writing on Color, Culture, and Identity.* Copyright © 1994 by Crossing Press. Reprinted by permission of the author. **p. 212:** From *Days of Grace* by Arthur Ashe and Arnold Rampersad. Copyright © 1993 by Jeanne Moutoussamy-Ashe and Arnold Rampersad. Reprinted by permission of Alfred A. Knopf, Inc. **p. 216:** Excerpts from *An American Childhood* by Annie Dillard. Copyright © 1987 by Annie Dillard. Reprinted by permission of HarperCollins Publishers, Inc.

Chapter 11   Psychological Disorders

p. 221: "The Auto Accident That Never Was," from *The Boy Who Couldn't Stop Washing* by Dr. Judith Rapoport. Copyright © 1989 by Judith L. Rapoport, M.D. Used by permission of Dutton Signet, a division of Penguin Books USA, Inc. **p. 227:** Reprinted with permission of the author, Quiet Storm. Originally appeared in *First for Women*, November 1, 1993. **p. 232:** From *The Beast: A Reckoning with Depression* by Tracy Thompson. Copyright © 1995 by Tracy Thompson. Used by permission of G. P. Putnam's Sons, a division of Penguin Putnam, Inc. **p. 235:** Allan Davis, "I Feel Cheated by Having This Illness," from *Menninger Perspective*, 1996, #3. Reprinted by permission of the author and the Menninger Clinic. **p. 243:** Text, pp. 349–357, from *Feeling Good: The New Mood Therapy* by David D. Burns, M.D. Copyright © 1980 by David D. Burns, M.D. Used by permission of William Morrow & Company, Inc. **p. 249:** Excerpt from *Welcome to My Country* by Lauren Slater. Copyright © 1996 by Lauren Slater. Reprinted by permission of Random House, Inc.

Chapter 12   Health, Stress, and Coping

p. 257: From *Days of Grace* by Arthur Ashe and Arnold Rampersad. Copyright © 1993 by Jeanne Moutoussamy-Ashe and Arnold Rampersad. Reprinted by permission of Alfred A. Knopf, Inc. **p. 263:** From *From Vietnam to Hell: Interviews with Victims of Post-Traumatic Stress Disorder.* Copyright © 1990 Shirley Dicks by permission of McFarland & Company, Inc., Publishers, Jefferson, NC 28640. **p. 267:** Reprinted from James Pennebaker, *Opening Up: The Healing Power of Expressing Emotion* (New York: Guilford Press, 1997). Copyright © 1990, 1997 by James W. Pennebaker. Reprinted by permission. **p. 273:** Excerpt from *Positive Illusions: Creative Self-Deception and the Healthy Mind* by Shelley E. Taylor. Copyright © 1989 by BasicBooks, Inc. Reprinted by permission of BasicBooks, a member of Perseus Books, L.L.C. **p. 277:** Excerpt from *Treating Chronic Pain: The Healing Partnership* by Aleene Friedman. Copyright © 1992. Reprinted by permission of Plenum Publishing, a member of Perseus Books, L.L.C.

Chapter 13   Social Thought and Social Behavior

p. 284: From *American Dreams: Lost and Found* by Studs Terkel. Copyright © 1980 by Studs Terkel. Reprinted by permission of Donadio & Olson, Inc. **p. 290:** Text from *Influence* by Robert B. Cialdini. Copyright © 1993 by Robert B. Cialdini. Used by permission of William Morrow & Company, Inc. **p. 297:** Brent Staples, "Black Men and Public Space." Reprinted,

Name Index

Subject Index